The Writer's Passage

a journey to the sources of creativity

Horst Kornberger

Horst Kornberger

First published 2008 by
INTEGRAL ARTS PRESS
PO Box 456, Hamilton Hill
WA – 6963, Australia
www.thewritingconnection.com.au

Copyright © Horst Kornberger, 2008
Copyright for the individual stories and extracts rests with the authors.
This book is copyright. Apart from any fair dealing for the purpose of private study, research, criticism or review, as permitted under the Copyright Act, no part may be reproduced by any process without written permission. Enquiries should be made to the publisher.

ISBN 9780980293111 (pbk.)
Dewey number 808.02

Edited by Janet Blagg
Cover art and design by Horst Kornberger

The Writer's Passage

for Jennifer
my partner on the journey of the poetic

Horst Kornberger

Contents

Acknowledgement — 7
Introduction — 9
Structure of the Book — 10
How to use this book — 11

1 Magical Language — 13
2 Echoes of the Sacred — 20
3 The Wishing Well — 29
4 Ladder of Dreams — 36
5 Fabulous Tales — 46
6 The First Song — 55
7 The Four Ages — 62
8 Parting with Paradise — 72
9 The Breath of Brahma — 82
10 Between Light and Darkness — 93
11 Baking the Stars — 104
12 The First of Friendships — 113
13 The Weighing of the Heart — 122
14 Burning Doubt — 132
15 Lyrical Kings — 142
16 A Journey of Epics — 155
17 The Lyre of Orpheus — 165
18 The Labyrinth of Light — 176
19 A Sober State — 188
20 Story Medicine — 199
21 Tongues of Fire — 208
22 Braiding of Words — 220
23 The Poetics of Battle — 233
24 The Grail Quest — 242
25 Troubadour and Troubairitz — 255
26 The Purgatory of Words — 268
27 The Alchemical Stage — 279
28 Landscape and Soulscape — 289
29 The Pact with the Devil — 300
30 Western Edge — 311
31 Tracing the Beloved — 323

32 Sermon of the East	334
33 Subtle Empire	343
34 Threshold Images	357
35 Choir of the New	371
36 The Imaginal Age	383
Bibliography	393
About the Author	396

Acknowledgement

This book was made possible only through the contributions and help of the following people:

Jennifer Kornberger, who first conceived the idea of a creative writing course and mothered it in all its stages. For being my partner on the journey of the word and for the many obvious as well as the many invisible contributions to this work.

Raymon Ford, who enrolled in a course with Jennifer and me many years ago and saw the possibility of extending our work into the world. Through his generous ongoing support we continue to realise our vision of the School of Integral Art.

Stefan Szo, our webmaster, whose insights into the subtle world of online communications and its possibilities to create new social forms mark him as an artist of the future.

Janet Blagg, my editor, who has a deep and soulful connection with the great stories of the world and a fierce eye for the 'right word'.

Katie Dobb, for pointing me towards the right title.

Adrian Glamorgan, for his meticulous note taking that helped me to gain perspective on my own teaching.

Ann Reeves, long-time supporter and fellow traveller whose close link with the impulse of our work brought far more than swiftly typed manuscripts.

Sue Johnson for proofreading additional chapters.

Maggie White, for her inspired suggestion to make Working the Word available as an online course.

Jenny Hill, for her support as a friend and inspiration as a colleague.

Scott Benjamin, friend and photographer extraordinaire, who brings colour to the life of our materials, online and printed.

I also acknowledge the following personalities whose contributions to the realm of language have shaped my own vision:

Rudolf Steiner, whose spiritual research, artistic impulses and many practical contributions have been the major inspiration of my life and work.

Paul Matthews of Emerson College, for first introducing me to the magic of creative writing as well as for inspiring some of the exercises in the first three chapters through his excellent book on creative writing, *Sing Me the Creation*.

Owen Barfield, who through his brilliant enquiry into the co-evolution of language and meaning has deepened my own understanding of the word.

Georg Kuhlewind, whose philosophic work has bridged the gap between word and logos.

John Gee, for his brilliant collection of literary texts made for the London School of Speech Formation and Dramatic Art.

Kenneth Koch, American poet and creative writing pioneer, who has contributed to the first three chapters through his book *Wishes, Lies and Dreams*.

Dawn Langman, Maisie Jones, Christopher Garvey and Jeff Norris from the London School of Speech Formation and Dramatic Art for introducing me to the spirit of the English language.

The many students of Working the Word whose creative writing appears in this book: Adrian Glamorgan, Ailsa Grieve, Ali McKenzie, Alison Ashton, Ann Harrison, Ann Reeves, Anna Minska, Anne Esbenshade, Anne Williams, Annie Wearne, Annette Mullumby, Anthony Hart, Antoinette van der Leeden, Barbara Edwards, Barbara Stapleton, Barbara Swingler, Bavali Hill, Bev Barker, Brenda Chapman, Caz Bowman, Cindy Innes, Coral Carter, Dale Irving, Desma Kearney, Diane Marshall, Edward Laurs, Elysia Tsangarides, Gilly Berry, Harriet Sawer, Helen McDonell, Janet Blagg, Jaya Penelope, Jean Hudson, Jeremy Sheldrick, Jill Whitfield, Jo Lunay, John Ryan, John Stubley, Judy Griffiths, Julie Dickinson, Karen McCrea, Kristina Hamilton, Lachlan McKenzie, Lia Eliades, Liana Christensen, Louise House, Maggie Brackenridge, Mags Webster, Martina Chippindall, Meirion Griffiths, Morgan Yasbincek, Nan Connell, Nandi Chinna, Pauline Mathews, Pen Brown, Peter Stafford, Renee Schipp, Rhea Pfeiffle, Richard Smart, Sean Burke, Sofia, Stuart Wallis, Sue Johnson, Sue McBurnie, Tineke Van der Eecken and Veronica Antalov.

Introduction

The Writer's Passage is based on a year-long part-time course I devised and taught in Perth, Western Australia. In it I told the literary biography of the world from the beginning of time to the present. My aim was not to provide information, but to stimulate the imagination into creative response. To this end I focused on the story that creativity herself wishes to tell: the biography of the poetic.

Working with this biography helped me to see that poets and their work are the expressions of a living being, whose life and destiny we have come to know as the history of literature. To engage with this destiny is an act of integration, an artistic initiation into the vitality of literature and the manifold ways of being human. For the attempt to write is inseparable from our attempt to be more thoroughly human, since what makes us most human is also what makes us most creative. In this way the work also serves as a course in personal development, undertaken through the medium of writing.

Every exercise in this book is an invocation of the poetic, a ritual to connect with what was most creative in the past. The shift of perspective demanded by such exercises is in itself deeply liberating. The scope of the soul is enlarged merely by trying on the soul-skin of a different time, culture and personality — to serenely reformulate the eightfold path of the Buddha or passionately hurl oneself into the battle fury of the Viking; to tangle with the verbal eroticism of Sappho or the righteous passion of the prophets. To become the pure Parzival of the medieval epics and then the devil in Goethe's *Faust* is an unmatched gymnastic for the creative soul.

In my book *The Power of Stories* I describe how many great myths contain at their heart a 'tale within the tale', in which the hero or heroine encounters their own story. In every case this meeting signifies the turning point: hearing their own story and telling the rest of it completes their quest. The same applies to writers. They too are on a quest. No matter if their grail is the completion of a poem, or a novel waiting to be written, they adventure between possibility and realisation, resistance and resolve. They look towards the completion of their project with the same intensity as Odysseus to his homecoming. They may be as haunted by their muses as Orestes by the furies or as desperate as Parzival in his long search for redemption. Like these heroes they are in need of a story: their story as a writer in the context of the greater tale — the tale that literature herself has told, and will keep on telling, by means of her poets and writers.

This book was created to provide an imaginative framework for this greater tale. Through it writers meet the poets of the past where they can still be met: in the act of creation, where abstract knowledge becomes personal experience; where the history of literature turns into the writer's own tale. This greater memory is the 'body of story' we need in order to be complete as writers and human beings.

Structure of the book

In The Writer's Passage you will re-create the most significant stages of human experience in our own writing. The course consists of thirtysix lessons.

The journey begins in the childhood of language. The first two lessons focus on developing the imagination in order to recharge the creative meridian at its most vital points: the realm of childhood wishes and the important phase of the folk tale.

Lesson three, Fabulous Tales, mediates between the childhood phase of language and the journey through time by exploring the realm of animal archetypes.

From there we turn to the powerful myths of creation. The creation of the world reflects the creation of the writer in us. Paradise is far from over and the great deluge is still ready to open the floodgates of the imagination.

After that, the course travels through historic time, following the trade routes of culture from the ancient Orient to the west: Exploring the sacred texts of Old India and Persia, the myth of Inana, the tale of Gilgamesh, the Egyptian 'Weighing of the Heart' and Hebrew texts.

These myths bestow a powerful charge — simply to hear them can be healing. To engage with them through creative writing intensifies the experience exponentially, bringing them fully alive with opportunities for creative growth.

We then meet Greek spirit through the love poems of Sappho, Homer's *Odyssey* and the great tragedies of Euripides. The journey continues with the exploration of Roman, Christian and Gnostic texts, Celtic and Germanic works.

From then on we encounter the epic of Parsifal, the Troubadours, Dante's journey through heaven and hell, the Persian Poet Rumi, Shakespeare, the Romantics, Goethe's Faust, Buddha's sermons, Chinese master poets Tu Fu and Li Po, Japanese Haiku and the Modernists.

The course is not an intellectual study, but a living recapitulation of human experience through the practice of creative writing. The journey through the past enables a liberation of creative potential to work powerfully into the present.

How to use this book

In The Writer's Passage you will engage with all the vital stages of world literature through your own creativity.

To fully engage with these stages I recommend that you work the lessons systematically from beginning to end. The imagination is like a fine muscle and the exercises in The Writer's Passage are designed to develop its strength.

There are a number of ways to approach the exercises in this course. One way is to leave your present circumstances behind and slip into the soul-skin of a bygone age. Doing this you become the composer of the Gilgamesh epic, or by choosing to write in the first person, Gilgamesh himself.

I call this approach *immersive writing*. Immersive writing means to fully engage with other ways of seeing and experiencing the world. We all too easily take the present mindset as the final verdict on reality. To effectively transcend the current paradigm, take every mindset you encounter in this course as a justified reality. Be Egyptian with the Egyptians and when in Rome, do as the Romans do. Remember that the gods were as real to the composers of the epic of Gilgamesh as bricks and mortar are to us.

This does not mean you have to stick to the story as it is. Feel free to explore more of the tale, find a different angle or change the narrative altogether. The great myths always existed in different versions.

A second option is to explore the relevance of these ancient stories to our time. Gilgamesh's struggle to come to terms with his own mortality is as pertinent today as it was in antiquity. You will readily find the theme in your own life and in that of others.

You may want to experiment with different approaches to find your own style. In all cases use your imagination rather than your intellect. Think in pictures rather than concepts. The exercises in this course will guide you to write down what you see and not what you think, to show rather than tell. Close your eyes for a moment and imagine a picture to form in your mind's eye, as though you are viewing a painting on the wall. Describe the picture, then let the story unfold - do not plan ahead. Stay in the moment and let yourself be surprised by what flows from your pen.

When doing the exercises, put aside the critical voice. Trust your imagination and let it lead you. Accept whatever you write. And no matter what comes out, remember, the first draft is sacred. You may write more responses, try different versions, but let your first draft take its rightful place.

On this count, poet Morgan Yasbincek passed on a good writing habit: keep all your creative writing in one book or file — poems, prose, ideas, thoughts, words and lesson material — so layers are set down one on top of another like in an archaeological dig.

You may also want to consider handwriting your responses first. The imagination is more apt to join the waltz of your wrists than the tap dance of your fingertips.

Each exercise is followed by one or two examples of student work. Read them carefully after you have finished your work; it is instructive to see how others have approached the same exercise. It will give you new ideas and broaden your creative horizon. After finishing the first exercise, continue reading and complete exercises as they arise. Refrain from reading the whole lesson before you write your response. It will help you to stay in the freshness of the encounter. Depending on your writing habits it will take you one to two hours to complete a lesson.

If you have the opportunity, share this journey with other writers. Form a group and meet regularly, working through the lessons. It is enlivening to read out your own work and inspiring to hear that of others. Writing can be an isolating activity and it is important for writers to find supportive community. A regular writing group can help you write regularly. Local writing centres can be of great help to find fellow writers.

Please note that The Writer's Passage is also available as an online audio course if you wish to take this journey in community with others and accompanied by a tutor. Visit our website: www.thewritingconnection.com.au for more information.

One more piece of advice before we start: If you are a beginner be patient with your first responses. Writing, like any other art, needs practice. This course is designed as a slow, step-by-step initiation into your creative capabilities. Working through these exercises will steadily stimulate your imagination and improve your writing over time. Trust the process.

1

Magical Language

In ancient times language was sacred. There was power in certain sounds; words had magical effect. Speaking the name of a Goddess or God could invoke their presence. A mantram was a doorway to the divine.

The cradle of every language is filled with spells and incantations. The earliest preserved text from Old German is the famous Merseburger Magic Spell, a spell to cure the broken leg of a horse. Nor have modern languages completely lost their magical properties; they still retain the power to move our inner world of soul. Who has not been spellbound by a particular poem?

Through the power of sound, every language shapes the reality of those who speak it. A language suggests a particular way of seeing the world. It directs our attention and guides our feeling. Let me give you an example. Consider the English word tree and its German equivalent, Baum. Superficially they mean the same thing, but the two words point towards very different experiences.

Speak the word 'tree' aloud. Feel its dynamic gesture. It rises upwards, a tall and straight word that emphasises the trunk. It is a word that makes us stand some distance from the tree and look at it. The German word Baum captures an entirely different reality. Baum is a round, encompassing word; there is no linearity. Baum draws us towards a large round canopy, into thick shade, a calm world of strength and maturity. Baum stands alone in a village square, sheltering wanderers. There are love hearts carved into its bark.

The Japanese word for tree is ke (pronounced a clipped *kee*). Ke is a precise word. It suggests a small tree, placed carefully into the silent perfection of a Japanese garden. It invokes the image of bonsai and reminds us of those few, masterful brushstrokes on the edge of a Japanese painting indicating neither tree nor baum but — ke.

Every language makes us see the world through a different lens, drawing our attention to a different reality and so shaping that reality. Not only through words, but the powers of sound held in the building blocks of language — the vowels and consonants.

The Landscape The Landscape of Vowels
Vowels have inwardness, they are an expression of soul. They express in different nuances how we feel about the world. The vowel *ah* (as in far) is our immediate

response to awe and wonder. When a magnificent landscape opens up before us we say ah because we feel it. In this moment our soul is entirely ah.

Imagine a landscape that inspires you with awe. With closed eyes, take a few moments to create the picture inwardly. Now speak the sound *ah* aloud. Then, still holding your inner landscape, utter the sound *oo* (as in you), and notice what happens. A long oo carries an element of fear, apprehension. It is a serious sound, deep blue in colour. While the ah makes us open up and step forward, the oo makes us inwardly take a step back. Now try the same with the other vowels — speak them aloud while imagining your landscape:

ee (as in sea)

eh (as in hem)

oh (as in low).

You may experience the *ee* as conveying lightness and vibrancy; it is an alert, fresh sound. It moves quickly, brightens things up.

The *oh* is a steady, slow, sympathetic sound. It is round and encompassing like the letter O itself. There is a generosity, a calm quality to oh that is quite different from the nervous agility of ee.

The *eh* has strength, it digs its heels in. It is self reliant; it makes us take hold of ourself and it separates things off for the sake of clarity. With *ah* we flow dreamily into the world; the eh brings us back to ourselves, awakening us.

Diphthongs

Vowels in English tend to be diphthongs, mixtures of pure vowels; they slide from one vowel to the next. Take the word 'may'. Speak it aloud and observe how the *eh* slides into the *ee*. The word 'low' starts with *oh* and slides towards *ou*.

The diphthong *au* (as in cow) is the king of sounds. It glides from *ah* to *oo*. The sound is grand and all-encompassing; serene, powerful. If you make the following experiment, you will see why. Articulate all the vowels: ah — eh — ee — oh — ou, paying attention to where they are located. You will find that the ah sits furthest back in the throat, and the other vowels move in sequence until the oo sits right on the lips.

The diphthong au travels from back right through to front encompassing all the other vowel sounds. If you listen carefully you will always hear the oh in the middle. Au is a sacred sound. In Sanskrit it is the holy aum or om: a syllable so sacred that it is a mantra in itself. In our language the aum continues as the amen.

The Shape of Consonants

While vowels express how we feel about the world, consonants describe the world around us. They sculpt the world by means of sound. Whereas vowels are soft and inward, consonants have an edge; they are distinct. Vowels merge; consonants keep their identity.

In language, consonants generally take the lead, guiding and directing the vowels towards expression. But without the vowel the consonant is empty, soulless.

Say B (as in bee). Say it again and leave all the vocalic sound out — the B becomes a mere husk, an empty sound bursting from the lips.

Say the following consonants aloud: C D F G H J K L M N P Q R S T V W X Z Sh. Feel how each consonant has a distinct identity. Some are closely related — like P and B. Some are solid, earthy — B D M N. Others are full of fire and movement — S F Sh.

R when rolled (as in the French language) has an airy quality. L has a liquid, watery nature. The good-natured B as in Baum, or baby, is a benevolent, big-bellied, sheltering sound. It is a steady friend but can be bold on occasion.

K is a less friendly companion. It has a cutting edge that likes clarity and confrontation. M combines tenderness and strength. Speak the sound gently and feel the humming on your lips. It is a nurturing, warm and gently pervading sound as in Mumma or Mum. It merges more easily than other consonants and has an unrivalled ability to hum at the ends of words as in blame, sham, dim.

Sh is mysterious, fierce sound; the magician among sounds, able to quiet a roomful of children, invoke awe, even fear. It can be abysmal (as in shadow), or bright (as in shimmering). Sh has the elemental power of a strong wind, of ships in storm or waves washing on the shore.

Onomatopoeia

The magic of consonants is revealed in words with an onomatopoeic character, such as croak or ooze. These words sound like their meaning; they are reminiscent of the ancient link between object and word. As words become more abstract they lose the link between sound and meaning: for example, national product.

The magical property of language is revealed in subtle ways. For instance, say the words short and long and examine their impact on you. In spite of its actual length (5 letters), short is a much shorter word than long (4 letters). Short owes its quality to the dynamic sh that is effectively cut short by the sudden t. Long is a relaxed, slow word. Long wants to continue its quiet momentum forever. When you speak it, feel how the ng draws you along in its wake.

Poets are always playing with words and their pure sound qualities. Take the r out of short and you have shot, a word calling up bow and arrow. Speak it and feel the swift arrow whirring through air before it hits the target t. Shot is the span of time from the moment the arrow leaves the bowstring until it hits its mark.

Some poets use onomatopoeia consciously to great effect. Read aloud, Gerard Manley Hopkins' *'God's Grandeur'* provides an almost continuous experience of the marriage of sound with meaning.

> The world is charged with the grandeur of God.
> It will flame out, like shining from shook foil;
> It gathers to a greatness, like the ooze of oil
> Crushed. Why do men then now not reck his rod?
> Generations have trod, have trod, have trod;
> And all is seared with trade; bleared, smeared with toil;
> And wears man's smudge and shares man's smell: the soil
> Is bare now, nor can foot feel, being shod.
>
> And for all this, nature is never spent;
> There lives the dearest freshness deep down things;
> And though the last lights off the black West went
> Oh, morning, at the brown brink eastward, springs —
> Because the Holy Ghost over the bent
> World broods with warm breast and with ah! bright wings.

The word trod is magnificent. The fierce t is thwarted by the r and then follows the melancholy oh until it finally drowns in the dullness of the d. Trod. The daring use of the vowel sound 'ah' brings a full unfolding of wonder and awe in the last line.

There is a world in almost every word. I like the word 'Vladivostok'. Vladivostok is a city somewhere in Russia. I have never been there nor do I know anybody who has. I know nothing about Vladivostok, but I love the way the word rolls and tumbles over my tongue. Other favourites of mine are luminous, peninsular, rhomboid.

Bring your attention to examine words and play with their sounds. Write down at least five words that you especially like because of their sound quality. Speak them aloud and consider why you like them. What qualities do they exude?

The Baptism of Names

The word most intimately related to us is our own name. It is our faithful companion throughout our life. Speak out your name and examine it for its qualities of sound — its vowels and consonants. Do their qualities match yours?

Now here is an exciting task: make up a totally new name for yourself — a name that does not exist in any language you know. Compose your new name out of your preference for certain vowel and consonant combinations. Try a few different possibilities. Here are some of mine — Shinnock. Mulami. Tasnak.

Read your new names aloud. Savour their sounds. Now that you have successfully baptised yourself in the waters of sound you will be able to rename other things.

Exercise 1: Re-naming

Rename the following: Teapot. Scissors. Sunflower. Daisy. Lion.

Create a totally new name for these objects. A teapot could be a kaloom or a pumpas. Use the qualities of vowel and consonant to characterise the object. Visualise it first. The teapot steaming on the table. The magic of language is at your disposal — the vowels and consonants are ready and waiting.

Read aloud the result. Is there a common quality to your words? Are they reminiscent of any particular language?

Exercise 2: Adding an Adjective

Take the word you have created for teapot, e.g. kaloom, and consider for a moment what qualities it refers to. Is it the smooth surface of porcelain, the round-bellied shape, or the steaming spout? Now add the adjective 'beautiful', to make it a 'beautiful teapot' in your new language. Thus, perhaps, lilas kaloom or binda pumpas. Try to make your two words sound as if they come from the same language.

Exercise 3: Making a Sentence

Expand the phrase 'beautiful teapot' into a sentence, the first sentence of a new and unknown language — This is a beautiful teapot. For example, Ta si lilas kaloom.

Now an ugly teapot: for example, Ta si graga kaloom. Read both sentences aloud and feel the contrast.

Exercise 4: Swearwords and Endearments

Your new language is taking shape.

Make up a swear word in that language and say it aloud, with feeling! Gastrokrom korumbab!

Create an endearment. For example: Lalloban banush.

Curses, Blessings and Spells

Swear words are closely related to curses; endearments to blessings. Both abound in the primal layers of language.

Exercise 5: Creating a Curse

Create a curse (2–4 lines) in your new language. For example:

> Kudra skune pitprolda sman
> Nudlenk fit stug rants Kram
> Duntlin duntlin stuglin smet
> A brandock skune pit ollkum ret.

Exercise 6: Making a Blessing

Now create a blessing and read it aloud with conviction. For example:

> Alum karalum tam, shalum tara to nan
> Lalom ta mano, shalum ta mano
> Lalom ta mano lam.

Exercise 7: Spell Binding

Take the blessing a step further to create a little spell — e.g., for the rain to fall abundantly, or for victory. For example, a spell for rain:

> Asdahl frere arus luken sine
> Prell soarn jarn arus sebel line
> Swantily, swantily
> Shunt ten saren-bley.

Exercise 8: Breaking the Spell

Translate your spell back into English.

> Gather in sky and link all hands
> Thunder roll and stamp all lands
> Cloud sisters, cloud sisters
> Unwind your hair of rain.

Exercise 9: Translation

Now that you have mastered the translation into English, translate the following passage into your language.

> This beautiful teapot is one of my greatest treasures. I love it so much. My grandmother gave it to me before she died. It always reminds me of her. Would you like a cup of tea?

Exercise 10: Poem in Tongues

Write a small poem (there is no need to rhyme) or piece of prose — something that nobody understands but you. For example:

> Eisla krell alout fornata. Say bell shastern serinta borint tal sand foralaine sand rabant. Caan brey ajornaus mus tol corrum fere sallas. Cal wolis present tant? Eisla tern frenn asorn sucsh blea.

Exercise 11: Translation of Tongues

Translate your piece back into English. For example, here is a translation of the prose above:

> The sky above is huge. So many stars swept in heaps and sheaves and fields. Let us walk slowly to the next stone. Whose voice will be heard? The night river ashen with moon.

Exercise 12: Multiple Translations

Use your poems in imaginary language as a catalyst for new writing. Morgan Yasbincek wrote a series of poems inspired by Exercise 11. Here is one of her translations.

translation ii by Morgan Yasbincek

the secret of your infinite will
is that it never loses itself
in fabrics

it resists containment by
listening within your hour

it has time to dry you
like a medicinal herb, to

add you to a concoction
of theatres

you are tossed and the current
carries you just so into the pot

spend everything you have
just in case this is your only moment

2

Echoes of the Sacred

Languages are powerful entities. In the past they were held as sacred and experienced as a gift of the gods. As modern human beings, we have the definite sense that it is we who speak, and we who give voice to what we think and feel. But in ancient times language had an existence beyond the individual — it had a will of its own — and it was the genius of the language that spoke through human beings.

Homer attributed his work to the Muse rather than to his own poetic genius, an attitude common among early bards. Many ancient literary works are anonymous because they were seen to be authored by the spirit of language — the bard was a tool for the spirit. Poets felt themselves overshadowed by the Muse, seized by a goddess, inspired by a force far greater than themselves.

Language has not entirely lost its ability to speak through us. In every good piece of writing, language makes its voice heard. Today it is not so much a matter of a poet being seized by ecstatic frenzies, it is more a case of being consciously co-creative with language. When this happens, poet and the genius of language both speak, enhancing each other's contribution.

The Mother of Rhythm

The feeling of being spoken through and being carried is strongly tied to rhythm. In language rhythm manifests as meter. Old poetry was metrical. (Rhyme came much later).

Old cultures had their endemic meters. The rhythm of language reflected the beat and pulse of life. Nordic verse with its strong stress on consonants readily catapults us into the clang of Viking battle. The even rhythm of the hexameter invites us into the Mediterranean light, engages us with the even proportions of Greek art, the lighter tone of Greek myth. Reciting the Kalevala we can feel ourselves transported to long winter nights, to two singers rocking ecstatically on wooden benches, singing the songs of Vainamoinen and Ilmarinen.

The Greeks still distinguished twelve different meters. Five of these are still known today. One of them is the iambic meter where one unstressed syllable is followed by a stressed syllable: ˇ —— This is the meter that Shakespeare uses.

'If <u>mu</u>sic <u>be</u> the <u>food</u> of <u>love</u>, play <u>on;</u>
Give <u>me</u> ex<u>cess</u> of <u>it</u>, that, <u>surfeiting,</u>

The <u>app</u>e<u>tite</u> may <u>sick</u>en, <u>and</u> so <u>die</u>.
That <u>strain</u> a<u>gain</u>! it <u>had</u> a <u>dy</u>ing <u>fall</u>…' (Twelfth Night)

Its polar opposite is the trochaic meter found in the Kalevala. Here one stressed syllable precedes an unstressed one: — ∨

'<u>I</u> am <u>driv</u>en <u>by</u> my <u>long</u>ing
<u>And</u> my <u>un</u>der<u>stand</u>ing <u>urg</u>es…'.

In the dactyl one stressed syllable is followed by two unstressed syllables: — ∨ ∨
In the hexameter six dactyls combine to one line as in Longfellow's 'Evangeline':

'<u>This</u> is the <u>for</u>est pri<u>me</u>val. The <u>mur</u>muring <u>pines</u> and the <u>hem</u>locks
Bearded with moss, and in garments green, indistinct in the twilight…,'

The anapaest begins with two unstressed syllables, followed by one stressed syllable: ∨ ∨ — as in Byron's 'Destruction of Sennacherib':

'The As<u>syr</u>ian came <u>down</u> like a <u>wolf</u> on the <u>fold</u>
And his <u>co</u>horts were <u>gleam</u>ing in <u>pur</u>ple and <u>gold</u>…'

The fifth survivor of ancient meters is the spondee, with two accentuated syllables providing weight: — — Hopkins's poem 'Pied Beauty' is heavily spondaic:

'…With <u>swift, slow; sweet, sour;</u> adazzle, dim;
He <u>fa</u>thers-forth <u>whose</u> beauty is <u>past</u> <u>change</u>:
<u>Praise</u> <u>him</u>.'

Strict meter is rare today. Rhythm has become secondary to content. But there are exceptions such as gibberish and nursery rhymes. Though not written in strict meter, rhythm predominates over meaning. Hence they are easily remembered and almost speak themselves. Once the first word is out all others come tumbling after (just like Jill in the famous rhyme).

The Cradle of Rhymes
In the nursery rhyme ancient, magical layers of language still echo. Nursery rhymes are much loved by children, who relive, through them, earlier phases in human development.

Nursery rhymes act like magical spells, charming us forever. They seize us the moment we hear them and never release us. When we have long forgotten other poems we still know the nursery rhymes by heart. There is no need to 'learn' them, and children seem to know them immediately: they meet them like old companions or lost possessions. In the nursery rhyme, as in magical language, sound, rhythm and repetition predominate over meaning. The rhymes are little rituals to be chanted in groups, compelling us to move, dance, step and clap. They are language learned by the whole body.

As in ancient texts, there is no traceable author. They might have started as a joke, a political pun or a pacifier, but their ancestry is noble — no less than the genius of the English language itself. The genius of the language seized an opportunity to speak itself and slip from the tongues of bards into the hearts of poets and children.

For children, nursery rhymes are the first truly artistic experience where the childhood of language meets the child. Each rhyme is an opportunity to dance with the genius of English — to be embraced by sound, carried by rhythm and invigorated by rhyme and repetition. They are the indispensable nursery of the poetic.

Gibberish

A close relative of the nursery rhyme is gibberish, a form of magical language enjoyed by children all over the world. It is like a younger sibling to the nursery rhyme, an even more playful and alive progeny of English.

> Eeenie meenie macka acka
> Hi di dominacka
> Stickeracka roomeracka
> Om pom push.

The exact wording changes from city to city, country to country. But the basic form, its rhythmical structure, remains the same from London to Adelaide, and New York to Cape Town. Here is a version from Melbourne:

> Eena meena micka macka
> Eyre eye omma nacka
> Icky chicky
> Om pom puss.

The way it asserts itself again and again in different locations is miraculous — like a little spell cast by language itself. It is English magical language, not Italian or Russian. The genius of the English language is active in every part of it. Compare it with the magical language you created in the last chapter and feel the difference.

In gibberish a very old and vital layer of the language has preserved itself — a layer closer to rhythm than sound. It is vital for the creative writer to engage in this layer of language because it is language at its most alive, comparable to the meristem of a plant. The meristem is where the plant is most alive: the point from which everything else develops. While the rest of the plant hardens over time, the meristem stays young and vital.

Gibberish is where language is its most green and juicy, where the genius of English sprouts anew! Read aloud the following version of the rhyme until it takes hold of you. Feel how it starts to speak itself and develop a will of its own. Let the rhythm carry you.

> Eeenie meenie macka acka
> Hi di dominacka
> Stickeracka roomeracka
> Om pom push.

Exercise 1: Gibberish

Now change the 'words' but keep it rhythmic. Leave your pen aside and try voicing different possibilities. Write it down when you feel you've got a good rhythmic flow. For example:

> Eenie beenie ocka locka
> Fe fi tocka tocka
> Tickerlacka woomaracka
> Om bom bush.

Writing down gibberish may feel alien to its nature. It is a form of language so alive its very essence is movement, change and re-creation.

Exercise 2: Weighing the Words

Now try the following experiment (and this time you may use your pen immediately). Replace some of the gibberish with 'proper' words. See how many real words this nonsense rhyme can digest before becoming incurably congested with meaning.

> Eeenie beanie soccer locka — works fine
> Eeenie beanie soccer player — definitely misses the goal!

The Nursery of the Poetic

Gibberish is the womb from which nursery rhymes are born. The rhyme emancipates itself gradually from its magical predecessor, but the links remain obvious. The gibberish at the beginning and at the end envelop the common English lines like a mother does her child:

Hickory dickory dock
The mouse ran up the clock
The clock struck one, the mouse ran down
Hickory dickory dock.

Bring to mind as many nursery rhymes as you can and recite them aloud. Give yourself permission to be playful and joyous. Here are some of my favourites: Georgie Porgie, pudding and pie; Jack be nimble, Jack be quick; Hey diddle diddle.

Exercise 3: Hickory Dickory Dock

Let us return to Hickory Dickory Dock. Leave the first and last lines but replace the middle lines, retaining the rhythm. Clap the rhythm several times and then and let the word fall into place, Try several verses, e.g.:

Hickory dickory dock
Ten numbers are on my clock
There used to be more, but two ran out the door
Hickory dickory dock.

Exercise 4: Nursing a simple Rhyme

Create a simple nursery rhyme of your own, as did **Barbara Reed**:

Eden went to market
To buy a little horse
She walked to the market
But rode home of course.

Exercise 5: Making a Nursery Rhyme

Now try a more elaborate version; example by **Jennifer Kornberger**:

How many miles to a mermaid's home?
As many as all the stitches you've sewn.
How many miles to the house of John?
Four and twenty before you've come.
How many leagues to the city of Grend?
More at the start and less at the end.
How many rings on the hand of a queen?
Only one, but it's never been seen.

Tongue Twisters

Some nursery rhymes are also tongue twisters. Recite this example:

> How much wood would a woodchuck chuck,
> If a woodchuck could chuck wood?
> A woodchuck would chuck
> All the wood he could chuck,
> If a woodchuck could chuck wood.

Exercise 6: Twisting the Tongue

Write a tongue twister. Choose a consonant and let it do its gymnastics with the tongue. Here is an example by **Helen McDonnell**:

> How much work would a work mate work
> if a work mate worked all week.
> If he worked all week
> he'd fall off his feet,
> if a work mate worked all week.

The House that Jack built

Some of the longer nursery rhymes revel in strict form and repetition. Enjoy the steady build-up of content of the House that Jack Built.

> This is the house that Jack built.
>
> This is the malt
> That lay in the house that Jack built.
>
> This is the rat
> That ate the malt
> That lay in the house that Jack built.
>
> This is the cat
> That killed the rat
> That ate the malt
> That lay in the house that Jack built.
>
> This is the dog
> That worried the cat
> That killed the rat

That ate the malt
That lay in the house that Jack built.
...
This is the man all tattered and torn
That kissed the maiden all forlorn
That milked the cow with the crumpled horn,
That tossed the dog
That worried the cat
That killed the rat
That ate the malt
That lay in the house that Jack built ...

Children have a strong affinity with repetition — they gain security from that which reliably recurs. Repetition is indispensable in magical language and ritual. It is present in all phenomena of life and is indigenous to the human soul where the new always contains the old. The house of our body is built in this way. Reciting a nursery rhyme like this is like participating in the process of growth. Inventing such a rhyme is like partaking in creation itself.

Exercise 7: The House that You Build

Model a nursery rhyme on the House that Jack Built. Start with one sentence — you do not need to know where it is going when you begin. Let it grow. Bypass adult impatience and enjoy the process. Build it up to around ten lines. Here is an example by **Sue McBurney:**

This is the land we live on

This is the sea that circles
the land we live on

This is the girl who swims
in the sea that circles
the land we live on

This is the friend
who holds the hand of the girl
who swims in the sea that circles
the land we live on...
This is the river that runs to the sea
and nourishes the tree

that dropped the stick
that was thrown for the dog
who belongs to the friend
who holds the hand
of the girl who swims
in the sea that circles
The land we live on.

The Key to the Kingdom

The House that Jack Built is layered like an onion. In the Key to the Kingdom the language imitates another growth process — the spiral — this time starting at its broadest, narrowing in, then out again.

> This is the Key
> This is the Key to the kingdom
> In that kingdom is a city
> In that city is a town
> In that town there is a street
> In that street there winds a lane
> In that lane there is a yard
> In that yard there is a house
> In that house there waits a room
> In that room an empty bed
> And on that bed a basket —
> A basket of sweet flowers
> Of flowers, of flowers
> A basket of sweet flowers.
>
> Flowers in a basket
> Basket on the bed
> Bed in the chamber
> Chamber in the house
> House in the weedy yard
> Yard in the winding lane
> Lane in the broad street
> Street in the high town
> Town in the city
> City in the kingdom.
> Of the kingdom this is the Key.

Exercise 8: Spiral Rhyme

Create your own verse using this spiral form. You may stay in the realm of childhood language, or use it as inspiration for a piece that lives in the realm of adult experience. For example:

This is the light that chants by Pen Brown

Aum is a rhythm in the light
in that light there is the chant
in that chant there is a heart
in that heart there is a sea
in that sea there is an island
on that island is a wood
in that wood there is a stone
on that stone there sits a man
in that man there beats a heart
in that heart there is the chant
in the chant there longs the light
light, light,
reaching for the light
light in the rhythm
rhythm in the chant
chant in the heart
heart in the man
man on the mountain stone
stone in the silent wood
wood on the sweet green island
island in the spiralling sea
sea in the world egg
world in the Creator's heart
heart in His ceaseless rhythm
rhythm in that secret chant
Chanting in the longed for light
Aum ….

3

The Wishing Well

Gibberish and nursery rhymes have many relatives that populate the kingdom of childhood, including play language, counting songs and all types of ditties and little poems. One of the most delightful is the wish poem.

> Rain, rain, go away
> Come again another day.

So simple and convincing — this wish makes the child in us feel that it could work! 'In olden times when wishing still helped one …' is the poignant introduction to some of the Grimm's fairy tales. Childhood is laced with wishes that often leave their traces in poetic form.

> Star light star bright
> First star I see tonight
> I wish I may, I wish I might
> Have the wish I wish tonight.

Exercise 1: Five Wishes

Take a moment to remember yourself as a young child, see yourself in your environment. Now write down at least five wishes you had (or could have had). Start each sentence with 'I wish'.

> I wish I had a red scooter
> I wish I could fly
> I wish I had a ladder to my secret room.

Exercise 2: The Wings of a Wish

Now choose one of your wishes and let it unfold in your imagination. Write a piece that explores what would happen if that wish could come true. Refrain from planning ahead. Let the wish unfold its full potential. Feel the wish build its own momentum and allow yourself to follow in its wake. For example:

> I wish I could fly. I wouldn't tell anybody at first that I really could fly. I would practise secretly behind the shed. At first I would lift off just a little bit. Then I would learn how to hover as high as the fence. At night I would pretend to go to sleep but then I'd open my window and fly up over the house. I'd fly down to Dan's house, over the power lines. I would knock on his window and take him for a ride, if he was not too heavy. It would be a secret. At my dad's birthday, I would tell everyone, 'I can fly.' Nobody would believe me. Then I would lift off. My mum would scream. Dad would shout, 'Come back — it's dangerous.' But I'd soar higher. There would be a huge commotion. Uncle Rob would call the police. There would be a fire engine …

Here is another example:

I wish I had an older brother. His name would be Dan and he would sleep in the top bunk. He would shine his torch on the ceiling at night and tell me all the things you do to stop robbers. He wouldn't get angry with me when I didn't know things. He would make a boat for us and we'd sail to Antarctica to put a flag in the ice and make things out of snow. The things we made would stay there forever. He would have a compass and always know where South was. He would walk with me to school and whistle and stare at Jason Teale and Jason Teale would just look at his shoelaces.

Every story has its own momentum. In these tales the momentum often has the story! Once a wish has mounted the winged horse of the imagination they can travel far together, especially in childhood where the reins of reality are not yet fixed. Wishes are brimful with potential. They yearn for the unattainable and long for fulfilment. They are always ready to unfold.

In creative writing we can give ourselves permission to explore this realm without fear of being unhorsed. An exercise like the last one may serve as a laboratory for the soul, a secure place to experiment with dreams. There is nothing to fear — the page is our safety net!

First Callings

Another common form of wish is the vocational wish. For the child, vocations present a doorway into the adventure of being an adult. Jobs and professions are powerful archetypes, surrounded by an aura of awe, endowed with mastery and magical status. In daydreams and play children wear them like clothes (and change them as often).

Exercise 3: Five Callings

List five vocational wishes you had (or could have had) as a child.

Choose one of these wishes and elaborate on it. Try to stay within the standpoint of the child (do not thwart your childhood imagination with the sentiments of adult reality). For example:

> I wish I was a jockey.
> I wish I was a trapeze performer in a circus …

> I wish I was a shop keeper. I would have a shop that sold everything. If someone wanted to buy ice cream or white bread or croissants I would have it in my shop. I would also sell dogs and fish-food and compasses. I would fold the fifty dollar notes and put them under the tray in my till. I would make a lot of money and camp in my shop at night. I would sell torches, too.

Poetic Tours

We can approach the next set of wishes with our adult voice. I call them geographical wishes and have found them very stimulating for the creative writer. The imagination is a born traveller, it is nomadic by nature. The geographical wish is directed towards the spirit of place:

> I wish I was in Tibet
> I wish I was in New York

Here we can explore a longing for a different landscape, for strange and adventurous places. It might be the wish to encounter the challenge of Mt Everest or the holiness of the city of Buddhas. As modern human beings we are world wise, our imagination is global. A name like Kenya conjures a flood of images that are very different from those associated with Tibet, Fiji, New York. Every place represents another way of being human. Deep inside we know the world is us.

Exercise 4: Poetic Tours

Explore one of your geographical wishes. Imagine yourself in your wish location. Find words that convey the experience of place. For example:

> **Wish Poem by Jaya Penelope**
> I wish I was in South India squatting on a flat stone by the lip of a river,
> spreading out my bright colours, my silks and my saris in the sun

I would crouch under an ancient tree with my pot of silver water and paint my feet with henna
I wish I was high in the holy Himalayas, where prayer flags flutter
I wish I was a red flag unfurled at the top of a fierce mountain pass
I wish I was a lonely road going nowhere through ice-hung trees
I wish I lived in a yurt on the high plains and drank mare's milk and slept in a raised hallway of red carpets, a nest of tangled limbs, lovers and children and a pack of dogs (and you'd come home to me, cat-coloured, and nightly I'd get tangled in your forest dark hair)

I Wish by Sue McBurnie

I wish I was in Villacabumba, the valley of longevity in the Ecuadorian Andes. The valley is flooded with clean white light and the air is fresh. People live to be very old and they work in the fields growing corn and sugar. They sit by the roadside at small wooden stores, chatting and drinking coffee. They walk up the mountainsides and drink water from mountain streams. They know the history of their neighbours, the sadness, the dark secrets. They remember births, weddings, deaths, and they tell stories. Their faces turn brown and wrinkled with age and smile lines are deeply etched. (But instead I am here, living by the sea and waiting for the smile lines.)

We can travel even further. Our imagination can take us anywhere, beyond our normal bounds. We can become a tree, a river or an otter. We can enter other forms of existence.

Exercise 5: Transformations

List three things you would like to be — if temporarily! Choose one wish and elaborate on it.

> I wish I was an otter
> I wish I was the Ganges River
> I wish I was a gum tree

Wish by John Stubley

I wish I was
A Thursday night
Cloud, floating and forming
And worldwide blown,
Shifting and shaping, free

From the ground,
Light and then
Brooding — with others —
Alone.

Wish by Jennifer Kornberger

I wish I was a goshawk hunting close to the sea
my wings wedged into the salt breeze, my eye
lit, my sight a thin beam of light probing the toss
of grass. I would drop like an empty shout
into the dunes to take what belonged to me.
The feathers on my innocent white throat
would clean themselves in the wind.

Wish poem by Antoinette van der Leeden

I want to be an opal
Darkly, deeply,
Wishing and waiting
For the tremor of light
In a moment of dripping rain.

The Life of Lies

Another way to liberate our creative potential is by means of the 'poetic lie'. Kenneth Koch explored this in exercises with children. A common lie might be an idea in the wrong place for the wrong purposes. But take it back to its appropriate realm and it will grow wings. We can do this by giving ourselves permission to lie. A wish prompts us to explore. A lie allows us to adventure. The wish is restricted by its own parameter of want or desire. Lies are unabashedly loose with the laws of reality.

Exercise 6: Five Lies

Write down five lies about yourself. Now expand on one lie. Follow the momentum of one lie into another. Here is a delightful set by **Anne Esbenshade**:

> I have an otter for a mother
> There is zip where my navel should be
> I don't float

Lies by Anne Esbenshade

I have an otter for a mother. My father met her in the Outer Hebrides on the night of the August moon. The light made a mystery that is hard to unravel. I do have an otter for a mother.

Lies by Morgan Yasbincek

My heart is blue and plays a tune like a flute. My mother was a swan and she was unable to sing. She died just as I was born and I died too. A split-second after I released my last breath a great blue dragon landed on my chest and called through seven rainbows to
, the blue flute-playing god. Now, when the moon is elliptical, I sit under it and write poems because it is what this blue heart commands.

Lies by John Stubley

I am a shell
on the beach waiting
for the tide
to come back in.
I am tap water
in an Evian bottle …

It is impossible to expand on one lie without telling more. Their lack of inhibition makes them good medicine for creatively restricted souls!

The Pedestal of Boasts

A close relative of the lie is the boast. Children boast often and blatantly; adults do so in more refined and ritualised ways.

Personally, I love boasts and I am good at them. I am one of the best boasters I know. Possibly the best. I'd love to show you one of my boasts, but it would only make you feel discouraged. They are too good. Here is a boast of one of my students instead:

The Boast by John Stubley

I am a Sierra Nevada mountain
man. I am a descendent
of Irish royalty and the English
that conquered them. I am
a Second Avenue
down-in-the-world
New York City

bum. I am
a wandering seer,
a rambling fool.
I am everything.
I am nothing.

Exercise 7: Time to Boast

Write a boastful piece. Enjoy the experience.

4

Ladder of Dreams

Wishes, lies and boasts stir us into creative fantasy and expand the inner life of the soul. They lead us into the realm of daydreams, that training ground for story-making. This realm is colourful and rich, but it is also illusory. Wishes, lies and daydreams are exhilarating but we can be swept away in their dreaming. They leave us longing for a different kind of dream, one that blossoms from the imagination itself. There are such stories — we call them fairy tales or folk tales.

The name 'fairy tale' first referred to the English tales with their leaning towards the elemental world, the world of fairy. The more popular German tales collected by the Brothers Grimm in the eighteenth century were called household or folk tales. (The Brothers carefully recorded the stories from country women who knew them by heart). Later they were all placed together under the title fairy tales.

Folk tales may be seen as the daydreaming of the world-soul; objective visions, modulated by the character of a particular folk culture. We could view them as remnants from the childhood of humanity, small in volume but mighty in content. They speak in pictures, the very language of the soul, and provide a powerful directive for the inner life.

Folk tales have an outward form that is determined by folklore and by their origin in a particular time and culture. I would like to acknowledge here the concerns of those who criticise folk tales on the grounds that they appear to present masculine and feminine stereotypes. If this is an important matter to you, I encourage you to address it creatively in the exercises to come.

For, cruel stepmothers and weak-but-good fathers aside, the essential dimension of the fairy tale is the human soul in the process of transformation. The soul is both prince and princess, king and queen. The happy marriage that concludes many tales speaks of the inner union of masculine and feminine aspects within the one human soul.

Wishing Tales

The two-edged sword of wishes often plays an important part in these tales. The story of 'The Fisherman and his Wife' explores the darker side of wishes and subjective dreams. It tells of a poor fisherman who lives with his wife in a pigsty near the sea. One morning the fisherman catches a large flounder. The fish is able to speak and it tells the fisherman that it is an enchanted prince. Most surprised, the fisherman returns his catch to the sea.

When the fisherman relates his strange adventure to his wife she is incensed because he has not asked for a wish. She insists he go back and ask the fish to turn their pigsty into a hut. The wish is immediately fulfilled and the fisherman and his wife enjoy their new life. But the fisherman's wife is soon tired of their small fortune. She fancies a castle and makes her husband return to the fish. No sooner is the new wish uttered than it is fulfilled. Now they live in a grand castle with servants and stables and parks and everything they could wish for. But the fisherman's wife is not happy for long. Now she wants to be king. Once more her husband has to ask the fish and again her wish is granted. But each time he returns to the shore the sea is darker and more turbulent.

Soon the fisher's wife wants to be emperor, then pope. The sea grows more and more turbulent but all her wishes come true. But even pope is not enough. Seeing the sun and moon rise she wishes to be like god. Her husband is frightened to ask, but he has to obey the pope. A storm is raging when he approaches the sea. The water is almost black. When the fish hears his request he replies, 'Go to her, you will find her back in the pigsty.' And there they are still living to this day.

We all know this story, experienced in small or large ways. Such a story portrays the condition of the human soul; it contains volumes of psychology, encompasses the teaching of the sages, and resonates with the wisdom of the Buddha and the Scriptures. Tales like the Fisherman and his Wife are circuitous. They spin their heroes up and down the wheel of fortune.

Folk Tale and Transformation

Most folk tales, however, break the pattern of stagnation. Rather than the main character being returned to where they started, they are lead through a process of transformation, the alchemical journey of the soul. On this journey the hero or heroine meets with challenges and hardship, and emerges victorious.

If folk tales were not part of your childhood it is time to administer a good dose of story medicine to your soul. These tales are essential to creative health and well-being, and are part of the imaginal wealth of any writer. The tales of the Brothers Grimm (as well as fairy tales from Russia and Norway and all around the world) are primary ingredients to a well-balanced library. If ever your imagination runs dry you can quickly refuel it from this source.

Writing a proper folk tale is not easy and we will not attempt it at this stage. (My book *The Power of Stories* treats this in great detail.) We will, however, use the household tale to gain inspiration for our own narratives. The tale of Ferdinand the Faithful and Ferdinand the Unfaithful will lead us into our first writing exercise.

Ferdinand the Faithful and Ferdinand the Unfaithful

Once upon a time there lived a man and a woman who so long as they were rich had no children, but when they were poor they got a little boy. They could find no godfather for him, so the man said he would just go to another village to see if he could get one there. On his way he met a poor man, who asked him where he was going. He said he was going to see if he could get a godfather, because he was so poor that no one would stand as godfather for him. 'Oh,' said the poor man, 'you are poor, and I am poor. I will be godfather for you, but I am so badly off I can give the child nothing. Go home and tell the midwife that she is to come to the church with the child.' When they all got to the church together, the beggar was already there, and he gave the child the name of Ferdinand the Faithful.

When he was going out of the church, the beggar said, 'Now go home, I can give you nothing, and you likewise ought to give me nothing.' Now when the child was seven years old, he went to play with some other boys, and each of them boasted that he had got more from his godfather than the other, but the child could say nothing, and was vexed, and went home and said to his father, 'Did I get nothing at all, then, from my godfather?' 'Oh, yes,' said the father, 'you have a key. If there is a castle standing on the heath, just go to it and open it.' Then the boy went thither, but no castle was to be seen, or heard of.

After seven years more, when he was fourteen years old, he again went and there was a castle on the heath and he used the key to open it and found within a horse — a white one. Then the boy was so full of joy because he had a horse, that he mounted on it and galloped back to his father. 'Now I have a white horse, and I will travel,' said he.

So he set out, and as he was on his way, a pen was lying on the road. At first he thought he would pick it up, but then he thought to himself, 'You should leave it lying there, you will easily find a pen where you are going, if you have need of one.' As he was thus riding away, a voice called after him, 'Ferdinand the Faithful, take it with you.' He looked around and saw no one, but he went back again and picked it up.

When he had ridden a little farther, he passed by a lake, and a fish was lying on the bank, gasping and panting for breath, so he said, 'Wait, my dear fish, I will help you into the water,' and he took hold of it by the tail, and threw it into the lake. Then the fish put its head out of the water and said, 'As you have helped me out of the mud I will give you a flute. When you are in any need, play on it, and I will help you, and if ever you let anything fall in the water, just play and I will reach it out to you.'

Then he rode away, and there came to him a man who asked him where he was going. 'Oh, to the next place.' 'What is your name?' 'Ferdinand the Faithful.' 'So, then we have almost the same name, I am called Ferdinand the Unfaithful.'

Now it was unfortunate that Ferdinand the Unfaithful knew everything that the other had ever thought and everything he was about to do. He knew it by means of all kinds of wicked arts. There was in the inn an honest girl, who had a bright face and behaved very prettily. She fell in love with Ferdinand the Faithful because he was a handsome man, and she asked him whither he was going. 'Oh, I am just travelling round about,' said he. Then she said he ought to stay there, for the king of that country wanted an attendant or an outrider, and he ought to enter his service. He answered he could not very well go to anyone like that and offer himself. Then said the maiden, 'Oh, but I will soon do that for you.' And so she went to the king, and told him that she knew of an excellent servant for him. He was well pleased, and had Ferdinand the Faithful brought to him, to make him his servant. Ferdinand the Faithful, however, liked better to be an outrider, for where his horse was, there he also wanted to be, so the king made him an outrider.

When Ferdinand the Unfaithful learnt that, he said to the girl, 'What? Do you help him and not me?' 'Oh,' said the girl, 'I will help you too.' She thought, I must keep friends with that man, for he is not to be trusted. And she went to the king, and offered him as a servant.

Now when the king met his lords in the morning, he always lamented and said, 'Oh, if I only had my love with me.' Ferdinand the Unfaithful, however, was always hostile to Ferdinand the Faithful. So once, when the king was complaining thus, he said, 'You have the outrider, send him away to get her, and if he does not do it, his head must be struck off.' Then the king sent for Ferdinand the Faithful, and told him that there was, in this place or in that place, a girl he loved, and that he was to bring her to him, and if he did not do it he should die. Ferdinand the Faithful went into the stable to his white horse, and complained and lamented, 'Oh, what an unhappy man am I.' Then someone behind him cried, 'Ferdinand the Faithful, why do you weep?'

He looked round but saw no one, and went on lamenting. 'Oh, my dear little white horse, now must I leave you, now I must die.' Then someone cried once more, 'Ferdinand the Faithful, why do you weep?' Then he was aware that it was his little white horse who was putting that question. 'Do you speak, my little white horse? Can you do that?' And again, he said, 'I am to bring the bride. Can you tell me how I am to set about it?' Then answered the white horse, 'Go to the king, and you will get her for him if he will give you a ship full of meat, and a ship full of bread. Great giants dwell on the lake, and if you take no meat with you for them, they will tear you to pieces, and there are the large birds which would pluck the eyes out of your head if you had no bread for them.' Then the king made all the butchers in the land kill, and all the bakers bake, that the ships might be filled.

When they were full, the little white horse said to Ferdinand the Faithful, 'Now mount me, and go with me into the ship, and when the giants come, say — peace, peace, my dear little giants, I have had thought of ye, something I have brought for ye. And when the birds come, you shall again say — peace, peace, my dear little birds, I have had thought of ye, something I have brought for ye. Then when you come to the castle, the giants will help you. Then go up to the castle, and take a couple of giants with you. There the princess lies sleeping. You must, however, not awaken her, but the giants must lift her up, and carry her in her bed to the ship.' And now everything took place as the little white horse had said, and Ferdinand the Faithful gave the giants and the birds what he had brought for them, and that made the giants willing, and they carried the princess in her bed to the king. And when she came to the king, she said she could not live, she must have her writings, they had been left in her castle.

Then by the instigation of Ferdinand the Unfaithful, Ferdinand the Faithful was called, and the king told him he must fetch the writings from the castle, or he should die. Then he went once more into the stable, and bemoaned himself and said, 'Oh, my dear little white horse, now I am to go away again, how am I to do it?' Then the little white horse said he was to load the ships full again. So it happened again as it had happened before, and the giants and the birds were made gentle by the meat. When they came to the castle, the white horse told Ferdinand the Faithful that he must go in, and that on the table in the princess's bedroom lay the writings. And Ferdinand the Faithful went in, and fetched them. When they were on the lake, he let his pen fall into the water. Then said the white horse, 'Now I cannot help you at all.' But he remembered his flute, and began to play on it, and the fish came with the pen in its mouth, and gave it to him. So he took the writings to the castle, where the wedding was celebrated.

The new queen, however, did not love the king because he had no nose, but she would have much liked to love Ferdinand the Faithful. Once, therefore, when all the lords of the court were together, the queen said she could do feats of magic, that she could cut off anyone's head and put it on again, and that one of them ought just to try it. But none of them would be the first, so Ferdinand the Faithful, again at the instigation of Ferdinand the Unfaithful, undertook it and she hewed off his head, and put it on again for him, and it healed together directly, so that it looked as if he had a red thread round his throat. Then the king said to her, 'My child, and where have you learnt that?' 'Oh,' she said, 'I understand the art. Shall I just try it on you also.' 'Oh, yes,' said he. So she cut off his head, but did not put it on again, and pretended that she could not get it on, and that it would not stay. Then the king was buried, and she married Ferdinand the Faithful.

He, however, always rode on his white horse, and once when he was seated on it, it told him that he was to go on to the heath which he knew, and gallop three times round it. And when he had done that, the white horse stood up on its hind legs, and was changed into a king's son.

The Picture Language of Story

Like many fairy tales, this one tells us at least two stories: the story of humanity through time and the journey of the individual soul. Both universal and intimate, these stories speak in the language of pictures.

It is important to realise that we are all of the figures in a fairy tale. We are not just Ferdinand the Faithful. We are the poor godfather, the king and the queen, the fish and the giants; we are the white horse that finds its voice in a moment of despair. (The white horse appears also in other tales as a trustworthy companion and counsellor in times of need.) The speaking horse points to the deeper knowing inside ourselves, to our intuition. Ferdinand the Faithful and the queen represent the essential and creative aspects of ourselves. Ferdinand the Unfaithful marvellously illustrates the ability of our lower self to put hurdles into our path and thwart our intentions.

This tale contains many motifs of particular interest to the writer. One is the sudden appearance at the age of fourteen of a key that opens a castle — this is the time when creativity starts to emerge. All writers have been handed this key, have unlocked their castle and found within it a white horse that made them think, 'Now I have a white horse I will travel.'

Whoever mounts this horse will find a pen lying across their path. And if they are writers they will receive their calling: 'Ferdinand the Faithful, take it with you.' They will pick it up. No matter whether this happens at fourteen or much later in life, picking up the pen will of necessity be followed by the appearance of the unwanted companion, the shadow at our heels.

This is the double, who in the case of Ferdinand the Faithful, 'Knew everything that the other had ever thought and everything he was about to do.' It is that aspect of our personality that makes us unfaithful to our calling, that aims to thwart our attempts, but in so doing also furthers them. Many writers know this companion well. It comes cleverly disguised in the form of doubt, the lack of confidence, the absence of good ideas, the inability to create. It hides itself in the cave of apathy or inner emptiness. Like Ferdinand the Unfaithful it makes the world conspire against us, convinces us our efforts are futile and our tasks impossible. And so they are without the help of an inner voice, a deeper kind of knowing that jumps the hurdles put in our way.

The pictures presented are often surprising and seemingly arbitrary. Ferdinand the Unfaithful disappears and the king is meted out what may strike us as an unjust fate. Looked at more deeply, however, these pictures reveal deeper aspects of the transformative journey.

The king exemplifies procrastination. His line, 'Oh, if I only had my love with me,' reveals his inability to act. First he is unable to fetch his bride and then unable to retrieve her writings. In the last scene he once more reveals his lack of creative courage. Ferdinand has to demonstrate the beheading before the king is willing to undertake it himself: he is only able to imitate. In terms of creative writing this reveals his inability to authentically create. He is a victim of cliché. Naturally this entity has to die in us for our full creative potential to unfold.

Another surprising turn is the sudden disappearance of Ferdinand the Unfaithful at the end of the tale. But this too makes sense when we look at the close link between procrastination on the one hand and the workings of our lower self on the other. They are as closely related as the king and Ferdinand the Unfaithful. When one dies the other dies too. And so it is in the tale. The king is beheaded and Ferdinand the Unfaithful disappears.

Consider Ferdinand's task to recover the writings of the queen. She, like us, is a creative writer. Like us she feels that some of her work is missing. To be a writer is to live with the conviction that some of our work is missing. We sense writings longing to be conceived and produced. And this is difficult at times, particularly for our ordinary self. The only way forward is by means of a more extraordinary self: some trustworthy emissary of the imagination to help recover our creativity — someone like Ferdinand the Faithful.

In other words our writing needs a hero or heroine. If they are real heroes they will attract adventures aplenty. All we need to do is to record their tales. Our challenge is to make such a hero or heroine join our imagination. One way of engaging such a heroine is by creating the right conditions.

Exercise 1: The Heroic Landscape

We can create the right condition for our hero by slowing our imagination to the speed of soul. This helps the right character to arrive. Start, not with the hero or heroine, but with their surroundings — the image of a landscape — and describe it in detail. It may be an oasis in a desert; towering mountains on either side of a fjord; a tangled tropical rainforest; a medieval village; a New York cityscape or some utopian settlement on Mars. Picture it as though it were a painting and describe it in detail. The more particulars you give the more potent your picture will be. Do not introduce your character yet.

If this is difficult, try the following: imagine yourself as a bird, flying high above a cloud covered earth. To begin with you see nothing of what lies below and know not where you are. Then slowly descend through the thick cover of white. Do not pre-plan what you will see. Let your imagination surprise you with a landscape. Describe what lies below in broad outlines, and then descend further. See more of the landscape and eventually alight in one particular place. Describe in great detail what you find there.

Monastery Garden by Janet Blagg

Across the valley you can see the monastery spread out on an acre of hillside. Along one side is a walled garden, its creamy limestone high and solid against the thin blue sky.

You enter the garden through a low gate, ducking your head to avoid the arch above. Within lies a wondrous juxtaposition of ordered form and joyous profusion of rampant plant life. Old fruit trees in lines, a tangle of climbing rose that is yearning for freedom, making its way over vegetable frames to merge its fragrance with lavender and hollyhock. Over by the kitchen door, the herbs, another wild profusion; thyme gone mad leaving all sense of time long gone.

Overlooking the rows of cabbages and tomatoes, their leaves pungent in the sunshine, is a wooden bench. On one side of it a sundial, on the other a well.

Exercise 2: The Distillation of the Hero

The landscape you created is a soulscape, the matrix from which your hero will be born. He or she is already in the scene, waiting. Now, let the hero appear. To do this properly revisit the landscape in your mind's eye, engage all senses, see the scenery in all its detail, then allow your hero or heroine to emerge from the background. Now let your imagination create a clear picture of your hero — the colour of their eyes, their posture, the way they smile or frown, the shoes they wear. Observe their clothes, look for minute details on their coat, a brooch, an unusual embroidery, a torn sleeve. See their hands. Are they large or small, rough or fine? How do they eat soup? If you give your character this imaginative substance, they will give you their story in turn, so be ready to record it.

Here is the continuation of **Janet Blagg's Monastery Garden:**

> On the bench, head bowed, sits a young novice, Ivan. It is his work to tend the garden, work he gladly accepted, but now he is not so sure. He is to reimpose the order in the garden that was let slip by his predecessor, who let everything go to the glory of god.
>
> With secateurs and pruning saw, Ivan is to remake the lines of precision and curb and tame, cut back the rambling rose. He sighs. There are roses in his own cheeks, an ardent foxfire in his eyes. He loves the wildness and the heady mix of scents in the walled garden. With long and sensitive fingers he feels for the locket at his throat, his mother's. It was her dying wish he give his life to Christ. He opens the locket, where her frail strength stares across into his father's heavy brow, the seeds from whence he came. He lifts his eyes to meet the creamy perfection of the rose, and the leaves of the trees moving in the wind beyond the protection of the stone wall, shifting and dancing in the breeze.

Here is another example by **Jennifer Kornberger:**

> He is a shambling long-haired youth with a face that is ready to smile and a voice that rides high when he is excited and low when he is calm. His clothes are ill-fitting and he seems to have packets and wads strapped to his body under his garments. When he passes through the forest part of it seems to sweep along with him as though the trees wished to follow in his wake. His glance always rests on

the furthest place. Houses and rooms do not hold him for long, he prefers to sleep outside. He plays a tin whistle gaily or sadly as the clouds decree. His name is Yentz.

Exercise 3: Beginning a Quest

Many great tales start with the hero or heroine leaving home to adventure with the unfamiliar. Stay in the mood of the household tale. Take away all modern trappings and watch your hero walk or ride into an unknown story. What are they leaving behind? (A poor father, a caring queen, a stern master?) What magical gifts from the past do they carry with them into the future? (A ring, a jacket from your mother.)

Stay with your story as it unfolds moment by moment, without planning ahead. Allow yourself to be continually surprised by what comes to meet you. Lead your hero into a challenge, and see what he or she makes of the situation. Remember, it is your character's story, not yours. I is not necessary to complete the story unless it presses towards conclusion. The young novice in Janet Blagg's tale begins his quest thus:

> He kisses the rose, turns. His feet crunch on the gravel, past the ornamental pond, on the path to the high gate. He takes the key from the chain at his waist, unlocks the gate, throws the key in a shining arc into the field beyond, pulls the cassock over his head and lets it fall, and walks across the field diagonally, against the grain.

Jennifer Kornberger's Yentz leaves home in his father's shoes:

> Yentz left home in autumn with his mother's blessing. 'Your feet are the same size as your father's,' she told him. 'Here are a pair of his shoes. See how they fit so well. Now go, my son, and see if you can find him for there has been no news whether he is dead or alive all these years.' Yentz kissed his mother and bade her farewell and promised to find news if he could. He strode out of the village in his father's shoes and took the road through the orchards. There were apples lying beside the road and Yentz stooped to pick them up. He put them in a little sack he had tied around his middle. Then he came to a crossroad. 'Well shoes,' he said, 'which road do we travel?' And the shoes started south and Yentz was mightily pleased at the way they knew where to go.

Exercise 4: The Hero's Tale (Optional)

Now let your hero tell you the rest of their tale. If you find this exercise difficult or beyond your creative means, remember you do not have to do it. Your hero will do it for you! It is their job, their very purpose in life, to tell their story. Listen and record them faithfully. Some writers find it helpful to always return to the same heroic storyteller, others create a new one for each tale.

5

Fabulous Tales

Ferdinand the Faithful dealt with the shadow aspect of the human soul. In a fairy tale we are always every character — the good and the bad, the industrious and the lazy, the stepmother, the king and the horse.

In Ferdinand the Faithful the soul's dance with its shadow is obvious; the choreography of light and darkness is spelled out. Fairy tales are adept at revealing the kaleidoscope of our inner life and demonstrating the integration of evil. Like their major heroes and heroines they are able to transform evil in unique and adventurous ways.

Legends and animal fables tend to specialise: the fable in the realm of human folly and the legend in the heroic and saintly. Legends often contain a kernel of historic truth which has undergone an imaginative elaboration. In Aesop's fables, we often find unsavoury aspects of human soul life portrayed by the animal world. A well-known example is the Fox and the Grapes.

> **The Fox and the Grapes**
> One hot summer's day a Fox was strolling through an orchard till he came to a bunch of Grapes just ripening on a vine which had been trained over a lofty branch. 'Just the thing to quench my thirst,' quoth he. Drawing back a few paces, he took a run and a jump, and just missed the bunch. Turning round again with a One, Two, Three, he jumped up, but with no greater success. Again and again he tried after the tempting morsel, but at last had to give it up, and walked away with his nose in the air, saying, 'I am sure they are sour.'
> Moral: It is easy to despise what you cannot get.

Animal fables are humorous, didactic and satirical. Fairy tales are born from the imagination but fables come from the intellect. Like the wolf in sheep's clothing, they wear imaginative elements to distract us from their purpose — which is to preach a moral. The common fare of fables relates human traits to particular animals. The fox is clever, cunning; the lion embodies courage, justice, the wolf greed. These relationships are deeply rooted in folklore and point far back to the powerful inspiration of the animal archetypes available to early humanity.

Animal Archetypes

In this lesson we will explore at a deeper level that which the fable is merely a sign for — the creative archetypes of the animals and their relationship to the human soul. Today such relationships easily slip into the realm of cliché — great poetic ideas that once were fresh with experience but now serve only as labels to indicate the experience. As creative writers we aim to re-enter the paradisiacal innocence of immediate experience to see the buffalo in all buffalo, the lion in all lions.

We are still linked to the animal world through those aspects of lion, bull and eagle that remain in us. All animals have left their gifts in our soul; they are the imaginal sphinx of our inner life. This sphinx is not silent; it willingly speaks to us in the wild woods of myth, where the bull within the bull is still alive, and the first of eagles still soars. Through the telescope of story we can still catch Bear trotting through the denser forests of mind. And if we are fortunate we might, like Rose Red and Snow White, find a bit of gold shimmering where the fur has rubbed off. For the bear is a mysterious creature. To the Ainu in northern Japan, the bear is a sacred ancestral being, ritually sacrificed at an annual feast. Bear clans are common in tribal societies all over the northern hemisphere. Bear is a powerful totem.

In all northern hemisphere languages the bear and the constellation of the Great Bear have the same name. The universal dreaming of the past baptised them both and an old knowledge slipped into the preservation of names in which we glimpse that ancient light shining through the rough coat of Bear's story.

All animals have such a coat — it is their coat of story, the cloak of myth. Through it we can see their true nature. As writers we are familiar with this coat of story; it plays a major role in how we place the animal in our imagination. Even today, we are mysteriously affected by certain animals. Some have the power to inspire awe, others repel us. Some come to us repeatedly in dreams or stories.

Consider all the animals that constitute your imaginal sphinx — animals that fascinate or repel you, animals whose presence is a message; animals you feel a relationship with, no matter what part of the world they roam. Mine are: Horse Otter Raven Snake Tiger.

Speaking Animals

In fables and household stories, animals speak. Their speech conjures an ancient memory of the animal archetype in communication with the human being. Tribal societies keep these communications alive via shaman, sacred rituals and animistic cults, but we have almost lost this capacity to commune with the animal realm. Most likely, the animals you listed will speak to you in only the faintest of voices.

One animistic cult however still exists in modern society, and may even be found in your own house. It is the Cult of the Cat. Cats are, to society generally, what your special animals are to you personally: an animal that still speaks; a totem pet, an archetype reduced to type. Cats communicate artfully; their primal language is of mood: likes and dislikes, closeness and rejection, soft paw and claw. Cats have a sixth sense for everything and a seventh for themselves. This makes them particular, often eccentric.

Each cat is individual. Like the lion, cats belong to the animal aristocracy. They have nothing but contempt for the servile attitude of dogs and the mundane routine of other animals. Theirs is an elevated life of chivalric exploits, elaborate rituals around the full moon, enticing songs, well-kept secrets, visionary dreams and premonitions of mice. There are few human soul traits that they do not reflect.

To the imagination cats represent the soul and its unfathomable ways. They are idols of the soul life, a magnet to all those signs of affection and ritual offerings of food from their human devotees. They elicit hymns of praise, a ritual indispensable to their cult. This is mainly an oral tradition, a kind of lounge-room benediction. The eighteenth-century English poet Christopher Smart made such a poem of praise about his cat Jeoffry — the following is only a small extract:

> For I will consider my Cat Jeoffry.
> For he is the servant of the Living God duly and daily serving him.
> For at the first glance of the glory of God in the East he worships in his way.
> For this is done by wreathing his body seven times round with elegant
>   quickness.
> For then he leaps up to catch the musk, which is the blessing of God upon his
>   prayer.
> For he rolls upon prank to work it in.
> For having done duty and received blessings he begins to consider himself.
> For this he performs in ten degrees.
> For first he looks upon his fore-paws to see if they are clean.
> For secondly he kicks up behind to clear away there.
> For thirdly he works it upon stretch with the forepaws extended.
> For fourthly he sharpens his paws by wood …

T. S. Eliot has explored the individuality of cats. In his *Old Possum's Book of Practical Cats*, he is a master of naming — Gumbie Cat, Rum Tum Tugger, Jellicle Cats, Mr. Mistoffelees, Macavity. Naming is an important act because name invokes character.

Exercise 1: Cat Names

Create a number of names encompassing a variety of cat characters. For example: Fortescue, Plum, Horatio, Scruffbucket, Madam Mao, Minnie.

Exercise 2: The Likeable Cat

Choose a likeable cat, name it and write a short piece in which its character and idiosyncrasies are illuminated. Write for fifteen minutes. Here is an example by **Jennifer Kornberger:**

> Paddley van Torc was an elegant cat who disliked any form of human hysteria, hustle or haste. Paddley van Torc trained himself in the art of ignoral. His ritual of ignoral was carefully crafted to shatter any superficiality he sensed in the society of humans. At gatherings he assumed a critical position on the Persian rug and raised his head slowly to catch drifts of meaning. Then he closed his eyes and allowed his whiskers to ruminate. Paddley van Torc then became impervious as stone, listening beyond the yib-yab of human voices to the deeper noises of life: the dog next door being ushered inside for the night, the wind parting day from darkness, the hunter's moon sliding up the autumn sky.

Exercise 3: The Disagreeable Cat

Now choose a rascally cat, name it, and write about it for fifteen minutes. Here is an example by **Adrian Glamorgan:**

> … Gutkin had a cat flap, and he intended to use it. Home was a place to hang up a fur ball, usually over his mistress's bed, but the cat flap was his ticket to adventure, a swinging turnstile of excitement. There were roofs to roam and Gutkin roamed them. Pigeon feathers he spat out after morning tea, and mice and small chihuahuas he'd mince by noontime. Gutkin never put on weight, only guile. His hunting only seemed to enlarge his eyes and sharpen his incisors. By midnight he was home, to meet Harriet coming home, stinking of Drambuie. Gutkin would purr, and Harriet (in fits and starts) snore, until first light.

Travelling with Animals

The mighty archetype of the lion has become domesticated in the cat. Cats are lovable but their power is limited, their voice faint. By contrast the horse is clearly audible. We can explore its archetype through our own inner experience of horse and then through its coat of story.

Exercise 4: The Corral of Meaning

Start with a clean page and write the word 'horse' in the middle. Then surround the word with the names of stories and myths and any ideas, facts and associations you might make about horse. This is the skeleton for the coat of story.

    Fury   The Black Stallion   Race horses   Centaurs
Horse-headed Kalki Avatar (incarnation of Krishna)   Apocalyptic Riders
Bucephalos (Alexander's horse)   Unicorn   Shadowfax (Gandalf's horse)
Riders in Vasilissa   Sound of horse hooves   Horse-shoes as good luck
C. S. Lewis's Horse and His Boy   **HORSE**   Marini's Horse sculptures
Horse-mad Girls   Peter Schaffer's Equus   Leonardo's horse studies
The Trojan Horse   Pegasus   White steed galloping on seashore
Durer's Knight, Death and the Devil   Durer's Apocalyptic Riders
Monty Roberts and the new method of horse training

We all have our own versions of this coat of story. Look at your page of images. Do certain pictures resonate with each other? What speaks most clearly to you?

Exercise 5: Writing on Horseback

Now build up the following imagination: First, create a strong inner picture of a horse or a series of horses. See it (or them) galloping. Let the horse come close so you can see its fine sensitive head; the grace of its whole form.
Now mount the horse. The horse trusts you; you are a fine rider. Trot, then gallop, united with the horse as it moves through the landscape. The landscape your horse travels through is also a soulscape. Write what you see from the back of your horse.

Here is an example **by Jennifer Kornberger:**

> I am grown into this horse. I am a muscle riding atop the substance of rhythm. We are faster than memory, my horse and I. See how we gallop past the broken houses, the houses of smashed windows and spent gardens, the streets where every post and fence wears its tight mask of graffiti. Not one seed from any dead flower do we take. My horse and I will outrun the fences, the cracked fibro, the telephone towers. We are travelling to the edge of the world to see the sun rise …

Horse and rider form a unique relationship. The rider guides the horse; the horse provides the power to fulfil the intentions of the rider. Horse and rider are in sensitive communication. The deep bond is also manifest in the image of the centaur.

Often we use the term 'spirited' for a horse because we recognise a kinship between our spirit and this powerful being. Teenagers, awakening to their own spirit, often become obsessed with the idea of horses. Let us now explore the archetype of horse through story.

Four Riders

For me, two stories involving horses are particularly charged. The four apocalyptic riders in the *Book of Revelation*, and *Vasilissa* in the Russian fairy tale, who meets the same four riders on her way to Baba Yaga's hut:

> The wood was very dark, and she could not help trembling from fear. Suddenly she heard the sound of a horse's hoofs and a man on horseback galloped past her. He was dressed all in white, the horse under him was milk-white and the harness was white, and just as he passed her it became twilight.
>
> She went a little further and again she heard the sound of a horse's hoofs and there came another man on horseback galloping past her. He was dressed all in red, and the horse under him was blood-red and its harness was red, and just as he passed her the sun rose.
>
> That whole day Vasilissa walked, for she had lost her way...But at evening she came all at once to the green lawn where the wretched little hut stood on its hens' legs. The wall around the hut was made of human bones and on its top were skulls ...
>
> As she stood there a third man on horseback came galloping up. His face was black, he was dressed all in black, and the horse he rode was coal-black...
>
> Then suddenly the wood became full of a terrible noise; the trees began to groan, the branches to creak and the dry leaves to rustle, and the Baba-Yaga came flying from the forest, riding in a great iron mortar and driving it with the pestle, and as she came she swept away her trail behind her with a kitchen broom.

Here is an excerpt from the **Book of Revelation**:

> And I saw, and behold, a white horse; and he that sat on him had a bow, and a crown was given unto him; and he went forth conquering, and to conquer.
>
> ...And there went out another horse that was red; and power was given to him that sat thereon to take peace from the earth, and that they should kill one another; and there was given unto him a great sword.
>
> ...And I beheld a black horse; and he that sat on him had a pair of balances in his hand.
>
> ...And I looked, and behold a pale horse; and his name that sat on him was Death...

Both accounts listen to the same archetype and are inspired by the imaginal meaning of 'horse'. In Vasilissa, the witch Baba Yaga and her fence of skulls recall the pale horse ridden by death. The horse can be seen as the intimate companion of the human spirit. Each horse in these passages represents a state of consciousness.

To me the white horse and its rider represent the primal, intuitive, all-penetrating wisdom of the remote past — the same wisdom (crown) that accesses the speaking world of the archetypes. This wisdom has been lost in stages, and remains only vestigially. The red horse, the colour of blood and passion, rides straight into conflict and warfare. It takes peace from the earth and wields a great sword. The calculating mind weighing its advantage (the scales) is the black horse; knowledge reduced to a bargaining, quantifying function. The last stage is the pale horse ridden by Death, with Hell on its heels. The intellect is severed totally from its cosmic archetype, the white horse.

Exercise 6: Four Horses

Ride all four of the apocalyptic horses, starting with the pale horse. Let it take you to its place, its imaginal location. Describe all you see from its back. Do the same with the black and the red horse and finally the white.

The White Horse by Liana Christensen

The white horse will not move. He simply stands stock still, legs braced, an occasional shiver running down his pure flanks. I try dismounting and gently tugging the silver bridle. The horse snorts, but does not budge. I re-mount and lean forward over his elegant neck to whisper encouragement into his pricked ears. Nada. We are going absolutely nowhere. I'm not by nature a cruel person, but eventually I gingerly try my spurs. The white horse rears up then crashes earthward, planting all hooves foursquare on the ground. Utterly immovable.

Centuries pass. I grow as still as the white horse. Mosses and lichens grow upon the beast's fetlocks, then gradually creep upwards until we are both greened over.

One morning, seemingly like any other, the silver reins disintegrate. The white horse begins walking towards lands unknown.

The Red Horse by Elysia Tsangarides

I am walking. Walking for some days searching for anyone, anything alive. The villages I pass are silent. I see something in the distance, so red it's like a burning furnace and I run towards it as if summoned, conjuring all the strength I have. My eyes focus and I see a horse. A red horse? My heart is pounding. There's no time for confusion, only action – necessary and with purpose I run. Finally I am next to her. She is quivering. I can feel the ache of her muscles as I feel my own. Drenched she is entirely in blood. Thick running blood. Not hers but that of others. I reach out my own trembling hand to caress her neck. My hand touches her red sweating skin and all her thoughts seem to be mine. Frightened I draw back but I can still feel her pain. Again I reach out. I see a river rich with blood, burning buildings, children screaming and when I open my eyes, I too am red with blood all over. We are the blood of the village.

The Black Horse by Karen McCrea

I have been summonsed. I am to go forth to plumb the depths of being. I call my steed, and he comes. He is power and purpose, flawless gleaming shadow, the stuff of inky night.

And so am I.

I mount him, he leaps and we are about our business. He steps, unhurried. We know where we are going and what we are doing. We measure the righteous, the good, the just. We are not much loved, but no matter, we will prevail nonetheless.

Bede - that is his name - stands his ground and only shakes his great Stygian head when shouting men with pitchforks or rifles try to turn his course. He merely waits when women or children, yes children, grasp his forelegs to stop his steps.

He is immoveable, immutable.

As am I.

We have no hurry, we have all the long dark night of the soul, every soul, to weigh our scales. On one side the heart and soul of man, on the other the light of the eyes of all the gods

Yes, we, the Black Rider and the Black Horse measure the light, the quality of light in any heart, in every heart. When a heart is found wanting, it's master should quail, should tremble, for in truth they already know what awaits in their own shadow. We take such a one into the long, long folds in the cloak of eternal night, to await the Pale Rider.

Pegasus

In Greek myth we meet two other horses: Pegasus who springs from the head of the slain Medusa, and the Trojan Horse — the cunning construction of Odysseus in his bid to conquer Troy. Forerunner of the new Greek thinking, Odysseus is the first hero to rely on the use of his intellect rather than his physical prowess.

The wooden horse is a picture of the Greek state of mind, while Pegasus is its artistic counterpart. In Pegasus the wooden horse grows wings, comes alive; it is the steed of the artist and poet, lifting the Greek mind above the ordinary into the realm of art and fantasy.

Exercise 7: Back on Pegasus

We will ride our own winged horse to the place where animals speak. Here we will connect with the animal that holds most power for us. In this place we do not speak about them, we must become them as we write.

Give voice to the animal that you feel a connection with, either through sympathy and awe or through fear and loathing. Write in the 'I' voice, exploring its archetypal dimensions. For example:

> I am whale. I sank beneath your dreams so long ago that you forgot the warmth of my blood coursing in the deepest places. I did not weep the sea from my body like you. I made it my sky and filled it with the might of old star songs. The pilgrimages I make along the ocean currents rotate the earth on its axis of salt. I take the air you breathe to the depths and when I move in the valleys of the sea it is the substance of my will heaving to a sure destination …

6

The First Song

In the last lesson we stepped from the created (the animals around us) to the creative (their speaking archetypes), exploring the world of primal creativity with what is creative in us. By artistic means (rather than the visionary powers of seers or saints) we divined the primal essence of the animals, making our way with the help of Pegasus, the winged horse of creative imagination, rather than the white steed of the initiate.

Now we leave the childhood of language to encounter the creation myths that form the foundations of tribal worship and the world religions. These myths are the gates through which we enter the biography of the poetic, and at these gates stand guardians who ask us to leave behind the spectres of our own time.

We need to leave behind modern conceptions that reduce the creation of the world to chemical reactions, divine ancestors to chaotic matter, the great strides of evolution to the accidental mutation of genes and survival of the fittest. All known creation myths point towards beings, presences and archetypes, not matter; towards creative intent, not accidental reaction. If such unimaginative notions are not decisively put aside, our access to the creative ancestors will be barred by the spectre of an ape, paradise will look like a nature reserve and the grand tales of the past will be reduced to the fancies of a naïve mind!

So let us take only what is essential for the voyage, and when we moor our ship at major poetic ports, show due respect to the inhabitants by adopting their garb and habits of thought. We can take on their nuance of feeling and as much of their experience of the world as our imagination will permit. As your guide I encourage you to mingle with the locals and meet the poets in their workplace — in the act of creation.

The first of these acts is the creation of the world itself.

The workplace of the first poets is graphically reflected in the creation myths of the Aboriginal people of Australia. The creative ancestors sang the land into being; their voices wove the fabric of this ancient continent. Each voice left its songline winding through the body of the earth. The story, the deeds, the biography of the ancestors have become mountain, waterhole and cliff. Knowing this song is to partake in the genesis of the land, its initial intent and meaning. Singing the songline links the land to its creator, invoking the power to restore wholeness.

The Aboriginal perception of the world being sung or spoken is shared with many other cultures. It is like a universal memory recalling the creative act. The Judao-Christian culture is no exception: the book of *Genesis* confirms the primal power of the word to create.

And the Gods said, 'Let there be light,' and there was light.'

The Elohim (the gods) do not ponder or build the world. They speak it. They said, 'Let there be light,' and there was light. As in the Aboriginal myths, it is the speaking that creates. *The Gospel of St John* summarises this experience in its opening verses:

> In the beginning was the Word,
> and the Word was with God,
> and the Word was God.
> The same was in the beginning with God.
> All things were made through it
> and without it there was not anything made
> that was made.

One American Indian creation myth begins with the howl of Coyote. Coyote starts to grow around its howl: first the mouth then the head, followed by the body and the rest of the world.

For the Hopi, creation begins with Tawa (the Sun god) and Spider Woman (the Earth goddess). Tawa rules the realm above and Spider Woman rules the magic below. Tawa and Spider Woman divide themselves into other gods and goddesses and eventually decide to make the earth. Side by side they make the first magic song: the song of rushing winds and flowing waters, the song of light and sound and life. Tawa forms thoughts in his mind and Spider Woman, chanting, takes clay and makes the thoughts take form.

To the ancient Greeks the goddess Gaia is the mother of all the gods and everything that there is in this world. She is the first born from the chaos of timeless expanse.

In the Finnish epic of the *Kalevala*, Ilmatar (Earth Mother) floats and labours in the waters before she shapes the world:

> Still the daughter of the Ether,
> Swims the sea as water-mother,
> With the floods outstretched before her,
> And behind her sky and ocean.
> Finally about the ninth year,
> In the summer of the tenth year,
> Lifts her head above the surface,
> Lifts her forehead from the waters,
> And begins at last her workings,
> Now commences her creations,
> On the azure water-ridges,
> On the mighty waste before her.
> Where her hand she turned in water,

There arose a fertile hillock;
Wheresoe'er her foot she rested,
There she made a hole for fishes;
Where she dived beneath the waters,
Fell the many deeps of ocean;
Where upon her side she turned her,
There the level banks have risen;
Where her head was pointed landward,
There appeared wide bays and inlets;...

Poetic Allies

We can explore the powerful and hidden place of creation for ourselves by means of a poetic ally. A poetic ally is a temporary muse or inner storyteller. We will give this inner teller the burden of telling this story. He or she will know what we don't. Such inner storytellers allow a more extraordinary self in us to access what our ordinary self cannot. They are indispensible tools for writers and story makers and I would like to encourage you to use them whenever needed: which is in all cases where you lack inspiration.

The poetic ally helps us to step out of our own mindset and into that of other beings, other times and cultures. This is particularly important when dealing with creation myth. Here we easily fall back on current ideas: if you use words like energy, particles, atoms, quantum, vibrations, matter, explosion and the like you can be pretty sure that you have used your intellect rather than your imagination. In all creation myths (save the one we have now) creation starts with a <u>who</u> rather than a what, beings rather than matter.

The White Elephant

To help you access these primal layers of knowing common to all humanity you will choose an ancient being who remembers the stories from long ago: the White Elephant.

Elephants are sacred, wise and known for their exceptional powers of memory. The Indian god of letters and patron of poets, Ganesha, is elephant-headed and uses his tusk as a pen.

The White Elephant carries the knowledge of the most distant past, but she will only divulge her secrets to those who know the rare and royal art of greeting. Only those who can bow with words may stand upright in her presence. Only those who can shape their language with respect are permitted to hear her words. This is why the White Elephant appears only to poets and writers.

Exercise 1: The Rare Art of Greeting

When you meet the White Elephant, bow three times before her, address her with the greeting she deserves, in language that befits her ancient royalty. For example:

> Oh keeper of deep wisdom who dwells in the green and umber words of the first earth.
>
> Oh mother of all hidden knowledge, smooth skinned one who inhaled the breath of the ancient gods.
>
> Oh rare one who is crowned with the mist of the first mist and wears the tusk of the first moon, I greet you in awe.

Exercise 2: The White Elephant's Account

Now that you have greeted the White Elephant and have been accepted by her, she allows you to climb onto her back. She will take you along the ancient path of her tales and tell you of the beginning; the first place, the creation of the world. Her story contains the genesis of all land and creatures, but not yet the human being, as in the **Sutra of the White Elephant by Jaya Penelope**:

> In the beginning, before the world was made there was an enormous ocean of milk, of seminal fluid, of star seed like tapioca frog's egg jelly'd pearls, like coconut pudding.
>   I was thirsty and I put my trunk down into the milk and stirred it. As I churned the milk with my trunk it began to swirl and bubble like a pot of chai.
>   A fountain of it sprang up and spat out one silver egg
>   From the egg came a divine woman, half maiden, half crone. She cut her feet kicking her way out of the egg; where she stepped there were bloody footprints that sprang into red river gorges, flowers, flooded gums, mango trees
>   But the divine woman was lonely and she longed for a mate
>   She sat down by the shores of the milk ocean and sang of the lover she wanted for herself — a song of the perfect lover who was as beautiful and broken as she.
>   She sang all night and stamped her feet and as she sang a being wove itself out of the red clay of her footprints
>   He was a monstrous god and he was beautiful — redwood trees, sequoia, karri and mallee stands sprang from his loins, green coconut groves swayed at his temples
>
>   The silver egg woman was delighted, she ordered him to lie down at once, she

climbed onto his back and together they flew

She rode him all night, and as they made love,
shoals of flying fish leapt from her mouth
buffalos from his thighs
great cats sprang from the Sahara of her collarbones
feathered things from their fingertips
their love-making was volcanic
and when they finally collapsed in an ocean of salt + blood + semen — they
had created the world
and everything in it.

The First Human Being

The White Elephant has initiated us into the beginning of the world, but she could not tell us about the origin of the human being. Only a human being can do that, one who is able to cross the abyss of time and listen to the song of human creation. In the Judao-Christian culture, Moses heard that song and gave his account in Genesis.

And the gods said, Let us make human beings in our image, after our likeness…

So the gods created human beings in their own image, in the image of the gods created they them; male and female they created them.

'Male and female' refers to the first Adam, long before the separation into sexes (Adam meaning not 'man', but 'human being'). Plato recalls the same condition in his Symposium where Aristophanes describes the hermaphroditic human of the primordial past.
   We can access these ancient memories by creating another poetic ally. This time it will be a human being.

Exercise 3: Story Teller

Find a poetic ally worthy of telling the story of the human origin. Imagine a storyteller you would like to hear this particular story from. They could be an elder or priest who in traditional societies had access to such knowledge: adventurers in inner realms who had made the journey to the underworld and back. Chosen by destiny, they had acquired a second life and communicated with gods and ancestors. Their memory extended further than that of the uninitiated. Their words carried weight. Alternatively it could be a child or a New York cab driver.

Describe your poetic ally in detail, perhaps naming the tests, deeds or sacrifices that made him or her worthy of such knowledge. Think of this description as a writing ritual, an imaginative invocation of a muse. The more reality you ascribe to them, the better the stories they will produce. If at any time a direct invocation proves difficult, start with the Heroic Landscape exercise described in Lesson Four and distil your poetic ally from his or her surroundings.

Tale Teller by Ailsa Grieve

He was sitting cross-legged upon the dirt. Different yet the same, everything under him was also inside and beyond him. When I looked to him I saw the dark water that I used to swim in as a child. It was deep within his heart. He wasn't afraid of it like I was though. I saw the dark water grow deeper in him, until I could feel the soft dark mud that my feet used to touch, settle into his vast character. In him, with eyes soft, I also saw the big blue sky. Lost and gazing, I wondered what he saw in me. I came to be sitting in front of him, me in my bright colours and extrusions, him in his mud and sky. He placed one hand on each of my shoulders and gently pushed me further into the soft dirt. I felt the ground rise up inside of me, and my eyes grow more affixed to him. He didn't say that there were many things I didn't know. I think that he didn't say anything at all. But in moments I saw white cockatoos flying through the backs of his eyes and out of his heart. Stranger still, they flew into mine. The flight of the cockatoos inside started me laughing, and we laughed together. At this point I realised that I didn't need to know. And that perhaps I was too young to hold the whole story. I had started a pathway though, this I knew, the dark mud, the blue sky and I.

There are many different accounts on the creation of the human Being. In the Finnish epic of the Kalevala, we met earlier in this lesson, the earth mother Ilmatar floats on the stormy sea before giving birth to Vainemoinen, the ancient singer and primeval craftsman. Here the first human being is a poet. Germanic myth tells us that Odin created Ask and Embla, the first human beings, from an Ash and an Elm tree.

In the Hebrew account the first Adam (human being) is not yet the Adam that God has breathed life into. And the breathing Adam is different again from the Adam (man) and Eve (woman) after the separation of the sexes. In Moses' telling God is aware of the loneliness of the first human being and decides to split 'it' into two. Plato tells it differently: it is the insolence and pride of the first hermaphroditic human beings that makes Zeus split them apart. In Indian creation myth Purusha, the first human being emerges from the golden egg and then offers him/herself as sacrifice to the gods, who create the present world from its vast body.

Exercise 4: The First Tale

Now it is time for your poetic ally to give her account of the creation of the human being. Ask her for a story. Make sure it is her story and not yours or the one you have learned at school. Forgo all current conceptions as in the previous exercise. Let your ally tell you about the primal makers and how they went about their sacred task. She will tell you the very tale you need to hear if you listen with respect. In most creation myths human beings, especially in their primal state, represent the masterwork of the original creators. Here is an example by **Jennifer Kornberger:**

> The twelve who ruled the placeless places gathered of one accord and the sound of their gathering was like the rushing of wind on a mountain and they drew close enough to grasp each other's hands, and in their dance they sang a song that poured their timeless being into time and each gave their most holy word, the word of their secret of their power that had never been uttered before into the arc of their dance and lo, the one who was to come was spoken and rose dreaming like sun in water as delicate as the bone of a bird, moist as the crest of foam and warm as a bud unopened is warm.

7

The Four Ages

The edifice of Western culture rests on two pillars: the Hebrew and the Greek myths. Both are fundamental to literature and art, philosophy and science.

Hebrew and Greek narratives offer very different accounts. The severe, and singular god of the Hebrews stands opposite to the multiplicity inherent in the Greek pantheon. The all-too-human attitudes and at times immoral inclinations of the Olympian gods make a refreshing contrast to the austere qualities of the Israelite deity.

The Greeks attributed the creation of the world to Gaia, the goddess who emerged first from the primeval being of Chaos. She was the mother of all beings including her spouse Uranus (Heaven, Sky) with whom she fashioned the world, the Giants, the one-eyed Cyclops and the Titans, a race of younger gods. When Uranus decided to banish the Giants and the Cyclops, Gaia counselled the Titans to rebel against their father.

Kronos, the youngest of the Titans, took the lead and castrated his father Uranus. Kronos then became the leader of the gods, but was vexed by the prophecy that he too would be overthrown by one of his children. Thus after marrying his sister Rheia, he remained mindful of the prediction and devoured his offspring as soon as they were born. When Rheia gave birth to Zeus, she handed her husband a rock wrapped in swaddling clothes, which he devoured instead of the babe.

Zeus was hidden in a cave in Crete. When he had grown to maturity he tricked his father into spewing out his siblings, the Olympian gods Poseidon, Hestia, Demeter, Hera and Hades. War soon broke out between the Titans and these newly emerged gods. The latter prevailed and Zeus became the ruler of the world.

The Four Ages

Greek mythology distinguishes four ages: Golden, Silver, Bronze and Iron.

The Golden Age is one of the most generic archetypes of humanity. It is a collective memory of the time before time, an age devoid of work, cares and conflicts. The Roman poet Ovid who lived and suffered in the constraints of the Iron Age remembers with longing the Golden Age in the beginning of his 'Metamorphosis':

> First was the Golden Age. Then rectitude

spontaneous in the heart prevailed, and faith.
Avengers were not seen, for laws unframed
were all unknown and needless. Punishment
and fear of penalties existed not.
No harsh decrees were fixed on brazen plates.
No suppliant multitude the countenance
of Justice feared, averting, for they dwelt
without a judge in peace. …
The towns were not entrenched for time of war;
they had no brazen trumpets, straight, nor horns
of curving brass, nor helmets, shields nor swords.
There was no thought of martial pomp —secure
a happy multitude enjoyed repose.

Exercise 1: The Golden Age

Recall the poetic ally you developed in the last lesson. Let your ally settle into a quiet place to tell you more about the Golden Age, and its inhabitants. Your poetic ally will speak in picture language and you will write these pictures down. Alternatively find a speck of gold in the age you live in.

The Golden Age by Dale Irving
Present moment.
Still. No wind. No birdsong.
Beamed in sun and moon.
Opening.
Closing.
Expansion, contraction.
Spectrum of colours.
Gesture. Word.
All as one.
Present moment.

The Golden Age by Sue Johnson
Quite suddenly, things are as they should be. I don't know why, but most often the Golden Age arrives as I travel alone in my car. The engine doesn't strain and pull, or need persuading, it flows with me. Its belly full of petrol, it flies along an empty two-lane road, gliding not driving, going whither it will. I relax, my body softens, my heart is open, the music on the radio cascades deliciously about me. I am gentle, I am kind, but also, yes, so powerful and so

competent. Beyond the window glass the children wave, the people smile. The day is rich with possibility.

The Greeks linked the passage from the Golden to the Silver Age to the Victory of the Olympian gods over the Titans, the transition occurring when Zeus dethrones his father Kronos. The myth of Demeter and Persephone explores the same transition within the human soul.

Demeter and Persephone

Demeter, a goddess of earth and fertility, was the daughter of Kronos and Rheia. She was the first spouse of Zeus, and their child Persephone was famed for her beauty and purity. Demeter took great pains to preserve the purity of her daughter and kept her secluded in the Olympian heaven. There the young girl played all by herself, content and without care until the god Eros found his way to the maid and persuaded her to leave the confines of her heavenly abode. Tempted by curiosity, Persephone left her mother's safe garden and while picking flowers on a meadow near Eleusis she was abducted by her uncle Hades and forced to become his queen in the underworld.

When Demeter found her daughter missing, she searched desperately for her for nine days and nine nights. On the tenth day when she heard the truth from the all-seeing sun god Helios, she forbade the earth to yield fruit. Humankind was left without food, and the gods without sacrifices.

Exercise 2: Demeter's Lament

In this exercise you will take Demeter's position. Imagine yourself as the goddess, realising that Hades, the dark lord of the underworld, has abducted your daughter whom you have protected from worldly evils. Try to inhabit, or at least imagine, her despair and give it voice in a lament.

> **Demeter's Lament by Annette Mullumby**
> oh my daughter of air and light
> of blue sky wheeling
> I cannot bear the thought of you
> locked in the mud cast of his body
>
> now he is Lord over all your territory
> has no regard for the way your rivers run
> for the gentle mounds and hollows of your body
> I fear his lust for the sun in you

I fall on rocky ground
pound until empty fists bleed
my heart a dull thud in fragile ribs

Demeter's Lament by Dale Irving
She held the flaccid hand, touched the cold forehead and found nothing of the bouyant, bonny child. Her heart filled her body with a heaviness that took her deep into earth's bowels, into fetid darkness.
Uniformed figures bore the gurneyed body on silent wheels.
Demeter sat alone.
Demeter clawed her breast. Dug through flesh, sinew and gore.
Dragged her galled heart from its sheath.
Dashed it to the floor.

Fearing that the earth would remain forever barren, Zeus demanded Persephone's return from the underworld. Hades obeyed. But before Persephone left, he gave her a pomegranate to eat that bound her to the underworld and to him. When Demeter heard of this ploy she threatened to withhold all fertility from the earth. The gods implored both Demeter and Hades and eventually a compromise was reached. Persephone was to spend two thirds of the year with her mother in heaven and one third of the year with her husband in the underworld.

The Greeks understood this story in two ways:

Firstly, Persephone represented the world soul and the fertility of the earth. The commencement of seasons after the unchanging spring of the Golden Age was related to her abduction. As long as Demeter's daughter resided in the underworld it was winter and the earth yielded no grain. When she returned in spring the earth adorned itself with flowers and fresh growth.

Secondly, Persephone was also understood as the archetype of the human soul. Before her abduction by the dark king of the underworld, Persephone resided in the purity of heaven, untouched by all earthly cares. After being made queen of Hades, she lost access to her heavenly origin.

The initiation cults at Eleusis near Athens were dedicated to Demeter and Persephone. In the temple rituals the soul's fall from grace and its subsequent entanglement in matter was ritually re-enacted to break the spell of the senses. It was understood that Persephone's destiny was everyone's destiny, that her fall was everyone's fall, and that her eventual return to heaven augured the human soul's liberation from the world of matter.

Exercise 3: Persephone's Lament

In this exercise you will assume the role of Persephone. As she is the archetype of all souls including yours, I suggest that you speak from your own experience.

This lament has two sides. One is the soul's discomfort and suffering in the world, the other the remembrance of its heavenly origin, a feeling for purity that has been lost, a sense that there are other, deeper dimensions to the soul. It does not matter if you agree or disagree with this notion. All that matters is that you agree with it for the duration of this exercise.

Persephone's Lament by Dale Irving
I cannot remember the scent, the ambrosial sweetness of walking through golden grasses. The picture is turning sepia, fading like an old Kodachrome print.
The memory is fraying, the sense of home a shabby couch lolling on the verge. Clichés of happy families, of Elysian days line up for patronage but they are empty phrases.
I look at my past like a stroke victim and cannot relate words to place or event.
I see the fading outline of my mother but cannot make out her face. I have no memory of that face, but know it was kind.
Kindness is a vestige of the past. A touch that doesn't inflict pain, a comment that doesn't rend my heart. It fades. It is insubstantial.
Taste, savoury or sweet, no longer excites my mouth.
I eat filthy things, scratched from fetid fissures.
At times I long to drink deep of cleansing water.
I remember the purity and gulp at faecal-flecked handfuls when the guard turns his head.
I have a memory of a gentle time but accept the curse, the flailed flesh, the present moment.

Persephone's Descent by Annette Mullumby
I am trapped in the earth juices
 of the Dark Lord
his touch scrapes my skin
my eyes are smeared
with the decay of leaves
my hair woven with roots
matted with fungi
I push through narrow
tunnels like a mole
my heart slows to a dull thud

no breath to breathe
the memory of light

The Silver Age and the Bronze Age

Persephone's fall led to the Silver Age that yoked humankind to labour on the land, a state close to the divine but not identical with it. Four seasons supplant the eternal spring and the first dwellings appear. Ovid tells us

> Jove first reduced to years the Primal Spring,
> by him divided into periods four,
> unequal,—summer, autumn, winter, spring.—
> then glowed with tawny heat the parched air,
> or pendent icicles in winter froze
> and man stopped crouching in crude caverns, while
> he built his homes of tree rods, bark entwined.
> Then were the cereals planted in long rows,
> and bullocks groaned beneath the heavy yoke.

The Silver Age was followed by the Age of Bronze which Ovid tells us very little about age except to say that that war and cruelty commence their reign. He meant that although the Bronze Age was violent and given to martial pursuits, it was not yet corrupted by greed and personal vice.

Exercise 4: The Silver and the Bronze Age

Employ your poetic ally to re-imagine the Silver Age and the Bronze Age.

The Silver Age is but one step away from perfection. The major alteration is the commencement of work, the need for humankind to fend for its livelihood, making the earth yield what she no longer provides of her own accord. The Bronze Age, barely mentioned by Ovid, introduces the vices of war. Juxtapose the two ages, identifying their differences.

> **The Silver Age by Annette Mullumby**
> Fastidious about cutlery
> can't stand a hint of tarnish
> must see herself grinning
> in the hollow of the spoon
>
> her mirrors sparkle
> free from the smudges
> of makeup dust dried pus
> in love with the way
> her teeth shine

constantly dyeing her hair
ash blonde dark roots threaten
puts her car through the car wash
at least twice a week

The Bronze Age (The Art of War) by Barbara Swingler
My worthy opponent, my fallen adversary----I salute you.
It could have been me, here on the ground, but this was not a personal matter; this was not a matter for our petty selves. This was a matter of Pride.
You died proudly, you fought to the end. Ever your sword in your hand, you loosened your grip not once. But in the end my arm was stronger, my sword victorious.
If we had fought as one we would have been formidable, unbeatable even.
But we were nourished by different milk and grew up apart.
Once more, I salute you.

The myth of Persephone explores the loss of innocence from the perspective of the human soul. The various myths surrounding the figure of Prometheus explore the deeper causes of decline that eventually led to the Iron Age.

Prometheus

Some stories tell us that Prometheus was the son of the Titan Iapetus, and others that he was a Titan himself. His name meant 'forethought' while that of his dull-witted brother Epimetheus denoted 'afterthought.'

In the war between the Titans and the Olympian gods, Prometheus sided with Zeus and helped him to gain victory. Later he rebelled and challenged Zeus's omnipotence. He tricked him at the inception of the sacrificial rites so that the best part of the sacrificial meat went to humankind rather than to the gods.

This angered Zeus who took fire away from humanity. Prometheus stole the heavenly fire from Olympus and brought it back to earth whereupon Zues was even more enraged and punished Prometheus by chaining him to the rocks of Caucasus. Every day he sent an eagle that opened Prometheus' chest and feasted on his liver. Every night the liver grew back.

In some versions Heracles frees Prometheus from his suffering. In others a dying centaur offers himself as a ransom.

The Pythagorean tradition credits Prometheus with making human souls immortal, elevating men and women into creators rather than creatures.

This tallies with what Plato tells us in his dialogue 'Protagoras': The gods made humankind and all other creatures out of clay and fire. Then they left it to Prometheus and his brother Epimetheus to complete the task by distributing the gifts the gods had bestowed. Epimetheus unwisely used all available gifts on the animals before he set to work on humankind. Birds were given wings to fly, horses had long legs for racing, cats were equipped with sharp teeth to bite and claws to scratch. Every animal was given a gift that served its nature. Every creature was covered in fur or scales or feathers or given shells to shelter in. The human being alone was left naked and defenceless. Prometheus took pity on humanity and stole the creative fire from the workshops of Athena, goddess of thought, and from the smithy of Hephaestus.

Equipped with the fire of thought and ingenuity, humanity was able to make up for what it lacked. Instead of fur and feathers, human beings received the ability to sew clothes. Instead of claws or hooves humanity was able to make tools. Through culture, art and craft, men and women achieved what nature had not provided. Like Prometheus, who in some myths also featured as the progenitor of humanity, mankind had been given the gift to create.

The price for the inner fire, for the spark of creation, for consciousness and self-consciousness is temporary decline. In revenge Zeus sends Pandora, a demonic woman made of clay, adorned with beauty by all the goddesses of Olympus and brought to life by the four winds. Prometheus warns his brother Epimetheus not to open the box Pandora is carrying. But Epimetheus succumbs and out spills evil, trouble, pain, disease and death. The lid is closed too late and only hope remains inside.

All these tales portray Prometheus as a curse and a blessing, as tempter and benefactor. The fall of mankind from its initial grace and the eventual rise to eternal being are both attributed to him. Creativity in particular has been his defining gift to humanity. It is not surprising that he has become the patron of painters, poets, sculptors, musicians, craftspeople, inventors, technicians, engineers and innovators.

Exercise 5: Prometheus Outspoken

The time has come for Prometheus to speak for himself: to reveal his motives, his vision, his passion, his great plans and his bold intentions. The fact that you are a writer or becoming one, clearly shows your kinship with this gifted, but rebellious god. You will not need a poetic ally. You can speak in Prometheus' stead. Write in the I-form. You can (like Goethe in a famous poem) make a speech in defiance of Zeus and the other gods who wanted to keep humankind in a state of childlike dependency. Or you can explain your motives to the human beings who benefited from your courage and beneficence. Feel free to rebel against my suggestions and find an original approach.

> **I Prometheus by Dale Irving**
> Every colour will sing. Hues, gradients, forms will flow from palette, to surface, to eye. The rainbow will flourish in our souls.

The weaver will warp and weft the cloth of generations.
The builders learn to blend, earth, wood, stone.
And I will sing humanity into its future, I will give the space to plan and fashion.
As every mood I will colour their days from indigo of night to the ecstasy of brilliant day. Every colour will sing.
And the future is possible.

The Iron Age

The Iron Age commences after the great flood with which Zeus plans to destroy humanity. Prometheus warns his son Deucalion of the disaster and instructs him to build an ark. Deucalion and his wife Pyrrha are saved. Taking stones and throwing them over their shoulders they create the humanity of the Iron Age, an age plagued by vices of every kind. Ovid links the moral decline of this age with the partitioning of the earth, with the love of gain and the mining of iron and gold.

>………………And last of all
>the ruthless and hard Age of Iron prevailed,
>from which malignant vein great evil sprung;
>and modesty and faith and truth took flight,
>and in their stead deceits and snares and frauds
>and violence and wicked love of gain,
>succeeded.—Then the sailor spread his sails
>to winds unknown, and keels that long had stood
>on lofty mountains pierced uncharted waves.
>Surveyors anxious marked with metes and bounds
>the lands, created free as light and air:
>nor need the rich ground furnish only crops,
>and give due nourishment by right required,—
>they penetrated to the bowels of earth
>and dug up wealth, bad cause of all our ills,—
>rich ores which long ago the earth had hid
>and deep removed to gloomy Stygian caves:
>and soon destructive iron and harmful gold
>were brought to light; and War, which uses both,
>came forth and shook with sanguinary grip
>his clashing arms.

Ovid describes history in terms of moral decline: as a gradual disconnect from the gods, the world, from others, and even from those closest to us.

...the guest was not protected from his host,
the father in law from his own son in law;
even brothers seldom could abide in peace...

Exercise 6: The Iron Age

As we still live in this age, many of the calamities described by Ovid are our own. As you have first-hand experience of the Iron Age you may tell the tale yourself. Alternatively continue with your poetic ally. Perhaps our own age has moved from iron to steel, from sword edge to machinery, from machinery to digital technology. This exercise offers great scope for the writer.

Iron Age by Gilly Berry
Tycoon upon a platform stands astride. High brow he sucks minerals from the bowels. Mines iron to wreck and ruin. Regard his room of jewels. Run your hands through them, cool, smooth. Drink the oil spillage. Admire the order: glittering guns, napalm, rockets, spearheads.

Iron Age by Annie Wearne
I'd like to paint the walls in vivid hues
To dance in shoes with metal taps as loud as life

I take up food and throw it in the pan...

The doorknocker of iron sounds out....
The fire is nearing
Empty the streets
It will eat us all!

8

Parting with Paradise

Early myths are foundational memories engraved on the global psyche. The form these memories take varies according to culture. Early humanity achieved access to this memory pool through identification with animal archetypes. The ancient Indians tapped their primal memory through the practice of yoga, the Babylonians through the study of stars; Egyptians through elaborate initiation rituals; and the Hebrews through the many layers of meaning related to their collective memories - narratives that only much later became fixed in scripture.

Our culture is left for the most part with the fossils of once vital narratives. But by developing the ability to think in pictures, we can bring them to life again. The poetic mind is predisposed to think in pictures, to divine deeper and manifold meanings. Like the antlers worn by the shaman, the poetic mind has its antennae tuned to the archetype and, like the Hebrew Cabbalist, it can make the particular transparent for the universal. With this in mind, let us use the archetypal pictures as catapults to our own writing.

I would like to acknowledge here that there are many writers who recoil from stories thickly covered with religious veneer. The fact that these primal tales have been used and at times abused by conventional religion should not prevent us from connecting with the vitality of tales that have been foundational to Western literature.

Paradise

Perhaps the best-known image of the Hebrew narrative is that of the Garden of Eden or Paradise, the Golden Age in the womb of the world we have already explored. Medieval paintings depict the Hebrew Paradise as a bubble, a womb, an enclosure, a walled garden, a blessed time in the beginning, a state of purity and wholeness, a seamless web enclosing humanity in the divine. The initial Adam who inhabits this garden is (as in Plato's account and Persian and Indian creation stories) both male and female.

Adam Naming the Beasts

This original hermaphroditic Adam has the power of naming. The Hebrew divinity brings all beasts before Adam to be named. It appears that naming and knowing are deeply related, one invoking the other. The original Adam still had this power of being one with the world. For him everything spoke, revealed itself in its name. The world was still poetic.

The English poet William Blake illustrated this capacity with two pictures: 'Adam Naming the Animals' and 'Eve Naming the Birds'. In Blake's vision, Adam has his index finger raised in a gesture of awareness while the animals pass by in line with his throat, the source of speech. Eve's head is surrounded by flocks of birds, a picture of thoughts flying in animistic form.

Another potent image is that of the two trees that stood in the middle of Paradise: the Tree of Life and the Tree of Knowledge of Good and Evil.

The image of the tree is also a generic memory. In Persian mythology the first human couple emerge from a tree. Germanic myth pictured the whole cosmos as one gigantic tree: the world-ash Yggdrasil.

Hebrew imagination supplanted the one world tree with two trees of opposite nature. Adam and Eve may take fruit from all the trees except for the Tree of Knowledge of Good and Evil which brings knowledge, but also brings death. The knowledge is not the naming/knowing of the primal Adam, the knowledge of the state of oneness, but a different kind of knowledge. What kind of knowledge is it?

Exercise 1: Two Trees

Your poetic ally has been to the centre of Paradise, has seen both the Tree of Life and the Tree of Knowledge of Good and Evil. Let your ally tell you about these trees. Record the words.

> **The Tree of Life by Mags Webster**
>
> She can only be a boab, pregnant with the water of life, holding herself erect while around her the wasteland shimmers with the bones of dead things. She is the sentinel on the horizon, proof that things can live while all around is

parched and desperate, the earth cracked and wrinkled. She is fleshy and strong, her fingers catch the moon in their basket. She rolls the planets round her middle; they want to drink the water from her. And just once, she'll let them — allow them to attach — she'll give them suck.

The Tree of Knowledge by Jennifer Kornberger

It is the sort of tree that you leave growing because it doesn't seem out of place in the garden, needs no trimming and doesn't appear to have an invasive root system. A good tree for the courtyard of a dental practice. But in the fruit, the seasons ripen. In the flesh of the fruit is the taste of everything halved, everything quartered, everything divided by time. The fruit is strangely weightless but in the mouth it becomes a leaden weight and casts you like a leaden sinker into a foreign water ...

The Serpent's Tongue

Closely allied to the image of the Tree of Knowledge is that of the Serpent who tempted Adam and Eve to eat from the forbidden fruit.

In Germanic myth the serpent takes the form of the trickster Loki, the deceptive companion of the Gods who brings about the ruin of the world. In Greek myth the same entity is ingeniously portrayed as the rebellious god Prometheus whom we encountered in the last lesson.

In the Hebrew tradition the fall from innocence is attributed to Lucifer, a splendid but rebellious angel who on account of overweening pride lost his high station. Lucifer insinuates himself into Paradise to tempt the primal couple Adam and Eve. Paintings often portray Lucifer as a snake, which is misleading as the ancestral Serpent of Paradise acquired its trait of sliding on the ground only *after* the Temptation. The Hebrew text suggests a subtle, beautiful and enticing creature that brings to mind the Dragon of Chinese tradition — a mighty, airy, warm and magnificent creature, bearer of good fortune. It also conjures up the rainbow serpent that features powerfully in Aboriginal creation, and the great plumed serpent of American Indian tradition.

In the Hebrew tradition the Serpent has fallen into disrepute — or that is how we have chosen to interpret the scripture. But perhaps there is more to this story.

Exercise 2: The Serpent's Tongue

The only way to discover more is to listen to the Serpent itself. Not the serpent that creeps on dusty ground, but a mighty, enticing creature.

Let the ancient Serpent speak. Listen carefully: it may or may not speak the truth. In either case write down what you hear using the 'I' form. For example:

> I am here to spin my greatness into you, breathe my pollen into your lungs, crouch among your ribs and curve them to my wild rhythms. Those who would bar my access would keep you as their child; wean you minutely on their pure pap. I say partake also of me: I will show you how to dance in ecstasy, how to plunge yourself into the wine of your own story.

When Adam and Eve eat from the Tree of Knowledge, they are banned from the timeless, placeless, carefree state of paradise. Now they have to fend for themselves, and acquire through effort what was freely given before.

Cain and His Descendants

In the tight staccato of the Hebrew narrative, the expulsion from paradise is quickly followed by one of the enigmatic stories in world literature: the story of Cain and Abel, the tale of the first murder.

Cain and Abel are sons of Adam and Eve. Abel is a nomadic shepherd, treading lightly on the earth. His brother Cain has shouldered the burden of making bread by dint of effort. He is the first to till the soil.

Both brothers sacrifice to their god. Abel's offering is accepted. But Cain's gifts are rejected. Angered, Cain slays his brother and so incurs the curse of becoming a fugitive. Leaving his native country he becomes the builder of the first city, a culture hero.

Cain's descendants are Jabel, Jubal, Tubal-cain and their sister Namah, early archetypes of being human that are well worth exploring for the writer.

Jabal

Jabal is a nomad who lives in a tent and rather than with sheep he is associated with the more powerful forces of cow and bull, sacred to many ancient cultures and still revered in India. Mythic consciousness experienced cow and bull as the focus of mighty forces. In Persian and Germanic creation myths the cow is instrumental in the creation of the world. To be a breeder of cattle means to master the sacred forces that express themselves in the cow. The cow is like an alchemical laboratory for the transformation of dead matter into life. Cows embody abundance and sacrifice: every part of their being is useful for human life — their dung for soil fertility, their milk and its by-products for nourishment, their meat, hide, intestines and horns. The breeders of the cow had a strong sense of the sacredness of their task.

Exercise 3: The First Cowherd

Be Jabal, the first breeder of cattle. Imagine yourself endowed with the task of tending the sacred cows and bulls. Talk about your office and holy task. Talk about the nature of the cow.

Jabal by Liana Christensen

People are always drawn to the sweet mysteries — the warm gust of yeasty breath, the clotted yellow milk, the firecakes from her fundament. All that is domestic and content as if somehow the Goddess can be brought to her knees before them and made to serve. She never serves. She is not servile.

Only I dared apprentice myself to the bitter mysteries — the goring horn, the leathered phallus, the crushing hooves. Only I faced down that which must be endured. Then — and only then — did those lustrous brown eyes turn on me and open.

Jubal

To be the first of musicians is a sacred and magical act. It is the attempt to recall the divine music of paradise with earthly means; to fashion matter and attune it to the heavenly harmonies. It is the striving to redeem mute wood and the baseness of metal in the beauty of sound.
The Greeks attributed the first instruments to the gods. In the beginning, all music is sacred. It is part of worship and ritual healing. Every instrument is one part of the lost body of Adam, every orchestra an effort to recall the sounds of Paradise.

Exercise 4: The First Musician

Choose to be Jubal. Gathered around you are those who wish to follow in your wake. Initiate them into the meaning of your art. For example:

Jubal by Jennifer Kornberger

The strings must be straight like the rays of the sun
and the wood must be curved like the belly of the moon

the hand that plays is a bird
you have played well if
even the stones listen.

Tubal-cain

Tubal-cain is the third brother. He is the magical craftsman of primordial time, the first alchemist and blacksmith; earth magician, transformer of earth, he is the archetype and ancestor of all artists. He masters the force of fire with the fire of his will. He brings the mixed blessings of ploughshare and sword, tool and weapon, progress and destruction. He has the power to work dead metal from the bowels of the earth and return it to its pristine state, to the warm, liquid blood coursing through the veins of the first Adam — purified; formless but ready to take shape. His work has long become our destiny. He initiated the use of metal tools and opened the way for the making of mining equipment and laptops. The Finnish epic of the Kalevala remembers him as Vainemoinen, the mighty smith, craftsman and unrivalled singer of magical spells, son of the earth mother Ilmatar.

Exercise 5: Tubal-cain

You are Tubal-cain. Speak to your followers of your mission and your motives. Let them know your vision.

Tubal-cain by Nandi Chinna

> In my mother's womb I felt the barely perceptible rumblings of heat and fire from the depths of the earth up through the soles of my mother's feet as she walked towards the river to bathe and collect water. As she walked the metals clanged and clashed, heated and were cooled; merged and were transformed beneath the surface of the earth. Their songs sounded, tap tap, ksshsh, knock knock, shake, spssh. The songs of alchemical processes barely perceptible moving up through the earth, through the soles of feet and into the amniotic fluid surrounding my body. The eerie high-frequency wailing of flickering flames harmonising with deep base knocking of metals. Calamity, harmony in time with the beating of my heart. I was born with the stories imprinted into my memory: a brand, a scar, a scythe and a sword.

Na-amah

Now let us consider Na-ahma. The Hebrew account is very sparse. It say only: 'And the sister of Tubal-cain was Na-amah.' We don't have a lot to go on but we must make the most of this mysterious name. Na-amah suffered the fate of all women in the patriarchal age. Her story melted into the background while her brothers took central stage. This is our chance to resurrect her.

Exercise 6: Na-amah

Tell us the story that has never been told of Na-amah, her life and work.

Na-amah by Pen Brown

I took seed and first brewed it and made it to drink. We poured it as a libation on the flat stone of an altar and into the deep circular Cups of Dedication … I would immerse my hand into the pot and feel the texture and the mad bubbles of new life. From this I knew in a dream of great beauty how to take the flat breads of my people and make them soft, make them swell up, fat and light, round like bellies.

I had discovered a drink to be used by the gods and by the gravely sick to cure their suffering when other herbs could not soften their pains. In my prime I treated chieftains and beggars and the odd queen or two and became a princess by title. I who had been chosen by the gods. Now do you see me, Baker, Healer, Brewer? …

Now do you recognise my face? Do you honour me, I who taught grain to give up its secret treasure of sunlight?

Na-amah by Ailsa Grieve

Na-ama came in a flash, her mother cried, the door slammed, and un-ironed unwashed words started rambling from the priest's mouth. Not only was she female of rare female descent, but also she was covered head to toe in fine hair. Her face was swollen, and she knew that, given a life of 35 years, she would never progress the mental age of 7. Na-ama knew that every colour represented a direction, and the browns were the tricky directions in between broader lines. At night she would walk a colour and speak with the keeper at colours end. She would first evoke ritual, of which she needed silk from jabel's tent, strings off jubal's instrument and metal from tubal's chest.

The Great Flood

We hear of the Great Flood in mythologies from all around the world: the *Epic of Gilgamesh*, the story of Noah, and in myths from South America among many others. The waters of this memory flow in powerful currents in the substrata of the soul: writers often experience strong emotion when writing of this event.

The flood represents a major turning point in human memory — one world ends and another begins. The mythical figure who leads the old into the new is Utnapishtim in the Gilgamesh story, Manu in India and Noah in the biblical text. All the stories offer pictures for processes that may have lasted millennia. Their concern is with the essential, moral dimension rather than historical accuracy — it is the fallen state of humanity that causes the floodgates to open.

In the Babylonian Epic of Gilgamesh, the surviving Utnapishtim himself describes the event of the great flood. The Babylonian tale resembles the biblical account, but Utnapishtim gives a more colourful description, with many gods taking part in the great event:

From Gilgamesh
I watched the appearance of the weather —
the weather was frightful to behold! ...
Erragal pulled out the mooring poles,
forth went Ninurta and made the dikes overflow.
The Anunnaki lifted up the torches,
setting the land ablaze with their flare.
Stunned shock over Adad's deeds overtook the heavens,
and turned to blackness all that had been light ...
All day long the South Wind blew ...
blowing fast, submerging the mountain in water,
overwhelming the people like an attack.
No one could see his fellow,
they could not recognise each other in the torrent.
The gods were frightened by the Flood,
and retreated, ascending to the heaven of Anu ...
Six days and seven nights
came the wind and flood, the storm flattening the land ...
The sea calmed, fell still ...
I fell to my knees and sat weeping...

Exercise 7: Opening the Floodgates

Tap into your own memory of the flood. Tell how it came about. What happened to cause the wrath of the gods? How did it all begin? Who was saved? Feel free to tackle the exercise in new and unexpected ways.

The Flood by Nandi Chinna

That crazy old dude has been up there hammering away on that hill for months. In fact I can't remember a time when he wasn't up there tinkering around with his junk, bits of driftwood, old cars.

   The council threatened to evict him. Reckon they'll send in the bulldozers. His neighbours complain his place is a fire hazard.

   You should see this crazy looking thing he's building. Some days it looks like a house, sometimes it looks like it will fly away with flapping canvas tarps and beams at weird angles. And sometimes it looks like it's part of the hillside and might quietly slip down the slope and swim across the ocean.

   He's one of those old folk who thinks that god is getting angry with us people living down the hill. Reckons we're too noisy.

The Flood by Helen McDonnell

The earth as we know it is doomed
Pain, torture, ruin.
We need a good clean out.
 Our souls need to be washed clean.
Enough yelling and screaming, I've had enough.
I have spoken and now I act".

The doors of the great heavens open and pour forth the tears of all the angels.
Their tears are full of love and hope.
They cry, they wash away the dirt and gloom.
You still do not learn.
This now becomes a raging storm.
The animals are frightened.
They have never seen such rage.
They run, they try to hide, they scream in fear.
Hold on, cling to me I will keep you safe.
I cannot, I am powerless.

Slowly one by one I see them fall.
They struggle.
They fight for their survival

but slowly they enter into oblivion.
The noise is deafening I cannot even hear my own thoughts.
I too am scared beyond belief.
I scream, I scream, I beg, I implore.
Save me.

   I fall, I fall deep into the waters.
   The water burns deep within my soul.

   Quiet. Stillness. Just being.
   We awake.
   Still. Quiet.
   What next?

9

The Breath of Brahma

India occupies a unique place on the map of the poetic. While cultures like Egypt or Babylon have faded into the past, the embrace of the gods has never ceased in the land of Bharata. Spiritual India is still alive.

An unceasing line of masters and gurus have kept contact with the divine, and it is this presence of the living master — the embodiment of the divine in human form — that is the backbone of the spiritual body of India. The blood that courses through this body is ritual: the symbolic enactment of spiritual reality. Ritual is the language of the cosmos; its heart is sacrifice and its soul devotion. Rituals, practised in temples or huts or as daily routine, are understood by gods and demons. They invite the presence of divinities and weave them into the fabric of life.

India has been laced with ritual for millennia. Its atmosphere is perfumed with incense and its history woven through with the achievements of ascetics and saints.

Indian Creation Myth

One major myth depicts Vishnu lying motionless on the thousand-headed cobra which is floating on an ocean of milk. His first deed is to emanate his divine counterpart and wife, Lakshmi, goddess of abundance and harmony. Then, from Vishnu's navel a pink lotus flower emerges on a long stalk. In the middle of the lotus Brahma is seated. He has four arms, each holding a book, and four mouths, each reciting from one of the books. These books are the four *Vedas*, the holy script containing the eternal laws.

The new-born Brahma immediately searches for the reason for his own existence, and that of the universe. Vishnu advises him to undergo fervent austerities. Brahma takes the advice and in intense meditation he creates the heat from which the gods and demons arise.

Once the gods are created they commence with the creation of the world. Vishnu turns into a tortoise and descends into the ocean of milk. On this tortoise shell rises Mount Mandara, the axis of the world. The serpent Visuki coils around Mandara. Led by Indra, the gods seize the tail of the serpent while the demons led by Vairocana seize its head. At Brahma's command they each start pulling the serpent. Mount Mandara rotates rapidly, churning the ocean of milk until the elements emerge.

This creation myth is like a seed containing four elements dear to the Indian tradition. One is the male–female aspect of the gods, represented by the emanation of saktis who are the female counterparts of the male gods. These saktis are aspects of the great mother, manifest in innumerable goddesses and also present in each woman. She is also the kundalini — the power residing at the base of the spine.

Next are the four Vedas, the holy scripture of India, primordial books existing long before the world began. They contain the grammar of the universe, the eternal laws to which gods, demons and human beings are equally subject. The third element is the great Indian passion — the quest for self-knowledge and the practise of austerities, exemplified by Brahma's search for enlightenment — and the fourth is the need for a teacher, a guru, in this case Vishnu, to guide the search. The student–teacher relationship is the central axis of Indian spiritual development.

The Sacrifice of Purusha

Another myth centres around the golden egg, 'Hiranyagarbha', which is as resplendent as the sun. The Lord splits the golden egg in two with the power of thought. The upper shell becomes the divine, celestial sphere and the lower becomes the material, earthly world. From this light-filled egg emerges Purusha, the primal human being, with a thousand thighs, a thousand feet, a thousand arms and a thousand eyes.

The final element is a grand ritual — the sacrifice of Purusha, who offers himself as sacrifice to the gods. The gods accept and turn every part of his body into a part of the world. Purusha is vast as the universe, containing everything that is, was and will be. Here is an example from the **Rig Veda:**

> A thousand heads had primal Man,
> A thousand eyes, a thousand feet:
> Encompassing the earth on every side …
> That Man is this whole universe,
> What was and what is yet to be…

This primal human being becomes the sacrifice in the ritual of creation. All created things derive from his sacred body.

> When with Man as their oblation
> The gods performed the sacrifice,
> Spring was the melted butter,
> Summer the fuel, and autumn the oblation.
>
> From this sacrifice completely offered

The clotted ghee was gathered up:
From this he fashioned beasts and birds,
Creatures of the woods and creatures of the village …

From his mind the moon was born,
And from his eye the sun,
From his mouth Indra and the fire,
From his breath the wind was born.

The Vedas contain many versions of this theme: the Indians were not dismayed by conflicting or incongruent stories. They understood them as representations of supersensible realities, not literal descriptions. All Vedic accounts agree on the vast dimensions of the initial human being and the act of sacrifice from which the world was made. They differ as to which part of the body of Purusha becomes which part of the world.

Exercise 1: The First Sacrifice

We have already worked freely with creation myth. In this exercise we focus on the holy sacrifice of the primal man or woman and the relationship of his/her body to the created world. Be specific with details — link the various parts of the divine human to the physical features of the world. For example:

The First Sacrifice by Harriet Sawer

Before the visible world was formed
it was She, the primal being, that breathed.
And the gods said 'Will you sacrifice
Yourself to be the world of form?' And it was
She who said 'Take me, and let me be the world.
Let my breath be the wind and the world's first song
and let my womb rock the fish in the deep black sea.
Let my heart become the first fire
that spews out mountains and valleys
and my blood become rivers, and my sinews
the twisting trees and the forests.
Let my mucus become the swamps
and my fingernails the flats and the plains
and my toenails the round clear lakes.
And let the hairs on my arms become the prairies whistling
and my nose form the first cave
filled with glow-worms and stars

and my lungs become the clouds in the sky
my intestines the twisting mangroves
my stomach the shallow waters
my hair the seaweed in the ocean
my bones the corals, and my teeth the rocks.
Let me be the world,' she cried. And it was.

The Indian pantheon contains some eighty million gods and goddesses. The major gods have many and often divergent attributes, according to their diverse functions in the workings of the world. Together with their divine female counterparts, the gods Brahma (creator) and Saraswati, Vishnu (preserver) and Lakshmi and Shiva (destroyer) and Kali (Durga) are the most important deities.

Divine Breath

Brahma, the creator of the manifested world, is present in all of nature as well as in the human being. He is the essence of the individual soul, the atma. Once his essence is experienced by the seeker, its presence is recognised in all other beings. He is present in the breath. With every in-breath, part of the divine Brahma is taken in; with every out-breath that part of the inner divine atma reunites with the world. Knowing this helps us to travel far back into prehistoric India, to a time when the air was still the body of Brahma and when breathing was a spiritual experience, a continuous ritual linking human beings with the gods.

To the ancient Indian, breathing was a way of knowing, just as our thinking is for us. But while our intellectual activity leads to a knowledge of the illusory world of the senses (maya), breathing led to a beholding of Brahma in the soul and in the world. To the ancient Indians, the outer world was merely maya, a thin veil cast over the vibrant presence of the gods Maya was experienced as insubstantial compared with the tangible reality of the divine. This was a time not of intellectuality but of wisdom gained by devotion to the gods and their representatives; the mere presence of a spiritual master could be enough to open the inner eye.

When breathing ceased to carry inner knowing, the yogic practice of pranayama (control of breath) was developed. The yogis began to achieve by dint of effort what had once been a natural state. The elaborate science of pranayama, however, is not the only way in which the sacred breathing of the past survived in Indian culture. Many passages in the holy scriptures of India mirror the breathing process in their poetic form. Here is an example from the **Upanishads:**

This earth is the honey of all beings, and all beings are honey for this earth. That radiant, immortal Person who indwells this earth and, in the case of the (human) self, that radiant, immortal Person who consists of the body, is indeed that very Self: this is the Immortal, this Brahman, this the All.

> The waters are the honey of all beings and all beings are honey for the waters. That radiant, immortal Person who indwells these waters and, in the case of the (human) self, that radiant, immortal Person who consists of semen, is indeed that very Self: this is the Immortal, this Brahman, this the All.
>
> Fire is the honey of all beings and all beings are honey for fire. That radiant, immortal Person who …

The first line is built on the activity of breath — turning the inside out and the outside in. The second part of the verse, repeated throughout like a mantric formula, does the same, asserting Brahma as the essence of the world without and the world within.

Exercise 2: Poetic Breath

Write your own version of this text. Keep the strict form and explore its possibilities. It is possible to simplify or omit the second half. If you include the second half do not lose the sense of breathing or the worship of Brahma as you create a ritual in words. Here is an example just taking the first part of the formula:

> Night is the honey of all beings and the honey of all beings is night. Oil is the honey of all beings and the honey of all beings is oil. The throat is the honey of all beings and the honey of all beings resides in the throat. Silence is the honey of all beings and the honey of all beings is silence.

Within Without by Liana Joy Christensen
The sand is the honey of all beings and all beings are honey for this sand
   The grain within the infinite
   sands without are one

The ocean is the honey of all beings and all beings are honey for the ocean
   The drop within the infinite
   droplets without are one

The plants are the honey of all beings and all beings are honey for these plants
   The seed within the infinite
   green without are one

The Breath of Conversation

The same pattern can be seen in student–teacher conversations, where breathing is transformed into the ritual of question and answer. The student exhales questions and inhales the wisdom of the teacher.

> Then Ushasta Cakrayana questioned him, saying: 'Yajñavalkya, explain to me that Brahman which is evident and not obscure, the Self that indwells all things.'
> 'This Self that indwells all things is within you.'
> 'But which one is it, Yajñavalkya, that indwells all things?'
> 'Who breathes in with the in-breath, he is the Self within you that indwells all things; who breathes out with the out-breath, he is the Self within you that indwells all things …'
> Ushasta Cakrayana said: 'Your teaching on this subject is exactly like that of a man who says: 'That is a cow, and that is a horse.' Explain to me that Brahman which is really evident and not obscure, the Self that indwells all things.'
> 'This Self that indwells all things is within you.'
> 'But which one is it, Yajñavalkya, that indwells all things?'

Reading such conversations sensitively, one becomes aware that their aim is not a definitive answer but the continuous weaving between the soul of the student (atma) and the enlightened essence of the teacher (brahma). The teacher is one of Brahma's representatives on earth and his wisdom is one of the many breaths of Brahma.

Exercise 3: The Nature of the Poetic Self

Imagine your are an Indian sage., a Guru of poetic lineage. Your beloved student approaches you with the question, 'What is the true nature of the self?' Give your reply. Here is an example:

> **The Nature of the Self by Penelope Brown**
>
> The Self is an indwelling eye. In it is reflected the lightning and the horse. The otter's hand and the panther's tooth.
> In it is the long ago print of a man in mud, running to fetch water. And the hand print of a woman in bread.
> The Self is a seed that a million years ago exploded to a star.
> The Self is blood and honey.
>
> **Nature of the Self by Ann Reeves**
>
> The self is the true nature of all things:
> The gift of your affection,
> The bestowal of your hand,

The deed done freely,
The door opened wide
These things are the true nature of the self.

The importance of the breath of conversation between student and teacher made is clear in the Bhagavad-Gita, India's famous work of epic poetry that preserves the words of Vishnu — in the form of Krishna.

Vishnu

Vishnu is beyond time; he strides from eternity to eternity as preserver of worlds. Between the great cycles of existence, when all that is manifested is breathed back again, he retains the immortal essences of all that ever was and will be. With the goddess Lakshmi he resides in paradise, surveying all that happens on earth. Artists depict him as a beautiful youth, blue in colour, but he has numerous manifestations and bears a thousand names.

Whenever the moral order of the world is in danger, Vishnu descends to earth in in order that the world may rise again. Then he appears as an avatar. Vishnu first takes the form of a fish, then of a tortoise, a wild boar, a half-human and half-lion avatar, followed by the dwarf avatar, Vamana. He then incarnates as the primeval hunchback and axe man Parashurama. Finally, he manifests in perfected human form as Rama and Krishna. The sequence from fish to reptile to mammal and finally human being parallels our modern understanding of evolution. The cause for the great leaps of evolution, however, is seen in the sacrificial descent of the divine.

The love and loyalty between Rama and his wife Sita have been immortalised in the great epic of the Ramayana. Krishna features in the Bhagavad-Gita — a work that contains the soul and spirit of Indian culture.

The Bhagavad-Gita

The Bhagavad-Gita is part of the long and complicated Indian epic of the Mahabarata, which describes the conflict between two royal families: the five sons of Pandu fathered by the gods and their hundred demonic cousins, the Kurus. Krishna is the counsellor and friend of one of the Pandaras, Arjuna.

The Gita captures a moment just before the final battle between the Pandaras and the Kurus. Arjuna, the mighty Pandara warrior and devotee of Krishna, despairs at the prospect of having to slay his own relatives. He addresses Krishna who assists him as his charioteer.

> Arjuna said: ... I feel the limbs of my body quivering and my mouth drying up. My whole body is trembling, my hair is standing on end, my bow Gāṇḍīva is slipping from my hand, and my skin is burning...

I do not see how any good can come from killing my own kinsmen in this battle, nor can I, oh Kṛṣṇa, desire any subsequent victory, kingdom or happiness.

.... O maintainer of all living entities, I am not prepared to fight with them even in exchange for the three worlds, let alone this earth. What pleasure will we derive from killing the sons of Dhṛitarāṣṭra?

Exercise 4: The Battle with Doubt

Imagine yourself before a major battle. Join Arjuna or choose another battles. No matter if you lead real warriors into a bloodbath or an army of arguments to a meeting at your workplace, feel the despair before the fight and the warfare of conflicting emotion in your heart. Explore what resists and what aids you in this moment. In what form does Krishna come to your aid?

> **Flight from Conflict by Liana Christensen**
> The noise is appalling. I can't think straight. Every fibre of my being vibrates with agony. All I want to do is flee to the cool, dim forest — the shade, the silence. Instead I step over the rivulet of blood coursing past the iron gates and enter his domain. If anything the roar intensifies and the forge bellows out the heat of a thousand suns. I see him there, by the flames. His skin gleams with sweat. His back is half-turned away from me but I can see he sits at ease near the conflagration, his knees open, his hands carving a spearhead from bone. I freeze on the threshold. Just as he begins to turn directly to me my tiny drop of courage evaporates and I take to my heels — fleeing, flying, tumbling down the stars to this place. I could never bear to see his face.

In the midst of desperation, Krishna dispels Arjuna's doubts. The result is the great teaching poem of the Bhagavad-Gita. In the following passage Krishna illumines Arjuna about the nature of Atma, the individual soul.

> The one who thinks that Atma is a slayer, and the one who thinks that Atma is slain, both are ignorant, because Atma neither slays nor is slain.
>
> The Atma is neither born nor does it die at any time, nor having been it will cease to exist again. It is unborn, eternal, permanent, and primeval. The Atma is not destroyed when the body is destroyed.
>
> O Arjuna, how can a person who knows that the Atma is indestructible, eternal, unborn, and imperishable, kill anyone or cause anyone to be killed?

The Bhagavad-Gita is a conversation in poetic form with Krishna initiating his devotee Arjuna in his wisdom and the paths of yoga. The royal road to the realisation of the higher self is the worship of Krishna through Karma-Yoga: the selfless fulfilment of one's duty (dharma) without attachment to the result, to profit or loss, pleasure or pain. The dialogue culminates in Krishna revealing his identity:

> How may I know You, O Lord, by constant contemplation? In what form are You to be thought of by me, O Lord? ...

> O Arjuna, I am the Atma abiding in the heart of all beings.
> I am also the beginning, the middle, and the end of all beings ...
> I am Vishnu among the (twelve) sons of Aditi,
> I am the radiant sun among the luminaries ...
> I am the moon among the stars ...
> I am thunderbolt among the weapons,
> I am Kaamadhenu among the cows,
> And the love among lovers ...

Exercise 5: The Manifestations of Krishna

Continue this revelation of Krishna's divinity using the 'I' form.

> **Krishna by Helen McDonell**
> I am all and nothing.
> I am the light of the world
> I am the dark of the night
> I am the love of all things
> I am the envy of all
> I am peace on earth
> I am the strength of all men
> I am the moon and the stars
> I am the thunder and the rain
> I am forgiving of all
> I am the memory of history
> I am hope for the lost
> I am the door to salvation
> I am all
> I am nothing
> I am that I am.

Shiva and Kali

Shiva and Kali are the fierce face of the divinity. Shiva destroys in order to renew. Through death and destruction he liberates the soul from bondage to the world and leads it to new birth. The eternal soul is benefited by the destruction of the maya of existence.

Shiva is the counterpoint to Vishnu the preserver. With his third eye continuously open, Shiva remains in constant meditation. He is the prince of ascetics, the champion of all who renounce the world of maya. Shiva is lord of the cosmic dance; stepping over demons, holding trident and tambourine in two of his four arms.

His consort Kali is often depicted naked, brandishing a blood-stained knife and a necklace of human heads around her breast, standing above Shiva who lies beneath her like a corpse. Initiates know that the heads are the false personas that must be cut off so that the true identity shines forth. Kali also has a hand that blesses and protects. It is said of her: 'Adore the terrible one.'

Exercise 6: Encounter with Kali

This is your chance to 'adore the terrible one'. Do it with all the poetic means at your disposal. Kali has many manifestations in the world of form. She is the transcended goddess and she is incarnate in every woman. Describe one of her many ways to liberate the soul.

Kali by Nandi Chinna

Kali Durga Namah Namah Kali Durga Namah Namah
I'm on a bus, my bags for pillows, my dresses worn one over the other. I see the people get on and off but still I sit. I'm on here till the end of the line. I'm camped out for the duration.

Once I had a home, a family, a love, but with one phone call all that was gone.

Out on the brick paving in the back yard I burned her things, papers, letters, dreams. The ashes I placed in an old ice cream container and wrote her name in black texta on the top.

Whatever I had left walked with me. What I thought was just gritty ashes and black despair sitting in my belly, aching as I lay alone in the winter bed, blankets and doonas piled up on top and temazapam and cask wine — was the beginnings of a new fire.

Now I don't collect. Now I move. I'm on a bus, my bags are my pillows. I wear my dresses one on top of the other. I don't get off. I'm here till the end of the line.

Kali by Lia Eliades

Kali skins me alive and leaves me bloody and lying without a protective sheath.
I draw back my lips to expose teeth and gums, "Thank you," I gurgle as blood pours forth.

Kali stands on my chest, dagger clenched in the hand of one of the thousand arms, and I can see through pupils glazed in blood, my heart, twitching still in her hand. My intestines twined around her fingers and through 100 arms entrails drape.

    My liver between her teeth, my ovaries dangle like earrings in her hair, uterus worn as a pinkie ring.

    Stomach lining fashioned into slippers and she dances; cracking my ribs, one, by one, machinating them to plover and powder.

    My lungs push out the sides and become a breastplate of spongy armour worn by the destroyer herself.
"But he did this to me; why is it I see only you? When he hurt me so."
    With one final yank of my hair, there pops free my skull and she pierces the sockets of my eyes with gold chains to hang from her neck.

10

Between Light and Darkness

India and Persia are sister cultures of antiquity. India delights us with her dreamlike innocence; her culture is a harmonious ritual in which gods, demons and humans rest in the unity of the cosmos: Brahma is in all things and all things are in Brahma. Ancient Persia stands in stark contrast — asserting all-pervading duality. Persian culture is awake to the conflict between good and evil, light and darkness; acutely aware of the place of human responsibility in the task of transforming evil into good.

The difference between the two is mirrored in their geographies: India blessed with a warm and supportive climate, fertile soil and abundant vegetation; Persia challenged by the contrast of vast deserts and fertile plains, biting winters and scorching summers.

Persian Creation Myth

Duality announces itself powerfully in the Persian creation myth. The supreme god Zurvan (Time) sacrifices for a thousand years to conceive a son. When he doubts the efficacy of his acts, the evil son Ahriman is born from his doubts. Another son, Ahura Mazdao, is born from the merit of his sacrifice. These two brothers will struggle with one another until the end of time when Ahriman is overcome and transformed.

Ahura Mazdao, god of light, created the first human being, Yima, and endowed him with magical gifts to sustain the world, including Kvarnah, which is the grace, the divine radiance, the glory, the heavenly charisma that is the mark of Persian heroes and kings. But tempted by Ahriman, Yima uttered the first lie and the heavenly Kvarnah fled from his brow in the form of a falcon.

In another version, Ahura Mazdao created the primal bull and then Gayomard, the first human being. The bull nourished Gayomard and both lived on the banks of the river that flowed from the centre of the world, each withstanding Ahriman's efforts to tempt them. Full of envy for Ahura Mazdao's glorious creation, Ahriman kills them both.

Ahura Mazdao fashions animals and plants from the dead body of the bull. From the seed of the dead Gayomard he grows a plant that after forty years splits into the first human couple: Mashie and Mashyane. Thus Ahura Mazdao curbs the power of evil and makes it serve the good. This grand motif of the struggle between light and darkness and the transformation of evil is elaborated in the details of creation:

> Ahura Mazdao creates birds and Ahriman fashions snakes.
> Ahura Mazdao creates bees, Ahriman fashions fleas, flies, bugs.
> Ahura Mazdao creates butterflies, Ahriman fashions spiders.
> Ahura Mazdao creates sheep, Ahriman fashions wolves.

Exercise 1: Dualism

The ancient Persian experienced outer nature as their own soul life — a moral web of good and evil. The modern human being is loath to divide the natural world into good and evil because the morality of the soul is experienced inwardly. As writers however we can stretch our imagination beyond the confines of the present and ad to this list of duality. Here is an example by Nandi Chinna:

> Ahura Mazdao created the wheel , Ahriman the internal combustion engine
> Ahura Mazdao created conversation, Ahriman the mobile phone
> Ahura Mazdao created forests, Ahriman clear felling
> Ahura Mazdao created abundance, Ahriman hunger
> Ahura Mazdao created generosity, Ahriman greed

Into this world of duality the human being is sent as a divine agent of tranfromation. Human beings can tame wolves and makes them into sheepdogs: the feared enemy becomes the trusted friend.

The Sacred Fire

In the myth of King Hushang we again see good arising out of the clash with evil. Hushang is one of the first kings of Persia. Once he was pursued by a monstrous beast and found himself deep in the mountains, confronted by a fierce monster. Having spent all his arrows, he takes up a stone and hurls it at the beast, who turns and flees. The stone hits a nearby rock and sparks a flame. Through his courage Hushang has discovered fire, and bestows the divine gift upon his people.

The worship of fire became central to the followers of Ahura Mazdao. It is the symbol of the Parsees' religion, and even today the holy flame is kept alive in the temples of Ahura Mazdao. Fire became the essential ingredient in all rituals, signalling the presence of Ahura Mazdao among the earthly elements, his emanation in the world.

The mysterious nature of fire acted like a gateway between the worlds, a language in which gods and humans could converse. Materially, it offered warmth, protection and light. It was at the centre of every dwelling, the power that bakes the bread and melts metal. It signified the power of the human spirit to illumine the darkness and dispel doubt; the courageous warmth of the heart to confront evil and to purge, mature and transform the coarse matter of the soul.

Hushang's story illuminates the dual functions of fire. Through the inner fire of courage he discovers external fire. Rather than flee from his evil opponent, he confronts him. Like Ahura Mazdao before him and the prophet Zarathustra after him he is able to transform evil into good.

Hymns and praise are integral to Persian culture. Praise is the soul's response to the presence of the divine and the grandeur of creation. As G. M. Hopkins once said, the human being 'is made to praise god.'

Here is a hymn from the *Avesta*, the principal Zoroastrian scripture. Note that the proper use of the word, in true and inspired speech, is as a potent weapon against the spirits of darkness.

> In the flaming fire we worship thee,
> Master of Wisdom, Lord of Light,
> Ahura Mazdao,
> O speak to us
> In the glory of the sun,
> Oh Lord of Life!
> From the regions of the north,
> Forth rushed Ahriman, the deadly,
> And the demons of darkness, the evildoers.
> Thus spake Ahriman, the deadly deceiver:
> Kill him, destroy him,
> Holy Zarathustra, Hated Zarathustra.
> Thus spake Zarathustra:
> The word of Ahura Mazdao is my weapon,
> With his word will I strike,
> The holy word of the Lord of Light
> The living word of creation!
> Forth fled Ahriman, the deceiver,
> And the wicked, evildoing demons

Exercise 2: Hymn to Fire

Write a hymn in praise of fire in true Persian style, exploring the dualities of the world.

Hymn to Fire by Bavali Hill

Oh Holy Flame, light of the world
Who brings light to the dark recesses of the mind and soul.

We worship thee.
From the ice regions of the North,
And the unknown territories to the South,
From the pestilence and plagues of the East
And from our demon enemies of the West
Oh deliver us!
Strike Ahriman the deceiver.
Cleave a path to our inner and outer deliverance
Cleft the rock, spill the blood of our enemies.
Oh Holy Zarathustra, most loved and feared.
Light the flame
Your word is law.
Your word is truth.
Thus Spake Zarathustra!

The Story of King Djemschid

Another mythical figure towering high in the tales of ancient Persia is King Djemschid. Until his reign, the people of Persia were hunters. One night Ahura Mazdao visited King Djemschid in a dream: the sun god was holding a golden dagger and stabbing it into the earth. Inspired, the king made the first ploughshare from his own sword. He and his people became sowers and reapers of grain. They learned to save the seed to plant next season. Nomadic life was left behind and villages were built.

This story marks a major step in human civilisation, an initiation into a new way of relating to the world. To be a farmer was to engage in an act of transformation, fulfilling the sacred command of Ahura Mazdao.

For the prehistoric Indian, the earth remained a veil of illusion and held little interest, but for the Persian it became a field of work. The Persian perceived nature as a moral reality arrayed in shades of light and darkness, indicating the presence of Ahura Mazdao and Ahriman. In all its manifestations, the world was a place of moral combat in which the individual was called upon to assist the forces of light.

Ahriman held sway in all that was dark, dull and heavy. He brought the biting cold of winter and the howling winds. He destroyed the harvest and withheld the rain. The earth is darkened and held captive by his demons. By contrast, ploughing, sowing, tending, reaping and storing became a holy service to the sun; every ploughshare a weapon of Ahura Mazdao, every furrow an opening of the dark and each seed a bearer of light. The ripening field was a feat of transformation and each harvest a victory, as expressed in this Persian hymn:

O Great Sun God
Ahura Mazdao
Help in the work to plough the earth.

Help in the battle Ahriman to bind
O great Sun God
Ahura Mazdao
Bring Light to the Darkness
Bring grain to the fields
Let the wolf become a dog
Let evil turn to good
O great sun god Ahura Mazdao

There is a great clarity and firmness in these hymns sung by warriors of plough and sword, a people decisive in their stance against the dark..

Exercise 3: Hymn to the Plough

Write a hymn of praise to the transformation of the earth. Decisive, bold, recalling the magnitude of the task, as in **Jennifer Kornberger's** example:

Into the darkness of humus
the dampness of clay
into the deaf and unmoving soil
I plunge the lance of the sun
the golden plough
so all the fastness of bound things is loosed
and the tethered cold is exhaled.

Hymn to the Plough by Allison Ashton

Salutations to the Supreme Warrior of Light,
Guardian of all that is sacred,
 divine instrument of transformation.

Take this blessed tool and fashion its path through the dar, yielding earth.
Create a river bed, a furrow for the seeds of life to lie therein,
nourished by the wells, by the rain,
warmed by the warmth of the blazing sun.

Guide my hand as it cleaves to the plough.
Steady my step as I wend my way.

Oh, Great One, I bow to your Supreme Creative Power.

This new way of life set the Persians apart from their nomadic neighbours who kept the old way and despised the people who gathered in villages. Hatred grew for those who cut into the earth with their ploughs and forced the ground to yield. The Persians in turn saw their neighbours as possessed by Ahriman, given to tribal warfare, evil rituals and cruel sacrifices. They experienced the plundering of their settlements, the killing and raping, and the burning of their fields as acts of darkness against the gods of light.

Legend tells us of a thousand year war between the people of Ahura Mazdao and the people of Ahriman. Protecting the land from invading hordes became as much a holy service as the practice of agriculture.

In the next two exercises we will explore the primal conflict between the first settlers and their nomadic neighbours. We will take both sides in turn. Give yourself permission to explore the sharp sword edge of the Iranian civilisation. Do not shrink back from the poetics of conflict.

Exercise 4: Persian Call to War

They are here again, pouring over the frontiers: destroying, raping, and killing. Call your village to arms and gather those who can fight. Invoke the power of light to bring victory over the forces of darkness.

Persian Call to War by Harriet Sawer

Come gather, people of the sun
For the shadows gather around us
And we must fight for the light.
The Turanians would drag us into the night
And would we let it pass, my shining people?
Would we let it pass?
Oh shining brothers, gather up your golden spears.
Oh shining sisters, make bread, that the sun may feed warriors.
Oh shining children, gather fuel, that we may forge our weapons.
We shall strike hard when we strike, my shining people,
Creeping from behind like a soft sunrise while our enemy sleeps.
We shall fight, every last inch of us willing to die, again and again
That the sun shall not be taken from us
That the splendid fire of our people shall burn
That our grains will shine golden
That our animals shall live safe in the field
That our gardens shall grow.
We shall pour over the hill, our spears the only light.
Oh Turanians! You know not!
It is WE that you fight!

Exercise 5: Turanian Call to War

From the height of the northern mountains you see the fertile land you once roamed unhindered. Now it is possessed by the hated Iranians who have divided the earth, cut her sacred body open forcing her to yield more than she willingly gives. They worship a foreign god who violates the spirits holy to your tribe, one who has destroyed the old ways sacred to your people. Call your tribe to arms and rouse them with your words.

Turanian Call to War by Harriet Sawer

It is a magic that we must call
the magic of the whole earth and the woods they cut
the soil they scar and the rivers they dam.
We call on you, our magic land, stand strong in us!
For they will come — the war-makers,
the soil-takers — the soul-breakers.
Come forth spirit,
We need a powerful dream.
The spirit of the wolf to come,
that wolf they would tame to
be the guardian of their woolly sheep.
Well we, the Turanians, not woolly sheep us,
see our teeth like knives, our claws,
see the pulsing thread of our dream magic,
that ties us together, into a warrior web.
We fight to be hunters.
We fight for the spirit of all beasts
untamed and untethered
in our spirit's land.

Here is a contemporary call by **Jennifer Kornberger:**

I call you, all nomads, all homeless, mortgageless, without degrees, without curriculum vitae, without a visa card, without a birth certificate; I call you to the forest, to the beach, to the desert; I call you to defend a grove untouched by the print of a Nike shoe, untouched by a page torn from supermarket junk mail, untouched by the invisible swords of mobile phone connections, untouched by the reach of the world wide web: I call you to defend a grove in silence, with bare hands, in the sight of falling leaves.

Zarathustra and Dughba

The several aspects of Persian culture culminate in the figure of Zarathustra: priest, prophet, law-giver and founder of one of the oldest religions on earth — Mazdaism. The original Zarathustra lived before historical times, and united the people of Persia in a common culture with monotheistic worship and elaborate laws long before Moses.

Zarathustra is the chosen vehicle of his god, Ahura Mazdao. His mother, Dughba, is graced with Kvarnah, the divine fire from the stars that descends unto the pure in spirit — the same grace that the ancient Yima lost when he uttered the first lie. But Kvarnah was not always a blessing, and Dughba's radiance caused the enmity of the Daevas, evil spirits inspired by Ahriman, who sent their armies of winter, plagues and storms against her. But no harm came to Dughba and her kin, and so the evil spirits tried to rouse the envy of the villagers against her. Because of her radiance she was accused of being a witch and had to flee her father's home. She became a refugee looking for a safe place.

Exercise 6: Dughba's Lament

Dughba's destiny contains many of the themes that women had to face for millennia: The persecution of female spirituality, the inner and outer homelessness of the spiritually gifted woman and the dire fate of all fugitives and refugees. Let one or all three of these themes inspire you to a creative response.

> **My Red Dress by Desma Kearney**
> I
> 'Banish all mirrors' — she said
> as if I could do that
> 'To live without a mirror' — she said
> 'Is to live without self'
> as if I would want that
> as if I would not
>
> an umbrella is not enough
> I told her — nor a sword
> nor a summer nor a lifetime
>
> II
> This red dress fits me like
> a crown of thorns. To all
> the imagined eyes resting
> on my lines, the shapes of this body
> are more than the shapes in my name

and beauty shows itself
in rills of dried blood
mapping on my face the will of the world
until I would rather be the cut precision of the dress
than the shape of the flesh of the woman beneath

Eventually she married and became pregnant with Zarathustra. But then her son became the target of Ahriman's host, the evil king Duran Suran, who made frequent attempts to kill the babe. But when he tried to stab the child with his dagger, his arm went lame. When he sent a servant to hurl the child into fire, the fire would not harm him; even placed in a wolves' den, the babe remained unharmed. Thrown under the hooves of stampeding cattle, he remained unscathed.

Dughba escapes with the child, and when Zarathustra is thirty years old, he is lead to a mountain top by an 'angel of good thought' where Ahura Mazdao shows himself in a vision and reveals his central doctrine: good words, good thoughts and good deeds. Zarathustra, having found his mission, converts Persia to the new faith. The new revelations draw all strains of Persian culture — the conflict between good and evil, the worship of fire, the sacred task of farming — into a coherent whole and a complex system of law.

Of course India had its spiritual directives too, but they were there from the beginning, like petals on the lotus of Indian divinity — the relationship to the spiritual was not a matter of choice. The followers of Zarathustra, however, made a conscious choice to worship Ahura Mazdao; a decisive act that brought each closer to the god and in opposition to other divinities. In ancient India each divinity is revered. But those who follow Zarathustra are called upon to distinguish: to take a stand for the light and fight for it. To take this stance has a powerfully awakening effect: it replaces the Lotus dream of India with the sobering contrast of light and dark, good and evil.

The laws Ahura Mazdao revealed to Zarathustra are a new creation in the history of the word. They are form-giving, shaping forces, demanding decisive action; a startling battle call for moral responsibility.

Creed of Zarathustra

The Zarathustrian creed which accompanies the laws is a major poetic act. Like the laws, the creed had a rousing effect. It is a moral, religious pledge distinguishing the old from the new, and light from darkness.

1. I curse the Daevas. I declare myself a Mazda-worshipper, a supporter of Zarathustra, hostile to the Daevas, fond of Ahura's teaching … I ascribe all good to Ahura Mazda …

2. ... I renounce the theft and robbery of the cow, and the damaging and plundering of the Mazda settlements.

3. I want freedom of movement and freedom of dwelling for those with homesteads ... I shall nevermore damage or plunder the Mazda settlements, even if I have to risk life and limb.

4. I reject the authority of the Daevas, the wicked, no-good, lawless, evil-knowing, the most druj-like of beings, the foulest of beings, the most damaging of beings ...

Zarathustra spoke the first creed. Every manifesto spoken since has been stamped by its decisive tone. The modern equivalent for the writer is the artistic manifesto — a pledge to aesthetic values and practices. Here is an extract from the *Imagist Manifesto* (1912) of Ezra Pound:

1. To use the language of common speech, but to employ the exact word, not the nearly-exact, nor the merely decorative word.

2. We believe that the individuality of a poet may often be better expressed in free verse than in conventional forms. In poetry, a new cadence means a new idea.

3. Absolute freedom in the choice of subject.

4. To present an image ... poetry should render particulars exactly and not deal in vague generalities, however magnificent and sonorous. It is for this reason that we oppose the cosmic poet, who seems to us to shirk the real difficulties of his art.

Exercise 7: A Writer's Manifesto

Write your own creed. State what you uphold. Be precise and bold.

Truth Manifesto by Janet Blagg

We believe that truth in all its complexity is preferable to the simple that is not true. That truth is reducible neither to pure relativism nor to absolutism. That it is useful to conceive of truth as a great and infinitely faceted diamond hanging in the centre of the cosmos, which reflects a different facet depending on where you stand to catch its beam.

That it is truth which is the many-splendoured thing, and the first pursuit, before freedom and even before love: for it is the first truth that the head must inform the heart and the heart must inform the head, or no good will come of it.

Manifesto by Shaktima Kotulla
A poem must be ripped from the heart
or poured from the soul.
It should beat like the heart of a passionate mother
or the veins of a soldier at war.
It should stand tall even in its meekness.
It should claim its right to life.
It should dance.

Time and Immortality

Zarathustra's vision also viewed time in a new way. Where Indian culture saw time as cyclic, emphasising that which remained the same rather than that which was new, for Zarathustra time was process leading to redemption, when all evil would be overcome and goodness restored in all creation. He prophesied the coming of the Sayoshant — the one who makes prosper and resurrects the body. The Sayoshant will overcome the bull of evil and prepare the drink of immortality.

The vision of the Sayoshant is like a balm on the wound of a divided creation. The Persian priests, the magi, have kept this prophecy as a sacred possession, patiently waiting for the appointed time when the Sayoshant is born. With this vision we leave Zarathustra's world and travel westward, to Babylonia.

11

Baking the Stars

Babylon has always been a melting pot of nations, conquering and being conquered. Its creation myth bears the birthmark of violence: the older, chaos-loving gods Tiamat and Apsu plan the destruction of the younger gods. Only Marduk has the courage to confront the monstrous Tiamat. In a fierce battle he slays her and from her corpse fashions the heavens and earth and all that they contain:

> He constructed stations for the great gods,
> Fixing their astral likenesses as the stars of the Zodiac.
> He determined the year and into sections he divided it;
> He set up three constellations for each of the twelve months.
> After defining the days of the year by means of heavenly figures,
> He founded the station of the pole star …
> That none might err or go astray.

The victorious Marduk assigns the stars to his fellow gods. Like a feudal lord of the cosmos he gives them their mission in the planetary spheres.

Babylonian Astrology

The stars were the dwelling place of the gods — the Babylonians' tall temples were observatories; they looked to the heavens for revelation and to divine the scriptures of the stars, the will of the gods.

The visible world became more real. For the ancient Indian the visible world was illusion; for the Persian it was a field of conquest. The Babylonian experienced it as a home, a tangible reality behind which the gods gradually disappeared. For some time they continued to perceive the gods in particular locations of the cosmos. Eventually this perception ceased and only the knowledge of their relation to the planets remained. The result was Babylonian astrology, an elaborate science of reading the directives of the gods by divining their heavenly relationships.

Our modern astrology is a thin derivate of the Mesopotamian art. Although the gods had begun to disappear, the Babylonian still had an soulful connection to the planetary realms and could interpret accurately what knowledge alone could not divine.

The earth was the tenth heaven, surrounded by the abode of the gods. For all major and minor events the stars were consulted. Certain harmonics between the planetary gods supported the building of houses or cities, others were auspicious for beginning wars or sowing crops.

The individual's horoscope was of particular importance. It was a map of the planetary relations at the moment of birth, charting the experiences of the newborn soul as it sojourned from its home in the heavens, through the planetary spheres, to its place of birth. The chart revealed the nature of the newborn soul, how it was received by the various gods in the spheres, and what the gods had given or withheld. The birth chart provided direction for education, diet, and all that pertained to the individual's destiny. It revealed how newborn souls stood in relation to the gods and determined their earthly tasks.

The Planets and their Spheres

Babylonian astrology has come down to us by way of the Greco-Roman Moon, Mercury, Venus, Sun, Mars, Jupiter and Saturn. Here are their Babylonian gods and some of their traditional associations:

Ninurta (Saturn) gathers all into seed, and presses the soul so that the spiritual essence can be reaped. Ninurta brings resistance but also the introspection and wisdom to be gained from encountering adversity.

Marduk (Jupiter) is a generous god who brings abundance, the gift of expansive vision and the skill to organise and rule.

Nergal (Mars) is the god of war and conflict, source of courage, champion of the new, of stirring speech and daring deeds.

Shamash (Sun) is the all seeing king of the planetary gods, the one who harmonises all the other qualities in the light of wisdom.

Ishtar (Venus) is the goddess of love in all its manifestations, inspiring inwardness of soul and a sense of beauty, grace and care.

Nabu (Mercury) is the god of scribes, communications, merchants and their transactions; the web that forms community.

Sin (Moon), god of procreation, supports the ability to reflect.

Exercise 1: The Seven Heavens

Imagine yourself a Babylonian, recalling your sojourn through the spheres and your meetings with all or any of the seven planetary gods. Write at least two pieces on your experiences: one that is positive and and one that is negative. Write each piece as an event or a short scene that unfolds in a picture of your birth chart, revealing in specific images its import. For example:

In a cleft of rock pieces of shale are skimmed off by the hand of Ninurta. He presses the grey shards into my knees, my spine; turns my head to the shale and places my mouth inside the rock, closes my jaws on the blue lapis. In my lips I feel the nerve of lapis lazuli, the deep vein reaching from teeth to bone and I know that in the seam of that blue are the names of the stories I will write.

Dancing with Ladyboy/ruled by Mercury by Liana Christensen
"Quicksilver! Quicksilver! Quicksilver!" the barker calls as I move through the market place, past the scribes scribbling furiously for the patient queues awaiting love letters, seals, poems, bills, prayers. The light fingered ones dart in and out of the alleys and the crowds, deftly gathering whatever takes their fancy. Warp and weft. I know the weave. I make my way to the tumblers, the acrobats, the pennywhistle dancers who play in the dust at the centre. The Ladyboy awaits me, that slight ironic smile. She/he holds out an elegant hand as I knew he/she would. I am drawn in to the dance.

Building the First City

The god Ea gave the Babylonian people the knowledge of brick baking and pottery. Clay was ample in the fertile land between the Tigris and Euphrates rivers and soon a great city arose. The gates of the city were tiled with magnificent reliefs, the walls wide enough for chariots to race along the top of them, and the temples reached towards the stars.

The baking of bricks and building of cities were sacred acts, performed according to the will of the gods. The design of the city mirrored the heavens above. Mighty walls surrounded the city like the zodiac encompassing the planets. The priest-king the representative of Shamas, the soldiers representatives of Nergal, the merchants of Nabu. The whole community replicated the hierarchies of heaven and the city itself was the pride of kings and commoners alike as this extract from the epic of Gilgamesh shows:

> Go up, Urshanabi, onto the wall of Uruk and walk around.
> Examine its foundation, inspect its brickwork thoroughly —
> is it not the brick structure of kiln-fired brick,
> and did not the Seven Sages themselves lay out its plan!

Exercise 2: Building the City

Place yourself in this first of cities where the effort of labourers, artisans and priests created the walls, houses, temples. What was your part? Write a piece inspired by this activity of city building.

Building the City of Shamash by Janet Blagg

In seven days was the city of Shamash raised, O beloved. Listen and attend, for I was there, the temple scribe, paid in silver and gold to record this auspicious and wondrous event.

On the first day were the bricks baked, ten thousand thousand of them from the red river clay. On this day the Northern Gateway — the first gate — the Shamash Gate was begun. All afternoon the priests sacrificed where the temple would be, a thousand goats, and their red blood mixed with the clay of the bricks and burned in the fiery furnaces. All day there was singing and dancing and feast-making, and when the last festive fire had burned down the First Gate was complete.

On the second day the first brick of the Temple of Shamash was laid and the bounds of the seven walls were beaten, on earth as above — from the Shamash Gate to the east: Nergal, Marduk, Ninurta; and to the west: Ishtar, Nabu, Sin — seven gateways radiating like the seven precious stones. When the last boundary post was set a silence descended on every soul alive. It was as though a holy fire filled our spirits. When dawn marked the end of the second day, the second gateway was complete.

And each day, as gateway, temple, bridge and dwelling was raised, and roads laid out and sewers dug, carousing revellers met the dawn at each newly completed gateway.

Seven gates to the City!

Building the City by Jo Lunay

The stars that spatter the sky and make me shine in the moonlight spoke to them and they came to gather me; my rich muddiness lying thick and heavy in rivers and on banks. They came and scooped me and shaped me into separateness — smoothed and folded me, molded me, then baked and fired me — I became so many pieces; separate, distinct and finally reunited to become one again as they stacked me and shaped me into walls …

The Encounter with Death

The building of brick dwellings and city walls marks a coming to terms with the solidity of earth. The wall is a boundary, a means of separation. In these massive constructions the Babylonian was building a sense of self and declaring a certain independence from the gods.

As the self awakens, the gods withdraw into the twilight of myth. Their presence is veiled now and the priest must mediate their will. In the wake of this fading, the realm of the dead takes on a new meaning. Death, which was once merely a transition from one world to another, now becomes a dreaded place. The underworld turns into a dark expanse issuing spectres of fear and doubt and ruled by a cruel goddess.

The encounter with death found powerful expression in the myth of the goddess Inanna (Akkadian Ishtar) and in the epic of Gilgamesh.

The Descent of Inanna

Inanna resolves to visit the underworld. This realm is locked by seven gates and ruled by her sister Ereshkigal, goddess of death.

> She placed twin egg-shaped beads on her breast. She covered her body with a pala dress, the garment of ladyship. She placed mascara which is called 'Let a man come, let him come,' on her eyes. She pulled the pectoral which is called 'Come, man, come,' over her breast. She placed a golden ring on her hand. She held the lapis-lazuli measuring rod and measuring line in her hand.

> Inanna summons her divine power, her adornments of glory and clothes herself for the Journey. She commands her servant Nincubura to wait for her at the entrance to the underworld and to beg the assistance of the gods if she fails to return. She comes to the first gate, which bars the netherworld from the living, and boldly demands entry. But Neti, the gate keeper, will not open the gate unless she leaves part of her power behind. At each gate she must relinquish some part of her being.

> And when Inanna entered, the lapis-lazuli measuring rod and measuring line were removed from her hand, when she entered the first gate, the turban, headgear for the open country, was removed from her head. 'What is this?' 'Be satisfied, Inanna, a divine power of the underworld has been fulfilled. Inanna, you must not open your mouth against the rites of the underworld.'

> When she entered the second gate, the small lapis-lazuli beads were removed from her neck. 'What is this?' 'Be satisfied, Inanna, a divine power of the underworld has been fulfilled. Inanna, you must not open your mouth against the rites of the underworld.'

> When she entered the third gate, the twin egg-shaped beads were removed from her breast. 'What is this?' …

> When she entered the fourth gate, the 'Come, man, come' pectoral was removed from her breast …

> When she entered the fifth gate, the golden ring was removed from her hand …

> When she entered the sixth gate, the lapis-lazuli measuring rod and measuring line were removed from her hand …

When she entered the seventh gate, the pala dress, the garment of ladyship, was removed from her body …

Stripped of her powers, she reaches the dismal world of the dead and seats herself on the throne of her sister. The seven judges of the underworld shout at her in rage. They look at her with the look of death and render her guilty. Inanna is turned into a corpse and hung on a hook.

Her servant Nincubura laments for three nights then begs the gods to deliver Inanna from the realm of death. Finally the god Enki consents to help and fashions ministering spirits from the dirt beneath his fingernails. The spirits descend and recover Inanna.

This myth is an initiation into the meaning of death. It allows us to explore the process of leaving behind, of giving up and of being stripped of the outer trappings, the accidental and inessential. The myth is resonant with the smaller and larger deaths that accompany our lives, the many thresholds into the new and unknown that we need to pass, and the radical change of dimension which is the large portal of death itself. To the Babylonians, the myth of Inanna showed their gods shuddering before the terrifying solidity of the dark earth.

Exercise 3: The Seven Gates

Use the descent as a stimulus for a piece that explores your own journey, into the underworld or through life. What do you give up as you pass through each of the seven gates? What of yourself do you leave behind?

There are many ways to approach this important exercise. The examples below from different students illustrate the variety of possible approaches.

Gate 1 by Jennifer Kornberger

At the first gate I leave my girdle of herbs, pau d'arco and olive leaf, golden rod and arnica. I leave the vials of water infused with the true names of flowers: elm, holly, iris and rock rose. I leave the dank green of spirulina, the zesty spit of vitamin C and the invisible fingerprints of my homeopathic remedies.

Gate 2 by Coral Carter

Here I cast off my obsessions, my fanatical neatness
clothes hung in the order of refracted light
hats arranged according to season
pots, pans and cutlery marshalled in rows of military precision
polished surfaces reflecting, reflecting, reflecting
every cup poured every pot stirred

my shoe collection: stiletto, mules, pumps, slippers, sneakers, runners, uggs, thongs, sandals, boots; beaded, shiny, matt, laced, buttoned and every one in its place —
I leave at the second gate

Gate 3 by Richard Smart

… I reach a lit room, this time covered in mirrors. The directions on the door read: 'Please leave Narcissus behind. Shave head and remove all clothing.' Naked and shaven, looking at my self in the mirror a version of myself appears out of my reflection. He's got thick blond slick-backed hair and he's wearing the latest fashion. He briefly stops his conversation on the newest mobile phone to give me some advice: 'Richo, Richo, Richo, dude check you out! Damn, you going for an ugly award or what!? They're not going to take you down there looking like that! Duuuude please!'

Gate 4 by Maggie Brackenridge

I leave dead eagles lying. Ambulance sirens — a drowned face — suicide Sunday — lover — Beauty Girl — overdosed. A lineage of grieving mothers, dead fathers — Popeye.

Gate 5 by Martina Chippindall

At the fifth all interior structures are pulled from around me. I fall through this gate, find myself amidst the rubble and all that defined me. Things must come and go. I cannot hold on.

Gate 6 by Rhea Pfeiffle

The next door is my front door. I must leave my heart. I open the door and behind it is the Welsh Dresser, adorned with family photos and children's art works like an altar. I hold my heart with my right hand and open the drawer that contains everything, half-worn batteries, inexplicable screws, keys to doors long forgotten and lego blocks. And I gently place my heart there. This is where it has always been.

Gate 7 by Pen Brown

Beloved: This is a chorus of sound. This is a thousand strings that I hold like ropes. Like a bell-ringer with a multitude of bells.

   This is every bird and bone, every moss and mollusk. Every rain drop. Every child. Every ant. This is the sound of every made and beautiful thing, before the making.

To pass through the Gate of Ropes and Strings, I must find and pull a particular sound … I reach out, and amidst the thousand calling ropes, through pure recognition, I find my own sound.

My heart note fuses to it instantly and as I move through the gate my note is drawn out of me, out of my throat, its entire length, like string, I gag and gag until it lies coiling and wild and streaming with sound behind me.

So this I must leave. This whole and secret sound of my made self. I attempt to walk, but find myself skimming in no known way for I have no legs or hands or feet …

Exercise 4: The New Inanna

Rewrite the descent as a story, as in the example by Brenda Chapman:

Inanna's Rebirth by Brenda Chapman

My mother drives me to the airport. I know I will never see my family home again. As we drive through the front gate, I recognise it as the first portal. My journey has begun.

We arrive at the airport and I kiss my mother goodbye. I know I will not see her again. 'Goodbye Mum, take good care.' Walking into the terminal, I pass through the second portal.

Checking my luggage in, I look down at my backpack filled with clothes, books and journals. My old guitar. 'You'll need this ticket to collect your baggage at the other end,' says the clerk. 'Thanks,' I say, and throw the ticket on the ground. I walk onto the plane, and pass through the third portal.

A few hours later, the plane lands. 'Make sure not to leave any items aboard the aircraft,' says the steward over the PA. I look down and see my mobile phone lying on the seat beside me. I pick it up and check it is turned off. I put it back down on the seat, walk off the plane and out through the fourth portal.

Standing in the airport, I am surrounded by people speaking a language I don't understand. They are begging and asking me for clothes and money. I give my jacket and shoes to a pregnant African girl who is wearing nothing but a sarong. In the doorway sits a tall thin man with four crying children. I pass him my wallet as I walk out through the fifth portal and onto the busy African street. It's 45 degrees and I am wearing nothing but a white sundress and a pair of sunglasses. I start walking out of town.

The sun has finally set but I have been walking all day on the hot sand. My feet are blistered and I wonder if I can go on. A dilapidated yellow car stops beside me. It has a smashed windscreen and no hubcaps or seat belts. I cannot see the driver, it's too dark. 'Give me your sunglasses and I will take you wherever you want to go,' he says. 'Thank you,' I say and hand him my sunglasses as I climb through the sixth portal into the back seat of the car.

After a few hours I see the full moon rising pregnant over the horizon.

'Stop here,' I say, 'this is where I get out.'

'I can't let you out here,' says the driver.

'Let me out.'

The car stops and the man turns to me. His large, moonlit teeth are glowing against his black face. I slip off my white dress, fold it and pass it to him. 'For your wife,' I say as I climb out of the car door through the seventh portal.

Now, I find myself surrounded by the vast West African desert. There's just me, the moon, and the little yellow car, driving off into the hot, fragrant night.

12

The First of Friendships

In the last chapter we encountered a goddess wrestling with death. Now we meet a human facing that same inevitability: Gilgamesh, the first tragic hero in the history of the word, whose story is the oldest known epic of humanity. Recorded in stanzas long before the Iliad and the Odyssey, the tale represents a major milestone on the road of human experience, the hero's quest for immortality, the celebration of the gift of friendship and the struggle with the fact of death.

Written down on clay tablets, the poem was excavated in the nineteenth century. Its account of the biblical flood caused a great stir, and it now stands among the major literary productions of humanity.

The Story of Gilgamesh

Gilgamesh is king of Uruk - divine and human, mythical and historic.

> Who can compare with him in kingliness? ... Two-thirds of him is god, one-third of him is human. The Great Goddess Aruru designed the model for his body, she prepared his form ... beautiful, handsomest of men ...

Gilgamesh is feared and adored by his subjects, but not loved. Ambitious to build great cities, he taxes the men with hard work and asserts his kingly rights over women. The people of Uruk complain to their gods, who decide a hero is needed to match Gilgamesh in strength and beauty. Thus they create Enkidu, a wild man, living in the wilderness and reared by the beasts.

> ... Enkidu, born of Silence, endowed with strength by Ninurta. His whole body was shaggy with hair, he had a full head of hair like a woman, his locks billowed in profusion like Ashnan. He knew neither people nor settled living, but wore a garment like Sumukan. He ate grasses with the gazelles, and jostled at the watering hole with the animals ...

A trapper spots Enkidu and is greatly alarmed. He asks help from the king, who sends Shamhat, a temple harlot, to seduce the wild man. Enkidu meets the woman and shares her company. When he returns to the wild beasts they shy away from him. Shamhat leads him to a nearby settlement. His hair is shorn, his body oiled and human clothes are made to fit his mighty limbs. He joins the shepherds, and with his formidable strength defends them against lions and wolves.

Soon murmurs from Uruk reach his ear. He is angered by the news of Gilgamesh's custom of enjoying the bride before her husband. He travels to the city to challenge Gilgamesh. Hailed by the discontented people, Enkidu bars the door to the bride's room. The heroes wrestle so 'that the doorposts trembled and the walls shook.' Gilgamesh proves the stronger. But the moment he throws Enkidu to the ground, the king's anger abates and both embrace as friends.

Gilgamesh and His Other Half

Gilgamesh is the hero-pioneer of individuality, the first to feel himself alone and separate from his people and the gods; a man of grand design, ambitious projects, of enterprise and pride in his achievements.

Enkidu is endowed with everything that Gilgamesh has lost. Reared in the wild, he is an echo of paradisal man, close to the gods and suffused with the grace that Gilgamesh lacks: the innocence of nature and kinship with the beast. In their love the old and new embrace and Gilgamesh finds what he has lost. He shares his throne with his beloved friend, they rule together and harmony descends.

Yet Gilgamesh is not content. For the sake of fame and ambition he decides to battle the demigod Humbaba, a fierce monster roaming in the cedar forests of Lebanon. Enkidu and the council of elders advise Gilgamesh against the adventure, but he remains steadfast.

Before his journey he visits his mother, the goddess Ninsun, who adopts Enkidu as her second son and ensures the support of the sun god Shamash for their perilous quest.

The two heroes make their way to the Cedar Forest and each day camp on a mountain top. Gilgamesh has five terrifying dreams about mountains crashing, raging storms, wild bulls and thunderbirds breathing fire. Enkidu, however, takes them as good omens and urges his friend on.

They enter the forest and are challenged by Humbaba, who vows to disembowel Gilgamesh and feed his flesh to the birds. Gilgamesh is afraid, but Enkidus' words renew his courage. The battle commences. The mountains quake and the sky turns black. In the middle of turmoil the god Shamash sends thirteen winds that bind Humbaba. The monster is captured and pleads for his life. Gilgamesh pities him, but Enkidu demands his death. Humbaba curses them both before Gilgamesh cuts off his head.

The two friends build a raft and return in triumph to Uruk. Gilgamesh's fame reaches even the heavens, and awakens the love of the goddess Ishtar. But Gilgamesh refuses her love, on account of the many lovers that she has ruined before. The goddess is incensed and asks her father Anu to send Gugalanna, the Bull of Heaven, to avenge her.

When Anu refuses, Ishtar threatens to allow the dead to devour the living. Anu consents and Gugalanna assails Uruk. The Bull of Heaven empties the river, dries up marshes and devours men. Gilgamesh and Enkidu battle the beast at the wall of Uruk. They slay Gugalanna and offer his heart to the god Shamash. When Ishtar cries out in anger, Enkidu throws the bull's hindquarters into her face.

The city celebrates the heroes, but Enkidu has a foreboding dream. He sees how the gods have decided that he must die to atone for the death of Humbaba and the Bull of Heaven. Enkidu curses the trapper and Shamhat who have lured him from the wild. Shamash appears and reminds him of the good that has come from this and Enkidu changes the curse into a blessing. Soon thereafter he falls sick and in a dream has a fearful premonition of his death.

> Listen, my friend, to the dream that I had last night. The heavens cried out and the earth replied, and I was standing between them. There appeared a man of dark visage … he seized me by my hair and overpowered me … capsized me like a raft, and trampled on me like a wild bull … Then he turned me into a dove, so that my arms were feathered like a bird. Seizing me, he led me down to the House of Darkness, the dwelling of Irkalla, to the house where those who enter do not come out, along the road of no return, to the house where those who dwell, do without light, where dirt is their drink, their food is of clay, where, like a bird, they wear garments of feathers, and light cannot be seen, they dwell in the dark, and upon the door and bolt, there lies dust. On entering the House of Dust, everywhere I looked there were royal crowns gathered in heaps …

Exercise 1: Enkidu

Before his death Enkidu remembers his life in the wilderness, when he ran free and naked among the gazelles, when the wolves were his friends, the nights his cover and the sunlight his raiment.

Imagine yourself Enkidu and write a recollection of your time among animals. Imagine yourself all sense, bathing in sensations of warmth, smells, dampness …

Enkidu by Jo Lunay

Sunlight on a puddle, wind ripples its surface and my mind topples in and down, down until I am standing again on the edge of the waterhole all those years ago. Bare feet sink into the mud as I nudge closer to the water's edge, shoulders rubbing with other hides. My eyes are also theirs as we cease our drinking and gaze across to the forest, deciphering the shadows into friend or foe.

The sun heats my hide and dew-turned-steam rises in a soft mist and with it that raw, earthy, sweaty-hair smell fills my nostrils; there is safety in it, familiarity, a wholeness.

Enkidu by Morgan Yasbincek

My birth came about hoof by hoof, hock by hock, shoulder by shoulder. It was the herd who created — stampeding, thundering, grunting as animals tripped on stone, heaving as they barged chest first into the water. The herd ran across day and night, day and night and when they stopped I was there, wet, cold. I suckled one of them, who nuzzled my first movements out of me with her muzzle, warm with breath. She had another suckling and together we butted at her udder. Together we slept on the dome of her veined belly. After some time I woke and found I was a clawed animal, the world a tantalising wind of aromas. I spent days padding after the perfume of honey, digging ants out of trees.

Enkidu dies, and Gilgamesh, hero and conqueror of cities and lands, who dared challenge Humbaba and the Bull of Heaven, stands helpless. Robbed of his friend, he mourns deeply:

> May the Roads of Enkidu to the Cedar Forest mourn you and not fall silent night or day. May the Elders of the broad city of Uruk-Haven mourn you. May the peoples who gave their blessing after us mourn you. May the men of the mountains and hills mourn you. May the pasture lands shriek in mourning as if it were your mother. May the cypress, and the cedar which we destroyed in our anger mourn you. May the bear, hyena, panther, tiger, water buffalo, jackal, lion, wild bull, stag, ibex, all the creatures of the plains mourn you.

The theme of friendship is at the core of Gilgamesh's tale. Only when individuality emerges is friendship possible. Blood ties loosen, and the love that tied family or tribe together gives way to a love based on the kinship of soul. Good friends are always part of us. Their gift is to reflect us as we truly are. Deeply familiar, we know them long before we meet them. The meeting is fated and the recognition mutual. A whole way of living in the world is tied to the presence of a particular friend.

Exercise 2: Lament for Friendship

Write down the names of at least six friends who have played a major part in your life. Picture them and note the feelings attached to each.

Now recall one of them. Savour the pictures and feelings. Imagine that this friend has gone irrevocably, perhaps died. Express your sadness, remembering the times together. For example:

Lament for a Lost Friendship by Janet Blagg

Shashi I might never see you again. You were free and full of your poetry and I loved you. There were flaws: how you were mean to Rowena; self-righteous and rarely fulfilled your promises. But I forgave all these, you were such a yay-sayer, so generous to me. Fetching me in the middle of the night all the way from Dromana with your daughter asleep on the back seat. But oh, I cannot look back without the reminder of how badly it all fell out.

Gilgamesh Lament by Judy Griffiths

This world has grown dim.
I wake to hear the magpies caroll as we so often did.
Their song no longer pierces me with that same joy .
I wait for the sun's rays to illuminate the tree's
uppermost branch, and I am not filled with its
burnished glory.
I have lost the intensity of hearing and sight, without
you beside me.

Your presence was a lens through which my life
garnered vitality.

Without you, I am dense; I am bland; I am shallow;
Even to my very breath.

The Quest for Everlasting Life

With Enkidu gone the spectre of his own death comes to haunt Gilgamesh. The prospect of his own mortality torments him night and day. Roaming the wilderness clothed in animal skins, he cries bitterly:
'I am going to die! — am I not like Enkidu? Deep sadness penetrates my core, I fear death, and now roam the wilderness.'

The riddle of death takes him on the quest for immortality. Gilgamesh resolves to search for Utnapishtim, the man who lived before the flood, who has been granted eternal life by the gods.

His pilgrimage is long and arduous. On a mountain pass he is surrounded by lions. Encouraged by a dream, he summons his strength and slays the beasts.

He arrives at the twin peaks of Mount Mashu at the end of the earth. Before him is a dark tunnel, barred by terrible scorpion men. Only when they recognise his semi-divine nature do they let him pass.

Then he wades through twelve leagues of darkness. After twelve double-hours the hero arrives at the Garden of the Gods, a paradisal place where trees are heavily laden with jewels. But the Goddess Siduri, the tavern keeper of paradise, bolts the doors. Gilgamesh bangs on the gates demanding entry on account of his divine origin, his great fame and his accomplishments.

I am Gilgamesh, I killed the Guardian! I destroyed Humbaba who lived in the Cedar Forest, I slew lions in the mountain passes! I grappled with the Bull that came down from Heaven, and killed him.

The Individual Self

Many traditional cultures saw a sense of self as a sin against the gods and the communal whole. In Babylonian culture, however, the gods withdraw and individuality asserts itself through heroic deeds and the erection of cities.

Gilgamesh is the forerunner of modern individuality, one of the first to acquire what is now a common possession: an independent sense of self. Gilgamesh has his name stamped on every brick, his life recorded on tablets of clay. His destiny is distinct from others; all his deeds are his own: they have shaped both the world and himself. The assertion of self through the proud recounting of deeds is a significant step in the journey of the word. Nowadays we are all like Gilgamesh, left by the gods to our own devices. We venture into the world and create our destiny.

Exercise 3: Gilgamesh

Write a piece that starts: I am Gilgamesh. Recount your heroic deeds, victories and accomplishments in the face of obstacles. View them from an imaginative perspective. Polish the mundane until it shines poetically. Search for the hidden myth in your biography.

Gilgamesh by Adrian Glamorgan

I am Gilgamesh, Adrian is my name. Builder of cities of youth, empires of middle age, father to a son. Was it not I who urged the march for reconciliation and 50,000 walked? Was it not I who challenged the government to make new occupational health and safety plans? And so, in the eventual way, these plans came to pass. Was it not I who called for support for Filipino workers, uniting? Did I not sing to a thousand people of the need for peace before the governors took us to war? ...

Gilgamesh by Jennifer Kornberger

I am Gilgamesh, I was on the early road
the one road where the sun
laboured red and bloody to rise
through the shard of night.
I am Gilgamesh, I was on the early road
the road where the wick of my star

was snuffed out by the fingers of Ishtar.
I am Gilgamesh, I was on the early road
the one road where my shoes melted
and now I stand before you, Siduri
and demand entry to your tavern!

Gilgamesh tells his tale but the goddess Siduri remains unconvinced.

> If you are Gilgamesh, who killed the Guardian, who destroyed Humbaba … who grappled with the Bull that came down from heaven, and killed him, why are your cheeks emaciated, your expression desolate! Why is your heart so wretched!

The hero who so proudly asserted his accomplishments now discloses the sadness of losing his friend and his desperation in the face of death.

> Six days and seven nights I mourned over him … I began to fear death, and so roam the wilderness. The issue of my friend oppresses me, so I have been roaming long trails through the wilderness … How can I stay silent, how can I be still! My friend whom I love has turned to clay. Am I not like him? Will I lie down, never to get up again?

Exercise 4: Confession

Painful awareness of his own mortality is the starting point for Gilgamesh's quest. What is the cause of your quest? What fuels your journey as a writer, a human being, a creative individual? What sadness, pain, shock, lack or need has sent you on your way?

Confession by Liana Christensen

I know exile. At eight years of age I was thrust from the kingdom of fairy. I wandered for most of my life as a wraith, starving, yearning, seeing only in others what I had lost so long ago that I failed to see it was mine to begin with. I grieve the unique, anonymous greatness of the uncelebrated ones. Those I love who have gone down unsung to their graves. For my own exile and pain — for the exile and pain of the world — I weep in bitterness and dwell in twelve realms of hell. Let me now enter the gates of paradise.

The Herb of Everlasting Youth

Gilgamesh asks Siduri the way, and the goddess warns him of the treacherous passage ahead. But seeing his resolve she points him to Urshanapi, the ferryman who crosses the waters of death. As he approaches the ferryman, he sees twelve stone Giants and in an outburst of anger destroys them. When he asks the ferryman to carry him across the water, Urshanabi tells him that the stone Giants were the means by which to journey across. Gilgamesh pleads with the ferryman and tells his tale of woe. Urshanabi takes pity on the weary traveller and advises him to cut 300 punting poles for the journey across the water.

When Gilgamesh finally crosses the river, Utnapishtim asks him the same questions as had Siduri and Urshanabi and again he repeats his lament. Then Utnapishtim tells Gilgamesh the story of the great flood and of how he was granted eternal life. He promises to give Gilgamesh the secret of eternal life if he passes a test: he is to stay awake for seven days and nights. Gilgamesh is confident, but falls asleep on the first day. Utnapishtim asks his wife to bake a loaf of bread for very day the hero lies asleep. When Gilgamesh awakes Utnapishtim shows him seven loaves of bread. Gilgamesh is devastated. Taking pity on him, Utnapishtim and his wife restore his health and clothe him in royal garments. As a parting gift Utnapishtim discloses to Gilgamesh the hiding place of the herb that restores youth.

Returning with the ferryman, Gilgamesh binds heavy stones to his feet and dives for the precious herb. He retrieves it from the depths and is overjoyed to have the secret in his hands. But alas! On his way back, a snake steals the herb and he returns empty-handed, his quest a failure. The story ends with Gilgamesh's return to Uruk with neither immortality nor eternal youth.

The goddess Siduri had spoken the truth when she advised him:

> When the gods created man they allotted death to be his fate. But life they retained for themselves alone. As for you, Gilgamesh, fill your belly with good things, be merry day and night, feast and rejoice. Let your clothes be fresh, bathe yourself in water, cherish the little child that holds your hand and make your wife happy in your embrace. This is the lot of man.

Exercise 5: Siduri's Advice

Take Siduri's advice to explore the limitations Gilgamesh must accept.

Siduri's Advice by John Stubley

Be content with Friday afternoons, with dreams about flying, with midnight phone calls just making sure. Be content with rain on the beach, with wall-to-wall silence, with trips that don't arrive at the end. Be content with jobs that fall through, friends that move on, and ideas that turn into the life that you live

Siduri's Advice by Jennifer Kornberger

Tolerate the dust that gathers on the piano, on the sill. Tolerate the dust that gathers in fine spun drifts over books and paint pots. Gather it gently into soft balls, mould it between your palms; it is all breath, all echo of something done and undone, the quiet embroidery of solid objects. Then blow it off your fierce palms out some open window.

The whole tenor of Babylonian culture echoes in the destiny of Gilgamesh. The gods withdraw behind the stars and the gates of everlasting life are closed.

13

The Weighing of the Heart

The Egyptians trace themselves to Ra, the shining one, the self-created god whose name was hidden, for it contained the power to create. When Ra said: 'I am Kephera at dawn, Ra at noon and Tum in the evening,' the sun rose for the first time in the east, traversed the sky and set again. When he named the god Shu, the wind began to blow. When he uttered Tefnet's holy name the rain fell. When he said Geb, the earth rose above the waters of the sea and when he called the name of Nut, the goddess of the sky stretched far and wide.

Naming all things, Ra created all that is. Ra himself descended among his people as the first Pharaoh, and ruled for many thousands of years, bringing peace and prosperity. As Ra grew old his bones became like silver, his flesh like gold. Bent by age he could no longer fight the dragon of evil lurking in the night. Younger gods had to help him.

Thoth, the god of wisdom and magic and Nut, the sky goddess, begat five children. The first was Osiris, then Harmachis, Set, Isis and Neptitis. (In older legends Osiris is the son of Isis.) The birth of Osiris was accompanied by miracles, and prophets proclaimed him the future king.

Isis and Osiris

Isis marries her brother Osiris and their father Thoth bestows all he knows upon them. It is said that Isis became the greatest magician that Egypt ever knew. To aid her husband in gaining the throne, she ascertained the hidden name of Ra. Possessing that gives her his power to create and the key to everything that ever was, is and shall be.

Having disclosed his sacred name to Isis, Ra resigns the throne and withdraws to the barque of the sun, in which he crosses Egypt each day.

Osiris becomes the new Pharaoh, and Isis his queen. They build the great city of Thebes and rule in peace. Isis teaches the people how to sow and reap wheat and barley, bake bread, cultivate date palms and tend the grape vines. She gives laws, and instructs the people in the building of temples and worship of the gods.

But their evil brother Set is envious of the throne and plots Osiris's death. He has a chest of precious wood made to fit precisely the proportions of Osiris. He then invites his brother to a feast and promises the chest to whichever god may fit it best. When Osiris lies down in it the chest is a perfect fit. Set slams shut the lid, nails it down and seals all cracks with lead. He flees and casts the chest into the Nile, which carries it out to the open sea. Eventually it is washed onto the shores of ancient Byblos, and is caught in the heart of a tamarisk tree, which grows around the precious load. So sweetly scented is the wood encasing Osiris that the king has it cut and made into a pillar for his royal house.

Isis searches for her husband everywhere. She traces the chest to Byblos, retrieves it from the pillar and returns with it to Egypt. But Set learns what she had done, and snatches the body of Osiris and tears it into fourteen pieces, scattering the parts all over Egypt.

Isis does not rest until she has found all but one of Osiris's parts. The fourteenth part, his genitals, were eaten by the fish of the Nile! By magic Isis recovers her brother's body in each of the thirteen locations and has thirteen temples built to enshrine his holy remains.

> Thy sister Isis put forth her protecting power for thee, she scattered abroad those who were her enemies, she drove back evil hap, she pronounced mighty words of power, she made cunning her tongue, and her words failed not. The glorious Isis was perfect in command and in speech, and she avenged her brother. She sought him without ceasing, she wandered round and round the earth uttering cries of pain, and she rested not until she had found him. She overshadowed him with her feathers, she made wind with her wings, and she uttered cries at the burial of her brother ... (from 'Hymn to Osiris')

After the burial the spirit of Osiris passes to the paradisal land of the dead, where he rules supreme and awaits the souls of the worthy.

The Egyptian Spiritual Life

The Egyptians saw their whole life as a preparation for reuniting with Isis and Osiris. Isis was their queen and a part of Osiris was buried within them. This part was their innermost essence, the immortal soul that had its abode in their heart. Only the pharaoh and initiated priests were able to awaken this essence during their lifetime. But what the initiated achieved while on earth, everyone was destined to experience in the afterworld, the world of the dead. Here the immortal soul, having traversed the netherworld, stood before the forty-two judges who would weigh their heart against the feather of truth.

This was the moment before the soul reunited with its true origin, the heavenly Osiris, when the deeds of a lifetime were weighed. The heavy heart of the dishonest sank on the scales to be snatched by Ament, the devourer of hearts, while the light heart rose and was welcomed as the new Osiris in the field of peace. In this final moment the words uttered during earthly life are reckoned of profound importance. Language had magical power. Words were sacred, and their misuse was sacrilege.

Imagine the ancient Egyptian, totally immersed in the tangible power of gods, priests and rituals. Imagine yourself infused with the prayers invoking the moment of judgement and read the following text aloud:

> He approacheth the Hall of Judgement
> O My Heart, my Mother, my Heart, my Mother,
> The seed of my being, my earthly existence,
> O stay with me still in the Hall of the Princes,
> In the presence of the God who keepeth the Balance.
>
> And when thou art weighed in the scale with the feather
> Of truth then render no judgment against me;
> Let not the Lords of the Trial cry before me:
> He hath wrought Evil and spoken Untruth …
>
> Behold O my Heart, if there be not a parting
> Between us, our name shall be one with to-morrow …

Taste that mood that is both joyful and serious. See yourself in the presence of the gods, about to undergo the weighing of the heart. Let your poetic imagination take hold of this scene.

Exercise 1: Addressing the Heart

In the first four lines of the text above the heart itself is named with the power of longing in language that carries a weighty simplicity. In four lines address your heart, beginning 'O my heart' or a similar phrase that will give the necessary distance without losing intimacy. For example:

> O my heart, quiet sun of a fierce land
> Blind singer, crosser of streams,
> Make me pause at each deed
> And weigh the stone of my words.

Exercise 2: The Weighing of the Heart

Create a series of pictures that speak of the deeds of your heart. Consider what the heart has been now that the weighing is at hand.

The Weighing of the Heart by Jaya Penelope

in the halls of the dead, the goddess comes
to weigh my heart
against the feather of truth
Oh mute heart
you have been voiceless
as a walled city,
drawbridge up,
arrows ready
to defend your citadel.
You have been an inland sea
with your velvet
chambers, anemone
mouths, your
red rivers.
You have been tinsel I have worn
on my sleeve
ready to give away
to the first pretty stranger
with syrupy eyes.
You have been a winged thing
singing in the branches
of an apple tree.
You have been hollow
and hungry, a thief
slipping over the back fence,
savage and full of blood,
an assassin with your hooks out.
I have buried you
in intricate Chinese boxes,
hidden you in
eggshell, lost you
as readily as
house keys

You have been bitten
in two, stuck
back together
with glue (or sticky-tape,
whatever was at hand) on more
than one occasion.
You have been boiled

in a broth
that was heavy
with loves
unspoken.
You have been
no
feather
weight.

The Weighing of the Heart by Desma Kearney

My grandmother was the keeper of the feather of truth
she had the world divided
held the light and dark of it in her own two hands
She had the seeing of a fearsome god
And no one entered her house
without being stopped at the doorway by her with her
rusty scales
She would rake her eyes across me, and hold out her
hand
for me to give her my heart to measure

In time I learned that only the innocent heart of a
forest animal
could balance against grandma's feather
(because the heart of a little girl
bears the weight that is rested in her)

When grandma died I was strange
and far from home — I rained
monsoons onto my knees
for a tasteless kind of love
where I cried — an old old place
(not memory or grief)
where I found her (a place where
we both should have drowned)
my heart is tear emptied and feather weightless
and she is forgiven her burden of judging the world.

The Temple Trials

The Egyptians longed for the realm of the dead as much as the Babylonians feared it. Death was their homecoming to the gods, the restoration of peace. The whole of

Egyptian life orientated itself towards the great revelation of the meeting with Isis and the recovery of Osiris in the soul. Life was a continuous prayer and a preparation for death.

For the common man and woman death was the only way to to reunite with the gods. But for the pharaoh and his priests, the temples offered the possibility of encountering Isis and Osiris in life. Each temple, holding one part of Osiris's body, opened a pathway to one aspect of his divine wisdom. Isis had her major centre of worship in Sais. Meeting with Isis and Osiris, the pharaoh knew how to follow the direction of the gods: a tendency toward tyranny is as rare among the Egyptian Pharaohs as it is common among the Babylonian kings.

We gain a glimpse of the influence of the temples when we consider that Orpheus, founder of the Greek pantheon, and Moses, creator of the Jewish religion, were both initiated in the temples of Egypt. Thales, first philosopher of antiquity, Pythagoras, father of science, and Plato all gained inner strength during long years of training in Egypt.

The spiritual seekers of antiquity made long and arduous journeys to seek admission to the mystery centres of Egypt, knowing that failure to pass the tests meant servitude to the temple. They faced severe trials, and spent long weeks in complete silence, fasting and praying, doing menial work, and partaking in rituals to prepare themselves.

Trial of Earth

After due preparation the novice had one last chance to withdraw. If he remains resolved he is led to a small passage cut into the temple rock. With only a small lamp, he squeezes through the narrow opening into a tight dark passage and hears the gates slam behind him. Now he is on his own and there is no return. Crawling and sliding on his belly he must make his way along a passage that seems endless. A sudden draft extinguishes his light. Blinded, he feels his panic rise. Is he lost? He pushes on, hemmed in, as though he were in a coffin of rock.

Threatened by the grip of stone, a host of fears surge up from his depths, amplified by every noise, sudden turn and jutting rock that bars his way. Amid the cacophony of terrors, fears and doubts the seeker finds an unknown strength or grows mad. All sense of time is lost.

Suddenly the passage ends in a bottomless pit. Groping, the novice searches for a way across. His fingers find an iron bar, the beginning of a ladder leading into an unknown depth. Slowly, carefully, he descends. The ladder comes to a sudden halt. He is left hanging, with no way forward and none back. Frantically searching the damp walls he finds a step carved into the rock. And another. Slowly he ascends again and soon walks upright in a spacious corridor towards a distant light.

Trial of Fire

Now his way is stopped by searing flames; a furnace bars his way. Summoning a courage almost beyond himself, the novice hurls himself into the heat and finds the flames an artful spectre of illusions.

Trial of Water

The passage darkens again and he wades in dark water, cold and dead. Deeper and deeper he sinks into the freezing pool. One slip and he is lost. He feels the cold seep into his limbs and slow his blood. His strength is fading. But against all resistance, he pushes on. Slowly the water abates. He reaches dry ground and a gate opens. He is welcomed by torch bearers, who wash and dry him and dress him in white linen.

Trial of Air

Finally the exhausted neophyte is led into a resting room where he falls onto a couch. He hears sweet music, a door opens and a woman comes towards him, arms outstretched to embrace the hero who has passed the tests. If he gives in, all is lost. He will remain a slave to the temple as he is to his desires. If he resists the temptation of sexual desire the trials are ended and the high priest comes to welcome him into the brotherhood of light.

Beyond this description there is scant knowledge, and female trials are entirely unknown, though there were priestesses of various rank.

The Egyptians evoked archetypal experiences by means of such trials: in modern life the same challenges meet us across a lifetime. Most of us will have experienced a long journey through the dark tunnel of time; tight confinement in adverse situations that make us crawl along the corridor of doubt. The trial of fire we have met in the struggle between fear and courage, when dreams are burnt to ashes and illusions crumble. And who has not almost drowned in the black waters of despair, or encountered the powerful dissolution of love?

Exercise 3: The Temple Trials

Write on the temple trials of earth, fire, water and air, and explore them as challenges of the soul. Take the Egyptian setting or explore the theme within the framework of contemporary experiences.

> **The Temple Trials by Morgan Yasbincek**
>
> Before I was sent forward into the darkness, the priest strapped a small hooded falcon onto my wrist. My wrist was bound with leather thonging and the bird rested there, its talons taking a calm grip. If I slipped or stumbled, the bird would panic and, tied to my arm, shred my flesh. If I remained calm the bird, the eyes of

my very soul, would guide me through. Perhaps out of necessity, within a few moments of crawling on my belly in the tunnel I became sympatico with the bird. We breathed together, became apprehensive together. We shared the instinct of a bird of prey, we shared the eye of the spirit. The tunnel seemed labyrinthal, with twists and turns on the way there were objects for me to contemplate — the scarab beetle made of lapis, the golden head of the great Sekhmet. In time I was grateful for the bird, sacred to Horus, who in truth eventually guided me out …

The Temple Trials by John Stubley

I entered into darkness
but darkness could not enter me.
I stepped into fire
but fire stepped aside.
I sank into water
but its weight could not sink me.
And when I resisted air
I started to breathe.

The Training of the Novice

All who came to seek the initiations of Isis knew the forbidding words inscribed beneath her statue in Sais: 'I am Isis. I am the past, the present and the future. No mortal can lift my veil.' They came to the temple to become immortal. Only those who discovered their eternal self were worthy to lift the veil of Isis. To wrest their immortal soul from the grip of matter they had to prepare themselves for many years. Thus the novice began his training under the strict supervision of experienced priests. Many years, often decades, were spent behind temple walls.

The novice first had to acquire knowledge of Isis, and learned to appreciate nature as her earthly reflection. Egyptian science was the first step. The students came to know the properties of rocks, metals and plants, the laws of sacred geometry and architecture, astronomy, mathematics and music. The most important of disciplines was the reading of the hieroglyphs — the foundation of all Egyptian wisdom and magic. The twenty-one major Arcana contained the sacred archetypes that composed the inner world of soul, the workings of nature and the relationships of the eternal gods.

After having gained sufficient strength and purity, the neophyte was led into the holiest of the temples and under the surveillance of fellow priests drank a potion to induce a death-like sleep. For the three days of the trance the soul wrested itself from the fetters of the body and found itself in the company of the gods. Then the priests guided the enlightened soul back into the body.

Exercise 4: Isis Initiation

In the sanctuary of the temple all the priests are assembled. Uttering a last prayer you drink the potion that induces deathlike sleep.

Your body stiffens as the incantations fade away, and your soul rises from the heavy weight of the body, from limitation and darkness.

You are born into the light, into the presence of the gods, face to face with Isis, a goddess as vast as the universe, who gives birth to time and space, sustaining all beings, upholding all that ever was, is and will be.

In your vision you experience her timeless body of light giving birth to her son and spouse Osiris. And as you witness this sacred birth, Osiris is born in you. You feel his being in yours and return to your body a freed soul. Penelope Brown powerfully evokes this in her piece below.

Standing before Isis

The waters of my body are falls of water and rain
The sea has made my eyes blue
Mists and rain, lake and pool, and mists and rain,
All this coming and going is a perfect language of tears
Every drop of water in Egypt has been breathed, wept, drunk, touched, or bathed in.
You, my brother, have drunk and wept the waters of my body
I offer again, my sister, the cup of my waters.

Every animal, every creeping beast have I suckled
I have bled milk into a million million mouths over and over
My clawed, scaled children.
Out of earth and sea have I lit their individual stars with my sacred spark, and
Pulling rivers and mountains have I made every tiny hair, I remember each eye and feather.
Myself, have I been born over and over into fur and sinew
I have lived on lakes and breathed in rivers
I, swimming and howling, have run towards the sun
Have flown and swum and dug,
I have been my children and my children have birthed me,
Human, woman, God ...
I am child and mother,
I give birth to myself in perfect circles
I love death, its coming and its going. I am life.
Look deeper, see before you the umbilicus of days
In my still centre dwells the golden boy with a Pharaoh's crown.

Whoever returned from this meeting with the goddess could say: 'In my still centre dwells the golden boy with a Pharaoh's crown.' Having seen Isis and birthed Osiris in his own soul the neophyte has become an immortal, and leaves the temple as an instrument for divine purpose.

When Egypt started to decline, the initiations lost their power. Isis lost her husband and son, and the temples lost their power to birth Osiris in the soul of the neophyte. But before it faded, the impulse to birth Osiris was saved by an Egyptian initiate whose name was Moses.

14

Burning Doubt

Egyptian culture derived its enduring stability from the temples. But the temple tradition encountered a remarkable challenge in the form of Pharaoh Ekhnaton, the first human being to develop a purely personal relationship with his god. In what we have of his writings we hear an intimate tone that is utterly new in the history of the word.

Ekhnaton held a bold and monotheistic view of a personal god in the middle of a polytheistic culture. He introduces a human-centred approach to sculpture and architecture, and poetry. His delight in the beauty of nature has modern overtones, as in his *Adoration of the Disk* (a hymn to the sun god that we will meet in the next lesson).

His new vision so shocked the conservative priesthood that his works were destroyed after his death, and his name erased from all inscriptions. He was a man before his time, and his intimate relationship with god resurfaces in the psalms of David and the Song of Solomon, while his artistic impulse toward a human-centred aesthetic found a place in Greek culture. But the seed of monotheism he sowed was taken up almost immediately by Moses, and firmly planted in the soul of the Hebrew people, who leave Egypt not long after Ekhnaton's death.

The Monotheistic Impulse

The priests rejected Ekhnaton's monotheism not because the idea was foreign to them, but because it belonged to intimate experiences that were strictly guarded behind temple walls: the birth of Osiris in the soul, the unifying essence of the soul, the 'I am.' To openly proclaim one superior god not only broke with tradition, it involved divulging temple secrets that could undermine the whole of Egyptian culture.

Moses' revolutionary deed was to save the Osiris impulse and make it the foundation of the Hebrew faith. And, as with every new step, something is gained and something is lost: while the birth of Osiris, of the 'I am' waxes, the awareness of Isis wanes. In the Hebrew religion, the great mother goddess falls away. She is not entirely lost; we can still divine her in Job, Proverbs and the Books of Solomon where she features as Wisdom, the female side of God. Later she appears in the Sophia of the Gnostics, the Shekina of the Cabbalists and the New Testament Virgin Mary, but she is even more veiled in the scriptures than in Egypt. The Egyptian still pursued aspects of matriarchal culture through the presence of Isis, but the Hebrews worshipped only the male god Jahwe.

The worship of a purely inward god, whose name is 'I am that I am', was a challenging innovation that enhanced the growth of individuality. This is a god opposed to all outer, pictorial representations, who appeals solely to the innermost essence, the 'I am' in his worshippers.

To the Egyptians the pharaoh was the outer representative of the self: he acted on behalf of his subjects and bore communal moral responsibility. The revelation of Moses gave moral responsibility to the individual. This courageous step into personal independence results in the diminishing of the power of an outside ruler or king. Though guided by their prophets in times of need, each person is called to rule himself or herself. In this way the Hebrews break dramatically with the hierarchical social structure of ancient Egypt and Babylon.

Jahwe, the particular god of the Hebrews, is directly accessible to his people through worship and through adherence to his law. He behaves like a strict father, guiding his often unruly children through a combination of miracles and punishments. Jahwe becomes the hierophant in the initiation of his people, and the destiny of Moses and his followers illustrates the stages of initiatory experiences on the path to selfhood — the birth of the 'I am' in the biography of the Hebrews.

This chapter follows the archetypal sequence of these initiatory steps so we may recreate them in our writing. Historically, these experiences pertain to a whole people. Today they are an element in every destiny that breaks with the old and ventures into the unknown and new.

The Birth of Moses

The Hebrews had come to Egypt during a great famine, as recorded in one of my favourite Bible stories — *Joseph and his Brothers (Genesis: 37–48)*. Initially welcomed because of the high office that Joseph held in the court of the pharaoh, the Hebrews soon fell into serfdom.

> And the Egyptians made the children of Israel to serve with rigour: And they made their lives bitter with hard bondage, in mortar, and in brick, and in all manner of service in the field: all their service, wherein they made them serve, was with rigour.

When the Hebrews multiplied in spite of these measures the pharaoh decreed that all newborn Hebrew males should be put to death. It was in this time that Moses was born. To save his life his mother made him an ark of bulrushes and cast it into the Nile. The floating baby was found by the pharaoh's daughter, who took the child under her protection.

Thus, Moses, the Hebrew, grew up as an Egyptian prince and was initiated into the temple. He experienced the birth of Osiris in his own soul. He is, however, aware of his Hebrew origins and greatly troubled by the burden of his people. When he witnesses an Egyptian beating a Hebrew, Moses is so incensed that he kills the Egyptian and consequently has to flee Egypt. He finds refuge in the wilderness of Sinai. Tending sheep there, he comes to Mount Horeb.

> And the angel of the LORD appeared unto him in a flame of fire out of the midst of a bush: and he looked, and, behold, the bush burned with fire, and the bush was not consumed …
> And the LORD said, I have surely seen the affliction of my people which are in Egypt, and have heard their cry by reason of their taskmasters; for I know their sorrows;
> And I am come down to deliver them out of the hand of the Egyptians, and to bring them up out of that land unto a good land and a large, unto a land flowing with milk and honey …

The Mission of Doubt

Moses receives his mission: he is to lead his people out of bondage. Like Zarathustra he is chosen by his god. But unlike the Persian prophet, Moses responds with doubt as to his ability to accomplish such a feat.

> And Moses said unto God, Behold, when I come unto the children of Israel, and shall say unto them, The God of your fathers hath sent me unto you; and they shall say to me, What is his name? what shall I say unto them?
> And God said unto Moses, I AM THAT I AM …
> And Moses said unto the LORD, O my Lord, I am not eloquent, neither heretofore, nor since thou hast spoken unto thy servant: but I am slow of speech, and of a slow tongue …

Doubt is a fundamental experience encountered by all who receive a calling. It has the initiatory character of a test that shakes the foundation of the personality in order to secure the person more thoroughly. We all know such doubts, in larger or smaller degree. They are always ready to arise when we take a new step, when we are called by a new task.

Nowadays we choose our own ideals, visions, projects (or do they choose us?) and while we may not encounter a burning bush, the burning is still experienced inside. When we chance on a new idea, we feel the inner burning in an irresistible urge to act and effect change.

Every good piece of writing is a calling. Long before it exists it entrusts us with the mission to give it birth, to liberate it from anonymity and lead it toward visibility. I have met poems that were almost as fierce and envious as the Old Testament God. The mission they imposed on me was not always easy and many a doubt stood in the way.

Exercise 1: Burning Doubt

Take Moses' encounter as a stimulus to explore the theme of being entrusted with a mission and the doubts and objections that arise.

The Burning Bush by Rhea Pfeifle

A vexatious seed has been planted
Unable to sprout
It lies wriggling,
itching

When I have no pen, no paper
Driving, making dinner
Clever spot-on words bubble up
from its domain
and I think happily
Yes, I can write,
I do have ideas

Later when I sit quietly
I scan the landscape
Of its domain
But all the words
Lie down flat,
Can't see them

It itches
Right in the middle of my back
Arms too inflexible
Nails too short

The Calling by Nandi Chinna

The calling is not words
the calling is what lies inside
the world of words
the calling is not a simple world

it is a kind of ache
it is a home for the homeless
it is a way of travelling
it is the road that is not there
it is not safe
the calling lies underneath
the relentless rising of suns and days
looking for jobs in newspapers
the opening of curtains
rain against windows
huddling beneath blankets
the world with no edges …

trawling its nets through incarnations
the calling is always singing
always knocking always tapping
always beating stories from dusty carpets
hanging in windy gardens
always waiting for me
to sit down with it at the table
to not fight with it
to make tea
to make friends
and to swallow it whole.

The Miraculous Rod

Moses returns to Egypt. He has been given a magical rod to perform signs in front of his people and the pharaoh. When we are committed to a task we find unknown strength or are unexpectedly aided by friends, even strangers. Events come to meet us unforeseen. Moses is thus helped by his eloquent brother Aaron to convince his people of his mission.

Aaron confronts Pharaoh with the demand of their god: to let the people of Israel journey into the wilderness. The Pharaoh has no intention of letting his serfs depart with all their herds and possessions and orders his overseers to burden the Hebrews with yet more tasks. Moses and Aaron return and perform a miraculous sign in front of Pharaoh, but the Pharaoh remains unmoved, and now the Hebrew god commands Moses and Aaron to bring plagues upon the land.

And Moses … lifted up the rod, and smote the waters that were in the river …
and all the waters that were in the river were turned to blood. And the fish that

was in the river died; and the river stank, and the Egyptians could not drink of the water of the river; and there was blood throughout all the land of Egypt.

Pharaoh yields a little, but then withdraws his consent again. And so Egypt is visited with a more severe plague, while the Hebrews are spared. After the waters turn to blood, frogs invade the land, then lice and flies. All the beasts of the Egyptians die, boils break out and pestilence. Severe hail destroys the harvest and locusts take what is left. Darkness descends for days on end and still Pharaoh resists. Only when the firstborn in each family dies, and with them his own son, does he give in. To this day the Hebrew people celebrate the deliverance from Egypt with the feast of Passover.

Plagues hold an eerie fascination for humankind, and the world is never rid of them. In the process of initiation they serve as a means of awakening. Their gift is the acute awareness that things are out of sync. They heighten the sense of crisis and call for decisive action. The power of the biblical account lies in the accumulation of plagues, their tight staccato, their dramatic urge toward a cataclysmic end.

Exercise 2: The Plagues

Write a list of plagues you see in the world (or yourself) and elaborate one.

The Plague by Bhavan Marshall

A plague of developers ravaging the landscape like locusts scourging the summer crop. A plague of urban sprawl with ever diminishing block size and Tuscan houses with bull-nosed front windows, no eaves. The sameness of ground hugging gardens, where no one dares plant a tree in case the leaves mess the lawn.

Ten Plagues by Adrian Glamorgan

I give you the plague of lies.
Of television without truth, talkback without mercy, parliament without honour.
Of B52s above, nuclear submarines below, missiles everywhere.
Every conversation heard by Pine Gap and Kojareena and Langley West Virginia.
I give you the pain of carrying a secret, the one that makes Aboriginal people invisible, and refugees hated.
I give you a man in Washington with unlimited power.
I give you the treachery of the rich.
I give you the incomprehension of the poor.
And the final plague: knowledge of all this, and not a blade of power to be felt in your little finger, only pity and numbness and pale excuses for your own sorry life.

Moses and his people leave Egypt, led by their god in a pillar of cloud by day and fire by night. Breaking his promise, Pharaoh pursues them; but Moses parts the sea and his people pass unharmed. When the chariots of Egypt follow, the sea closes and drowns both horses and men.

The Wilderness of Choice

The Hebrew people find themselves in the Sinai Desert, a dead and hostile wilderness that contrasts sharply with the fertile plain of the Nile delta. Water and food are scarce and for many of the Hebrews, a return to servitude in Egypt seems preferable. The people begin to murmur against Moses and Aaron. But when the crisis comes to a peak, the god Jahwe rescues his people by miraculous means: Moses smites a rock with his rod and water pours forth, while manna (heavenly food), rains from heaven to sustain his people. And when the people again murmur against Moses, again they are saved by the grace of their God.

Exercise 3: Leaving things behind

(Exercise inspired by Jan Teagle Kapetas)

When we embrace the new we often leave the old behind. Exchanging the familiar for the unknown, we leave cities, friends, lovers behind.

Make a list of things that the women left behind in Egypt; what you yourself have left behind in your life. You might use this exercise to lament the loss of Isis, the great mother goddess whose splendour has been obscured by the new god leading Israel. For example:

> The sweet waters of the Nile
> The dusty village street
> The two date palms in the front yard
> The reed hut daubed with clay
> The beaded curtains
> The sacks of barley hanging from the roof
> The brimming pots of oil …

The constant wrestling between the god and his people comes to a climax when Moses and his congregation reach Mt Horeb, the place of the first revelation. Encamped below Mt Horeb the whole nation witnesses Jahwe's descent. Moses is called up the mountain to receive God's commandments, but he is away too long. His people have had enough of this invisible god who abhors outer depiction. While Moses is on the mountain, they fall back to the cult of idols. They combine their treasures to make an idol, a golden calf — a visible god.

This seems to me an account of schizophrenia in the soul life of a people. Nowadays the divergence between ideal and reality is a matter of fact in the world around us as well as in our own inner life when our best intentions are left high on the mountain of our aspirations while our lower self dances around the golden calf of commodities.

Exercise 4: The Golden Calf

Picture Moses on the mountain, while his people are dancing in a mad frenzy around a golden calf of their own making, an idol and illusion. Take this image as a stimulus to describe a situation you have observed in the world around you or in your soul life.

Golden Calf by Annette Mullmby

With the caress of your fingertips
I will give you everything you want
but you do have to press the right buttons
I will organise, codify, modify and commodify you
I will elude and delude you
sedate, unmake and create you

I will introduce you to the phantoms on Facebook
the twits on tweeter
the wanna be godlings on avatar
I will distract and waylay you
memorise and terrorise you
induce and seduce you
I'm your glamour girl glueing you to your seat
The computer suitor come to marry you
in unholy dreadlock

Even the resistant ones eventually succumb to my charms
Me incrementally creeping into your unconsciousness
You see I'm so easy once you get the hang of me
Soon you all will be dancing to my iTunes!

Dancing around the Golden Calf by Janet Blagg

I close the front door, set my bags on the kitchen table. Shoo cats, not interested. I unpack the Baileys, the Black Forest Torte, King Island double cream, white castello — nothing that needs cooking.

I run the bath, light candles and incense, and put clothes ready for when I emerge. Black over-the-knee stockings, and French knickers. I strip off in front of the mirror and gaze at my body, at the flesh of my belly.

I've had enough of self-denial, of this is bad for you, that'll kill you, that's exploiting your brothers and sisters, this will inflame your pitta! I don't care any more.

Because tonight, in my scented bath, a glass of wine in one hand and a book in the other —

I am the White Queen, and I'm drinking my own health

I am the Red Queen, and I'm drinking what I want

I am the Black Queen, and you can call me the Whore of Babylon for all I care!

The Mouth of Anger

The wrath of the god Jahwe is upon his people and Moses avenges his god with sword and deed. The biblical text is sparse with words but we need not be. I am interested in the power of anger to unleash the tongue, in the creative wrath and rage of words. I have seen even timid and extremely tongue-tied people find powerful verbal expression in anger. The floodgate opens and a barrage of words tumbles from the lips.

Exercise 5: The Mouth of Anger

Take your lead from the previous exercise. You have watched the dance around the golden calf. Enough is enough. Feel the righteous anger well up in you and unleash a barrage of words, insults, etc. Avoid all clichés (such as four letter words). Be creative and original in your wrath. Try to stay in poetic mood, in spite of the theme. For example:

> **The Anger Of Moses by Cindy Innes**
> You flea ridden, lice infested, pomegranates for brains, slime ridden stones for feet, hewed tree trunks for backs, frog eyes, rattails for hair, swine sounds from your laughter, your evil stench defies the lowliest of lizards that shrink and decay from your breath.   You sloppy bottomed women with no muscles to walk with but simper and sit with mouths parted red with betel juice waiting to be pandered to and you dung filled men planted like broken trees, leafless and birdless . No use!

The Letter of the Law

Much in the new revelation was truly revolutionary and the people struggled to change their ways in keeping with this new way of life. The law decreed by Jahwe took the place of outward authority. The Hebrews were by no means the first to create elaborate laws and regulations, but they were the first to accord them an importance that made the presence of a king or prince unnecessary.

The law is the presence of god among his people. It regulates all manifestations of life down to the finest detail. This system of regulation had an effect on the Hebrew peoples similar to the effect that years of learning had on the Egyptian temple novice. It was a continual religious practice that fine-tuned the soul for the revelations of a purely inner god.

Nowadays we have become our own lawmakers, and the source of regulation resides within us.

Exercise 6: The Law of Letters

Make your own inner system of law more conscious. Set down your convictions as a writer in the form of ten decisive commandments. Use 'Thou shalt' (or shalt not), or 'You shall' (or shall not) for strength of conviction. For example:

Thou shalt make writing a priority and keep a journal
Thou shalt never judge thy first draft
Thou shalt honour all thy literary productions
Thou shalt not covet the writing style of thy fellow writers
Thou shalt witness the productions of thy fellow writers and praise them
Though shalt honour thy days of writing and prefer them to all other times
Thou shalt not kill thy enthusiasm with clever arguments.

15

Lyrical Kings

In the last lesson we met the Egyptian pharaoh Ekhnaton as a religious innovator and revolutionary. In this lesson we are meeting him as a pioneer of the poetic. There is little left of his poetry as everything pertaining to his reign was systematically destroyed. But one of his works has survived: The famous 'Adoration of the Disc.'(1375 BC).
Like Ekhnaton himself 'The Adoration of the Disk' (by disk he means the sun) is a work out of time and place, sounding an entirely new note amid the choir of early literary works. It is a hymn sung in praise of the sun god Aton, the supreme divinity that Ekhnaton championed above all gods. As the pharaoh, Ekhnaton saw himself as Aton's representative as well as the actual, spiritual son of the sun god.
There is a new and intimate tone in this hymn: the love that Ekhnaton bears for Aton (even his name echoes that of his god) is that of dedicated son to a loving father. It is suffused with a deep and unwavering trust that translates into the poet's admiration for all of Aton's works. His delight in the beauty of nature (seen as the revelation of his god) has modern overtones:

> Thy dawn — O Ra — opens the new horizon,
> And every realm that thou hast made to live
> Is conquered by thy love — as joyous Day
> Follows thy footsteps in delightful peace.
>
> And when thou settest, all the world is bleak;
> Houses are tombs where blind men lie in death;
> Only the lion and the serpent move
> Through the black oven of the sightless night.
> Dawn in the East again! the lands awake,
> And men leap from their slumber with a song;
> They bathe their bodies, clothe them with fresh garments,
> And lift their hands in happy adoration …

Thou are in my heart,
And there is no other that knows thee
Save thy son Nefer-kheperu-Re Wa-en-Re,
For thou hast made him well-versed in thy plans and in thy strength.

The world came into being by thy hand,
According as thou hast made them.
When thou hast risen they live,
When thou settest they die.
Thou art always thy own self,
For one lives (only) through thee…
All work is laid aside when thou settest in the west.
But when thou risest again,
Everything is made to flourish…

Exercise 1: Hymn to the Sun God

I suggest that in this exercise you transport yourself back to Egypt. Imagine you are a young Pharaoh; feel yourself as the son of the sun god Aton, the great creator and sustainer of Egypt, a world engaged in ritual and rites, where sacred temples tower high over mud-brick cities. Imagine your world one long oasis, traversed by the sun god every day, woken by his light, sustained by his beneficence. Picture the daily rhythm of Egypt attuned to your father Aton. Feel yourself elated, held and carried in the knowledge of your kinship to this god. And most importantly, imagine your god visibly traversing in his sun barque. Write from this place and engage in praise.

Hymn to the Sun by Renee Schipp
Paint the world into being
take me from the night of myself
with a pinpoint of light
lean on the world
with rayed love and make it new

brush stroke on branch
each leaf lit
birds ignite into song

in the darkness
I read your presence
star by star
my shadow selves

the moon becomes
a promise
a mirror
of another morning

in the darkness
I run my mind
over galaxies
their brailled
stories of epic endings
and renewal

in the darkness
I am sealed into solipsism
but with you
with you
I will radiate
in bright filaments
radiate
once more

paint the world into being
ignite with your pinpoint
of light
what is best in me
lean on the world
held new in you
again

Hymn by Annette Mullumby
you creep through
my window
shred the darkness
shake awake my
sleep sodden limbs
I tug the curtain aside
allow your gold
to flood my face
my heart quivers
as you grace my room
with the lilt of your dance

Ekhnaton's religious innovation transformed into the teachings of Moses not long after his death. His poetic innovation took longer to resurface. His personal, and highly poetic relationship to the divine had to wait centuries for another courageous and innovative ruler: King David

Psalms

There are many to whom the word psalm brings up fraught memories of Sunday mornings in church; of sombre books read by sombre people for moral edification. But King David, the most famous composer of psalms, had little in common with many of those who quote his work — just imagine the king dancing naked in front of the whole congregation as he returns the ark to Jerusalem. David's psalms are among the most sublime productions of world poetry, a form of love poetry addressed to his god, and they pioneer the interior dimension of the soul. Passionate and intimate, psalms arise from the heart.

While Moses follows his god as a child follows his father, David is in a lifelong love relationship with his divinity. To him the creation of psalms is a form of courtship, and poetic verse the most effective form to converse with his god. The god of David loves poetry.

Psalms are spontaneous prayers inspired by particular situations. They well from the heart in extremes of anguish or joy. To appreciate them fully we have to see them in the context of King David's life.

King David

Shortly before David's kingship the Hebrews had given up their direct governance by their god and opted for a king to defend them against the Philistines. The first king is Saul. The Israelite God soon rejects him for his weakness of character, and then sends the prophet Samuel to Jesse, whose youngest son David is secretly anointed king.

The spirit leaves Saul and takes residence in the heart of David. From this moment, Saul is increasingly plagued by demons and burdened by depression. His advisers search for a musician to ease his gloom. They hear of David, who is a harpist of extraordinary skill, and bring him to court. When David plays, the king's depression lifts, and before long the young musician is indispensable.

War then flares up against the Philistines whose champion Goliath is a man of gigantic size and strength. None dares answer his challenge to single combat until David hears the giant openly scorn the god of Israel and decides to face him. He kills Goliath with one shot of his shepherd's sling. Seeing their champion defeated, the Philistines lose courage and flee. The victory is celebrated and the women dance and sing in honour of David.

Saul is alarmed by David's popularity, and begins to envy him. At one point he even hurls a javelin at his young musician. Later he plots against David's life by sending him to battle. But David is favoured by his god and succeeds in all his exploits.

Eventually however, David must flee from the court. The shepherd, secret king, harpist, poet, giant-slayer and military leader becomes the captain of a band of outcasts. Pursued by Saul and never at peace with the neighbouring tribes, he often finds himself in great danger.

Psalms of Agony

During such times of desperation, David composes psalms invoking the comfort of his god. Psalm 22 is unsurpassed in its description of agony. It also holds a prominent place among the messianic prophesies. The king's pain transformed by his poetic gift becomes a vehicle for a greater suffering than his own. The psalmist becomes a visionary, the king a prophet. Here is an extract from this psalm:

Psalm 22
My God, my God, why hast thou forsaken me? why art thou so far from helping me, and from the words of my roaring?
 O my God, I cry in the daytime, but thou hearest not; and in the night season, and am not silent …
 I was cast upon thee from the womb: thou art my God from my mother's belly.
 Be not far from me; for trouble is near; for there is none to help.
 Many bulls have compassed me: strong bulls of Bashan have beset me round.
 They gaped upon me with their mouths, as a ravening and a roaring lion.
 I am poured out like water, and all my bones are out of joint: my heart is like wax; it is melted in the midst of my bowels.
 My strength is dried up like a potsherd; and my tongue cleaveth to my jaws; and thou hast brought me into the dust of death.
 For dogs have compassed me: the assembly of the wicked have enclosed me: they pierced my hands and my feet.
 I may tell all my bones: they look and stare upon me.
 They part my garments among them, and cast lots upon my vesture.
 But be not thou far from me, O LORD: O my strength, haste thee to help me…

The line 'I am poured out like water, and all my bones are out of joint: my heart is like wax; it is melted in the midst of my bowels' is unrivalled in its poetic intensity and agonising beauty.

There is a direct line between Ekhnaton's Adoration of the Disk and the psalms of David. But there is also a marked difference. Ekhnaton adores a visible god. His Aton is still embodied in the sun. Jahwe is an entirely invisible deity. No image can do justice to the 'I am that I am'. Outer representations are idolatry, a fall back into older and outdated forms of worship. David's Jahwe is a deity exclusively accessible to the soul. The relationship is intimate, dedicated, highly personal and at times passionate.

Exercise 2: Psalm of Agony

A psalm allows the composer to address his or her deity from a place of personal need. Imagine yourself to be David, or anyway in dire need. Address a god or a goddess, your own muse, guidance, inspiration or higher self. (There is no need to believe in the divine for this exercise. It is enough to *imagine* it.) Charge your language with the conviction that your word will enlist the help you desire.

If this proves difficult (as it sometimes is) write a psalm about this difficulty (which can be agonising) as Anna Minska has done in the second example below.

Psalm by Mags Webster
My bones are dry with the ache of loss.
   Stack-sided walls surround my head. I plunge into the well; the fog drowns out my feeble cries.
   I am pricked by a thousand small agonies but the blood never shows. Behind the smile is the void. I am as hollow as a flute which will never be played again.
   From my box of darkness I raise a hand to you. The lid is too heavy now for me alone.
   I have not wanted to ask for your help, but I have nowhere else to go, and you are the only one left who is strong enough for this.

Post to Pillar by Anna Minska
I do not believe in the god of churches
or more accurately, the churches of men,
- their dogma handed down as faith -
and my postmodern education has liberated me
from fancies of being shepherded.
I weave my own web of philosophies
to live by and can quickly articulate some well-spun thesis by which to justify
a religiously chaste life.
And yet, behind the crisp page some unsolicited passion palpitates:
I yearn to be wed to that pillar of light
that upholds me when academia crumbles down
unsubstantiated by spirit

David soon wins respect and support. He becomes the champion of the poor and discontented. Saul, however, pursues him incessantly. David always escapes, and is repeatedly given the opportunity to slay Saul. Once he even manages to take the king's drinking cup and spear as he sleeps, but he is never tempted to kill Saul, and when the king is eventually killed in battle, David grieves sorely for him.

After Saul's death David is the new king. He soon establishes the kingdom of Israel as a major power with Jerusalem as its capital.

Psalms of Joy

Psalms are by no means only products of agony or repentance. Their first and foremost function was the ecstatic joy in the presence of the god. Like the adoration of the disk, psalms are hymns to the divinity, albeit a divinity that is become inward and invisible. The result is an intimate, direct and close rapport, a dialogue across the threshold between humanity and the divine. In his ecstatic psalms, David celebrates his love for his god: his heart bursts forth in praise and his words dance and leap in veneration.

> **Psalm 104**
> Bless the LORD, O my soul. O LORD my God, thou art very great; thou art clothed with honour and majesty.
>   Who coverest thyself with light as with a garment: who stretchest out the heavens like a curtain: Who layeth the beams of his chambers in the waters: who maketh the clouds his chariot: who walketh upon the wings of the wind: Who maketh his angels spirits; his ministers a flaming fire: Who laid the foundations of the earth, that it should not be removed for ever.
>   Thou coveredst it with the deep as with a garment: the waters stood above the mountains. At thy rebuke they fled; at the voice of thy thunder they hasted away … He causeth the grass to grow for the cattle, and herb for the service of man: that he may bring forth food out of the earth; And wine that maketh glad the heart of man, and oil to make his face to shine, and bread which strengtheneth man's heart …

Exercise 3: Psalm of Joy

Write a psalm of joy to your deity and revel in all the praises you can. Remember that in contradistinction to the Ekhnaton's hymn a psalm addresses an invisible god. Take it as a purely imaginative exercise if you have religious reservations and see where it leads.

> **Psalm by Jennifer Kornberger**
> Which organ of my body holds a cup of praise?
> How do I sing into a day flapping with chores?

There are no veils or candles at hand
and holy hours are not marked on my clock.
I have only my tulip bulbs
nudging their blunt spears above the potting mix
so tightly wound with praise they shatter my morning haste.

Psalm – child leaving a church by Renee Schipp
I read you once
in morning light
from the side of a hill
in a tiny town

the leaves palimpsestic
lit screens of green, background sounds
of hymns from the hall

I knew you
had not betrayed me
when I turned my back on that
congregation

the birds stirred
in their silent stratas
the stream curved, invisible
in the rock
and we remained

return to me now
like you lived for me then
let my mind not reason
you obsolete, left
alone with hollow grief

may you surface
cellular, resplendent
as I open
hold me, help me be

I will wait
commit to waiting
commit to opening

hear my invitation
return to me

King Solomon

David's son Solomon becomes the next king. He inherits his father's poetic ability. Unto this day his reign is remembered as the golden age of his nation. Solomon becomes famed for both his wisdom and his wealth. Enlisting the help of the king and architect Hiram he builds the great temple in Jerusalem. In Hebrew and Moslem faith he is held to be a prophet. Legends celebrate him as astronomer and accomplished magician. Tradition credits him to be the author of three canonical book: The Proverbs, Ecclesiasticus and the Song of Songs.

The Song of Songs

In the Song of Songs the relationship with the male god of the scriptures finds its feminine counterpart in one of the most beautiful passages of world literature. The song is written as a conversation between bride and groom and has become famous for its celebration of love.

Traditionally it is interpreted as an expression of love between god (the bridegroom) and his chosen people (the bride), or as the passion of the Hebrew initiate (Solomon) for the female wisdom of god — the Shekina of the Cabbalists, the Isis of the Egyptians. There are also those who see it in terms of the courtship between Solomon and the Queen of Sheba. As a great piece of art, it has no problems being all three simultaneously.

The relationship between man and woman reflects the nature of divine love. The bold use of imagery is reminiscent of a time when the sacred and the profane were not yet separated. The language is direct and pictorial, the similes refreshingly unusual, sometimes strange to modern sensitivities.

Song of Solomon: 2
The Bride speaks:
I am the rose of Sharon, and the lily of the valleys.
   As the lily among thorns, so is my love among the daughters.

   As the apple tree among the trees of the wood, so is my beloved among the sons. I sat down under his shadow with great delight, and his fruit was sweet to my taste. He brought me to the banqueting house, and his banner over me was love.
   Stay me with flagons, comfort me with apples: for I am sick of love. His left hand is under my head, and his right hand doth embrace me. I charge you, O ye

daughters of Jerusalem, by the roes, and by the hinds of the field, that ye stir not up, nor awake my love, till he please. The voice of my beloved! behold, he cometh leaping upon the mountains, skipping upon the hills …

Song of Solomon: 7
The Bridegroom speaks:
How beautiful are thy feet with shoes, O prince's daughter! the joints of thy thighs are like jewels, the work of the hands of a cunning workman. Thy navel is like a round goblet, which wanteth not liquor: thy belly is like an heap of wheat set about with lilies. Thy two breasts are like two young roes that are twins. Thy neck is as a tower of ivory; thine eyes like the fishpools in Heshbon, by the gate of Bath-rabbim: thy nose is as the tower of Lebanon which looketh toward Damascus. Thine head upon thee is like Carmel, and the hair of thine head like purple; the king is held in the galleries.
How fair and how pleasant art thou, O love, for delights!

Exercise 4: A Song of Songs

Explore this unashamedly abundant realm of pictures. Let the bride address the bridegroom and vice versa. Take poetic license and use daring similes and untried metaphors for the sublime experience of love.

Remember that the main purpose of this kind of poetry is not a personal one (you will have ample opportunity to explore the individual human dimension later). Write the first part of this love song to the female aspect of the divine, and then let her respond to your courtship:

Song of Songs by Jennifer Kornberger
She speaks:
My beloved makes the night a song of molten brass; he is the gamelan and I am the shy wood chosen for the melody buried in its grain. My beloved rings like a bell in the valley, raising the mist into the crowns of trees. He branches like a tree and his limbs contain the sap that is clear like rain.
He speaks:
My beloved is a hill and a city with seven gates. She is the street trembling with horses and loud with chariots of kings. The morning listens to her speech and the evening bows in the dark.

Eros by Renee Schipp
your face is a white sail
that sets me running
like a boat before

a cyclone – why the need
for peace?

the snap and catch
of your cloth
lifts me into the light
of your life, sets me skimming
away from myself
toward broader
horizons

you body
is the briny vessel
full of fish-scales and fins
full of ropes and scrape
skidding away from the place
of islands

your iris
pulls anchor in me
away from mapped territories
full of fences
to where flying fish leap
and dragons unfurl
at the curling lip
of the world.

Solomon's reign is marked by political expansion and the accumulation of much wealth. Israel becomes a mighty nation, often at war with its neighbors. Keen to find allies, Solomon marries foreign princesses. To please his wives he builds altars to their deities. When he sacrifices to these deities he incurs the wrath of his native god. Solomon is given to understand by his god that his kingdom will be torn apart after his death as a punishment for his idolatry.

This may be the reason why his later poetry is tainted with sadness, disillusionment. The king is aware of the incumbent loss of all that he has achieved. In Ecclesiasticus lines like *Vanity of vanities, saith the Preacher, vanity of vanities; all is vanity* and *"I have seen all the works that are done under the sun; and, behold, all is vanity and vexation of spirit* are a constant refrain. Below is a celebrated passage from the same work:

> To every thing there is a season, and a time to every purpose under the heaven:

A time to be born, and a time to die; a time to plant, and a time to pluck up that which is planted;
A time to kill, and a time to heal; a time to break down, and a time to build up;
A time to weep, and a time to laugh; a time to mourn, and a time to dance;
A time to cast away stones, and a time to gather stones together; a time to embrace, and a time to refrain from embracing;
A time to get, and a time to lose; a time to keep, and a time to cast away;
A time to rend, and a time to sew; a time to keep silence, and a time to speak;
A time to love, and a time to hate; a time of war, and a time of peace.
What profit hath he that worketh in that wherein he laboureth?...

For that which befalleth the sons of men befalleth beasts; even one thing befalleth them: as the one dieth, so dieth the other; yea, they have all one breath; so that a man hath no preeminence above a beast: for all is vanity.
All go unto one place; all are of the dust, and all turn to dust again.

Something that was still vitally alive in Ekhnaton's poetry and that came to full bloom in David's psalms has withered in Solomon. As writers we should not shy away from such experiences, but embrace the end as wholeheartedly as the beginning. With this in mind let us experiment the mood of the above two passages in our own writing.

Exercise 5: Song of Loss

Assume a resigned stance of loss. Allow you imagination to taste from the bitter cup of disillusionment. Lament this world, give voice to your disappointment and the fact that everything comes to naught. Attempt a piece that reflects on a similar mood. Note there is no need to get depressed while writing about depressing views.

Song of Loss by Annette Mullumby

your forest of curls
now brittle sticks

the sway of your walk
a puppet's jerk

your breath the taste
of burnt toast

your skin rough bark

your words fall apart
I kick the letters
into the gutter

your mesmerising smile
a torn gap in the bulwark
of your face

your warm belly
my hands
once quivered over
now cold marble

Lament by Ann Reeves
Why adore the rose when tomorrow her petals turn brown?
Why water that bush at all then, only to watch the blossoms fall?
Shall I burn my yoga mat, knowing my joints will ache eventually?
Put down my pen, watch the paper curl in the heat?
Shall we turn those boatloads upside down, save them the agony of those eternal camps?
Why not stones in my coat pockets now, at the winter's shore?
Why wait for another sunrise?

The Un-poetic by Tineke Van der Eecken
We are dirt and dirt we turn into
Love and turn it into hate
Feed and become the one starving
Breed and find everyone dying
Conceive and discover a warzone
Connect and be pierced by divide and conflict
Find and suddenly be lost
Inspire and realise you are dry and unhappy
Greet and be the uninvited
Adore and become the outcast

There is no such thing as beauty
when it's shadow dirties
your very soul.

16

A Journey of Epics

Two epics stand at the inception of Greek culture: the *Iliad* and the *Odyssey*, written by the great poet of antiquity, Homer. Together they provided a vision that constituted the very heart of Greek cultural identity. For a long time Greek education centred on the learning, reciting, dancing and ritual performance of Homer's verses. Long passages were known by heart by many, and wandering bards recited the entire tale in a kind of singsong verse, accompanied by the lyre. Written in hexameter, the most harmonious of metres, each verse echoes the subtle interplay between the rhythms of heart and breath.

Both epics start with the ten year war against Troy. The *Iliad* centres on a few days in the last year of the siege. Its primary subject is the wrath of Achilles and the consequences of that wrath. It begins:

> Sing O daughter of Heaven, of Peleus, son of Achilles
> Him whose terrible wrath brought a thousand woes to Achaia
> Many a stalwart foe, did it hurl untimely to Hades …

The *Odyssey* tells the adventures of Odysseus on his long journey home to Ithaca, a journey which takes as long as the war itself.

The contrast between the two epics is personified in their heroes. Achilles is the son of a goddess and a human father, the last of the superhuman heroes. His mother bathed him in fire to make him invulnerable, except that immunity failed at the part of his heel where she held him. With his supernatural strength he is the invincible champion of the Greeks.

Where Achilles is the last of the great heroes, Odysseus is a pioneer of human prudence and cunning.

> … that ingenious hero who travelled far and wide after he had sacked the famous town of Troy. Many cities did he visit, and many were the nations with whose manners and customs he was acquainted; moreover he suffered much by sea while trying to save his own life and bring his men safely home …

In the end it was the inventiveness of Odysseus that won the war, not the prowess of Achilles. His cunning idea of the Trojan horse accomplishes what ten years of warfare failed to do.

In their character, too, the two heroes differ sharply. Achilles is entirely given to his emotions and immediate reactions. He is passionate and impetuous, and consideration and thought are alien to his nature. The whole of the *Iliad* is about Achilles' anger and its consequence. By contrast, Odysseus overcomes one challenge after another through his well-considered actions and cunning. He heralds the new consciousness, he is a thinker when everyone else is still given to immediate action.

The Adventures of Odysseus

After ten years of warfare, Odysseus and his men are keen to return to their home. But a storm drives them off course and some of their fleet is lost. The remaining ships are driven towards the land of Libya, where Odysseus sends men ashore to get provisions. They are met by the Lotus Eaters, a friendly people who live on a honeyed fruit that makes them forget all earthly concerns. The men partake of the fruit and forget their mission. Their wish to return to their comrades and their longing for home and family are drowned in the sweet bliss of the drug.

Odysseus has to bring them back by force. The men weep all day long and have to be tied down to keep them from jumping overboard.

Exercise One: The Lotus Eaters

Imagine yourself one of the explorers. Feel the drug loosen your fears; experience the great release of forgetting and letting go, the warm embrace of bliss and contentment. Describe the ecstasy of the experience and the painful awakening from drowsy sleep.

The Lotus Eaters by Adrian Glamorgan

In this silver sliver-sparkling shiver of pleasure, I sit and chew the hairy leaves of the lotus. I feel pinpricks on my tongue, reassuring. I eat more. The sun is motionless, held in space as its glow ebbs and throngs in the moment. I am in the pleasure heat just after climax, in the stillness of the winter midnight with the ember burning down to the soft-eyed nothingness, the faraway look, the islands of charcoal. And now there is the grinding, elephantine opening of a door. It is someone from outside, beyond eternity, ripping these green leaves from me, shaking me, pulling me back and fore, punching my ribs, clapping their hands, dousing me in water. Taking me from this forever place, bringing me back to now. I feel the weight of my bones, my hands, my arms; the drum-roll of my heart. I feel the gasping of my lungs; see the nakedness of sunlight, of clouds across the sky. I see the faces of warriors demanding I join their reckless, endless journey. Be gone! I cry. Leave me here! I know what nourishment feeds me! I am done with petty villages and dung fires, with sheep amongst the stones! This is my place, my mother, my lover, my deathbed …

The Island of the Cyclops

Now the wind drives the fleet to the island of the Cyclops, a fierce race of giants, each with only one large eye in the middle of their forehead.

Odysseus and his crew explore the island. They find a large cave and in their hunger fall upon huge slabs of cheese stored in a corner. In the midst of the feasting, the Cyclops Polyphemus returns to his cave. Seeing the intruders he closes the entry with a huge boulder. He grabs a few of Odysseus' men, dashes their heads against the rocks, tears them to pieces and devours them before their horrified companions.

The rest of the crew he spares for future meals. When the giant asks Odysseus his name, the prudent hero tells him, 'Nobody'. To placate him, Odysseus offers the giant the wine the sailors had brought. The giant soon falls into an intoxicated sleep. Odysseus and his men quickly carve a huge spear from a wooden beam and, after dipping it into the fire, they ram it into the Cyclops' one and only eye.

Maddened by pain, the Cyclops grabs for Odysseus and his men. But blind, he cannot catch them in the vast expanse of his cave. Despairing, he calls his fellow giants for help. Hearing his cries they ask who is attacking him. 'Nobody is attacking me,' he answers. 'If nobody is attacking you, you don't need our help,' the giants reply.

The next morning Odysseus and his men escape by tying themselves beneath the bellies of the giant's sheep. Back on his ship, Odysseus for once abandons his usual restraint and proudly calls out his true name to Polyphemus. Knowing his enemy's name, the blinded giant appeals to his father, Poseidon, to avenge his humiliation, and from that day the sea god commands his winds to drive the fleet off course.

The Isle of Aeolos and the Land of the Lastrygones

Odysseus comes to the island of Aeolos, the warden of the wind, who entertains him hospitably. As a parting gift he gives Odysseus a sealed bag, containing all the winds that might hinder his return to Ithaca, and warns him not to open the bag until he is safely home.

Odysseus does not disclose the contents of the bag to the crew, who sail day and night unhindered towards Ithaca. But when Ithaca is in sight and Odysseus is asleep the men, feeling close to the end of their journey, take a peep into the sealed sack. That moment, the winds escape and blow the ship far from Ithaca, to the land of the Lastrygones.

Land of the Lastrygones

The ships enter a harbour and some men go ashore. They are seized by cannibals and killed. The Lastrygones hurl rocks from the cliffs and sink all the fleet except Odysseus's ship, which are anchored further away.

Circe and the Island of Aeaea

After this close escape the ship is blown to Aeaea, ruled by the enchantress Circe. When Odysseus sends his men ashore, she turns them into hogs. One escapes and reports to Odysseus, who immediately sets out for the rescue. On his way to Circe's palace he is met by the god Hermes, who gives him a flower to protect him from her spell. When Circe realises that Odysseus is immune to her magic, she offers him her love. He in turn extracts an oath from her never to harm him and commands her to restore his companions to human form.

Odysseus stays many years with Circe, who bears three sons with him. But he longs for home, for his wife and his son. When he cannot be constrained any longer, Circe advises him to make the journey to Hades, to the underworld, to ask the blind seer Tiresias for advice.

Descent to Hades

In the underworld Odysseus follows the advice of Circe and sacrifices a young ram and a black ewe. The spectres of the dead drift towards him, begging for a drink of the warm blood. But Odysseus wards them off until the shade of Tiresias appears. He drinks the sacrificial blood and warns Odysseus not to touch the cattle of the sun god when he visits Sicily and tells him about the troubles in Ithaca, where Penelope struggles to keep arrogant suitors away and where their son's life is in danger. When the shade of Tiresias fades, Odysseus encounters many of his former friends and learns about their destiny and death.

Exercise 2: The Descent to Hades

Like Odysseus you have come to the end of the world. You have made the blood sacrifice the dead drift towards you. Whom do you ward off and whom do you allow to drink and converse with you? What is their destiny in the underworld? Do the dead have insights that you need?

> **Tiresias speaks by Jennifer Kornberger**
> Give me blood, Odysseus, let it grow into me like red sap, let me feel again what it is like to command flesh, to inhabit solidity, to press earth into a mound. Give

me blood, Odysseus, let it grow into me like red sap, let me feel again what it is to command flesh. I crave the coursing of blood within a moving pillar of flesh. away with the held breath, this body of stilled branched wind …

Teresias speaks by Karen McCrea
This place is dark, cold, clammy. The walls press on me, the wet clay path under my feet draws the heat from me as voracioulsy as any leech draws blood. It seems there is nothing here; no light, no warmth, no sound other than the indecent torrent of my own blood hammering in my ears.
I feel it before I see it - a presence, the raw want of it pulsing in the darkness. Someone is there.
I try to still the clamor of my breath so I can hear. My skin prickles and my hair is actually standing on end. Every sense is hyper-alert.
"Karen".
The voice of my father crashes on me, like surf smashing on the shore. He begins to take shape in front of me. It is my father, and not. He doesn't quite have substance, weight. He is a shadowghost, a hologram. He reaches a bony hand to me, to touch my face. This hand, once strong and warm is as cold as his grave, and his touch marks me like a knife. He sees and is saddened. His eyes, dark pools in sunken pits, hold the only life in him. He gazes on me whilst I wrestle down the urge to turn and run from this specter, this not- father. He knows.
"Karen."
I cannot look at him.
"I told you once, that it takes only one person to change the course of someone's life. Sometimes, just a moment with one person. You know this now. There have been several moments, several 'one persons' for you. As you go on with your journey, for you aren't quite done yet, remember this. One person, one moment. Keep your heart open to this, your eyes, your ears, your mind. Remember, you are that one person. Be generous with your moments. They grow upon themselves and create the path as you walk it. Remember."
He looks at me. Again, I feel his hunger, his need. I take my bag and from it I give him all the nourishment I have.

The Sirens' Song

When Odysseus leaves Aeaea, Circe warns him of the Sirens, those creatures who lure sailors to their deaths with their enticing voices:

> Therefore pass these Sirens by, and stop your men's ears with wax that none of them may hear; but if you like you can listen yourself, for you may get the men

to bind you as you stand upright on a cross-piece half way up the mast, and they must lash the rope's ends to the mast itself, that you may have the pleasure of listening. If you beg and pray the men to unloose you, then they must bind you faster.

Odysseus is determined to hear their song. He follows Circe's advice, and while the sailors row with plugged ears, Odysseus is exposed to the lure of the singing and is consumed with unbearable longing. Raging in his bonds he begs his sailors to undo him. But they are deaf to his frenzy.

Exercise 3: The Sirens' Song

You are Odysseus tied to the mast of your ship. Describe the Sirens' song. How do their voices take hold of you? What do you feel? Hearing the song while tied to the mast offers a unique opportunity to experience ecstasy and agony at the same time.

The Sirens' Song by Adrian Glamorgan

Three, four sirens to a rock, drying their bare wings. I caught the eyes of one, all white around a startled lizard stare. No love or hearth in these skeleton crones, dazzling breasts, lice-infested hair; I have seen more beauti—

The first one calls, and my body flexes, uncontrollable, my back almost snaps with the pleasure and confrontation. She sings full throated, ululating, and her sisters join her … It is the song of my mother's womb. It is the silk gown being unknotted, and the rolling pelvis of love. It is the soft massage of the back after battle. It is the call of family across the last league before Ithaca's shore …

Sirens by Caz Bowman

Bask in the ecstasy of pretence!
My ears are plugged with warm wax that I may remain firmly connected with reality.
You would revel in the tantalising seduction as she entices you.
Come to me.
You would cast aside the threads that connected us.

I watched you, dear one, as you danced and swayed to the sweet, hypnotic call.
Seduced, you basked in the ecstasy of that pretence!
Long mane of hair, promises of eternal bliss.

You saw your souls entwined and you lunged for the shore
Oblivious to the jagged rocks
Tore away the ropes that had secured you.

I heard that song, stripped of the honeyed promises
Bound to the prow. I watched you go.

Scylla and Charybdis

The next challenge comes with the monsters Scylla and Charybdis, who guard a tight passage through which the ship must sail. The only way to pass unharmed is to steer exactly in the middle. Any deviation exposes the sailors to the grip of either monster. The Greek notion of balance between polar opposites finds pictorial expression here.

> Then we entered the Straits in great fear of mind, for on the one hand was Scylla, and on the other dread Charybdis kept sucking up the salt water. As she vomited it up, it was like the water in a cauldron when it is boiling over upon a great fire, and the spray reached the top of the rocks on either side … the men were at their wits ends for fear. While we were taken up with this, and were expecting each moment to be our last, Scylla pounced down suddenly upon us and snatched up my six best men. I was looking at once after both ship and men, and in a moment I saw their hands and feet ever so high above me, struggling in the air as Scylla was carrying them off, and I heard them call out my name in one last despairing cry.

Exercise 4: Scylla and Charybdis

The passage between Scylla and Charybdis is a situation we frequently experience in life, when we must steer our course between two extremes. Explore it through a personal experience, in pictorial or mythical terms.

Scylla and Charybdis by Jennifer Kornberger

It's not a monster, it's a mobile phone. You need one, you can't function without one today. What if you are in danger, late at night, and the Scylla clan are lurking on lonely highways. What if you're going to be late and the meeting is important?

It's not a monster, it's a phone tower. You need one, you need to be in contact. Those electro-magnetic waves keep you from dropping out of the net of humanity, keep you from the free fall of Charybdis, the abyss of alone.

I row between the mobile phone and the phone tower, wearing a poem pinned to the oar of my arm.

The Man in the Cage by Louise House

I know a man in a cage. He sits by me. His cage is steel and bars. It is cold and heavy. It encloses him completely. He doesn't know he is in the cage.

In the cage he wears chains and they hurt. I lean in from time to time and put ointment on the wounds where the chains rub. He doesn't really notice but maybe the pain goes away for a while.

The man in chains in the cage looks forward only. He sees nothing but the horizon. He keeps his eyes forward and fixed on the horizon. The man in chains in the cage walks on a black treadmill. He clanks the chains and carries the heavy steel cage as he trudges on and on and on. He looks solidly, only forward, at the horizon.

The man in chains in the cage on the black treadmill is tired, very tired. He has been carrying the cage for a long time. He didn't start in chains but they seem to have grown like a metal vine, encapsulating leg and sinew, arms and chest. They bind his wrists and cut into the flesh. Each year they grow stronger, bigger, tighter and cut in more. He used to feel them, but now the pain is always there so he doesn't really notice.

How can he? If he stops to notice, he will cry and then he wont be able to see the horizon. If he stops to notice and cries, he will need to look about and he might lose his balance. If he looks about and loses his balance he may stumble and fall off that black treadmill into goodness knows what. There must be only a black nothingness there. That thought is fearsome to the man. He cannot have that thought. So he does not look. He continues to walk, laden, every day.

He was given that cage. It looked golden then, and encrusted with jewels. Precious, shining, beautiful- glorious to behold. It was passed to him by The Man Who Knew. Was it really golden or was it the hue of the spectacles he wore on his fresh hazel eyes?

Where did that grinding black strip of tar come from? There was once only the greenest of grass. So green. So green.

Were the chains hidden? He says not. The golden cage was surrounded by a flower garden of marigolds, blood red poppies, purple iris and the lightest of white alyssum.

The climate changed.

I lean in from time to time and dress the wounds for the walking man with the lined face and the scarecrow hair. He is getting tired. He does not laugh. He never takes his eyes from the horizon.

He has forgotten who I am. He can only see the horizon and he must get there. He just must. I am sad, but I cant stay in that cage anymore. I got so thin I nearly died but being emaciated allowed me to escape through the bars. I overbalanced and I fell onto rocks and into pea soup. I found driftwood from other shipwrecks and it saved me. Just bits of simple wood.

I cant get back in that cage but I cant leave the man chained inside, trudging on to his horizon. So I will walk alongside (though sometimes skipping off in my red shoes and dress with a flounce) and lean in from time to time and I'll dress the wounds.

The Nymph Calypso

The few remaining sailors come to Sicily. As instructed by Tiresias, Odysseus gives strict orders to his men not to kill the cattle sacred to the sun god Helios. But food is scarce and the winds fails. Unable to leave the island, the sailors kill one of the sacred cows. Odysseus refuses to partake of the meal. The winds return, but as soon as they

are on the open sea a storm sent by Helios shatters the vessel. Odysseus alone survives and drifts for days, clinging to a beam of wood.
Exhausted he is washed up on the Island of Ogya. Calypso welcomes him, falls in love with him and keeps him there seven years. She offers him the immortality of a god if he stays with her. But Odysseus is determined to return to Ithaca.

Exercise 5: Calypso

You are Odysseus and Calypso has just offered you immortality (or something else you desire). Explain to her why you must reject her tempting offer.

Calypso by Caz Bowman

Stay with me where time no longer exists
Be with me and indulge your every desire
Here there is no yesterday and no tomorrow
Today, now is all you will know.

Egos massaged hourly.
Halls of mirrors to delight.
Luscious ice cream made with the cream of unicorns.
Lotus juice to wet your lips
Tall glasses of
Adoring audiences
Indulgent maidens
Hedonism day and night.

Calypso by Ann Reeves

Stay. Tarry. Linger.
Let my blessings fall about you, cloak you in heaven's graces.
I will anoint you, deify you, grant you world-all.
Strong I'll make you, your beauty will go before you, perfumed and golden,
To dazzle all who gaze upon you.

Resist? You cannot. What I offer is rich beyond worldly measure.
To stay means to stay forever youthful,
your strength unmatched, your years without number.
To leave is not to court death, it is to *be* death.
Turn to me, turn to love, turn to life everlasting.

The End of the Odyssey

Odysseus builds himself a raft and leaves the island. The watchful Poseidon spots his enemy and before Odysseus reaches safe harbour a storm shatters the raft and the hero is left floating helplessly in the raging sea. He is washed ashore on the fabled Island of the happy Phaecian. There he is found by Nausikaa, daughter of King Alkinous, and is hospitably received at her father's court. During the welcoming feast, Odysseus reveals his true identity and tells all that has befallen him after the sacking of Troy. The king takes pity on him and returns the weary traveller by means of a magical ship to Ithaca.

Odysseus finds his palace under siege by men wooing his wife Penelope. Aided by his son Telemachus, he takes bitter revenge on the intruders. He reunites with Penelope and makes a long pilgrimage to rid himself of Poseidon's anger.

17

The Lyre of Orpheus

The Greeks revelled in a whole train of gods, heroes, nymphs and other fabulous creatures whose quarrels and love affairs intrigue us. Greece is the artist among the ancient cultures; its gods are passionately portrayed in sculptures and artefacts, and its mission is encapsulated in the myth of Perseus and Medusa.

The Medusa is the ancient, snake-haired deity with the power to turn to stone anyone who gazes upon her. When Perseus undertakes to slay her, Pallas Athene, the goddess of wisdom, equips him with a mirror-like silver shield. Perseus approaches the Medusa while she sleeps. He steps carefully backwards, looking at her reflection in his shield. The moment her snake-covered head is severed from her body, Pegasus, the winged horse, rises from her remains and takes to the air.

Medusa is a picture of the old instinctive knowing or clairvoyance that the Greeks had to overcome in order to attain the new capacity of intellectual thought. The shield is a picture of the intellect and its capacity for reflection — something we see flowering in the achievements of the Greek philosophers — while Pegasus represents art, fantasy and imagination. The winged horse captures the inspiration behind all the artistic endeavours of Greek culture.

The First Lyre

The lyre is a symbol for the poet, and the creation of the first lyre is linked to the Greek god Hermes, patron of merchants and thieves, a son of Zeus. The fleet-footed god Hermes is cunning and at a tender age steals cattle from his brother Apollo. He brings them to his cave and slaughters a bull. Ever inventive, the young god fashions strings from the intestines,takes a tortoise shell and stretches seven cords across it to make the first lyre.

Apollo has in the meantime discovered the theft. The wise god immediately guesses who is to blame. He finds and confronts his fleet-footed brother.

When, Apollo, however, beholds the lyre his brother has made, he gladly exchanges his herd for this wonderful instrument. The Lyre becomes Apollo's emblem, and with his music he brings harmony and softens discord. Later he passes the lyre on to Orpheus, son of a river god and a muse.

Orpheus is a musician, poet, mystic and priest. Hearing his songs, wild animals become tame, trees bend to him and even fierce men grow gentle. Orpheus was one of the Argonauts; his music gave strength to the rowers and calmed the raging wind. When their ship passed by the sirens, Orpheus's song was the sweeter and the sailors' lives were saved.

Orpheus and Eurydice

Orpheus is best known for his love for his wife Eurydice. Soon after their marriage Eurydice is bitten by a snake and dies. Orpheus is inconsolable and journeys to the underworld to retrieve her. Even the gods of the dead are softened by his music, and Hades and Persephone agree to let Eurydice return with him, on condition that he not look back as Eurydice follows him out of the underworld.

Orpheus agrees and leads the way. But when the gate to the upper world appears, Eurydice stumbles and utters a cry. Startled, Orpheus turns back to look at her, only to see her fade back into the underworld. He has lost her again and this time forever. Virgil describes this moment in his *Georgics*:

> Wildly he grasped at shadows, wanting to say much more,
> But she did not see him; nor would the ferryman of the Inferno
> Let him again cross the fen that lay between them.
> What could he do, where go, his wife twice taken from him?
> What lament would move Death now? What deities hear his song?
> …
> As a nightingale he sang that sorrowing under a poplar's
> Shade laments the young she has lost, whom a heartless ploughman
> Has noticed and dragged from the nest unfledged; and the nightingale
> Weeps all night, on a branch repeating the piteous song,
> Loading the acres around with the burden of her lament.

Orpheus's lament seems more intimate than Gilgamesh weeping over Enkidu. It rends the heart. I experience Gilgamesh's pain at an awed distance. Orpheus's tragedy feels much closer.

Exercise 1: Lament for lost Love

As Orpheus you have gone to the utmost extreme to save your love. You almost succeed but at the last moment your precious love is snatched away. Your world is torn in two; you have lost a part of yourself.

Write a lament for a lost love. Hold Orpheus's lyre over your heart and let the chords of grief accompany your song.

A lament to lost love by Penelope Brown

I find you in fragments
in the surgeon's hand
in the poet's paper that grasps the wind
in the cat's green eye, blinking in the grass

I find you and lose you
again and again
in the smell of baked bread
in that sip of laughter
in the crunched sheets fragrant with soap and sunlight
of my empty bed
I find you only to lose you over and over
in the face of a stranger
in the cave of a hermit who no longer speaks
who no longer looks upon the sea

When I stand upon the mountain
imprinted with the shadows of owls
and awash with moonlight
I open my mouth in a cry
The clocks fall off the walls of my kitchen
the fridge defrosts like a storm
and I am frozen in my starlit loneliness

Lament by Jennifer Kornberger

The world is stretched with longitude
time zones slap against each other like waves
the world is gridded with latitude

I could hopscotch my way to you once
not needing a map, a globe
but a silent shroud
has been pulled over our communications

The gem in the belly dancer's navel was lost
and in the morning small creatures had made
a new grid over the earth.

Lament for lost Love by Louise House
I had it in my hand…just there. Clear, full of the coolest fresh water. A glass so fine the angels would want it for their own. So suddenly it slipped from my fingers.
The water splashed in slow motion, over my shoes. Drops, puddles, water flowing - now a river. A river carrying me away.
A river of tears, full of rocks and stones and wood and trees. Faster now, into the rapids. I am whirled about, helpless, battered, drowning.
But no, not drowning. That would be too swift , too easy. Then the pain would cease. The pain of a thousand pinpricks, of axe and sword on head, on heart.
There are only jagged bleeding words. My wounds stung with salt water when I reach the sea.

Orpheus continued his mission, establishing the first temples and the priesthood of ancient Greece. As founder of a new worship, he is opposed by the Thracian women, who adhere to older cults. In a mad frenzy they tear Orpheus apart. When his head continues to sing, they throw it with his lyre into the river. Head and lyre float to the island of Lesbos, where they are buried. Here myth joins with historical reality. For the great poet Sappho is born here many hundred years later, and in her songs the lyre of Orpheus comes to life again, and his lament for Euridice echoes through her poetry.

The Tenth Muse

Sappho was born in the seventh century BC in Myteline on the small but prosperous island of Lesbos. She was an aristocrat, and married a rich merchant with whom she had a daughter.

As a poet Sappho was an icon of public veneration by her early twenties. After a short banishment due to her political affinities, she established herself as a mentor for young women. Wealthy families sent their daughters to her for an education in which graceful conversation, poetry and song mingled with an unashamed eroticism.

Sappho is the first lyrical poet. Love poems were written before her, but they lack the intimate and highly refined awareness of Sappho's work; their lyrics are accidental to life. With Sappho, life is accidental to poetry! Lyric (the word derives from lyre) is her sole mission, and a continual falling in love is the prerequisite for poetic creation.

Sappho is also a pioneer of interior life. Love poetry functions like a midwife for the tender fledgling of inner awareness. She charts the map of the lover's soul through changing mood, attraction and passion. Her verse is the first chapter in western psychology, each poem an attempt to draw the soul from the underworld of emotion into the brightly lit contours of the word. In her verse is the Greek passion for youth and grace, and a celebration of the beauty of female form.

At last
You have come
and you did well to come
I pined for you.
And now you have put a torch to my heart
a flare of love —
O bless you and bless you and bless you:
you are back . . .
we were parted

And another example:

The moment I saw her
Love
like a sudden breeze
tumbling on the oak leaves
left my heart
trembling

Sappho is among the first poets to explore the tender interior dynamics of the soul, with similes like that of trembling oak leaves.

Exercise 2: The Subtleties of Attraction

Put yourself in Sapphic mode to experience the goddess in the young woman. Imagine yourself as a mature woman enamored by the beauty and grace of a young girl. Like Sappho, try to find similes that illumine the subtleties of attraction, passion and love.

In the Sapphic mode by Anne Williams

Arising from the sea
like Aphrodite
grace sliding like cool water
from every limb.
You stoop to tie your sandal.
I envy the warm leather that protects your step
and clasps it closely.

sappho by morgan yasbincek

you may have lain with artemis herself I think
for i felt your shadow as it fell upon the gate

only hers can marry such wilderness and grace, and
i can tell now by the attitude of your chin, the
depth of your supernal notch what kind of poet you will be

a wolf lurks in your haunches, a doe in your breast
and your eyes hold the only question I may never
be able to answer

we have yet to speak and even with the advantage
of age and station i am already preparing
for our first dialogue to collapse
me like water into ground

artemis, whatever becomes of this love,
let her perfection take me mercifully

Sappho by Jeremy Sheldrick
She was taller than the rest
her brows rising like a shy moon
above the others ...
Already she had a murder of
giggling admirers
they would tickle her to watch
pink flood her cheeks
... my heart was at a wedding,
    staring, unable to speak.

The Seesaw of Love

Often Sappho's poetry turns to the seesaw of emotion, the pull and push between the souls of lovers; the longing, pining and courting, the hope of fulfillment and the ecstasy of embrace.

    I could not wait
    Yesterday you
    Came to my house
    And sang to me.
    Now I
    Come to you.
    Talk to me. Do.
    Lavish on me
    Your own beauty.

For we walk to a wedding,
As well you know.
Please send away
Your maids. Oh may
Heaven then present me
With all that heaven ever meant for me.

Exercise 3: The Persuasions of Poetry

Like Sappho, address the one you love; savour the tension between hope and fulfillment. Persuade your love with the power of your verse.

Vignette in Sapphic Style by Anne Williams

You came towards me
and in my house
all the doors flew open.
Stay longer.
Tonight I will beg the stars
to freeze.

Sappho speaks by Jennifer Kornberger

I watched you carry the jug of water from the spring
There were drops of water on your arm
And you stepped with care over white stones.
But I was brimming
and walked from one window to the next
without stopping.

Jealousy

Jealousy is a powerful incentive for both love and poetry. The depth of attachment is its measure of pain. Sappho meets jealousy when her beloved girls leave school for marriage. The body is a barometer of the agony in letting go in the poem below.

I more than envy him
He is a god in my eyes, that man,
Given to sit in front of you
And close to himself sweetly to hear
The sound of you speaking.
Your magical laughter — this I swear —
Batters my heart my breast astir —

My voice when I see you suddenly near
Refuses to come
My tongue breaks up and a delicate fire
Runs through my flesh; I see not a thing
With my eyes, and all that I hear
In my ears is a hum.

The sweat runs down, a shuddering takes
Me in every part and pale as the drying
Grasses, then, I think I am near
The moment of dying

Exercise 4: Jealousy

Follow the thread of jealousy in your own emotions. Observe like Sappho the intensity of envy and loss, and express them in words.

That Silver Tongue of Yours by Janet Blagg

You bring me his letters as trophies
To impress me with his oafish verse and metaphor.
O girl, I poured my fire into you
Polished that silver tongue of yours
Made it leap in verse and song and on my sun-drenched thigh.
And now it is for him?

I would not take it back, not one honeyed moment
But it is nearly winter
And this velvet cloak I promised would be yours —
I will keep it for myself to stand alone in.

Sappho: Your Leaving by Barbara Stapleton

I sit here with you
Drinking out of these delicate cups
With their fluted rims
My teeth are on edge
Set hard in a skeleton grimace
All my bones become chalk
Ready to crumble
As you prepare
To set sail.

When Sappho is more than fifty she falls in love with the dashing young sailor Phaon, who returns her love but then leaves her. Sappho despairs and follows after him until finally she recognises the futility of her desire to win him back, and leaps from a cliff into the sea. She lived for the poetry of love, and now she dies for it.

The charismatic Sappho is another Orpheus. Much in her destiny mirrors the fate of the Thracian singer who found death in the mad frenzy of enraged women. Sappho is consumed by her passion for Phaon. And though she is not torn to pieces, her body of work is: her poems were torn from ancient documents and her books destroyed by the bigotry of later times. Even her name was erased, her memory eradicated.

Scraps of her poetry turn up now and then — in the paper stuffing of mummified crocodiles and other unlikely places. She is the first martyr of poetry, and her destiny is a reminder of the violent fragmentation suffered by the female soul as patriarchy asserted itself across the ancient world.

The Apotheosis of Love

In another great work of Greek literature, Plato's *Symposium*, a group of Athenian literati discuss the nature of love. Here Socrates admits that all he knows about love he learned from a woman named Diotima. He outlines her explanation of the stages through which love evolves, starting with the physical attraction that a mature man might feel for a younger man or boy:

> When a man, starting from this sensible world and making his way upward by a right use of his feeling of love for boys, begins to catch sight of that beauty, he is very near his goal. This is the right way of approaching or being initiated into the mysteries of love, to begin with examples of beauty in this world, and using them as steps to ascend continually with that absolute beauty as one's aim, from one instance of physical beauty to two and from two to all, then from physical beauty to moral beauty, and from moral beauty to the beauty of knowledge, until from knowledge of various kinds one arrives at the supreme knowledge whose sole object is that absolute beauty, and knows at last what absolute beauty is.

Exercise 5: The Nature of Love

Prepare a speech in honour of love. Give your insights into what love truly is, in either philosophical or imaginative terms.

> **Apotheosis of Love by Ann Reeves**
> If love be of this earth
> Then I know love,
> Love of the green, the bud, the flower, the fruit.

If love be the swirls of my ravening soul that sings to the sun,
Howls at the moon and hungers mightily,
Then I know it.
And if love be the racing of my heart when I bed a man,
That love too I know.
And if love be a yearning, a reaching out and a cry seeking an echo from out of the heavens,
Seeking an answer to the very best in me,
Seeking the blessing of Yes to the questions in my heart,
Then that is true love – it is love of my life.
And that too, I know.

The Nature of Love by Karen McCrea
This question! It has fired the loins of men, stirred their hearts and inflamed their souls, but it has no answer that can be told one to another.

Rather, the question has to be lived, and lived at full tilt, perhaps even recklessly at times, though not necessarily for there are many paths.

Many other passions are mistaken for love - it is not piety, passion or romance. It is not protection nor intellect. But it can contain all of these things, and perhaps must, at some time.

It is the lowest and the highest of all things. A mother's love for her babe is the same, whether the mother be woman or she-wolf. Love is that, and more than that. It is the same force that moves rutting buffaloes as rutting men - love is that and more than that. It is the same song that fills the night whether from the throat of the nightingale or the throat of Orpheus. Love is that and more than that.

It is bigger than the nets of fishermen, and it is bigger than the net of Indra. It is sharper than the sword of the battlefield, sharper than the sword of Gilgamesh; it is sweeter than any honey, wilder than any pride of lions. It will change you, crack you, wisen you, anneal you, perhaps over and over until you are more burnished than any gold.

And, it is more than that.

It moves you from the small love of ruthless need to the wide open heart of a wise God, manifest everywhere. And then - then you know you will never know the end of it, for there is none. This is love.

Liberation from the Tragedy of Love

Alcibiades is one of the guests at the Symposium. He is the most handsome young man of Athens, desired by many of those at the party. Alcibiades tells the whole assembly how he, the handsome youth, became enamoured with the much older Socrates and tried to seduce the philosopher, only to be thwarted by Socrates' dedication to virtue and inner beauty. The young Alcibiades is left lovesick, and admires the old man all the more for his steadfast dedication to what he preaches.

> On the one hand I realised that I had been slighted, but on the other I felt a reverence for Socrates' character, his self-control and courage; I had met a man whose like for wisdom and fortitude I could never have expected to encounter. The result was that I could neither bring myself to be angry with him and tear myself away from his society, nor find a way of subduing him to my will. It was clear to me that he was more completely proof against bribes than Ajax against sword-wounds, and in the one point in which I had expected him to be vulnerable he eluded me. I was utterly disconcerted, and wandered about in a state of enslavement to the man the like of which has never been known.

The conduct of Socrates reverses the tragic destiny of Sappho. Dedicated to the contemplation of absolute beauty, the philosopher liberates himself from the tragic ties of love. Plato's philosophic contemplations on Socrates complement the poetic productions of Sappho. Together they comprise the span of experiences that the Greek soul was capable of in its age of glory.

18

The Labyrinth of Light

Odysseus strikes a new note in the chorus of ancient heroes. Through his prudence and clever thinking he pioneers the emerging intellect. He is not the only Greek hero to do so. Through his intellect Theseus liberated Athens from the cruel tribute exacted by Crete — the yearly sacrifice of twenty young Athenian women and men, to be devoured by the bull-headed Minotaur in the labyrinth of King Minos. Theseus slew the Minotaur and with the help of a ball of thread, given to him by the Cretan princess Ariadne, he found his way out of the labyrinth. The thread is an image of human thought, by which we can find orientation in the bewildering passages of the soul. Theseus overcomes the old clairvoyant forces symbolised by the bull-headed Minotaur through the new capacity of thought.

But the new light of thought is not without its shadow. For all that is gained, much is lost. The tragic dimension of this loss is powerfully explored in the myth of Oedipus

The Story of Oedipus

King Laius of Thebes and his queen Jocasta are childless. The King consults the oracle of Delphi and is told that this is in his favour, for if he ever had a son, he would kill his father and marry his mother. The king is alarmed and shuns the bed of his wife to avoid the prophesy. Jocasta, feeling rejected, makes her husband drunk and so tricks him into intercourse. When a son is born the king pierces the babe's feet with a nail, and orders a servant to abandon him in the wilderness. The servant however, takes pity on the child and hands him to a shepherd of Corinth. The shepherd nurses the child back to health and presents him to his own king and queen. Lacking an heir, the royal couple of Corinth adopt the child and name him Oedipus (wounded foot).

Oedipus grows up as a prince of Corinth and remains ignorant of his origin. At a feast he is taunted by drunken friends because he does not resemble his parents, and he is beset by doubt. To gain clarity he consults the oracle of Delphi. But when he approaches the sanctuary, the priestess cries out 'Away with you. You are cursed. You will kill your father and marry your mother.'

To avoid the prediction Oedipus resolves never to return to Corinth. He takes the road to Thebes. At the same time King Laius is travelling from Thebes to Delphi. The king is coming to the oracle to ask for advice because a Sphinx is troubling Thebes, killing travellers who fail to answer her riddle. In a narrow pass between Delphi and Thebes the two travellers meet. The king calls out to the stranger to make way for his betters. Oedipus retorts that he acknowledges no better than the gods and his parents. The king orders his charioteer to drive straight on. The chariot passes close by and the wheels crush Oedipus's foot. Enraged, Oedipus hurls his spear, kills the charioteer, puts the king's attendants to flight and wrestles with Laius. He tangles the king in the horses' reins and whips the horses until they drag him to his death.

Ignorant of the fact that he has killed his father he continues his journey. Outside Thebes he is challenged by the Sphinx, a creature with a lion body and the head of a woman. She transfixes wanderers with a riddle that no-one has yet solved: 'What being with one voice has sometimes two feet, sometimes three and sometimes four, and is weakest when it has the most?' Oedipus correctly answers: 'The human being.' Devastated by defeat, the Sphinx leaps over a cliff.

Exercise 1: Meeting the Sphinx

Sphinxes inhabit the myths of antiquity. The Egyptian sphinx combined a human head with elements of lion, bull, and eagle. The Greek sphinx was a mixture of lioness and woman. In this exercise you are waylaid by a sphinx. What does your sphinx look like? What is her challenge? Does she pose a riddle? And if so, do you know the answer?

Meeting the Sphinx by Karen McCrea

Weary, battered, grimy, I was close to home, longing for my bath and bed. I wanted only to rest and hoped fervently I would not cross paths with the creature said to lurk about these parts. Of course, that was not to be. I found my way suddenly blocked by the startling appearance of a huge figure, rising, rising into the sky. It was a fearsome thing, and at first I could not fathom it at all. It had a long sinuous, glistening body, slick, wet and smelling so sweet, so warm ... I shook my head. The thing was mesmerising me, making me lose my wits. Its face, high above me seemed to be unset, shifting, looking first like a woman, beautiful, soft, warm; then a man, darkly handsome, then a wolf, teeth bared and slathering, then a snake, tongue flicking, darting, tasting the air around me. This grotesque then spouted arms, breasts, a flat female body, a long male phallus, claws where fingers should be, and on and on, changing in front of my eyes, making me feel breathless and dizzy. I shook my head, the better to think, and understood, I had met The Sphinx...

The Thebans welcome their liberator with great honour. When news of Laius' death reaches the city, Oedipus is invited to be the new king. He accepts the crown and marries the widowed Queen Jocasta. The prophesy is fulfilled.

Oedipus is much respected by his people. Jocasta bears him two sons and two daughters and all seems well. But eventually a plague visits Thebes. Oedipus sends messengers to Delphi and the oracle's advice is to find the murderer of King Laius. Oedipus, ignorant of his own involvement, curses the murderer, and vows to find and exile him.

Oedipus Rex

Sophocles' famous play *King Oedipus* commences at the moment Oedipus begins his search for truth. He becomes the first detective, ignorant that he is looking for himself. Oedipus calls for the blind seer Teiresias. The prophet, knowing the terrible truth, is unwilling to come. Forced by Oedipus to testify, Teiresias accuses him of the murder. Oedipus is incensed and accuses the prophet in turn. Soon other witnesses arrive and more evidence comes to the fore. The attendant who survived the attack on Laius is brought before Oedipus. He is also the shepherd who saved the wounded child from destruction. Soon the evidence is overwhelming. Oedipus realises the terrible truth: he has killed his father and married his mother. He is both brother and father to his children. Trying to escape the prophesy, he has made it come true. Oedipus hurries to his wife, but Jocasta has hanged herself. Despairing, Oedipus takes a pin from her garment and pierces his eyes until he is blind.

Exercise 2: Oedipus

King Oedipus of Sophocles is one of the most compelling tragedies of all time. Take up your pen and record Oedipus' despair when he realises what he has done. See him with his bleeding eyes and give voice to a despair that will move an audience to compassion and fear.

Oedipus by Nandi Chinna

Cut my eyes
pierce my skin with knives
cut off my hands
that made this deed
cut off my feet that carried me here
to this place of no return
cut off the organ that has
lain with my mother
and born children that are both
my sons and my brothers

I am lost

Oh horror that I have walked in a circle
away from the oracle's fire
and blindly into its inferno
are all men my father?
when I meet him in the street
how will I know it's him? ...

Cast me out beyond the city's walls
I want to suffer
I want to wander
on desolate mountains
and re-run this tragedy
over and over in my dreams
run it over, run it dry
until I am nothing but dust.

Oedipus's Lament by Janet Blagg

That man was me.
That man was me.
I see that bright morning, the mountain pass. I looked into my father's eyes before I cut him down. That man was my father.
And Jocasta, darling wife — how often did I gaze into your warm brown eyes as I sank into your strong arms?
That man was me.
Everything I sought to escape came marching fast to meet me.
And now — what? — am I to see these eyes forever?
So help me, I will not, you vile old gods of Fate.
I shall look upon no man again.

Oedipus keeps the vow he has made and exiles himself from Thebes. With his faithful daughter Antigone he wanders as a homeless beggar through the country. Eventually he finds refuge with Theseus, Duke of Athens. After many years the oracle declares him blessed and proclaims that his remains will bring a good fortune to the place in which they rest.

Antigone

After Oedipus' death, Antigone returns to Thebes, where her brothers are contesting the rulership. Eteocles has proclaimed himself ruler and Polyneices gathers an army and attacks the city. The brothers kill each other in combat, and Creon, brother of Jocasta, becomes the new king. His first order is to bury Eteocles with all honours, and to leave Polyneices unburied.

To leave a man unburied violates the laws of the gods and prevents the soul from finding its rest, but no one dares oppose the new king — except Antigone. Under cover of night she heaps earth on her brother's body. When the guards discover the deed she is gone. Creon is incensed. Someone has dared to disobey his first decree! He orders the body to be exposed again, and when Antigone returns to repeat her act, she is captured.

Antigone is fearless in her own defence. Death does not frighten her. The laws of the gods must be obeyed before the laws of men. Her mission is one of love for her brothers and she will not repent. The passage from Sophocles' play Antigone is a compelling expression of courage and honour:

> CREON: Do you plead innocent or guilty to these things?
> ANTIGONE: Guilty. I deny not a thing.
> CREON: … Did you know an edict had forbidden this?
> ANTIGONE: Of course I knew. Was it not publicly proclaimed?
> CREON: So you chose flagrantly to disobey my law?
> ANTIGONE: Naturally! Since Zeus never promulgated
>   Such a law. Nor will you find
>   That justice publishes such laws to man below.
>   I never thought your edicts had such force They nullified the laws of heaven …
>   And I, whom no man's frown can frighten,
>   Am far from risking Heaven's frown by flouting these.
>   I need no trumpeter from you to tell me
>   I must die. We all die anyway.
>   And if this hurries me to death before my time —
>   Why, such a death is gain. Yes, surely gain
>   To one so overwhelmed with trouble.
>   Therefore, I can go to meet my end
>   Without a trace of pain. But had I left
>   The body of my mother's son unburied
>   Where he lay — ah! that would hurt. For this,
>   I feel no twinges of regret. And if
>   You think I am a fool, perhaps it is
>   Because a fool is judge.
> CREON: You wait and see! The toughest will is first
>   To break: like hard untempered steel,
>   Which snaps and shivers at a touch when fresh
>   From off the forge …
>   This girl, already versed in disrespect
>   When first she disobeyed my law, now adds
>   A second insult — vaunts it to my face …

Creon is challenged by a young woman who is both his niece and the intended bride of his only son. Their dialogue represents a major step on the long road towards freedom and conscious choice. Antigone fulfills her mission in full consciousness of the consequences. Her destiny redeems that of her father Oedipus.

Exercise 3: Antigone

In dramatic dialogue explore the conflict between Creon and Antigone or a similar confrontation between official authority and civil courage, pride and determination, ignorance and conscious action.

Antigone by Nandi Chinna

CREON: What have you got to say for yourself young lady?

ANTIGONE: My actions speak my mind.

CREON: Do you realise how much this is going to cost? We've lost three days work and all those men are sitting out there doing nothing. They still have to get paid you know.

ANTIGONE: Do you think I care about your stupid money?

CREON: Are you coming down or do we have to drag you?

ANTIGONE: You think you can come in here with your suits and your maps and your silly machines. This is my house and youse can all fuck off. Go on get off my land.

CREON: Look lady I've got a job to do so will you just open the gate so we can get the machines.

ANTIGONE: You whitefellas think you can come in here and do what you like, traipsing in and out of my yard. No respect. Leaving your rubbish, digging holes, cutting trees. This here is aboriginal land. Nothing's changed in 200 years. You still think you got the right to come in without asking.

CREON: Listen it's not your land ok. It's government land and we've got a job to do. If this goes on any longer we'll be pressing charges.

ANTIGONE: Press what you like. Press a button and blow up the whole bloody country. This is my place. I live here and I deserve some respect.

CREON: John, will you go and call the police.

Creon condemns Antigone to be interred in a sealed tower until she dies of hunger and thirst. Confronted by his son Haemon, who is to marry Antigone, he remains unyielding, and father and son part in enmity. The blind seer Tiresias comes to warn Creon, but the new ruler remains unmoved. Only when the Thebans plead with him to listen to the prophet, does he relent. But it is too late. Antigone already has hanged herself, and Haemon, seeing his bride is dead, kills himself in front of Creon. Returning to the palace, Creon finds that the news of his son's death has preceded him and his wife the queen has killed herself. Creon's pride has brought his downfall.

Plato's Apology

Drama played a major part in Greek culture. Attending a dramatic performance was a kind of religious experience, a minor initiation with therapeutic benefits; its value as entertainment was secondary.

There are four major Greek playwrights: Aeschylus, Sophocles, Euripides and one who sadly burned all his dramatic works — Plato. His gift for drama however appears like a phoenix in his dialogues. Plato's stage is the philosophical conversation, his plot the search for truth, his cast the Athenian intelligentsia, his hero, Socrates.

We met Socrates already in the *Symposium*. Now we examine his contribution in the dance of destiny, intellect and freedom. Oedipus was fated before his birth. Antigone rose to conscious choice in the light of divine law and familial honour. In Plato's *Apology* we come to a further stage in the drama of human freedom. The aged Socrates is charged with impiety, a crime punishable by death in Athenian law. His accusers are the good citizens of Athens, who blame Socrates for corrupting the youth with his disrespect for time-honoured customs.

The *Apology* reveals the full humanity of Socrates, as well as his lifelong passion: the search for truth. His address to the court reveals his powers of reasoning, personal integrity, humour and fine sense of philosophic irony, as in this passage from the beginning:

> What effect my accusers have had upon you, gentlemen, I do not know, but for my own part I was almost carried away by them; their arguments were so convincing. On the other hand, scarcely a word of what they said was true. I was especially astonished at one of their many misrepresentations: the point where they told you that you must be careful not to let me deceive you, implying that I am a skilful speaker. I thought that it was peculiarly brazen of them to have the nerve to tell you this, only just before events must prove them wrong, when it becomes obvious that I have not the slightest skill as a speaker — unless, of course, by a skillful speaker they mean one who speaks the truth. If that is what they mean, I would agree that I am an orator, and quite out of their class.

In his defense, Socrates recounts how his quest for truth started when the oracle at Delphi publicly declared that he, Socrates, was the wisest of all men. This pronouncement astonished no one more than him, he said, who had always been acutely aware of his ignorance:

> I set myself with considerable reluctance to check the truth in the following way. I went to interview with a man with a high reputation for wisdom, because I felt that here if anywhere I should succeed in disproving the oracle and pointing out to my divine authority, 'You said that I was the wisest of men, but here is a man who is wiser than I am.'
>
> Well, I gave a thorough examination to this person — I need not mention his name, but it was one of our politicians I was studying when I had this experience — and in conversation with him I formed the impression that although in many peoples' opinion, and especially in his own, he appeared to be wise, in fact he was not. Then when I began to show him that he only thought he was wise and was not really so, my efforts were resented both by him and many of the other people present …

Socrates continues his search by questioning artists and craftsmen, but comes to the same result. They all think themselves in possession of some truth that on careful examination is unfounded. He realises that the oracle proclaimed him the wisest of men because he at least is aware of his ignorance, while others pride themselves on shallow illusions.

Thus Socrates makes it his task to question the beliefs and half-truths of his fellow citizens, as a holy service to Apollo, the god of the oracle. His passion for truth brings him the admiration of young people and like-minded followers, but incurs the enmity of established citizens who see their reputations damaged by his questioning.

Like Antigone, Socrates is not afraid of death. Far from repenting, he clearly states his determination to continue the mission he has begun. In fact he represents his activity as a benefaction to the city.

> For this reason, gentlemen, far from pleading on my own behalf, as might be supposed, I am really pleading on yours, to save you from misusing the gift of God by condemning me. If you put me to death, you will not easily find anyone to take my place. To put it bluntly (even if it sounds rather comical) God has assigned me to this city, as if to a large thoroughbred horse which because of its great size is inclined to be lazy and needs the stimulation of some stinging fly. It seems to me that God has attached me to this city to perform the office of such a fly; and all day long I never cease to settle here, there, and everywhere, rousing, persuading, reproving every one of you. You will not easily find another like me, gentlemen, and if you take my advice you will spare my life.

Exercise 4: Socrates

Imagine yourself Socrates, in front of the court of Athens. You have the opportunity to once more address the court before the final decision. With one succinct speech give voice to your convictions, your passion for the search for truth; for the philosopher to challenge the status quo and awaken the community to the pursuit of higher ideals.

Socrates by Mags Webster

... I look around and I see scholars, priests, judges and seers. The collective might of your minds hangs like drapery around the room: in swags and folds, puckers and pleats, wrinkles and robes. How could such wisdom not recognise truth? I am a simple man; I do not have the words capable of dressing up my sentiments. My knowledge is not costumed in rhetoric, my convictions are unadorned, Your speeches to me, gentlemen, are clothed in superior vestments; I swear I cannot even begin to part the layers. So I stand before you, naked as the words I speak. You do not have to strip me to get at my truth.

His bold and brilliant speech, in which he frequently proves the ignorance of his accusers, does not endear him any further. The death sentence is pronounced, which he receives with equanimity. When friends try to persuade him to avoid execution by fleeing Athens, he refuses to thwart the laws of the city he has tried to obey his whole life.

The Death of Socrates

Plato deals with Socrates' death in his dialogue *Phaedo*: Before his execution Socrates talks to his friends about death.

He explains that the true philosopher shuns common pleasures such as food, drink, sex and fine clothes to focus on the attainment of justice, goodness, beauty, truth. In other words, the philosopher's main occupation is to die to all the pleasures derived from the body and awaken to the eternal part of the soul. While in the body, this eternal element can only be partially realised. For the philosopher, death is the final liberation from all obstacles that separate him from his goal.

Socrates then explains what he expects in the afterlife - how the soul after death will live in the state it has prepared for itself during life:

> ...When a man dies, his own guardian spirit (Daimon), which was given charge over him during his life, tries to bring him to a certain place, where all must assemble, and from which, when they have been sorted out by a process of judgement, they must set out for the next world under the guidance of one who has the office of escorting the soul from this world to the other.....
>
> The wise and disciplined soul follows its guide and is not ignorant of its surroundings; but as for the soul which is deeply attached to the body...it is

only after much resistance and suffering that it is at last forcibly led away by its appointed guardian spirit. And when it reaches the same places as the rest, the soul that is impure...is shunned and avoided by all... and it wanders alone in utter desolation until certain times have passed, whereupon it is borne away of necessity to its proper habitation. But every soul that has lived throughout its life in purity and soberness enjoys divine company and guidance, and it inhabits the place that is proper to it.

Exercise 5: Last Words

Imagine yourself in a similar situation as Socrates. What do you have to impart to those who have gathered around you? What are your convictions about life after death? And how does that which comes after relate to the life you led before?

Last Words by Nan Connell

I begin this new journey at the banks of the River - already
the Ferryman is waiting
the small boat bobs in the water - my Soul
is being transported on a white stallion

he paws the ground - impatient
for the freedom that awaits - soon
we will gallop through the forrest
i will enter the spirit of the trees

the birds - free
to fly - dive and sing
my Soul - poised
has a singular purpose - a destination

a welcome like no other awaits us

we are coming Home

Socrates redeems the tragedy of Oedipus. In both destinies the oracle of Delphi plays a decisive part. But while Oedipus cannot escape his ignorance, Socrates, knowing his ignorance, exceeds all others in wisdom.

Blinded by his intellect, Oedipus stumbles into the labyrinth of tragedy. Trying to avoid the prophesies, he brings them about. Socrates, on the other hand, consciously fulfills the oracle's pronouncement and fearlessly completes his mission as a martyr to truth.

The Function of Drama and Poetry

Plato preserved the memory of his beloved teacher in his philosophical dialogues. However, the philosopher who burned his own plays had strong reservations about poetry, which in his opinion, served illusion rather than truth. As a political philosopher he wanted poetry excluded from the ideal state.

Aristotle, his immediate pupil, championed a different view. In his *The Art of Poetry* he examines Sophocles' King Oedipus as the most representative play. Unlike Plato, he does not discount the ability of poetry and drama to reveal the truth. On the contrary he states:

> The difference between the historian (someone who writes about reality, i.e. the truth) and the poet is not that the one writes in prose and the other in verse. The difference is that one tells of what has happened and the other of the kinds of things that might happen. For this reason poetry is something more philosophical and more worthy of serious attention than history. For while poetry is concerned about universal truth, history treats of particular facts.

Aristotle recognised that dramatic plays brought about catharsis, a purging of the soul, by evoking powerful emotions such as compassion and fear. To watch a tragedy was a healing experience for the whole community and hence beneficial for the state.

Exercise 6: The Purpose of Poetry

Write a short treatise on the function of drama and how it affects society. What does drama do? Does it serve truth or illusion? Is it beneficial to society? Do plays have a healing effect on those who watch them?

> **In Defence of Poetry by Karen McCrea**
> How, without poetry,
> can the breath of God
> lift the birds
> to fill the sky with weeping?
> How, without poetry,
> can ghosts be captured
> so they may be remembered by those who need them?
> How, without poetry, can grassy fields drink the blood
> of the slain?

How, without poetry, can winter be cruel and summer, rosy?
How, without poetry, can truth be told uncloaked from lies?
How, without poetry,
can the heart move
to brimming
with love, and joy, and rage?
How, without poetry,
can children grow
lute strings in their hearts?
How, without poetry, can the intervals
fill with silence?
How, without poetry,
can the illuminated
squeeze through mouse-holes to fill the world
with light?
How, without poetry,
can love break the shackles and sing?
How,
without poetry, can we love?

It is interesting to note that the highly poetic Plato dismissed the function of poetry in his ideal state while the prosaic Aristotle, who preferred meticulously reasoned treatises to lively dialogues, championed it.

With Plato and Aristotle the mission of the Greek intellect — presaged through heroes like Perseus, Theseus, Odysseus and Oedipus — came into its own. Aristotle gathered science, philosophy, rhetoric, law and literature, and organised this nowledge into a meaningful whole. His pupil and friend, Alexander the Great, spread Aristotle's achievements throughout the civilised world. As the pupil of Aristotle, he longed for a meeting of east and west, a merging of cultures. Rather than subduing the conquered nations, Alexander honoured their cultural contributions and integrated them in his vast cultural schemes, founding the city of Alexandria as a new centre of global learning.

19

A Sober State

When Alexander died, his generals divided his vast empire between themselves. But soon a new political power rose in the west: the Roman Empire. The Romans were a pragmatic people, and as sober as the Greeks were inspired. Their success rested on their clever martial tactics and diplomacy — traits apparent in their earliest myths and records.

According to tradition a princess had been imprisoned in a tower by her usurping uncle in order to prevent her future children succeeding to the throne. The god Mars, however, visited her and she gave birth to twins: Romulus and Remus. The king ordered the twins to be abandoned in the wilderness. A she-wolf suckled the helpless babes until a shepherd found them and brought them to his wife.

When grown to manhood, Romulus and Remus avenged their mother, overthrew the usurper and founded the city of Rome at the place where the she-wolf had suckled them. Romulus gathered a troop of outcasts and became the first king of Rome. But he and his men lacked wives, and their Sabine neighbours refused their daughters as marriage partners. So Romulus arranged a horse race between his followers and the Sabines and when the race was at its most dramatic, the Romans abducted the Sabine daughters. Open warfare ensued, but as the two armies prepared to clash, the Sabine women threw themselves between the warring men, proclaiming that they were happy to stay with the Romans. Hostilities ended and an agreement was reached that satisfied both parties.

This story contains motifs typical of Roman conduct. The Romans were a warlike people: the first king traces his ancestry to the god Mars himself. The she-wolf suckling the brothers symbolises their fierce courage and conquering instinct, and it became the emblem of Rome.

In the abduction of the Sabine women we see a strategy that couples the Roman sense for tactics with their diplomatic skill. A culture that has as one of its founding motifs the abduction of women also reveals itself as a patriarchy that is likely to be particularly enduring. Throughout their history the Romans repeat again and again this pattern of conquest followed by skilful diplomatic agreements.

The Greeks were inspired artists and thinkers. The Romans were a thoroughly practical people: capable engineers rather than gifted sculptors; brilliant lawyers, rhetoricians and politicians rather than original philosophers. They excelled in organisational feats such as the creation of complex laws, political systems and highly efficient armies.

But while the Romans conquered the Greeks politically, the Greeks conquered them culturally. Most Roman gods are mere copies of the Greek pantheon: Zeus becomes Jupiter, Ares becomes Mars, and Aphrodite is Venus. Roman temples and sculptures are stiff replicas of the Greek originals and Roman poetry mostly imitates the work of Homer, Sappho and Pindar. The most original contributions of Rome are engineering feats — roads, bridges, aqueducts and baths — and the creation of law and a republican constitution.

The Mission of Law

Roman law is not inspired by a god like Jahwe or a king like Hamurabi. It is a pure expression of the newly emerging individual and his (not her) rights as a citizen, an equal among (male) equals. After the passing of the last Roman king, the Republic and its laws guaranteed freedom from tyrannical suppression and ensured the rights of the individual. This position is well expressed by **Cicero (106–43 BC):**

> True law is Reason, right and natural, commanding people to fulfil their obligations and prohibiting and deterring them from doing wrong. Its validity is universal; it is unchangeable and eternal. Its commands and prohibitions apply effectively to good men and have no effect on bad men. Any attempt to supersede this law, to repeal any part of it, is sinful; to cancel it entirely is impossible. Neither the Senate nor the Assembly can exempt us from its demands; we need no interpreter or expounder of it but ourselves. There will not be one law at Rome, one at Athens, or one now and one later, but all nations will be subject all the time to this one changeless and everlasting law.

Exercise 1: The Life of the Law

Law and poetry are not easily matched. The Roman law, however, was a creative act and Cicero, in his legal enthusiasm, almost waxes poetic in its praise. Let us do the same and in a spirited speech or impassioned piece of writing explore on the idea of equality that stands behind republican law. Alternatively explore the downside of binding laws, of over-regulation, super administration, and state control.

The Law by Liana Christensen

Law is not one thing; it is many. I love not the law that pits adversarial sophistry to sophistry with no relation to truth.
I love not the law that infinitesimally divides, attempting mastery of that which is essentially uncontrollable.

I love not the law that is unjust.
But, oh, when cities crumble, when people's apocalyptic savagery spills the blood of a whole race, when lives are worth less than the election game . . . Oh, then, my heart cries out, where is the Rule of Law? Justice must prevail.

The initial Roman ideal is the free citizen dedicated to the Republic, determined, unperturbed by emotions, in control of affairs, prudent and ready to act for the benefit of the state. The following ode by Horace (65–8 BC) gives a good picture of the stability considered one of the major virtues of a true Roman.

Not the rage of the million commanding things evil,
Not the doom frowning near in the brows of the tyrant,
Shakes the upright and resolute man
In his solid completeness of soul;

No, not Auster, the Storm-King of Hadria's wild waters,
No, not Jove's mighty hand when it launches the thunder;
If in fragments were shattered the world,
Him its ruins would strike undismayed.

Exercise 1: The Roman Matron

Roman women had few political rights in this martial and patriarchal culture. It is worth considering, therefore, what ideals a Roman matron might have expressed.

The Roman Matron by Nandi Chinna
Not by fires
or sons becoming men
not by daughters given away
not by skies that offer no rain
not by the call of soft words
beauty, sweet music
not by stones on rocks
not death by sword
are we perturbed

strength is in grain and meat and water
metal hammered in hot fires

we have no rights
but the rights of the moon

the power of our blood
spilled in childbirth
our mothers daughters sisters
born on this fertile land

our men will gladly die
for Rome and for us
we will gladly live

The Roman Matron by Mags Webster

I'm longing for the time when he is dead and I can truly stand alone for the first time. No longer the daughter, no longer the wife. While he is out proclaiming his strength it is I who stay cloistered, controlling our wealth; telling him what to wear; overseeing our business in the fields. The men take his orders because the words have passed from my lips into his. When will the men of Rome realise it is more dangerous to keep women within the home than allow them freedom among their peers? This whole city is fractured by the silent power of our rage.

The Republic

The city-state of Rome remained a republic for almost five hundred years, slowly conquering all neighbouring nations and eventually holding supreme power in the Mediterranean world. As an empire, however, the Republic faced many challenges, among them the constant danger of powerful politicians taking control of the state.

The first to succeed in such a bid for power was Gaius Julius Caesar. A gifted rhetorician, charismatic politician and successful leader of military expeditions, he allied himself to two other influential Romans: Crassus and Pompey. The three soon wielded more power than the Senate. Caesar became consul and conquered Gaul (France), and was the first Roman to set foot on English soil. His report of his military conquest became a bestseller and classic of Latin literature.

The three men soon had a falling-out, however, of which Caesar emerged as the sole victor. When Pompey fled to Egypt, Caesar pursued him with his fleet and arrived in Alexandria to be presented with the head of Pompey — betrayed by his Egyptian allies. This was not the only surprise Egypt held for Caesar. A precious carpet was brought to him as a gift, and within it, the young princess Cleopatra. She had smuggled herself into his presence to enlist his help against her usurping brother. Fascinated by her beauty, brilliance and courage, Caesar became her lover and reinstalled her on the throne of Egypt.

When Caesar left Egypt, Cleopatra was pregnant with a son. This was not merely the incidental love affair of a successful general with a charismatic woman. Through Cleopatra the customs of ancient Egypt with its god-kings took hold of Caesar and through him, Rome. Already over-powerful, Caesar was infected by ideas of hierarchy and returned to Rome determined to achieve total control.

The Senate was soon reduced to a puppet-cabinet and Caesar gave himself supreme life-long power. The Republic was over. Even Caesar's friends were alarmed, and a group of conspirators, led by Brutus and dedicated to the ideals of the Republic, killed Caesar outside the Senate.

But the murder was not universally approved. For Caesar had not been a brute tyrant; he was a careful politician with great public appeal; a brilliant rhetorician, gifted writer and capable administrator; and a commander much loved by his troops. He had been generous to his opponents (he initiated the principle of clemency) and enjoyed much support in the general populace. Shakespeare captured the loyalty to Caesar in the speech of Mark Antony, given immediately after the assassination.

> ANTONY: Friends, Romans, countrymen, lend me your ears;
> I come to bury Caesar, not to praise him.
> The evil that men do lives after them;
> The good is oft interred with their bones;
> So let it be with Caesar. The noble Brutus
> Hath told you Caesar was ambitious;
> If it were so, it was a grievous fault,
> And grievously hath Caesar answer'd it.
> Here, under leave of Brutus and the rest, —
> For Brutus is an honourable man;
> So are they all, all honourable men, —
> Come I to speak in Caesar's funeral.
> He was my friend, faithful and just to me:
> But Brutus says he was ambitious;
> And Brutus is an honourable man.
> He hath brought many captives home to Rome,
> Whose ransoms did the general coffers fill:
> Did this in Caesar seem ambitious?
> When that the poor have cried, Caesar hath wept:
> Ambition should be made of sterner stuff:
> Yet Brutus says he was ambitious;
> And Brutus is an honourable man.
> You all did see that on the Lupercal
> I thrice presented him a kingly crown,
> Which he did thrice refuse: was this ambition?
> Yet Brutus says he was ambitious;
> And, sure, he is an honourable man.
> I speak not to disprove what Brutus spoke,
> But here I am to speak what I do know.

You all did love him once, not without cause ...
But yesterday the word of Caesar might
Have stood against the world; now lies he there.
And none so poor to do him reverence.
O masters, if I were disposed to stir
Your hearts and minds to mutiny and rage,
I should do Brutus wrong, and Cassius wrong,
Who, you all know, are honourable men:
I will not do them wrong; I rather choose
To wrong the dead, to wrong myself and you,
Than I will wrong such honourable men ...

Exercise 2: Brutus' Speech

Now consider Brutus' perspective and write his speech. Use all the rhetorical devices your imagination can muster to convince the citizens of Rome of the necessity of your deed.

Brutus' Speech by Penelope Brown

Friends, Romans and Countrymen,
Today my hands are bloodied,
But not my conscience.
Today I have killed a friend, but I have not killed a friend of Rome.
I raised my hand and in so doing, have I raised Rome.
For the higher Caesar climbed, the lower Rome fell ...
There are those among you who will say I was no friend to Caesar. Let them know their error.
I have been a greater friend to him than any man among you. By my hand I have saved that which he himself loved more. I have done no wrong.
My fault lies in one thing — my friendship for Caesar was not as great as my love for Rome!

But Brutus' intentions to reinstall the Republic fail in the political turmoil after Caesar's death. Caesar's stepson Octavian takes control of the empire and establishes himself as Caesar Augustus (Caesar's name becomes the title of all subsequent emperors). It is during Augustus's reign that Roman literature reaches its zenith in the work of Virgil (recall his passage on Orpheus in chapter 16), Horace and Ovid.

Ovid - The Women's Poet

The decidedly male tone of Roman culture echoes through almost all its literary productions, leaning always towards masculine themes. But there is one exception: Ovid. Like his contemporary Virgil, Ovid is a master of the Latin tongue. But unlike Virgil he is intensely interested in the female psyche and excels on the topics of both love and women. His elegant style has made him canonical reading for scholars and poets throughout the ages, and his *Metamorphosis* provides a brilliant summary of Greek and Roman myths.

In his own time Ovid was both popular and controversial. His unabashed writing on matters of love so incensed Caesar Augustus that the poet was banished from Rome and died heartbroken and homesick on the very fringes of the Roman Empire.

Among Ovid's earliest works are the *Heroides*, a collection of fictional letters written by Greek heroines that had been left by their lovers — Ariadne to Theseus, Penelope to Odysseus, Dido to Aeneas and Sappho to Phaon. Such a letter offers a special perspective into the depth of the female soul. Consider the way the poet begins the letter from Sappho to Phaon:

> When these letters, from my eager hand, are examined
> are any of them known to your eyes, straight away, as mine?
> Or would you not know where this work came from
> in short, unless you'd read the name of its author, Sappho?
> Indeed, perhaps you ask why my lines alternate,
> when I'm more suited to the lyric mode:
> my love is weeping: it's elegiac verse that weeps:
> I don't set any of my tears to the lyre.
> I'm scorched, as a cornfield burns, its rich crop set alight
> by a wild south-easterly, bringing lightning.

This short passage summarises the whole tragic course of Sappho's love affair with a much younger man, and one who is by no means her mental or emotional equal.

Exercise 3: Heroides

Write such a letter using any heroine of your choice, ancient or modern. This may be a good opportunity to add Penelope's perspective to the tales of Odysseus or to explore the theme of Sappho further.

Dear Phaon by Janet Blagg

Soon you will hear of my mortal death and I want to reassure you that it was not for unrequited love. You know me better I think.

Certainly I loved you — you the most beautiful of boys and certainly I have pursued you — some say foolishly — but you were my Siren and I would not be tied to any masthead.

Phaon, it was a wondrous couch we shared that golden Autumn long; how could I not shout after you when you turned your back and left without a word? Leaving me to weep after those white thighs of yours, re-membering them …

But these winter days at sea have brought a different Siren song. Farewell my dearest boy, there is another fire for me. Aphrodite herself is singing. Newly armed she is leaping with her ten white dolphins on the flinty high-capped waves of the wine-dark Aegean below my cliff. She is calling me, her lover, she is calling.

Farewell dear boy, love well. Sappho

Letter to Phaon by Lia Eliades
I wish to write this letter backwards my love
I breathe water, the rocks smash my head, the splash, falling up through the air to the cliffs edge, I stop, I stare off into the eternal sea, I shuttle backwards away from the edge stumble fall up and run backwards some more.
I wind my way through chaotic seaside walled towns, I swallow your name back from peoples ear's.
I speak backwards to everyone, I beseech, "NoahP? NoahP!? I ask.
Question marks hang alongside the vacant responses.
"Ochi Ochi, no, no," they shake heads side to side and go back to putting holes into nets laid upon their knees. The boats throw fish back into the sea. Fishermen empty their nets and row boats empty backwards to the shore.
The blisters on my feet mend, my robes and finery become cleaner, my pace assured, my poise in place. I am confident in finding you, just a misunderstanding that can be understood.
I pick up the basket of wine and bread that I dropped by the bridge. The basket hangs heavy on my arm again as I slip back into my house, my cloaks ribbons get untied and re-hung with a flourish, I walk to the window, I look down the garden lane.
With your back to me you grow in size, your gait haughty your hat dragged off your head, you are in my doorway our tongues go back into our mouths, you - unsqueeze me. We stand and drink each other in, we smile and we cry, we promise to meet again soon at the bridge.
"You love I," say you, I believe you.
"Back be will I," I can trust you.
We are wrapped and rolled in arms and fine silks, an eternal lovers embrace - you in I, I in you.
And it is like this that we stay still

Emperors and Tyrants

Augustus continues Caesar's political ambitions and allows himself to be revered as a god. Subsequently many Roman emperors saw themselves as divine beings over and above the restraints of mere mortals. Some forced their way into the surviving temple mysteries of Egypt and Greece, exposing themselves to experiences that, unprepared, they were unable to integrate. The result was a number of dangerously inflated and deranged personalities. Caligula, Commodus and Nero have become proverbial for excess and destructive aberrations.

Not all emperors followed this path. Augustus, for example, was able to integrate personal ambitions and use his organisational skills to secure the empire's constitution for several hundred years.

But Nero murdered several wives, as well as his own mother. His orgies and sexual excesses were legend and early Christians suffered greatly under his rule — fed alive to wild beasts to amuse the masses or used as torches to light Nero's gardens while he enjoyed their suffering.

Interestingly, Nero saw himself as a major poet, and gave long recitals of his poetry from which nobody was permitted to leave. When part of Rome burned during his reign, rumour spread that he watched the flames while reciting poetry on the roof of his palace. It was even said that he had ordered the fire lit to gain inspiration for his poetry.

Exercise 4: Nero's Speech

You are Nero, all-powerful emperor, and you did indeed order Rome to be burned for the sake of one immortal poem. Justify to a small circle of followers the sacrifice of the lowly and mundane for that one great poem. Take the opportunity, if you like, to write a really bad poem.

Nero's Speech by Nandi Chinna

Citizens of Rome
Who among you can deny
that a poem from the gods
is worth more than
streets, market places
mere buildings cannot compare
to the sweet soporific melody
of line and stanza
rhyme and recall
you have lost your houses
your children are
burned alive in their beds
your dogs and cats have fled

and drowned in the Tiber.
The fruits of your labours
are in ruins

I stand above the inferno
my muse alight with flame
the cries of the dying
release my nightingale
ideas are born and fly out
from my silken tongue
what greater honour than to
choke on the smoke
of divine inspiration
to collapse under the falling timbers
of literary greatness …

Nero by Liana Christenson
I don't expect anyone to understand. You are not granted the capacity to approach the sublime realm that is my allotted and fitting place. But I discern in your dull, coarse faces, some faint traces of loyalty, so I shall bend over and shine my light upon you, open up the bowels of my blessedness, and grant you the rare grace of my faeces, perfumed more finely than all the coffers of Araby. Know that a God goes among you! I see you bow your heads in fitting humility. Very well then, I shall extend my most magnanimous glory and bestow upon you the opening lines of my finest epic:

> Roseate imps are leaping and turning
> the temples are smoking and
> Rome it is burning

When Nero is eventually cornered by his enemies, he commits suicide. His last words are *Qualis artefix pereo*. 'What an artist is lost in me.'

The inflated ambition of emperors to be gods characterises one side of an increasingly decadent empire. On the other side is a general sense of disillusionment, loss of trust and the erosion of old ideals and time-honoured religious beliefs. The once confident Roman attitude towards life gives way to a mood of cynicism, disillusion and stoic resignation, well captured in the following piece by Seneca (4 BC – 65 AD):

> After death nothing is, and nothing death:
> The utmost limits of a gasp of breath.
> Let the ambitious zealot lay aside
> His hopes of heaven; whose faith is but his pride.

Let slavish souls lay by their feat,
Nor be concerned which way or where
After this life they shall be hurled:
Dead, we become the lumber of the world,
And to that mass of matter shall be swept
Where things destroyed with things unborn are kept:
Devouring time swallows us whole,
Impartial death confounds body and soul.
For Hell, and the foul Fiend that rules
The everlasting fiery gaols,
Devised by rogues, dreaded by fools,
With his grim grisly dog that keeps the door,
Are senseless stories, idle tales,
Dreams, whimsies, and no more.

Exercise 5: Roman Disillusionment

Imagine yourself a Roman in imperial times. You have experienced the vagaries of life, the disillusion with politics; you are disgusted by inflated emperors pretending to be god and acting less than human.

You are learned enough not to believe in the all-too-human gods of antiquity and the shallow hopes of those who seek salvation in the many sects that claim the day.

Write a piece that explores the mood of disillusionment with political lies, naïve beliefs and shallow reasoning. Give voice to the realm of resignation.

Roman Disillusionment by Mags Webster

Was there a time when there was hope? When there really was a meaning to things? What was the struggle for, where was the purpose to the journey? What use to me are gods and emperors when I stand here in the ruins of my own skin, sadness sticking to me like wet leaves? My shoulders are dull and heavy, pulling my head down into the dust where thousands of feet have marched, have stumbled, have fallen. I am fallen among ghosts and corpses and dust. I am level with the aching world.

20

Story Medicine

To understand the contribution of Christianity to literature we must first examine its roots in the prophetic tradition of Israel. The gift of prophesy was common among the Hebrew people, and the psalms of King David himself were often prophetic.

One of the most influential prophets was Elijah. After his long battle with Jezebel and her worship of Baal he departed the earth in a fiery chariot, leaving his 'cloak' to his pupil Elisha. Not a literal cloak, but the endowment of spiritual power that has inspired the Hebrew prophets of antiquity.

The prophets engage in powerful word work. They speak with the strength of conviction and the sureness of having been sent by their god. Frequently visited by vision, they have an immediate experience of the divine and record it in a language unmatched for its visual intensity, as for example in this initiatory vision of the prophet Ezekiel (1: 4):

> Then I looked, and behold, a whirlwind was coming out of the north, a great cloud with raging fire engulfing itself; and brightness *was* all around it and radiating out of its midst like the color of amber, out of the midst of the fire. Also from within it *came* the likeness of four living creatures. And this *was* their appearance: they had the likeness of a man. Each one had four faces, and each one had four wings. Their legs *were* straight, and the soles of their feet *were* like the soles of calves' feet. They sparkled like the color of burnished bronze. The hands of a man *were* under their wings on their four sides; and each of the four had faces and wings. Their wings touched one another. *The creatures* did not turn when they went, but each one went straight forward.
>
> As for the likeness of their faces, *each* had the face of a man; each of the four had the face of a lion on the right side, each of the four had the face of an ox on the left side, and each of the four had the face of an eagle. Thus *were* their faces.

Exercise 1: The Prophetic Vision

Put on the coat of Elijah: you are visited by a vision. Describe what you see when the heavens open and you feel yourself in the presence of your god or goddess. Be inspired by the vivid imagery of Ezekiel's account.

The Prophetic Vision by Jennifer Kornberger

A great cloud lowered around me like a whale descending and I put up my hand and the belly of the cloud was split and the splitting was a rending between worlds, a crack that separated a living branch from a dead branch. And out of the cloud came a being with two faces, one joined to the other and one face shone like a goblet held by a queen and was the colour of the rising sun and the other face was that of a howling dog. And there issued from the face of the rising sun a sound of water, a murmuring of waves and a waterfall and from the face of the dog there issued great howls that rent the earth and did battle with the noise of the waters.

The Burning Bush by Janet Blagg

I climbed a rusting staircase that spiraled up the side of a steep cliff, the sea boiling below me and the water green and red where great animals breached its writhing surface. And at the clifftop there grew a bush and as my body brushed its seed heads, each one burst into flame so that the whole bush was alight and I was afraid. But I was not burned; it was a cold fire.

And beyond the bush stood a doe, quivering, with eyes of velvet. And in the blackness of those eyes I saw a great figure, tall as a poplar, and the sky behind was curdling, milk and mica, as though stirred by a great wind. And in the silence the figure spoke and her voice came to me as if from the core of old rock. I heard it in my bones. A day and a night passed between each syllable and I cannot say what were the words they made. But like rock my heart cracked open; the lava is pouring still.

The prophets not only convey their visions; they serve as a conscience among the straying people. Acutely awake to the moral decadence of their time, they spoke out against idolatry, and those who were shallow in their worship and given to outward show. In this passage from Isaiah (1: 13), God speaks through the mouth of the prophet to his people:

> Bring no more vain oblations; incense is an abomination unto me; the new moons and sabbaths, the calling of assemblies, I cannot away with; it is iniquity, even the solemn meeting. Your new moons and your appointed feasts my soul hateth: they are a trouble unto me; I am weary to bear them. And when ye spread forth your hands, I will hide mine eyes from you: yea, when ye make

many prayers, I will not hear: your hands are full of blood. Wash you, make you clean; put away the evil of your doings from before mine eyes; cease to do evil … Come now, and let us reason together, saith the LORD: though your sins be as scarlet, they shall be as white as snow …

The prophets upheld the integrity of Israel in times of inner confusion and outer misfortune. They were witness to the intentions of god and announced the coming of the Messiah to crown the mission of Israel. Political as well as religious hopes were attached to his coming, though the prophets foresaw no powerful leader in the worldly sense. Their account points in a different direction, as in Isaiah (53: 3):

He is despised and rejected of men; a man of sorrows, and acquainted with grief: and we hid as it were our faces from him; he was despised, and we esteemed him not. Surely he hath borne our grieves, and carried our sorrows: yet we did esteem him stricken, smitten of God, and afflicted.

Prophetic Women

There are also many women who prophesy such Miriam, sister of Moses while the prophetess Anna in the Luke Gospel. Luke also tells the story of Mary, pregnant with Jesus, visiting her cousin Elisabeth, pregnant with John the Baptist. When they meet, Elisabeth's child stirs for joy and she breaks forth in prophetic speech:

… and said, Blessed art thou among women, and blessed is the fruit of thy womb. And whence is this to me, that the mother of my Lord should come to me? For, lo, as soon as the voice of thy salutation sounded in mine ears, the babe leaped in my womb for joy … And Mary said, My soul doth magnify the Lord, And my spirit hath rejoiced in God my Saviour.

For he hath regarded the low estate of his handmaiden: for, behold, from henceforth all generations shall call me blessed. For he that is mighty hath done to me great things; and holy is his name. And his mercy is on them that fear him from generation to generation. He hath shewed strength with his arm; he hath scattered the proud in the imagination of their hearts. He hath put down the mighty from their seats, and exalted them of low degree …

Three things are particularly striking about this passage. The first is that the women are pregnant in both body and spirit. The second is the communality of their prophesy, its divinely inspired conversation: they are not solitary like their male counterparts. The third how Mary's prophesy resembles Christ's Sermon of the Mount.

John the Baptist

The last prophet of the Jews is the first prophet of Christianity — John the Baptist. He rises amidst political unrest and religious expectancy. The Judea of his time was a protectorate on the fringes of the Roman Empire: the Jews had enlisted the Romans to their aid against the tyranny of Hellenistic rulers. But now the Republic had become an empire ruled by men claiming to be god — which was absolute anathema to the Hebrews, whose god allowed no other deities.

John the Baptist is the last prophet of the great style. His abode is the desert wilderness. He is clothed in rough camel hair and a leather girdle. His food is locust and wild honey. Like a searing flame he appears in the midst of confusion. His words have power, and masses come to hear him. He preaches baptism through the repentance of sin and prophesises the coming of the Messiah. He urges his followers to repent their greed for personal gain, their shallow worship, their idols, their lack of faith, their concern for only earthly matters. The fire of his words purges his listeners and shakes them into moral awakening.

His righteous anger flares hot against the Pharisees and Sadducees — the religious and political establishment among the Jews.

> But when he saw many of the Pharisees and Sadducees come to his baptism, he said unto them, O generation of vipers, who hath warned you to flee from the wrath to come? Bring forth therefore fruits meet for repentance: And think not to say within yourselves, We have Abraham to our father: for I say unto you, that God is able of these stones to raise up children unto Abraham. And now also the axe is laid unto the root of the trees: therefore every tree which bringeth not forth good fruit is hewn down, and cast into the fire. I indeed baptise you with water unto repentance: but he that cometh after me is mightier than I, whose shoes I am not worthy to bear: he shall baptise you with the Holy Ghost, and with fire … he will burn up the chaff with unquenchable fire. (Matthew 3: 7–9)

When he finally dips the repentant pilgrims into the waters of the Jordan they are vouchsafed a vision revealing the moral fibre in the fabric of their lives. They leave the desert inwardly reborn.

Exercise 3: The Sermon of John

Sermons are powerful word work. Language and speech at its most immediate and best. Be the Baptist, and hurl your holy indignation against the travesties of priests (or contemporary equivalents); call the masses from their lethargic sleep to repent their sin.

The Sermon of John by Mags Webster

I'm sick of the fact that no one listens to me. Why do I waste my time with you people. Look at you — how much did you pay to come here tonight? $500 a head? Was it worth it? Or maybe 500 bucks gives you the chance to be seen with the right people, in the right clothes, with your professional wives and professional walkers. And perhaps you believed the hype about me — how inspirational I am; what privations I've endured; how I can motivate people. Therefore you don't want to be the only one out of your friends, your peers, your competitors, your enemies who missed out on my speech — the only one I'm making here on my 10 city tour. And will you listen to a word of it? Will there be anything you take out into that cold night which will change the way you are and the way you see other people? You are described as the A-listers, the elite. It means nothing. It means only that you can afford to be here. And this is not the real world, ladies and gentlemen — the real world is out there in the wet and the cold, with real blood and real tears. This luxury, this excess, this life à la carte — it is an illusion. Wake up before it is too late.

The Prophet by Lachlan McKenzie

Each day I will sit in the Heart of the City, in the Sight of The King, and each day the guards will take me back. I will not speak for my message is exhausted of words. I will sit and in reflection I will lead an example of quiet thoughtfulness, for only by example will my message be heard.
In the Sight of our vain King I will sit daily and in my thoughts I will slowly peel the gossamer onion of our time- ever simplifying- and each day as the guards remove my body from the Heart of the City, the King will see a man pass who is each day younger and more beautiful than the last.

The mission of John ends when Jesus appears among the crowds to be baptised by him.

> But John forbad him, saying, I have need to be baptised of thee, and comest thou to me? And Jesus answering said unto him, Suffer it to be so now: for thus it becometh us to fulfil all righteousness. Then he suffered him. And Jesus, when he was baptised, went up straightway out of the water: and, lo, the heavens were opened unto him, and he saw the Spirit of God descending like a dove, and lighting upon him: And lo a voice from heaven, saying, This is my beloved Son, in whom I am well pleased. (Matthew 3: 13–17)

This is the moment that Jesus becomes the Christ and embarks on his mission. The spirit leads him into the wilderness, where he is three times tempted by Satan. Returning from his trials he gathers his first disciples and starts to teach and heal all over the countryside. His fame spreads and multitudes gather to hear him speak.

The Sermon on the Mount

Christ's first speech, the Sermon on the Mount, stands in great contrast with the preachings of the Baptist. John cleansed souls from their past and made way for the new. The revelation of Moses and the law of Jahwe echo in his words. Christ's sermon is very different in tone. The Christ presents himself not as a prophet, a messenger of the divine, but as the fulfiller of prophesies. He speaks with unprecedented authority of the god within. His teachings transcend the law. He calls for a radical change and the awakening of inner authority. The sermon begins with a series of almost mantric benedictions (Matthew 5: 3–12).

> Blessed are the poor in spirit: for theirs is the kingdom of heaven.
> Blessed are they that mourn: for they shall be comforted.
> Blessed are the meek: for they shall inherit the earth.
> Blessed are they which do hunger and thirst after righteousness: for they shall be filled.
> Blessed are the merciful: for they shall obtain mercy.
> Blessed are the pure in heart: for they shall see God.
> Blessed are the peacemakers: for they shall be called the children of God.
> Blessed are they which are persecuted for righteousness' sake: for theirs is the kingdom of heaven.
> Blessed are ye, when men shall revile you, and persecute you, and say all manner of evil against you falsely, for my sake.

Rich as these words are, many layers of meaning in the original Aramaic language that Jesus spoke are lost in translation. According to native Middle Eastern mysticism, each word has at least three translations and many different levels of meaning. Christ calls for a new attitude of soul that exceeds the requirements of traditional law.

> For I say unto you, That except your righteousness shall exceed the righteousness of the scribes and Pharisees, ye shall in no case enter into the kingdom of heaven. Ye have heard that it was said by them of old time, Thou shalt not kill; and whosoever shall kill shall be in danger of the judgment: But I say unto you, That whosoever is angry with his brother without a cause shall be in danger of the judgement. (Matthew 5: 20–23)

The Sermon's very heart is the call for the divine nature within every human being, that innermost essence that is able to turn greed into generosity, hatred into love.

> Ye have heard that it hath been said, An eye for an eye, and a tooth for a tooth: But I say unto you, That ye resist not evil: but whosoever shall smite thee on thy right cheek, turn to him the other also. And if any man will sue thee at the law,

and take away thy coat, let him have thy cloak also. And whosoever shall compel thee to go a mile, go with him twain …

Ye have heard that it hath been said, Thou shalt love thy neighbour, and hate thine enemy. But I say unto you, Love your enemies, bless them that curse you, do good to them that hate you … (Matthew 5: 38–44)

John's sermons were a call to repent from the sins of the past. Christ makes a mantric invocation of the true self within each human being. Matters of moral conduct are addressed as the natural, creative, expression of the fully awakened self — the uncensored revelation of the divine within the human self.

Exercise 4: The Sermon on the Mount

Imagine the divine — the source of all authority — vibrantly alive within you; make your sermon a revelation of this innermost self. Begin with a series of benedictions (Blessed are …).

Sermon on the Mount by Janet Blagg

Blessed are the wounded, for in their attempt to breathe the air of freedom they
   shall make the world anew;
Blessed are the drowning, for they shall know the value of a piece of straw and
   give praise for the ground beneath their feet;
Blessed are the poor, for they shall know the joy of seashells and fallen leaves, of
   friendship, song and winter sun;
Blessed are the children, and the child at the heart of every soul, for the child is
truly greater than the man.

Sermon on the Mount by Nandi Chinna

look into the space between
inhalation and exhalation
and let go there
untangling like a net of thoughts
drifting out
on the receding tide to
the place inside you
small on the outside
huge on the inside
that expands to encompass
the whole world
breathe it in
breathe it out

and in the space in between
falling into the gap
between theory and practice
is the path that is not there
walk upon it with trust
and it unfolds like a map
it's not on tv
not in a book
it's there in the space
behind closed eyes

The Parable

Fifty-one parables are recorded in the scriptures and there were surely many more. The founder of the Christian faith is one of the most productive story makers of all time. In fact he is the first fully-fledged story maker I know of.
The Old Testament contains only few parables. Plato produced one or two parables, and so did Confucius. But Christ's constant creation of tales is unprecedented. It is interesting that his followers have focused on his few sermons (Christ as a preacher) and missed his profuse story-making (Christ the poetic innovator and forerunner of story-makers). The parables of Christ are immediate Story Medicine, situational and remedial; they are poetic improvisation on the roadside, at the dinner table, the inn; unpremeditated and straight from the heart. By means of simile and metaphor they convey complex insights and spiritual realities in language that everyone can understand. They leave the listener free, suggesting a truth without preaching it, as in these two short examples describing the Kingdom of Heaven.

> Then said he, Unto what is the kingdom of God like? and whereunto shall I resemble it? It is like a grain of mustard seed, which a man took, and cast into his garden; and it grew, and waxed a great tree; and the fowls of the air lodged in the branches of it.
>
> And again he said, Whereunto shall I liken the kingdom of God? It is like leaven, which a woman took and hid in three measures of meal, till the whole was leavened.

Luke is particularly rich in parables, among them the parable of the prodigal son (Luke 15: 11) and of the great banquet (Luke 14–16).

Exercise 5: The Kingdom of Heaven

The transformation of lifeless concepts into enlivening pictures is the poet's domain. A parable allows us to practise this art. Find at least three metaphors, similes or pictures to describe the kingdom of heaven.

The Kingdom of Heaven by Kristina Hamilton

The Kingdom of Heaven is like a bowl of fruit with seven varieties of colour, form and sweetness. I will describe them to you:

1. The Passionfruit. Passion always comes first. Without it, nothing follows. The seeds of passion are many — tangy, a bit crunchy, but surrounded in sweet syrup.
2. The Pear. It divides itself into two halves quite easily. This and that. Hither and thither. Take me hither, sweet pear.
3. The Apple. Your centre is a star, a temptation to the heavens.
4. The Kiwifruit. So thin-skinned you are, but so sweet beneath.
5. The Peach. Your skin tickles me.
6. The Banana. Long and curved like the sickle of the moon.
7. The Cherry. Round and red with just one stone — a heavenly reminder of the Bowl of Life.

The radical teachings of Christ soon brought him into conflict with priests, rulers and scribes, culminating when he raises Lazarus, brother of Mary Magdalene, from the dead, described in John (11: 43):

> And when he thus had spoken, he cried with a loud voice, Lazarus, come forth. And he that was dead came forth, bound hand and foot with graveclothes: and his face was bound about with a napkin. Jesus saith unto them, Loose him, and let him go.

From this point the chief priests and Pharisees plotted his death. Their concern was in part for political stability, but to understand the ferocity of their reaction we need to consider the ancient Mystery traditions. The Egyptian priesthood expunged the memory of Ekhnaton for divulging secrets they wanted kept behind temple walls. The raising of Lazarus can be seen in a similar light. Here the central act of temple initiation — spiritual rebirth after three days of deathlike sleep — is performed publicly, challenging hierarchical traditions and heralding a new era of spiritual independence.

When Christ suffers death on the cross and after three days is resurrected, his spiritual impulse takes hold of his disciples (like the mustard seed of his parable) and his power to use the word creatively is likewise resurrected in the poetic productions of his followers.

21

Tongues of Fire

Christ's power to use the word creatively is resurrected in the work of his disciples, beginning with the event of Pentecost:

> And suddenly there came a sound from heaven as of a rushing mighty wind, and it filled all the house where they were sitting. And there appeared unto them cloven tongues like as of fire, and it sat upon each of them. And they were all filled with the Holy Ghost, and began to speak with other tongues, as the Spirit gave them utterance … Now when this was noised abroad, the multitude came together, and were confounded, because that every man heard them speak in his own language. And they were all amazed and marvelled, saying one to another, Behold, are not all these which speak Galilaeans? And how hear we every man in our own tongue, wherein we were born? (Acts 2: 1–8)

This passage links the outpouring of the Holy Spirit to a major poetic event: speaking in other tongues. I have always experienced poetry as a kind of universal language: it reaches beyond the confines of national languages. Poems speak to everyone because everyone recognises in them the language of their innermost self. Another great example of 'poetic Christianity' is in the opening verses from the Gospel of St John:

> In the beginning was the Word, and the Word was with God, and the Word was God. The same was in the beginning with God. All things were made by it; and without it was not any thing made that was made. In it was life; and the life was the light of human kind. And the light shineth in darkness; and the darkness comprehended it not.

The Pentecostal event is the first outpouring of divine creativity. In the many paintings that depict it, Mary the mother of Christ occupies the central place, the Apostles pictured around her in the same way they were gathered around Christ before the Crucifixion, reflecting an ancient tradition that saw the Holy Spirit as the Christian manifestation of the feminine wisdom of the Old Testament — Sophia — and Mary the new representative of this wisdom, the earthly vessel of the Holy Spirit.

Exercise 1: Tongues of Fire

In a sermon for or a poem, take the the theme of Pentecost as a preparation for what is to come in the future, when the inspired and artistic use of language will once more overcome what separates human beings from one another.

The Tongues of Fire by Ann Harrison

I walked into the room and they all sat quietly. No one spoke. The silence roared. I could feel the tension, the derision, the accusations ,the pent up emotion. I wanted to walk out and leave the silence to speak only to them. This I could not do. I stood and greeted all present and I began to speak, to lay out the mosaic of events for all to hear and see. The silence changed to a babble of acknowledgement. The word was manifest. The spirit was amongst them and they cried in angst for the judgement they had metred out to one and all. The word had explained. The word had united. The word healed .

Tongues of Fire by Jennifer Kornberger

The world is @ a new address
wireless, it makes its own connections
tongues of fire flit in the air
words have been cloned with oxygen
I'm breathing your message
remember, I'm case sensitive
so Capitalise on my invisibility.

The Letters of Paul

Pentecost marked the beginning of much word work. Once the flame was lit among the first disciples, the fire of inspiration spread far and wide. One of the most avid writers of early Christianity was Paul, initially a passionate and active persecutor of the new Christian sect. After his epiphany on the road to Damascus, the former Pharisee became the untiring apostle of the young church, establishing Christian communities across the Roman Empire.

Paul keeps in contact with the communities through writing letters remarkable for their personal tone. In them we meet Paul's unshakeable faith, founded in his personal experience of the resurrected Christ. But in spite of his closeness to Christ (or maybe because of it) Paul is often argumentative, impatient and angry at his Christian brothers and sisters.

Letters are a perfect literary form for his message. They combine intimacy and distance. The writing voice is immediate, full of urgency, but received as a letter the content can be pondered over time and gradually integrated. Letters slow down the conversation, allowing a careful response and informed judgement.

Writing to the Corinthians on the theme of community and love, Paul soars to poetic heights. He describes the ideal Christian community in terms of the human body (community) and its parts (members), in which everyone finds their place through their individual contribution.

> For to one is given by the Spirit the word of wisdom; to another the word of knowledge by the same Spirit; To another faith by the same Spirit; to another the gifts of healing by the same Spirit; To another the working of miracles; to another prophecy; to another discerning of spirits; to another divers kinds of tongues; to another the interpretation of tongues: But all these worketh that one and the selfsame Spirit …

The passage culminates in the invocation of love as the essential ingredient of community.

> Though I speak with the tongues of men and of angels, and have not love, I am become as sounding brass, or a tinkling cymbal. And though I have the gift of prophecy, and understand all mysteries, and all knowledge; and though I have all faith, so that I could remove mountains, and have not love, I am nothing. And though I bestow all my goods to feed the poor, and though I give my body to be burned, and have not love, it profiteth me nothing. Love suffereth long, and is kind; love envieth not; love vaunteth not itself, is not puffed up, Doth not behave itself unseemly, seeketh not her own, is not easily provoked, thinketh no evil; Rejoiceth not in iniquity, but rejoiceth in the truth; Beareth all things, believeth all things, hopeth all things, endureth all things. Love never faileth: but whether there be prophecies, they shall fail; whether there be tongues, they shall cease; whether there be knowledge, it shall vanish away …

Exercise 2: Letter to the Community

Write to a community about the nature of social life or the importance of mutual love (or any other quality essential for the harmonious working of community). Find metaphors for the functioning of the ideal society.

On Community by Anna Minska

Isn't it peculiar how we have not yet stood face-to-face, said hello, exchanged names, shook hands – all the customary introductory greetings – and yet I know you are there. Out There. In here. I know you well. I love you completely. Funny, isn't it, how there can be recognition before seeing, kinship before relationship, community before contact. How else does one explain the conversations hovering about the footpath, the deep commitments floating outside time? It is something about journeying towards the middles of things; each of us, on our own epic voyage to the Heartlands. It is something about being born into the perimeter of the world and learning, through trial and tribulation, triumph and treachery, that setting out – setting off inwards – is imperative to carve out the true depths of things. Perhaps we collect ourselves, each other, along the way. Perhaps we reflect, for a moment, the scope of what has already been and what is yet to come. A community of mirrors. A network of temporary travellers... someday, somehow, if we are brave enough, soft enough, we arrive at the core. The heart of things. We have collected our true colours and we wear them proudly, joyously, humbly. We love our own reflection. We love. We are home.

Letter to the Community by Jean Hudson

Mothers, do not keep your young locked up in air-conditioned houses, surrounded by plastic toys, television and computers.

Let your children run free. Allow them to feel wet grass between their toes and sand on their feet. Let them hear birdsong and smell flowers in the forest. Allow them to climb trees and splash in puddles. Do not keep them indoors because you are afraid of dangerous people. Forget about the cleaning and the laundry. Go outside with your children. Take off your shoes, fly a kite, and maybe build a sandcastle. Do not instill your own fears into your children. Let the child within you come forth.

Sophia and the Writings of the Gnostics

The Christianity we have come to know through the canonical writings of the church comprises only a section of what was once a far more diverse response to the impulse of Christ. That diversity does not reflect the status that Paul assigned to women:

> Let your women keep silence in the churches: for it is not permitted unto them to speak; but they are commanded to be under obedience, as also saith the law.
> And if they will learn any thing, let them ask their husbands at home …

Attitudes like this are not founded in the initial teachings of Christ. But male church leaders favoured the texts of selected male disciples, and feminine spirituality suffered the same fate as that of many Christian sects that were eradicated or suppressed in later times.

One of the most widespread and poetically vibrant approaches to Christianity was Gnosis, which drew on elements of the Greek and Hebrew religions, as well as Hindu, Buddhism and Zoroastrism. Gnosis means 'knowing' and emphasises personal experience and originality of thought and expression. A 'knower' was not considered mature until they had reworked their teacher's knowledge into an original contribution

— a far cry from obediently accepting the received word. Gnosis had its centre in Alexandria, the city founded by Alexander to bring about the fusion of Western and Eastern culture.

Central to Gnosis is the story of Sophia, the female counterpart and heavenly wisdom of God who, according to the scriptures, partook in the creation of the world. *In Proverbs 8: 22*, Wisdom speaks of herself:

> The LORD possessed me in the beginning of his way, before his works of old. I was set up from everlasting, from the beginning, or ever the earth was. When there were no depths, I was brought forth; when there were no fountains abounding with water. Before the mountains were settled, before the hills was I brought forth: While as yet he had not made the earth, nor the fields, nor the highest part of the dust of the world. When he prepared the heavens, I was there … and I was daily his delight, rejoicing always before him.

Christian Gnosis respected feminine and masculine spirituality and regarded Mary Magdalene as one of the closest disciples of Christ. In the *Pistis Sophia*, discovered in the eighteenth century, the resurrected Christ teaches his disciples about the fall and restoration of the Sophia. Mary Magdalene features prominently in this discourse, in which Christ relates how the divine Sophia was lured by envious deities into the dark chaos, where she was ceaselessly oppressed. Christ, however, returned her to her place of glory and restored her *pleroma* — the fullness of her wisdom. Freed from the power of chaos, the Sophia sings her praises:

> Light has become a crown on my head and I will not be without it, nor will the emanations of Darkness steal it from me. And even if all matter moves I will remain silent. And even if all material things are destroyed and remain in chaos and darkness, I will not be destroyed. For the light is with me and I myself am with the light.

I understand the teachings of the Pistis Sophia first as the macrocosmic restoration of Wisdom through the deeds of Christ, and second as the purification of the human soul through contact with Christ. The soul becomes pure, or 'virginal' again and so is able to reflect the wisdom that permeates the cosmos. Individual soul merges with the world soul.

In *'Thunder, Perfect Mind'*, one of the Gnostic scriptures found in Nag Hammadi, we sense the power of feminine spirituality that emanates from this invocation in which the Sophia speaks for herself:

> Do not be ignorant of me.
> For I am the first and the last.
> I am the honoured one and the scorned one.

I am the whore and the holy one.
I am the wife and the virgin.
I am the mother and the daughter.
I am the members of my mother.
I am the barren one and many are her sons.
I am she whose wedding is great, and I have not taken a husband.
I am the midwife and she who does not bear.
I am the solace of my labour pains.
I am the bride and the bridegroom, and it is my husband who begot me ...
I am the utterance of my name ...

Exercise 3: Invocation of the Holy Sophia

Let the paradoxs of Thunder, Perfect Mind inspire your own invocation of the Sophia. Spiritual experience resists confinement by the logic of intellect. This is an invitation to liberate yourself from conventional concepts. I recommend that you repeat the first two lines of the text above as a poetic catapult. Use the 'I am' form and let the Sophia speak for herself:

Invocation of the Sophia by Edward Laurs
Do not be ignorant of me.
For I am the first and the last.
I am the shadows and reflections.
I am the rhyme and the curse.
I am the rug at your hearth and the rock in your sandal.
I am the balm on your burns and the sting of the wasp.
I am the sweetest wine and the oldest water.
I am the purring kitten and the roaring lion.
I am the perfume and the rot.
I am the smile and the slap!
I am the golden dream of hope and the chilling spectre of endless nightmares.

Mary Magdalene

Mary the Mother of Christ embodies the Sophia before the fall. Mary Magdalene exemplifies the restored Sophia; her destiny mirrors the fall and rebirth of feminine wisdom. She is the sinner (as in alienated from the spirit) who through love for Christ reaches purity again. Her soul reflects the world soul. She is the 'woman who knew all' as she is often referred to in the Gnostic tradition, and one of the major proponents of an intimate, feminine and poetic Christianity that has been suppressed since its inception. Christ freely acknowledged her wisdom:

> When Maria finished saying these words, he said: 'Excellent, Maria. Thou art blessed beyond all women on earth, because thou shalt be the Pleroma of all Pleromas, and the completion of all completions.'

Peter, founder of the organised church, resented Mary's wisdom, and the fact that she seemed to be preferred by Jesus:

> When Jesus finished saying these words ... Peter leaped forward, saying to Jesus: 'My Lord, we are not able to suffer this woman who takes the opportunity from us, and does not allow any one of us to speak, but she speaks many times.'

This attitude is even more apparent in fragments that survive of the recently found *Gospel of Mary*. Mary has just related to the other apostles something Jesus had told her:

> But Andrew answered and said to the brethren, Say what you wish to say about what she has said. I at least do not believe that the Saviour said this. For certainly these teachings are strange ideas.
>
> Peter answered and spoke concerning these same things. He questioned them about the Saviour: Did He really speak privately with a woman and not openly to us? Are we to turn about and all listen to her? Did He prefer her to us?
>
> Then Mary wept and said to Peter, My brother Peter, what do you think? Do you think that I have thought this up myself in my heart, or that I am lying about the Saviour?
>
> Levi answered and said to Peter, Peter you have always been hot tempered. Now I see you contending against the woman like the adversaries. But if the Saviour made her worthy, who are you indeed to reject her? Surely the Saviour knows her very well. That is why He loved her more than us ...

Peter's attitude, supported by the ethos of the time, became the trend of the Christian faith. The result was the crippled Christianity we have inherited, devoid of heavenly wisdom and the feminine qualities of soul.

Exercise 4: Magdalene's discourse on the Sophia

Give voice to Mary Magdalene, the 'woman who knew all'. Let her, who has had authentic experience, describe the Sophia, the heavenly Wisdom, the female side of God. Look for a poetic form appropriate to those who are led by love and wisdom.

From: The Magdalene does Seven Drawings by Jennifer Kornberger

In the small clearing
between two breaths
a tree grows imperceptibly.

When the light is ripe
the heart breaks into pictures.
Then it will be fire —
fire that seeps
like the fine, fine blood
of planets,
rhythmic
combustible.
You will know fire
because it will give
you its tongue,
it will take up its abode
at the kernel and at
the edge of things;
set its camp in the desert,
in a skull,
a maverick or a saint.
Fire will draw on you
with the damp fingers
of a child,
announce its intentions
in the script of the seasons,
at the rim of the sky where
cirrus cloud dissolves and returns
turns towards the earth;
and fire will know you —
the way your dark resin
catches light and because
you remained still
while it wrote
its name on you.

The Book of Revelation

Another disciple beloved of Christ was Mary Magdalene's brother Lazarus, author of the Gospel of St John and the Book of Revelation. Through John, Gnostic concepts such as the Logos as the major power in the creation of the world entered into the fabric of the Bible.

The Book of Revelation, one of the most poetic productions of early Christianity, has troubled many Christians with its visionary energy and intensity. I see it as a deep description of initiatory experiences. One of its most famous passages (*Revelation 12*) is the vision of the Sophia:

> And there appeared a great wonder in heaven; a woman clothed with the sun, and the moon under her feet, and upon her head a crown of twelve stars: And she being with child cried, travailing in birth, and pained to be delivered. And there appeared another wonder in heaven; and behold a great red dragon, having seven heads and ten horns, and seven crowns upon his heads. And his tail drew the third part of the stars of heaven, and did cast them to the earth: and the dragon stood before the woman which was ready to be delivered, for to devour her child as soon as it was born. And she brought forth a man child, who was to rule all nations with a rod of iron: and her child was caught up unto God, and to his throne. And the woman fled into the wilderness, where she hath a place prepared of God, that they should feed her there a thousand two hundred and threescore days.

A passage like this has many layers of meaning: one is the dramatic process that always accompanies the birth of the higher self in the soul. Another is the travail of the world soul, of the eternal feminine wisdom, as it is persecuted and attacked by the powers of chaos.

Exercise 5: And there Appeared a great Wonder

Imagine yourself a gnostic vouchsafed with an overwhelming vision that illumines the spiritual conflict that in the depth of your soul, every soul and the world-soul simultaneously. Use your imagination and allow it draw on the potent imagery that has inspired the writer of the apocalypse.

> **And there Appeared a Great Wonder by Ann Reeves**
>
> A man with a gaze stern and soft,
> Without compromise yet ever forgiving
> In one hand is a rosebud, blushed red.
> In the other a serpent, dreamy, indolent.
> The man sets down the rose, the snake too.
> The rose becomes seven, perfection and pure.
> The snake coils on itself,
> takes time unto itself.
> In its grasp, time is constricted, made tighter, harder, brittle.
> As the serpent uncoils,
> time clatters to earth,
> splits into fragments.
> Men hurl themselves upon the grit of seconds, of minutes.
> Greedy, grasping, piling hour upon hour
> in their own miserly hordes.

They scratch and snarl, hiss and spit,
stealing the very thing they will squander.
The seven roses breathe sweet perfume,
perfect in their fullness.

And There Appeared a Great Wonder in Heaven by Sophia
A tiny boat upon the high seas
Lifted skyward by huge waves
Smashed into thousands of pieces
Splintered across the ocean

People like tiny dots
Flung into the cold grey darkness
Bobbing, drowning…
barely clutching wooden debris

Then a bright light shone in the darkness
A siren echoed into the night
A great splash sent
circles of life to waving hands
Roping them in
Covering them
with blankets of hope

Fishers of men
and women and children
Drowning in a sea of tears
Rescued by the hand of love
Landed on the rock of becoming

The Book of Revelation is full of potent images — consider the four riders of the apocalypse we met in chapter five, and the last great picture presented by John: the heavenly Jerusalem (Revelation 21–22):

> And I saw a new heaven and a new earth: for the first heaven and the first earth were passed away; and there was no more sea. And I John saw the holy city, new Jerusalem, coming down from God out of heaven, prepared as a bride adorned for her husband …
>
> And he carried me away in the spirit to a great and high mountain, and shewed me that great city, the holy Jerusalem, descending out of heaven from God, Having the glory of God: and her light was like unto a stone most precious,

even like a jasper stone, clear as crystal; And had a wall great and high, and had twelve gates, and at the gates twelve angels, and names written thereon, which are the names of the twelve tribes of the children of Israel …

And the twelve gates were twelve pearls; every several gate was of one pearl: and the street of the city was pure gold, as it were transparent glass. And I saw no temple therein: for the Lord God Almighty and the Lamb are the temple of it. And the city had no need of the sun, neither of the moon, to shine in it: for the glory of God did lighten it, and the Lamb is the light thereof …

And he shewed me a pure river of water of life, clear as crystal, proceeding out of the throne of God and of the Lamb. In the midst of the street of it, and on either side of the river, was there the tree of life, which bare twelve manner of fruits, and yielded her fruit every month: and the leaves of the tree were for the healing of the nations.

The heavenly Jerusalem is John's vision of a new earth. It is the most daring prophesy: a new world born from the old; the future of the earth and humanity inseparably linked. The heavenly Jerusalem contains the moral essence of the physical world, depicted in terms of precious stones and in the sum of all achievements wrought through human effort, symbolised in the cubic shape of the city.

The vision of the heavenly Jerusalem is the concluding picture in the Bible, and resonates with the Bible's opening picture — the Garden of Eden — also representing the earth. The heavenly Jerusalem is the higher octave of Paradise. Eden was a garden, a gift, bestowed by the divine. To John, the heavenly Jerusalem is a city, a place built and achieved through human effort inspired by the Christ.

Exercise 5: The Heavenly Jerusalem

Take the passage from the Book of Revelation as a stimulus for your own vision of a future earth and humanity. Follow the writer of the Apocalypse and use pictures rather than concepts. Use the phrase 'And I saw a new heaven and a new earth' as an entry formula to set the mood.

I saw a new Heaven by Nandi Chinna
We will be made of steel
one day we will be made
of plastics and re-buildings
of molecular chains and revisions
rewritings of skin and organs
and bones

we will be under surveillance

our lives documented
at railway stations
in shopping centres
at airports

we will be movie stars
of the surveillance epic
we will never go unnoticed
even if we believe
that we have no talent
the cameras will roll
and we are the un willing
participants in this documentary

and when this epoch
is at its end systems fail
green shoots erupt
through concrete
branches of trees
smash glass and birds
make nests in computer terminals
there is always a back up
into history a camera
recording the growing
of moss on streets.

22

Braiding of Words

Ireland was one of the few civilised places of the ancient world not conquered by the Roman armies, and its indigenous culture thrived for a long time undisturbed on the western fringe of Europe.

Ireland has a long spiritual history. In prehistoric times large circles of standing stones bore witness to the ancient worship of the sun and the first attempts to punctuate time with a calendar of stone. Then around 400BC, Celtic tribes from the east settled, merging with the old culture: the Celtic priest absorbed the former megalithic spirituality without extinguishing the primal power of its mysteries. The druids, as the priests were known, had a strong hold on the population through their powers of magic and healing. Much of their training was undertaken in great secrecy and went on for twenty years and more.

The Druidic Training

To become poet, singer and harpist was the first stage on the path to Celtic priesthood — knowing the old stories and being able to make new ones. Poetry and song were considered much more than entertainment. The great stories united the people through the memory of a heroic past; they stirred up courage and rekindled hope. Tales also served as a means of healing, for the individual and the community. A bard was also priest, doctor, psychologist, political adviser.

The young bards would be apprenticed to a master singer, or minstrel, who they followed from place to place and court to court. Some minstrels had a whole school at their heels. Even as late as the sixth century, Christian–Irish monks underwent Bardic schooling, and Columba (d. 597), the great Irish saint and missionary, had many years of bardic training. Ollam, one of the most famous of wandering bards, knew about three hundred and fifty songs by heart — some the size of the Odyssey. The singers were loved for their gifts of story making and telling, but feared for their word magic.

Taliesin

Scotland and Wales too were places of Celtic culture. The Tale of Taliesin (a Welsh version of Merlin) may serve us as an example for poetic initiation practiced in Celtic tradition.

The story begins with the sorceress Ceridwen and her ugly and doltish son Morfan. In order to address her son's disadvantages, the enchantress resolves to make him into a great bard by means of her magic arts.

> Ceridwen brews the cauldron of inspiration, gathers herbs, boils them for a full year, muttering incantations to create a brew that will yield inspiration (and the wisdom of the ages) to the first who tastes it. Her boy-servant Gwion tends the fire and stirs the brew. But on the last day of the work, three drops of the boiling liquid fall on his thumbs and when he puts his thumb into his mouth for relief, Gwion, instead of Morfan, receives the poetic gifts of the ages.
>
> Fearing Ceredwins revenge he runs away. But the sorceress soon comes after him. Using his new magical powers, Gwion turns himself into a hare, but Ceridwen turns herself into a fierce greyhound. When he changes himself into a fish, she becomes an otter. When Gwion becomes a bird, she pursues him as a hawk. Finally Gwion turns into a grain of wheat, but Ceridwen changes into a hen and swallows the grain. Soon, Ceridwen falls pregnant, though she did not lie with any man. She realises that the baby is Gwion, and she and Morfan resolve to kill the babe as soon as it is born. But when the baby is born, he is so beautiful that Ceridwen cannot kill him. She sews the child into a bag and sets him adrift on the sea.
>
> Meanwhile, the notoriously unlucky prince Elphin is fishing for salmon at his father's weir on May Eve. His father Gwyddno, lord of the land, has sent him there to turn his luck on a day that has always yielded a great catch. But he catches nothing. When he throws his net one last time, he hauls in a leather bag. Opening it, he beholds the beautiful child and cries out, 'Taliesin!' (which is Welsh and means radiant brow.) 'Yes, Taliesin will be my name,' replies the baby 'How is it that a baby can talk?' marvelled Elphin. And Taliesin, already a bard, replied in verse:
>
>> Once I was a handsome youth
>> Tutored in the hall of Ceridwen …
>> Learned I grew in ancient laws
>> And in the speech before words.
>> For the wisdom I gained
>> I had to flee from her hall
>> From the anger of Ceridwen
>> Her terrible call of revenge
>> I fled and shifted my shape

Since then I have been a hare
And the shape of a crow
And a green frog
High I jumped with roe-bucks
Over the thickets barring my way
I have been a raven of prophetic speech
A cunning fox, a sure swift and
A squirrel hiding in vain.
I have been the red deer
And hot iron hammered in fire
I have been the keen edge of a sword
And the cry in the midst of battle
I have been a struggling bull, a bristling boar in a ravine
I have been a grain of wheat and was eaten and born again
Put in a bag I floated on the sea
I know I have come to light again.

Taliesin remembers all that he has been. A born poet and destined to become a druid, he recalls what others forget: his initial oneness with the world. Before he was born he drank from the cauldron of Ceridwen, a sorceress and witch. But the hag mask merely hides the radiant face of the Celtic goddess of poetry and inspiration, Ceridwen. Through her initiations Taliesin has become a bard.

Exercise 1: The Cauldron of Ceridwen

Let us approach Ceridwen, goddess of wisdom and poetic inspiration. Let us drink from her cauldron of imagination and remember all that we have been before we were born. For example:

Cauldron of Ceridwen by Ali McKenzie

I have been the foulest of plagues and the most sacred of spells.
I have been an insect sheltering in the skull of the world.
I have been the fallen body of my ancestors reclining in the underworld.
I have been the daughter of both a coven and a conquering warrior.
I have been rebirthed and transformed.
I have been the horns of an antler and the corpse of a crow.
I have been the spirit of a dove and a suppurating wound.
I have been locked within stone and woven into a great web.
I have been the froth on a milky star and the grief of a nation.
I have been the wisdom of light and the mist of mourning.

Druid and Nature

The name Taliesin signifies more than a single individual. Like Arthur, Merlin or Gawain, it points to a rank or office, and dates back to the first bearers of those names. Each generation had its Arthur and Taliesin.

When baby Taliesin tells Elphin all he has been — hare, fish, crow, frog, roebuck, the raven of prophetic speech — it testifies to the druid's ability to merge with nature and become one with its beings and elements. A striking example of this close relationship with nature in all its manifestations is preserved in the old Irish Rann of Amergin. Read it out loud and imagine how it would feel to be all the things.

> **The Rann of Amergin**
> I am the wind that blows over the sea, Ah-ro-he!
> I am the wave of the sea, Ah-ro-he!
> I am the sound the sea makes, Ah-ro-he!
> I am the ox of the seven combats, Ah-ro-he!
> I am the vulture upon the rock, Ah-ro-he!
> I am the ray of the sun, Ah-ro-he!
> I am the fairest of plants, Ah-ro-he!
> I am the wild boar, Ah-ro-he!
> I am the salmon in the water, Ah-ro-he!
> I am the lake in the plain, Ah-ro-he!
> I am the word of knowledge, Ah-ro-he!
> I am the spear-point of battle, Ah-ro-he!
> I am the god who kindles fire in the head, Ah-ro-he!
> Who makes wise the company on the mountain?
> Who makes known the ages of the moon?
> Who knows the secret resting place of the sun?
> Ah-ro-he!

Both bard and druid experienced these states of oneness. While Taliesin remembered all that he had been, this writer merges with the here and now of wind and wave, vulture and rock. 'I am' rather than 'I have been'. Repeating 'I am' at each line gives a mantric quality that is further strengthened by the Ah-ro-he until the poem acts like an invocation. We feel as if the bard becomes the very things he describes: he braids himself into the fabric of nature by means of word magic.

Exercise 2: An Ancient Rann

Let us braid ourselves into the fabric of nature. Write a piece where each line starts with 'I am' and ends with 'Ah-ro-he!' or some other exclamation. Feel how the repetition carries you and how each line asserts your oneness with all the beings that surround you.

Ancient Rune by Nandi Chinna

I am the dark night — shhhhh
I am the city sleeping in its bed — shhhhh
I am the humming of electrical wires — shhhh
I am the whirring of white goods on standby — shhhh
I am the somnambulist walking through quiet rooms — shhhh
I am the hissing of wheels on tarmac — shhhh
I am the wind whistling through car windows — shhhhh
I am the journey at dawn through wet streets — shhhh
I am the rustling of dawn birds — shhhh
I am the leaves of trees absorbing the sunlight — shhhh
I am shards of grasses shedding their seeds — shhhh
I am germinating underground and reaching for light — shhhh
I am water seeping down through the earth — shhhh
I am the footsteps walking through wet grass — shhhh
I am the taste of water trickling over stones in a creekbed — shhhh
I am the inhalation — shhh
I am the exhalation — shhh

The Tale of the Bard

When Elphin returns home with the babe, he and his wife take good care of the foster child. With a bard in his house his luck turns for the better.

At that time Maelgwn was high king of the country. When Taliesin reaches thirteen years of age, Elphin is invited to a feast at the court. At the dinner table the courtiers boast about the beauty of Maelgyn's queen and the unsurpassed skill of his bards. Elphin replies that his own wife was just as beautiful and virtuous as the queen and that his bard Taliesin surpasses those of the court. When the king hears of Elphin's claims, he imprisons Elphin in the dungeons and sends his lecherous son Rhun to seduce his wife and prove him wrong.

Taliesin, however, has a vision of what has happened to Elphin. He informs his foster mother and together they trick Rhun and so ruin the king's ploy. The king however will not let Elphin go until his bard has competed with his own.

Taliesin soon arrives at the court and with his supreme magic stupefies the king's bards. When asked by the king who he is, Taliesin gives the following account:

> Primary chief poet am I to Elphin. And my native country is the place of the
> Summer Stars. John the Divine called me Merlin, but all future kings shall call

me Taliesin. I was nine full months in the womb of Ceridwen. Before that I was Gwion, but now I am Taliesin. I was with my king In the heavens When Lucifer fell into the deepest hell. I carried the banner before Alexander. I know the names of the stars from the North to the South … I was in the ark with Noah,… I witnessed the destruction Of Sodom and Gomorrah. I was Partriach to Elija and Enoch. I was in Africa before the building of Rome. I came here to the remnant of Troy. I was with the Lord in the manger of the ass. I upheld Moses through the water … I was at the Cross with Mary Magdalene … I received the Muse from Ceridwens Cauldren….

I was instructor to the whole universe. I shall be until the judgement on the face of the Earth …

Taliesin who remembers the whole biography of humanity as a personal experience, reveals the depth of his Bardic initiation. Such claims might seem boastful or strange, but to students of the word they sound a familiar note. By means of our poetic imagination we have travelled on a similar journey. We too have been present at the fall of Lucifer, at the flood, and have given voice to Mary Magdalene …

Exercise 3: The Tale of Taliesin

Boldly testify as to who you are as a poet. Recall your poetic biography; the places you have been, the situations you have inhabited with your imagination. Use themes that have spoken to you in this book; themes that have shaped your poetic self. Start with: 'I am' or 'I was.'

The Tale of Taliesin by Janet Blagg

I was there with Cassandra in the dark temple when the treacherous Apollo spat in her mouth. I was with Joan when the king's men and churchmen lit the faggots beneath her and I was with Socrates, laughing at the first performance of bitter Irony. I wept with Eve when she was cast from her beloved garden. I was in the tomb with Antigone, mourning the end of honour, and with Inanna I waited at the gate of the dark sister. I sat down in the desert with Gnostics, men and women who knew that they too were God.

I was there, O beloved, at every point at which History stopped, if only for a moment, and just stared.

Taliesin by Edward Laurs

I am Taliesin:
I scuttled across the dreamtime with the great spider, defining this land.
I cheered as Gilgamesh hurled Enkidu into the Sumerian sand.
I beheld the sun shining at Salisbury before the stones were raised.

I cultivated the mysteries of Isis in the pyramids.
I ate the cloned fish of the Nazarene.
I launched the javelin under Zeus' eyes at Olympus.
I sat in the forest and learned the secrets of happiness from the Prince who was whispered it by a flower.
I saw the first biting rat that began the dark night of Europe's rot.

I am Taliesin by Ann Reeves
I was a boy when Adam lost a rib.
I was with Abraham when he made that choice.
I was a builder of Solomon's temple.
I carried the tray for the Baptist's head.
I counted the gold in the purse won by Judas.
I thrust the spear into He on the cross.
I mourned at the rock that covered that cave.

The king remains unconvinced and demands a contest between Taliesin and his bards. His bards however can do nothing but mumble in Taliesin's presence. Then Taliesin commences his song of the wind. And as he sings the winds start to blow and become a storm. The storm rages with such violence that the walls of the castle shake. King Maelgwn quickly frees Elphin from imprisonment. Here is the beginning of Taliesin's song:

Taliesin's Song of the Wind
Discover thou what is
The strong creature from before the flood,
Without flesh, without bone,
Without vein, without blood,
Without head, without feet;
It will neither be older nor younger
Than at the beginning …
Great are its gusts
When it comes from the south;
Great are its evaporations
When it strikes on coasts.
It is in the field, it is in the wood,
Without hand and without foot,
Without signs of old age,
Though it be co-eval
With the five ages or periods;
And older still,
Though they be numberless years.

It is also so wide;
As the surface of the earth;
And it was not born ...
It neither sees, nor is seen.
Its course is devious
And will not come when desired
On land and on sea
It is indispensable.
It is without an equal,
It is four-sided;
It is not confined,
It is incomparable;
It comes from four quarters;
It will not be advised,
It will not be without advice ...
It is sonorous, it is dumb,
It is mild ...

It is astounding how thoroughly the bard knows the wind and how intimately he observes and experiences it!

Exercise 4: Song of the Elements

Choose an element of nature — water, air, earth; clouds, mountains, a tree, fire, rivers, lakes, a patch of land — and give it the treatment Taliesin gave wind. Avoid modern abstraction and scientific explanation. Stay with immediate experience; sense the 'being' of your element.

Spinifex by Nandi Chinna

I am spinifex
I am fluorescent green laughter
I am the warm blanket
that is spread on sand
it snuggles down warm
is held together
my roots are tunnels of life
they spread like veins and arteries
beneath red deserts
they deliver into the cool
fault lines in rock
they are the strong limbs

of my thorny crown
I am god and the Devil
I appear soft and inviting
like the most delicious rest
but touch me and you will
cry out in alarm
chaplets of blood will tattoo your skin
blades of pain behind your eyes
Ha! I am the chameleon
the joker the jester the clown
I hold down the world
like a net without me
the earth would blow away
a hundred million sand particles
drifting into space
forming lonely galaxies
in the orbits of stars
I am a home
I draw circles in spirals
in the sand around me
imitating the tracks of snakes
tiny animals huddle beneath me
if not for my benevolence
they would burn and fry
evaporate into the deepest blue sky
their souls longing for the cool caverns
of my stems and roots
Oh! I can be cruel
I can pierce the jaw bones
of lost sheep who perish
of hunger and thirst
I can slice the pads of
foraging wallabies lame and bleeding
Ha! I will stop the walker in their tracks
you can't get through here
a barbed gate protects the sacred places
I am also the healer
the balm the helper
at night I am trampled by tired kangaroos
who curl up in my wiry windless warmth
I keep the soil moist
so that others can germinate and grow

I am baskets I am fish traps
I am the weaver of the world.

Song of Sound by Ali McKenzie

I am the sound,
The smallest vibration
Parting the air,
An elastic wave on vocal velvet,
Released, collected, dispersed
On musical tones.
A net of repose
Drowned voices.

I am sound,
Stretched and coiled, crowded waves
Echoed, absorbed and held together
Through audible focus and
Intense impression,
A noise of notes
Irregular patterns and
Jagged edges.

I am sound,
A smooth sensation
The pitch of a splash
The plunge of a roar
The well of deep and
Delicate touches
A funnel of tiny bones
An unborn murmur.

Taliesin is able to summon the wind because he knows the wind. The song is an invocation, magical wordwork. His words carry power. At his command the wind comes to his aid. In Celtic countries the power of the word to change reality continues into Christian times. Under this new influence the magical spell turns into the wishing spell and the wishing spell into prayer.

A wishing spell is less direct. The authoritative command is supplanted by faith in the goodwill of words. The prayer is even less direct than the wishing spell, seeking the aid of the intermediary angels and saints. A vast heritage of prayers, blessings, hymns, incantation, wishes and spells was preserved by peasant folk and carefully passed from generation to generation.

Thanks to the research of Alexander Carmichael in the Outer Hebrides, a portion of this heritage has been preserved. The charm of the poetic spells and prayers he recorded lies again in the harmonious merging of pagan and Christian elements. The wish charm below is a good example of a pagan wishing spell, loosely tied to the Christian 'Our Father'.

Good Wish
Wisdom of serpent be thine,
Wisdom of raven be thine,
Wisdom of valiant eagle

Voice of swan be thine,
Voice of honey be thine,
Voice of the son of the stars.

Bounty of sea be thine,
Bounty of land be thine,
Bounty of the Father of heaven.

Exercise 5: Irish Wishing Spell

Create a wishing spell, using the same structural pattern as the above: 3 times 3 lines, each triad starting with the same word. Enjoy the strict form. (Limitation can be a great liberator.) For example

Blessing by Janet Blagg
Stone of the peach be thine
Stone of the river too
Stone singing in the heart of the fire, for thee.

Ocean of emerald be thine
Ocean of naked joy
Ocean sighing, lapping all night at thy shore.

Song of the sea in thy heart
Song of the earth in thy breast
Song of the wind in thy bones, in thy mouth, in thy breath.

Two Christianities

Consciousness of this intimate relationship with nature survived longer in Ireland than in any other part of the Western world. For many centuries it co-existed and eventually merged with the Christian impulse. The many legends woven around St Brigid fuse Christian and pagan elements. Like the Celtic goddess Brigantia, St Brigid hung her wet cloth on a sunbeam to dry and like Christ she turned water into ale, healed the sick and made the dumb speak. The close connection of Irish spirituality with the Palestine story appears too in the legend that St Bride (who lived five hundred years after Christ) was the midwife of the Virgin Mary and Godmother of Jesus.

St Patrick is often credited with bringing Christianity to Ireland, but in fact Christianity existed in Ireland long before. This first impulse of Irish Christianity focused on the goodness in human beings and worshipped Christ as Lord of the Elements, present in every part of nature.

St Patrick was, however, the first to establish the Roman Catholic Church on Irish ground, a form of Christianity which emphasised the hierarchically organised church, the sinfulness of the human being and the fallen state of nature. For the Roman Catholic Church the cross stood mainly for death. The Irish monks added the circle or sun sign, balancing death with the symbol of resurrection: the circle representing the omnipresence of Christ in nature and in the human being.

To the early Irish monks the division between a heaven above and a nature below that was devoid of spiritual beings was utterly alien. They lived, breathed and prayed in a world permeated by nature spirits and angels, and ruled by the resurrected Christ. Gathered in monastic settlements, monks formed brotherhoods and sisterhoods of equals dedicated to the spiritual quest. Couples and families often formed part of the community and celibacy was voluntary rather than enforced.

In many of these Irish monasteries, learning and culture were kept alive for centuries while the rest of Europe fell into a state of barbarism after the fall of the Roman Empire. The Book of Kells illuminates the artistry and skills of monks who dedicated their lives to the creation of manuscripts. Some of the larger monasteries had choirs of up to three hundred voices, and singing went on continuously, day and night.

The Braiding of Words

Present in many Irish prayers and blessings is the weaving of spiritual reality into the everyday. The division of above and below; elevated spiritual beings and lowly matter, does not exist in the Celtic conception. The saints, angels and even Christ can be artfully braided into the fabric of the world with words and poetic incantations.

In this atmosphere of religious devotion arose poetry in praise of god and nature. The extract from the benediction below bears witness to the powerful merging of Christian belief with the worship of nature. It is radiant with the verdant, fresh green of Ireland itself.

Praised be the rain and dew
Praised be all spirits
Praised be the nights and days
Praised be darkness and light
Praised be cold and heat
Praised be frost and snow
Praised be the lightning and the clouds …

Exercise 6: Praise

Write a piece which braids the love of nature with enthusiasm for the divinity. Start each line with the words 'praised be' and add as many benedictions as your heart will yield. Note the subtle ecstasy that takes hold of your soul in such a feast of praise.

Praised be the rain on the rooves
Praised be the recycling bin
Praised be the mice who do not enter the house
Praised be the tilt of the roof
Praised be the passive solar house
Praised be the architects of all sound houses
Praised be the clean clouds filing in from the Indian Ocean
Praised be my friend's life and death
Praised be my son's breath

23

The Poetics of Battle

For a long time the Norsemen — Vikings — lived isolated north of the civilised world. In primitive dwellings in the inhospitable lands of Denmark and Scandinavia they battled fierce winters and the long Arctic nights. In the early Middle Ages the seafaring warriors became the terror of the civilised world, journeying as far as the Mediterranean and the Black Sea.

A warlike people, they preserved their own brand of imagination and gave birth to a vibrant mythology untainted by the veneer of civilisation. Myths and legends that wove the destiny of gods and human beings, of giants, dwarves, witches and elves, into a fabric of dramatic tales.

Nordic myth is potent with images, like a sword drawn in words, like thunder and lightning, or dark clouds opening onto a mighty, tragic panorama of conflict and destruction. Contrast and tension predominate in the Edda, the Icelandic texts that preserves many of the ancient sagas.

The Wala

The Voluspa is the oldest and most important part of the Edda. It is sung by the Volva or Wala, the prophetess and visionary of the Germanic world. The Wala tells the great tale from the beginning of the world to its end. She was the healer and sorceress, the spirit woman whose knowledge encompassed the past and the future, and she stands for all women who held power among Germanic tribes. Even the god father Odin has to invoke the spirit of a dead Wala in times of dire need.

The Wala could end famine and banish illness. Her powers were feared and her insights demanded. Among the Nordic people she played a major role as the link to the gods and in divining their will. In the Erik's Saga, the arrival of such a seer is described:

> She arrived in the evening with the man who had been sent to escort her. She was dressed like this: she wore a blue mantle fastened with straps and adorned with stones all the way down to the hem. She had a necklace of glass beads. On her head she wore a black lambskin hood lined with cat's fur. She carried a staff with a brass bound knob studded with stones. She wore a belt made of touchwood, from which hung a large pouch, and in this she kept the charms she needed for her witchcraft. On her feet were hairy calfskin shoes with long thick

laces which had large tin buttons on the ends. She wore catskin gloves, with the white fur inside. When she entered the room everyone felt obliged to proffer respectful greetings …

The composer of the Voluspa was such a woman and the Edda is her visionary account. The many dramatic tales of Odin and Thor were first woven on the loom of the female imagination.

The Giant Ymir

According to the Wala, the world begins with a large abyss, an enormous gap between Muspelheim, the land of eternal cold, and Niflheim, the land of warmth and light. When the ice melts, the primeval giant Ymir is born, followed by the first cow, Audhumbla, the mother of all beings. When she licks the ice, Buri is born from the drops from her tongue. Buri is the father of Bor who is the father of the Nordic gods Odin, Vili and Ve. Here is the Wala in her own words:

> Silence I ask of the Sacred Folk,
> Silence of the kith and kin of Heimdal:
> At your will, Valfather, I shall well relate
> The old songs of men I remember best.
>
> I tell of giants from times forgotten,
> Those who fed me in former days:
> Nine Worlds I can reckon, nine roots of the Tree,
> The wonderful Ash, way under the ground.
>
> When Ymir lived long ago
> Was no sand or sea, no surging waves,
> Nowhere was there earth nor heaven above,
> But a grinning gap and grass nowhere.

Mark the repetition of consonants in the third stanza: *Was no sea or sand, no surging waves*. Alliteration is typical of Nordic writing as the hexameter is of Greek. Now read the third stanza out loud, stressing the repeated consonants. Stand and stamp with your foot as you speak, and feel the strength, the rising power of will, the tenacity of rhythm and surge of courage that pulses through Nordic poetry. This is a language that heats the blood, inspires courage, a language that summons the warrior to war and heroic exploits — the hallmarks of Nordic myth.

The gods Odin (Wotan), Vili and Ve are quick to slay Ymir. Tearing the giant's body apart they create not only the world but also the unending conflict between the race of giants descending from Ymir and their own race of gods, the Aesir.

The World Tree

Te Germanic tribes saw the world as a gigantic ash tree, Ygg-drasil. Some of its seven roots reach deep down to the Norns, the three mighty goddesses who guard the past, present and future as they weave the destiny of gods and men. Other roots reach to the fountain of youth and to the well of the giant Mimir who guards the most secret knowledge.

The tree is always green and the whole world rests in its shade. Its topmost branches are clothed in clouds of light and heavenly dew falls upon its leaves. Its mighty trunk connects the world of giants, gods and men. Countless animals live in and on its branches; a golden cockerel sits on top to warn of giants. An eagle surveys the whole tree and between his eyes is perched a hawk. Four stags devour the foliage and bark of the tree, and Nidhoggr, a dragon, gnaws at its roots. The squirrel Ratastock darts constantly between the dragon and the cock, creating discord.

Exercise 1: The World Tree

Become a prophet and create your own version of a world tree that encompasses the universe. Use picture language and avoid explanation.

World Tree by Lachlan McKenzie

For every leaf a day, and every tiny piece of powdering mist in morning's first ray, a man, a woman, a child.

The dewdrops run together as cities, then empires waging war down sapling boughs.

Every bud and twig a story built from the choices of men, and every branch the destiny of a people, and the greater branches are nature and the shape of man, and of woman herself

The World Tree by John Stubley

My world tree was a big old jarrah
lying down its roots and leaves and sighs
in the middle of a clearing
it shadowed for itself. It stood
and bent and reached with the sideways song
of cold water creeks flowing and tumbling
through a path of lowdown sky.
I'm sure it spun and danced in the night —
shedding the half-finished tree-house
my brother had gently wedged
between its sunburnt branches
for me …

Trees and groves were sacred to all Germanic tribes, and Odin himself created Ask and Embla, the first human beings, from an Ash and an Elm tree. Odin (Wotan) is head of the Aesir. His powers surpass those of all other gods and he is the master of magic and poetry, of prophesy and the meaning of the Runes, the alphabet of the gods.

The Quest for Knowledge

Odin gained his knowledge in the beginning of creation by hanging himself for nine days on the world tree, sacrificing himself to himself.

> Wounded I hung on a wind-swept gallows
> For nine long nights,
> Pierced by a spear, pledged to Odin,
> Offered, myself to myself:
> The wisest know not from whence spring
> The roots of that ancient rood.
> They gave me no bread, they gave me no mead:
> I looked down; with a loud cry
> I took up runes; from that tree I fell…
> Learned I grew then, lore-wise,
> Waxed and throve well:
> Word from word gave words to me,
> Deed from deed gave deeds to me.
> Runes you will find, and readable staves,
> Very strong staves …
> Know how to cut them, know how to read them,
> Know how to stain them, know how to prove them …

Odin's passion for knowledge leads him to the depths of the world tree, where the giant Mimir guards the fountain of wisdom. Determined to taste from the well, Odin plucks out one of his eyes to pay for the drink.

This quest for magic knowledge is shared by gods and men alike. Riddles and word games were means to test true knowledge and hence the real power and standing of gods, dwarves and men. Here is a riddle by the hammer wielding god Thor:

> THOR: What are clouds called, that carry rain,
>   In all the worlds there are?
> ALVIS: Clouds by men, Hope-of-Showers by gods,
>   Wind-ships by vanes
>   By giants Drizzle-Hope, by elves Weather-Might,
>   In Hel Helmet-of-Darkness

Exercise 2: Solving a Riddle

Question: What are the winds (or seas or mountains) called in all the worlds that exist: the world of human beings, gods, vanes (gods of a different race), giants, elves and hel (underworld). For example: Storms by women, breath-brides by gods, thin-wings by vanes, Fliff-fluffs by giants, Ruffleflem by elves and Flungstergroins by the inhabitants of hel

What are mirrors for? by Jeremy Sheldrick
Among Gods the mirror was the world of semblance
Among Men the mirror was a source of great love
Among elves the mirror was an unfolding story
Among dwarves the mirror was a way to look at the ceiling
Among giants it was a way to look at the floor

The Ecstasy of Battle

Odin is first and foremost the god of battle; master of warlike passion who seizes the warrior with holy fury. When thunder rolls and lightning flashes, he is the leader of the wild hunt, riding into battle with his host of dead warriors. He inspires ecstasy in battle. For the ancient Norse, war was a religious experience that brought the gods closer. The warrior felt the breath of Odin in the ecstasy of fight; felt a strength beyond himself as the hammer of Thor thundered through his blood and the Valkyries rode at his side.

Death in battle was the highest ideal. Seized by ecstatic frenzy, warriors hurled themselves into battle, seeking death or victory. They were accompanied by Odin's messengers, the Valkyries, spirit women. In the moment of death the hero saw the brilliant Valkyre at his side, seizing his soul and carrying it to Valhalla, the abode of the gods, to join Odin's host of fallen heroes. In Valhalla the heroes train every day for the great and terrible battle at the end of time, when the giants will mount their final attack. In the evenings they feast in the great golden hall of Odin.

Women too were warriors. Freydis commanded her own ship. On an expedition to Vinland (America) while visibly pregnant, she confronted a whole tribe of Scraelings (native Americans) alone. With a sword she tore open her clothes and slapped the blade against her naked breast. The sight so shocked the advancing Scraelings that they turned and fled.

Exercise 3: The Battle Fury

Use your imagination to enter a state of frenzy, every fibre of your body longing for battle. Grip your sword, axe and shield and hurl yourself into the fight, seeking victory or death. Savour the clash and thunder.

Battle Fury by Jennifer Kornberger

She is running beside me. She shows me how to breathe with her, long and clear, she shows me how the glint of light on my silver lipped axe will grow when it tastes blood. She points to the one I will slay and the one who will slay me. She is the roar in my throat. I swing the silver, I am the axe and the howl, I am the arc of blood surging into her arms.

The Ecstasy of Death by Ailsa Grieve

We were to run beyond our sight.
into the raw cusp of the horizon.
i took my heart thick into my hand
held it to the wind, and showed it my path.
and then i ran because there was nothing else to do,
the stars and gods awaiting me,
after a battle that had been whispered to me every dawn since the beginning.
we moved from running into the white morning cloud to running with our eyes closed,
to have them open would be to murder ourselves.
only age-old tradings with the wind granted us a straight line of passage.
and as I entered my opponents awaiting sword i called upon my star,
to take me home and birth me again, to birth me again to run.
to always run in the misty battle.

Thor and Loki

Thor is a son of Odin. He drives a chariot drawn by goats and his strength is unmatched. His magical hammer Mjolnir is a thunderbolt that he hurls against the giants and that always returns to his hand.

Loki is one of the most intriguing figures of the Nordic pantheon. He is a constant companion of the gods, and they often seek his advice. A spirit of fire, his wit and cunning are sometimes helpful, sometimes destructive. Loki is a trickster and fond of disguises. He loves to exploit the weakness of the gods and often misleads them with false advice. His tongue is quick in slander and he lacks all sense of honour and moral conduct. In the end it is his wile that brings destruction to the gods.

The Twilight of the Gods

The twilight of the gods began with the death of Baldur, the second son of Odin, so handsome in appearance that he shone like light. He was the kindest of the gods and loved by all. When he had a foreboding dream, his mother, the goddess Frigg, asked all beings never to harm him. She received pledges from fire, water, wind, stone and metal, bird and beast — all but the small and harmless mistletoe. The gods thought Baldur was invulnerable, and threw swords and lances to test his immortality. But the scheming Loki knew that the mistletoe had not sworn to Frigg. He cut it into an arrow and persuaded Baldur's brother Hodur to throw it at him in jest. Baldur was hit and died. With the radiant Baldur gone, kind-heartedness, happiness and justice vanished from the world and the doom of the last great battle approached.

The twilight of the gods, Ragnarok, is unique to Norse myth. The gods are mortal and perish at the end of days when the giants attack. On this day of doom Loki is unbound from his chains, the giants raise their arms and, allied with the Fenris Wolf and the Midgard Snake, with evil witches and malignant dwarfs, they attack Valhalla.

Odin rides his eight-legged steed Sleipnir into the battle against his arch enemy the Fenris Wolf, but the beast devours him. Vidar, his son, avenges his father and tears the wolf apart. Thor slays the Midgard Snake, but dies from her venomous fumes. The battle rages and the world ash shakes as gods and giants kill each other. Loki and Heimdal slay each other and fire spreads across the world. Then darkness falls and all is gone. The ancient world has perished and the Wala recounts in her prophetic vsion:

> Brother shall strike brother and both fall,
> Sisters' sons slay each other,
> Evil be on earth, an Age of Whoredom,
> Of sharp sword-play and shields' clashing,
> A Wind-Age, a Wolf-Age, till the world ruins:
> No man to another shall mercy show …
> Yggdrasil trembles, the towering Ash
> Groans in woe; the Wolf is loose …
> The sun turns black in the summer after,
> Winds whine. Well, would you know more?
> Earth sinks in the sea, the sun turns black,
> Cast down from Heaven are the hot stars,
> Fumes reek, into flames burst,
> The sky itself is scorched with fire.

The twilight of the gods is one of the most dramatic events in the world of myth. The mortal gods and their arch enemies the giants, confront and kill each other. Fire, earthquake and tidal waves destroy the world.

Exercise 4: The Twilight of the Gods

Write about the violent end of the world, the battle of all battles, when monsters rise and even the gods are overcome. Imagine yourself as a Wala seeing this vision unfold. Use Nordic names or invent new ones.

The Last Battle by Mags Webster

The axe is at work in the forests murdering the trees. Will I have time to get home to you, my love, before the axe falls on me, on us all? The sky is torn, the jagged clouds rage across the horizon, a weak sun spills pale honey over the destruction. My ears are infected with the cries of men dying in the mud; my shoes are stained red with their agony. And still I run home, to you, so that I may touch your cheek and hold you to me. The promise of a thousand Valhallas is not as powerful as you — I have broken from the ranks of the glory-hunters and left them to the old ways of the old world. I do not fit there any more. Out of this tumult will come a new understanding; and it will speak with your voice and be called by your name.

The Twilight of the Gods by Julie Dickinson

Your certainty and your comfort are stripped away.
Your knowing, your language even self definition dissolves.
A history, a ring of relatives cannot support you now —
Map, dictionary, rule book are useless in this blank unknown.
Will I step forward, to engage this raw green foreignness
Will backward longing capture me, or
Will a sense of curiosity, of adventure, lure me on?
Wait …………… pause …………
'Inaction is death.'
I breathe deeply …… I raise my heel …..

A few gods survive the Ragnarok, and the earth, drowned in a deluge, rises again, refreshed and green. Vidar leads the new generation of gods toward a new time, and Baldur returns, bringing justice and law.

The twilight of the gods portrayed the fading of the Germanic vision, the death of a world peopled with gods and giants, witches and dwarves, monsters and benevolent spirits. Their world vanished, along with the world of their gods. But there remained hope that in the future their vision would return and with it the gods, a hope centred around the figure of Vidar, Odin's son who slew the Fenris Wolf.

Exercise 5: Vidar

Write about Vidar, the waiting god who survives the end of the world — a sign of hope, a beacon of light, bringer of a new vision, a new world.

Vidar by Veronica Antalov

Silent one
Where do you dwell?
Could we brush against you
and not even know
We welcome you in our lives
We are waiting, expectant
We are knowing
Walk among us
Spread your soles on our earth.

Vidar by Shaktima Kotulla

Willows weep beneath the earth
Doves circle with bloodied claws
Mountains move to hide

A wind pulls all vapors from the air
The air pulls all life from things
With the coming of change
The change has come

All things are undone
Waiting to die into a sleep
That will dream them
Real again.

24

The Grail Quest

When Germanic peoples destroyed the last remnants of the Roman Empire, Europe returned to a feudal society, combining the newly acquired ideals of Christianity with a Germanic rigour of conquest. The Romans had conquered with organised armies and the Germanic peoples had fought in tribal groups. Now a new ideal emerged: the medieval knight journeying alone in search of renown.

While the knight is also engaged in larger battles to fulfill his feudal obligations, his real mission only emerges on his individual quest, unsupported by family, tribe and companions. He pits himself against potent foes and against loneliness. Relying on his own strength he faces inner and outer battles as he meets his destiny.

Quests were undertaken in search of adventure, in defense of honour, for the love of a lady or in pursuit of worldly wealth. But the highest ideal was the quest for the Holy Grail, combining outer and inner effort in the search for true identity and spiritual attainment. Wolfram von Eschenbach described the archetypal stages of this quest in his epic *Parzival*, written around 1200, but set 300 years earlier. Parzival pioneered modern individuality. Though clothed in medieval garb, his adventures resonate with contemporary challenges.

Legends of the Holy Grail

In the background of the many tales of questing knights hovers the sublime image of the Holy Grail. Numerous legends were told of its origin. According to one, the Grail was the most precious stone in the crown of Lucifer, long before his fall from heavenly grace. When, seduced by his own pride, Lucifer battled God, the stone was struck from his crown and fell to earth. A chalice was later carved from the stone and was the very chalice Christ used at the last supper.

In this version of the legend, Joseph of Arimathea collected the blood of the crucified Christ in the chalice and kept it as his secret possession. When Joseph was interred in a tower by zealous Jews, to die without food or drink, the Grail kept him alive for years until he was freed by the Romans when they conquered Jerusalem. Joseph then gathered a small community of Christians, among them Mary Magdalene, and fled to France to avoid further persecution. According to one tradition they made their way to Glastonbury, England, as in Tennyson's version:

The cup, the cup itself, from which our Lord drank at the last sad supper with his own. This, from the blessed land of Aromat — after the day of darkness, when the dead went wandering o'er Moriah — the good saint Arimathean Joseph, journeying brought to Glastonbury, where the winter thorn blossoms at Christmas, mindful of our Lord. And there a while it bode; and if a man could touch or see it, he was heal'd at once, by faith, of all his ills. But then the times grew to such evil that the holy cup was caught away to heavens and disappeared.

In Parzival the Grail is returned again to Earth when angels bestowed the holy vessel on the first Grail King, Titurel. Wolfram's Grail is a rare and miraculous stone kept in the remote castle of Munsalvaesch:

A warlike company lives there. I will tell you how they are nourished. They live from a Stone whose essence is most pure. If you have never heard of it I shall name it for you here. It is called 'Lapsit exillis'. By virtue of this Stone the Phoenix is burned to ashes, in which he is reborn … Further: however ill a mortal may be, from the day on which he sees the Stone he cannot die for that week, nor does he lose his colour … Such powers does the Stone confer on mortal men that their flesh and bones are soon made young again. This Stone is also called 'The Gral'.

Parzival

Parzival is a complex epic, the hero's quest interwoven with other tales and encounters. It begins with the adventures of Gahmured, Parzival's father, and his knightly adventures in the Orient. On his return, Gahmured wins a great tournament and the hand of Herzeloyde, Queen of Waleis. Their marriage is short as Gahmured soon leaves for new adventures and is killed through treachery.

The Queen, who is with child, is seized by violent grief and vows to protect her son from the dangers of knighthood. When Parzival is born she withdraws with a few servants to a remote forest wilderness. There, Parzival grows up in ignorance of his royal descent and his father's fate. Roaming through the forest one day he chances upon three knights. Seeing them in the splendour of their armour, the naïve boy takes them for angels and falls to his knees. One of the knights explains to him the calling of knighthood. Parzival returns home determined to become a knight and to join the company of King Arthur's Round Table.

Herzeloyde reverts to cunning. She dresses the unsuspecting Parzival in fool's clothing and gives him a pony that stumbles with every step, hoping that if her son is mocked by all, he will soon return to her. She gives him a few last words of advice: never cross a stream that is murky and always kiss a lady and take a ring from her (she means to take her for a wife).

When Parzival leaves, Herzeloyde dies of grief. Parzival knows nothing of this and rides on into the world. He comes to a little rivulet that a hare could easily have jumped over, but seeing the water is murky he follows it for hours downstream. Only when it has grown into a deep, broad river with clear water he crosses over.

Soon after, he sees a pavilion in the forest. Looking inside, he sees the lady Jeschute asleep on a couch (her knight Orilus is off seeking adventure). Again remembering his mother's advice, he kisses the sleeping lady, who wakes up alarmed to be confronted with a handsome lad trying to take the ring from her finger. Parzival succeeds in taking the ring and helps himself to food and drink before he leaves.

When Orilus returns, he is convinced that his wife encouraged the lad to more than what was seemly, and stung by envy he punishes Jeschute with neglect for many years.

The Pure Fool

In this phase of the story we meet the theme of the pure fool. Parzival is untutored and is, to begin with, utterly unfit to meet the world.

This is a new theme in the history of myth. Previous heroes were well equipped for their task and fitted into the world they inhabited, but not Parzival. He begins his journey with nothing but scant and misleading advice from his mother. Missing the meaning, he takes things literally. The handsome youth possesses only formidable strength and purity of heart, but these attributes do not prevent him from making a fool of himself and affecting others in adverse ways.

When Parzival in his motley dress reaches the camp of King Arthur, he causes much merriment among the pages and squires. He finds the court in disarray. Ither, the famous red knight, has challenged the Knights of the Round Table to single combat. But none of the knights present dares meet the formidable challenger. Parzival immediately offers his service. Though nobody takes him serious, he approaches the red knight on his knock-kneed pony. Ither thinks the lad in fool's clothes is a bad joke, and butts Parzival with the side of his lance, knocking him from his horse. The incensed youth hurls his javelin at the vizier and kills the Red Knight, unaware that he is his own cousin. His ignorance has caused a death.

Exercise 1: The Pure Fool

Look to your own life for situations that resemble Parzival meeting the world as a fool. They may be humorous, like his crossing of the stream, or deadly serious, like the duel with the Red Knight.

The Pure Fool by Liana Christensen

It's a fool's errand, it's true. Nonetheless. Dig this well. You will see layers of fear, stratas of ignorance. The walls will be encrusted with the effluvia of sophistication. The overly refined. Dig. Dig till you are dropping with exhaustion then summon the will to go on digging. Eventually you will come to fresh earth, honest soil. Do not pause in your labours. Dig still. If you are to be blessed, then one day when the sky is a far circle of blue above you and your old life is entirely gone, the pure, clear water will flow. You will kneel and drink from the holy well. You will become the pure fool.

The Pure Fool by Nandi Chinna

The pure fool
wears old clothes
out of style before they reach
the good Samaritans rack
the pure fool
tried an after school job
with a huge vacuum cleaner
strapped to her back
she smoked a joint beforehand
and spent hours chasing specks of dust
the pure fool
drove a car across the country
it fell apart and she
tied it back together
with wire and string

words enter her ears
and fall out of her mouth
forgotten
she cannot see
what all the urgency is about
she follows a great Osprey
along the evening shore …

Parzival mounts Ither's horse, but not knowing how to direct the steed, he is carried away from Arthur's court. At nightfall he arrives at a Castle whose lord welcomes the weary rider and, recognising Parzival's qualities, takes him under his care. Parzival stays many months with his new-found tutor and learns knightly conduct and courtly manners. Among the teachings he receives is one that will bring him much hardship later on: he is advised to refrain from asking questions.

When his training is complete, Parzival leaves to seek further adventure. His destiny leads him to a besieged city, where the young queen valiantly resists the army of a neighbouring king who wishes to force her into marriage. Parzival aids the defenders and with his prowess in battle soon turns the tide. The young knight and the queen fall in love and soon the marriage is celebrated. Their innocent purity is revealed when we learn that the couple only discovered the secrets of intimacy in the third night of their marriage.

The Grail Castle

After a while Parzival, still ignorant of his mother's death, feels a longing to visit her. He takes leave of his wife and sets off for his former home, the forest of Soltane. Parzival is so troubled by longing for his beautiful wife that he allows his horse to take the path it pleased. In the evening he comes to a mountain lake. A barge is anchored near the shore and men are fishing, among them a kingly looking figure.

Parzival asks for lodging and is invited to stay the night. The castle is more magnificent than any he has seen. He is well received but notices the sorrowful mood of all the courtiers. His armour is removed and he is given a beautiful silk cloak by Reponse de Schoye, the sister of his host, King Anfortas.

The great hall is lit with a hundred candelabras. Parzival is seated next to Anfortas, who is obviously in much anguish. He can neither sit nor lie, only recline, and despite the heat from the fire he is wrapped in thick furs. Despite his suffering, the king welcomes Parzival kindly. Suddenly a large door opens and a squire enters with a lance dripping with blood. All sink to their knees, moaning loudly until the squire has gone again. Then follows a procession of twenty-four maidens. Finally Reponse de Schoye enters, carrying the Grail. The Grail is placed before the king and each knight receives whatever nourishment he most desires.

> Whatever one stretched out one's hand for in the presence of the Gral, it was waiting, one found it all ready and to hand — dishes warm, dishes cold, new-fangled dishes and old favourites …
> 'There never was any such thing!' many will say. But they would be misled by their ill temper, for the Gral was the very fruit of bliss, of the sweets of this world and such that it scarcely fell short of what they tell us of the Heavenly Kingdom …

Parzival gazes at this miracle in amazement, but remembering his teaching, he refrains from asking about the meaning of the ceremony and the suffering of his host. Even when the king presents Parzival with a costly sword, saying: 'Since God wounded me, you are the one fitted to wear this sword,' he remains mute, despite the promptings of his heart. Parzival refrains from asking questions. The feast ends and Parzival is led back to his room. Exhausted, he falls into a tormented sleep and wakes the next morning to find the castle deserted and all the company gone.

Exercise 2: The Grail Castle

You are a knight on your way to the Grail Castle. Your experience may differ greatly from Parzival's. Describe the castle and whatever meets you there in detail. Approach the writing in the way a hero approaches an adventure: do not plan ahead. Be surprised at every step of your encounter. Stay in the moment and let your imagination feed you with one picture after another. Do not explain what you see, but let us marvel at the strange and miraculous events you observe.

The Grail Castle by Penelope Brown

I rode a night like a black pool, unaware of light, struggling to balance and unable to see the stones or the grass, just the wild calls of animals came to me and the nostril blowing and chunk chunk of my horse's hooves. It was a night so long and so black it was without end. Until I saw a single tree trunk lit up amidst the shadow as though some waif had lit a lamp and let it stand there and beyond that a yellow hill and above that a sky as bright and blue as day. As I entered past that lighted tree I felt my body grow still and centered, a great ease came over me and my horse's hooves became muffled as though she walked in soft turf. I also felt warmth as though I was lit, as though a sun was risen and glowing but no sun saw I in that enchanted sky. I dismounted and walked to the top of the hillock. All around the darkness still was, yet here was only warmth and radiance.

 I felt a movement to my right and had no response within to take up my sword, I left it un-drawn and instead I felt a hand slip into mine and turned to see a smiling girl, not more than sixteen years, at once, as I turned to meet her, a garden sprang up and then walls around us and all manner of stones and things of wood to make a castle as pale as sand. No thing was solid for I could see through every wall and all things from dogs to tables to tapestries to drawbridge were transparent and lit from within.

The Grail Castle by Richard Smart

Blackened night, so black there's no way of seeing in front of me. All I can make out is the white steed I ride upon, bare back. Galloping headlong I feel anxious, and yet part of me is quiet, for it seems the horse knows where to go. Suddenly, we have arrived in front of a huge castle; the gate is down, we are invited in. I am greeted by white-clad women, earthly yet ethereal. They lead me to a great hall of feasting and dancing. Then, in front of me on the table, I see a beating heart with a dagger impaled in it. Blood fills and then oozes over the white plate it sits upon. A black servant comes to clean it up, apologising for the mess, and I let him know it's all right. All my friends and family are seated close by, each eating a heart in silence. Shocked, I stand up but am shackled by chains. I pick up the heart in front of me up and fling it at the dancers, but they just carry on dancing, oblivious. I push over my table but everyone continues to eat. Another black servant enters and asks me what is the problem. I say, look around you, it's weird. He replies, yes sir, this is what you ordered — is there a problem? I tell him I want to leave. He replies, sorry sir, you must finish your heart. This is the rule of the castle. I reluctantly begin to eat and soon I am consumed by the same silence as my fellow guests.

When Parzival has his visionary encounter with the Grail and the suffering King Anfortas, he is well educated in matters of knightly etiquette and knows how to refrain from asking questions out of curiosity. But all he has learned and acquired from the culture of his time prove insufficient when faced with the spiritual reality of the Grail and the suffering of a fellow human being.

After he has left the castle, he learns that he could have ended the cruel suffering of Anfortas simply by asking: 'What ails thee?' But following the convention he was taught, he failed.

Kundry and the Wheel of Fortune

Continuing his journey, Parzival chances again upon the knights of King Arthur. By now he has won great renown and King Arthur asks him to join the Round Table. A great feast is given in his honour but amid the celebration, Kundry, Messenger of the Grail, rides into the camp. She is hideous in appearance. Kundry denounces the king for accepting Parzival as one of his knights, then curses Parzival for his lack of compassion with Anfortas, for failing to ask the question that would have ended the king's suffering. Only a moment before Parzival had thought himself at the height of his career. Now he faces a grim reversal of fortune. Feeling unworthy, he leaves Arthur's court to seek the Grail Castle and ask the redeeming question.

As the Messenger of the Grail, Kundry confronts Parzival with the painful news of self-knowledge. Such knowledge typically comes at the height of success to turn the wheel of fortune. Kundry has many disguises. All are ugly for she mirrors the unacknowledged shadow, the dark unredeemed side of the psyche. She may appear as an enemy, a sudden turn of fortune, a fear or an obsession. She may have an outward representative or take purely inward reality. Kundry is the great awakener, the hideous benefactor who urges us on and points to forgotten aims and unfulfilled obligations.

Exercise 3: Kundry

Invoke Kundry's powerful awakening presence in writing. Recall or invent an experience where you (or someone else) have met with her.

Kundry by Nandi Chinna

Kundry chased me
I was on a train
I had no shoes
in fact I despised
the very notion of shoes
Kundry sat in the opposite seat
I could feel her bristling
cactus needle stare
her hair was white from birth
it was matted with sticks
and stained with desert red
I stole furtive glances …

In a room people sit
with their eyes closed
they are deep breathing
they are levitating sound to the ceiling
the sound rises up from their bellies
like bees they can't prevent from swarming
that fly out into the space
a hive of sound wings beating
sounds out of people

Kundry is in my stomach like vomit
I run from the room and down
the hill to a bridge where
green water rushes underneath
holding my bruises
I open my mouth and Kundry
spews out a white scream
a black scream a blue green
purple scream she is out.

I collapse onto the splintered boards
the bruise is pale
the wound is open
Kundry holds me gently
she strokes my hair.

Kundry by Barbara Edwards

"If there is anyone here who knows a reason why this man and woman should not be joined in holy matrimony - let him speak now or forever hold his tongue." The church is overflowing with eager wedding guests, the couple at the front dressed in regalia, the day is set, the future beckons...

Will I speak? I slowly rise into the silence of the congregation: "Not one, but many reasons..." I begin. "Where do you want me to start?"

The Journey of Doubt

After his meeting with Kundry, Parzival's sole desire is to redeem Anfortas. But he cannot find the Grail Castle. For many years he journeys, fighting jousts and acquiring yet more fame, but the castle remains hidden from him. He loses all trust in God, feels unjustly treated by destiny and cannot find any meaning in his failure. At odds with the world he feels the painful prick of doubt and despair.

Exercise 4: The Never-ending Journey

The journey through the grey-lands of life can be long and arduous. At one time or another everyone encounters doldrums, tunnels without light, stretches without green. The journey seems unending and the quest in vain. Explore this theme. Find pictures that illustrate the long road

The Grey Quandary by Ailsa Grieve

grey long stretches of wild ocean
interlaced with long grey stretches of land
both must have gone on forever, I'm not sure
but what i do know, as I've said, is the colour was grey
grey wash to the tips of the oceans current
grey depths to the grey murky waters underneath
grey barges that toiled grey midnight horns
while they quarried things, untold things, varied things
from long grey shore to long grey shore
it was as if the moon had been half turned down
or ghosts of half invisible dragons were blocking its golden reign
at the time though i wasn't aware of the colour, i wasn't conscious of the grey
i was tottering through the mazes collecting odd scribbles that i needed to finish
the nights calling on this boat, off that one, onto the next, collecting from the
shores of the long lands things i can't even remember to call into form now,
but things that filled my arms in odd bundles, juggling sometimes as i rushed to
keep pace with myself.

and as the night barge sounded to bring nights end, the captain echoed with news for me
the news was a letter that my love wasn't going to be waiting for me at nights end, that he had decided that he didn't love me anymore.
and so at days dawn i finally realised the grey of my landscape
the foreboding storm clouds, the monotonous passageway of disenfranchised boats
the mourning wail of horns across harbours
the strips of land so long you could only ever walk in lines
and the objects i collected
just coils and odd bits of broken dreams

One day he meets the hermit Trevrizent and takes lodging with him, asking advice and guidance in his search for the Grail. Trevrizent tells him that such a search is in vain, unless the seeker is called by the Grail. Not knowing Parzival's identity, or his former encounter with Anfortas, Trevrizent tells Parzival the whole story of the Grail, from its fall from the crown of Lucifer to its bestowal on Titurel, the first Grail King, and grandfather to Anfortas. Trevrizent himself is the brother of Anfortas. He became a hermit in order to devote himself to praying for the healing of the wounded king. He tells the tragic tale to Parzival.

> 'Sir, there was a king who went by the name of Anfortas, as he does today,' he said. 'The agony with which he was punished for his pride should move you and wretched me to never-ending pity! His youth and wealth and pursuit of love beyond the restraints of wedlock brought harm to the world through him. Such ways do not suit the Gral. In its service knights and squires must guard against licentiousness: humility has always mastered pride ...

Anfortas was called to be the Grail King when he was still occupied in the pursuits of erotic love and ill-suited to be the keeper of this holy office. His passion for a woman became his downfall; in a joust fought for the lady he incurred an incurable wound in his testes. Too strong to die and too weak to live, he suffers unending misery.

The Wound of Anfortas

The king's tragic fate exemplifies the modern tension between sexuality and spirituality. In the remote past this tension did not exist, as sexuality was sacred and integral to life; primarily a religious experience, love was directed toward the gods. When modern individuality emerged the gods withdrew from direct perception and the ecstatic closeness of religious experience was lost. Only in the love between two people did a faint echo of the ecstatic union with the divine remain. Personal love became the substitute for former religious experience.

Some mystics began to avoid sexuality altogether and redirect the longing for union back to its original source: the divine. But this kind of celibacy was not required of the Grail Kings. They married according to the directions of the Grail and combined spiritual life with earthly tasks.

Anfortas however sought sexual adventures against the directions of the Grail. He pursued an inappropriate relationship and so incurred his terrible wound. Suffering extreme agony, he becomes a prototype of human ailments caused by eroticism for its own sake. In every human being there is both a pure, striving Parzival and a flawed Anfortas.

Trevrizent continues his tale with the coming of a young knight who, in spite of seeing this suffering, fails to ask the question that would have brought healing to the wounded king. Parzival realises the full magnitude of his failure. He reveals his identity to the hermit and asks him for help.

Thus moved by compassion, Parzival begins to accept his responsibility and reconcile himself to his fate and God. He leaves the hermit as a spiritually matured man, soon finds the Grail Castle and asks the redeeming question, 'What ails thee?' Anfortas is restored to health and Parzival becomes the new Grail King. He joins again with his wife, who has in the meantime given birth to twins.

Exercise 5: What Ails Thee?

To ask the right question requires compassionate awareness and presence of mind, purity of heart and depth of experience. A true question is an expression of who we truly are and bridges the gap between us and another human being.

To answer such a question requires equal depth. Had Parzival asked the question at his first opportunity he would have learned all that Trevrizent later imparted to him: a story that included the fall of Lucifer and the destiny of the grail. Anfortas' suffering is only meaningful in this wider context.

Now is your chance to ask the redeeming question: What ails thee? You may ask this question to anyone who suffers from a wound, physically, emotionally or psychically; caused by misdirected love or some other problem. What is their answer? The first example below is written by an 84 year-old student:

What ails thee? by Pauline Matthews
' Friend what ails thee?' And I replied: 'Life after death.'
And he asked again, 'Friend what ails thee?'
And I replied. 'Death after life' and then came only silence.

The Question by Jennifer Kornberger

For years I did not ask the question. I did not want your messed up rooms, your journals with every nightmare carefully recorded. Didn't want you growing on me like mistletoe, like *Nutsyia floribunda*, all grinning and golden and heavy with nectar.

But, unasked, the question bore its own weight, became a stone, became a mound.

When I asked the question I saw it was hidden in rain water, in lemon grass tea, it was stirred in dahl. It melted like a stock cube in soup.

You asked what herbs I used. It was the question in flakes, in powder, ground in a mortar.

When the cancer had eaten nearly all, the question became as light as breath. Just breath sculpting an answer without words, shaping it with geometric precision through a fog of morphine.

What Ails Thee by Ailsa Grieve

she yelled out to the sea, the sea held in a cave,
the cave clasped in the palm of her hand 'what ails thee?'
so that from all the waters and untold deep quarters
just her own echo returned but with no glee.

she cried out to the moon, the moon held by stars,
the stars hooked tight to the pen in her hand 'what ails thee'
and as she wrote to the cosmoses, sonnets of this
only the same question replied to be.

she called to the vastness, the vastness travelling so fast,
and resting for a while on her back 'what ails thee?'
and the vastness returned all crippled and burnt
that nothing ails me as thee.

and so she sewed a small basket
with wools warm and life like
and she placed herself inside
inside with a candle and scents of sweet mantles
and she whispered to me as of thee
.. 'what ails you?'

Parzival is one of the last mythical heroes. He solves the tension between earthly and heavenly love through his purity and strength. He and Anfortas are both forerunners of our modern consciousness. In the ninth century they appeared as separate personalities. In the contemporary human being they exist simultaneously: the pure striving fool and the wounded king. Parzival lacks maturity and compassion. Anfortas lacks the pure, determined striving of the true spiritual seeker. Kundry brings them together. She forces Parzival on his quest for maturity and so teaches him to ask the question that redeems the king.

25

Troubadour and Troubairitz

The tension between sexuality and spirituality that bound the destinies of Anfortas and Parzival was in later centuries experienced ever more inwardly as twin forces in a single soul. William IX, duke of Aquitaine and the first troubadour we know of, is described by a thirteenth century biographer as

> '…one of the courtliest men in the world and one of the greatest deceivers of women. He was a fine knight at arms, liberal in his attention to ladies and a fine composer and singer of songs.'

The topics of William's songs — from coarse descriptions of sexual intercourse and his own prowess to the refined subtleties of romantic love — were as diverse as the scandalous incidents of his private life. His own marriage did not stop him from abducting another nobleman's wife and he was threatened with excommunication by the pope.

Eleanor of Aquitaine

William's grand-daughter and heir to his large realm was Eleanor of Aquitaine. Highly educated, adventurous and of independent spirit, she was the most powerful woman of her time. Betrothed in her teens to Louis VII of France, the weak and bigoted king was a bad match for her.

When the second crusade against the Turks was proclaimed, Eleanor led her own knights into campaign. She and her ladies started the crusade from Vezelay, the legendary burial site of Mary Magdalene.

The crusade failed, and rumours of her love affairs soon led to her divorce from the French king. Six weeks after the separation Eleanor married Henry Plantagenet, soon to be King of England. When that marriage failed, Eleanor returned to her own lands and established her famous Court of Love. Lovers, poets and scholars congregated around the great queen to create a cultural centre which pioneered a new and refined conduct in courtly manners and affairs of love.

Eleanor fostered the civilising influence of love at her court. Through her patronage the first medieval romances were written — Tristan and Iseult, and Lancelot and

Guinevere — and it was she who commissioned the first Grail Romance, Chretien de Troyes' Parsival.

The Art of Courtly Love

As if to counterbalance the impulsive nature of men like her grandfather William, Eleanor inspired a code of courtly love, written down as rules by Andreas Capellanus in his *Art of Courtly Love*. Here is a selection:

> Marriage is no real excuse for not loving.
> Love is always a stranger in the home of avarice.
> It is not proper to love any woman whom one would be ashamed to seek to marry.
> A true lover does not desire to embrace in love anyone except his beloved.
> Every lover regularly turns pale in the presence of his beloved.
> A new love puts an old one to flight.
> Good character alone makes any man worthy of love.
> He whom the thought of love vexes eats and sleeps very little.
> A man who is vexed by too much passion usually does not love.
> Nothing forbids one woman being loved by two men or one man by two women.

Exercise 1: Rules of Love

Add to the set of rules or change them according to your own insights into the *Art of Courtly Love*.

> **Rules of Love by Nandi Chinna**
> Love takes time to become real.
> Passion and good sex do not always mean great love.
> Love peels off skin, cracks shells, holds up mirrors.
> Love is not blind. It sees everything and still miraculously loves.
> Love makes cups of tea, has conversation, watches tv, makes gardens and is glad to hear the car pull into the driveway, the footsteps approaching, the arms wrapped around, the soft kisses.

The courts of love in medieval Europe served to refine the interchange between men and women and encourage the emergence of love poetry. Romantic love was *not* a theme for medieval poetry and love affairs were not deemed worthy of poetic treatment before this time. Marriages were made to cement alliances and for economic reasons. Poetry was written in the honour of God or in celebration of heroic deeds. Slowly however the life of the soul claimed more attention and the complications of romantic love became a major theme. The emergence of this new kind of love is powerfully depicted in the legend of Tristan and Iseult.

Tristan and Iseult

Tristan is sent to Ireland to fetch Iseult the Fair as a bride for his uncle, King Mark. The marriage is one of political alliance and Iseult only unwillingly leaves Ireland, all the more reluctantly since Tristan had earlier killed Morold, her former fiancé, in combat. Iseult the Fair therefore harbours ill feeling towards the young knight who is sent to fetch her. On the return voyage, however, the two drink from a love potion that knits their hearts forever. From then on, their lives suffer from the tension between their moral obligations and the demands of their love.

Gottfried von Strassburg describes their first signs of love, sensitive to the intimate realm of the soul and the battle of conflicting feelings:

> But one heart had they — her grief was his sadness, his sadness her grief. Both were one in love and sorrow, and yet both would hide it in shame and doubt. She felt shame of her love, and the like did he. She doubted of his love, and he of hers. For though both their hearts were blindly bent to one will, yet was the chance and the beginning heavy to them, and both alike would hide their desire.
>
> When Tristan felt the pangs of love, then he bethought him straightway of his faith and honour, and would fain have set himself free. 'Nay,' he said to himself, 'let such things be, Tristan; guard thee well, lest others perceive thy thoughts.' So would he turn his heart, fighting against his own will, and desiring against his own desire. He would and would not, and, a prisoner, struggled in his fetters. There was a strife within him, for ever as he looked on Iseult, and love stirred his heart and soul, then did honour draw him back. Yet he must needs follow Love, for his liege lady was she, and in sooth she wounded him more sorely than did his honour and faith to his uncle, though they strove hard for the mastery. For Love looked smiling upon his heart, and led heart and eyes captive; and yet if he saw her not, then was he even more sorrowful …
>
> Even so was it with the maiden: she was as a bird that is snared with lime. When she knew the snare of love and saw that her heart was indeed taken therein, she strove with all her power to free herself, yet the more she struggled the faster was the hold Love laid upon her, and, unwilling, she must follow whither Love led.
>
> (trans, J. I. Weston, London: Nutt, 1899)

We see deeply into the souls of the lovers, feel the innocence and purity of their love. Both are victims of a power greater than themselves. They battle valiantly against their emotions, but love asserts its demands.

Exercise 2: Love Unruly

Take your lead from Tristan and Iseult and describe the many opposing emotions that often accompany the feeling of love. Draw on your own experience or use a fictional character.

> **The Moment of Love by Liana Christensen**
>
> This moment - tango class, wide-eyed, breast to breast, hip to hip, our bodies awkward, new to the steps. Our eyes and hearts parsing a new language.
>
> This moment - do I imagine this feeling, do I take the dance of love which enacts passion and read into it real, personal love?
>
> This moment - you come to me too late for in my uncertainty I have taken another lover. And I am still uncertain but dare to ask "Have you come here for love? If so, I'm sorry, but you're too late. And your response told me all I needed to know.'
>
> This moment - I do not double deal. I did not double deal. But when you dropped by months later I told you the plain truth. "If you feel something from me it is not just your imagination. It is real. But I do not, will not, double deal. And I do not, will not, ask you to put your heart on ice."
>
> This moment - at a friend's wedding I listen to the priest and my heart moves within me. I must forsake the one I'm with and fly to you.
>
> We dance, we dance wildly at the wedding feast, but honour is still served.
>
> There are farewells and tears to be cried.
>
> This moment - you tell me "You are the one" and all my being melts.

The lovers meet in secret until King Mark discovers them. Both are condemned to death on account of their disloyalty, but Tristan escapes on his way to the galleon and rescues Iseult. They hide in the forest of Morrois, where Mark discovers them lying in sleep. They make peace and Iseult returns with Mark, while Tristan seeks adventure abroad. But in spite of all precaution destiny unites and separates them again and again. Eventually Tristan marries another lady, Iseult of the White Hands, to forget his former love, Iseult the Fair. For a while all is well. But then war breaks out and Tristan is mortally wounded. He knows that nobody can heal him, but Iseult the Fair. The Queen is sent for and immediately departs to aid her knight. His jealous wife, however, tells Tristan that Iseult the Fair is not coming and the knight dies. When Iseult the Fair arrives and finds Tristan dead, she too dies. The mortal remains of the lovers are brought back to Cornwall and buried in the same chapel, united at last.

To the medieval soul, complications in romantic love act like pain in childbirth. Through it the intimate feeling life is born and with it the poetry we know as the songs of the troubadours and the troubairitz.

The Paradox of Love

Oscillation between conflicting feelings assists the birth of soul. Love becomes the awakener and its many paradoxes a much explored topic of medieval poetry, as in the contradictions in this piece by Jean de Meun:

> Love is a troubled peace, an amorous war —
> A treasonous loyalty, disloyal faith —
> A fear that's full of hope, a desperate trust —
> A madman's logic, reasoned foolishness —
> A pleasant peril in which one may drown —
> A heavy burden that is light to bear —
> A healthy sickness and most languorous health —
> A famine swallowed up in gluttony —
> A miserly sufficiency of gold —
> A drunken thirst, a thirsty drunkenness …
> A bitter sweetness, a sweet-tasting gall —
> A sinful pardon, and a pardoned sin …

Exercise 3: The Paradox of Love

Use your own experience to write a piece exploring the paradox of love.

The Paradox of Love by Rhea Pfeiffle

> Love is an endearing pain
> A tragic joyfulness
> An ecstatic boredom
> And a liberating burden
>
> How can Love that initially promises
> Glorious transcendence
> Deliver in the granularity of everyday.
> The roots of love
> Dig into the cornflakes
> Wind around the drains of the dishwasher
> And push through the lattice of the laundry basket
>
> The heights of its meaning
> Encased in dinnertime conversations
> Along with 'so how was everyone's day?'
>
> Its fragility exposed to

Unthinking scowls
Barks
Casual neglect

And its potential
Needing to be grabbed
With one hand
Along with the car keys
As you're flying out the door
Every morning

The Paradox of Love by Mags Webster

Love consumes you while you are consuming it. Love is sherbet on the tongue; the sweetness that causes decay; the long cold beer that makes you thirsty for more; a fat oily chip poking out of newspaper, going eat me eat me, teasing you with the promise of its taste; the deliciousness of something you are not meant to have; that extra chocolate; one more helping of macaroni cheese just like your mother made it. Love is meant to make your belly feel tight, your throat feel constricted; it gives you heartburn. It is overripe fruit: bruise the peach and the bruises manifest all over your flesh. Love is the sweetest hangover: it makes you want to drink to the end of the bottle then lie back, smiling your joy out loud.

The Troubadour

The power of romantic love awoke the medieval personality to the depth of its soul-life, a depth that harboured both treasures and pitfalls. William of Aquitaine experienced the extremes of both but in his life was unable to transcend his often violent passion, whereas subsequent troubadours escaped his destiny through the conscious practice of courtly love, culminating in the adoration of an unattainable lady. By choosing a love remote enough to prevent requitement, the troubadour kept himself in a state of inspiration. The lady became a doorway to the eternal feminine, spiritual attainment and poetic productivity.

To fully appreciate the poetic aspirations of the troubadours we must recognise them as the first attempt by the male to reach the depths of the soul through courtship of the eternal feminine. Poetry was central to this project, for the 'readiness of speech' demanded of the lover — an ability to express himself with words — was proof of both soul and worthiness.

The Cathar Movement

The troubadours emerged concurrently with the Cathars, a religious movement that practised a form of Christianity considered a dangerous heresy by the church. Cathars believed that good and evil coexisted from the beginning of time and that the human being is sent by the powers of light into the realms of darkness to transform it. To the Cathars the whole of nature, including the human body, dwelt in this realm of darkness from which the human soul could liberate itself through a pure life. They believed that human beings descending to earth left their pure essence, a heavenly sister, back in the world of light. To reunite with this heavenly counterpart was the aim of both Cathars and troubadours. The former achieved it through living a pure life and the latter through the sublimation of love and the practice of poetry. Awareness of this higher self within was the troubadour's point of contact with his muse. The ability to express himself in song testified to this purity of love. Through this practice of restraint and dedication he redeemed the ailing Anfortas, and through his 'extreme readiness of speech' he redeemed the tongue-tied Parsival.

When the Cathar movement was destroyed and tens of thousands were burned on the stake, some of their traditions survived in the poetry of the troubadours, many of whom were inspired by Cathar ideals. Troubadours used their art to both hide and reveal Cathar beliefs.

Not all troubadours followed pure ideals, but many did, exemplified by Geoffrey de Rudel: he fell in love with the Countess of Tripoli, whom he had never seen, through the praise that he heard of her. He made songs about her, and through the desire to see her he took the Cross and set out to sea. On the voyage he fell ill, and was carried as a dead man to an inn in Tripoli. The news was told to the Countess, who came to him and took him in her arms. And he praised God and thanked him for having let him live to see her. And so he died in her arms, and on the same day, she became a nun because of the grief of his death.

Here are two stanzas from a song written to his distant love:

> When now the days are long in May,
> I love to hear the birds far distant,
> And when the song has died away.
> I dream about a love as distant.
> Deep in my longing am I drowned.
> The songs, the hawthorn-bloom around,
> warm me no more than winter-snow …
> Love has no joy that won't betray
> except this love that lies so distant.
> Such charms no woman can display
> in any land that's near or distant.
> So lovely, gentle, pure, she's crowned:
> to see her close, a captive bound
> by Saracens, I'd gladly go…

Such notions may seem unrealistic, ideal, even abstract. But to the troubadour they were real, allowing him to enter his own soul through fervent longing. His absolute dedication that would shun neither death nor captivity for a glance of his beloved reveals a passion both earthly and mystical.

The Troubairitz

Aristocratic women, often far more educated than their male counterparts, also wrote and we know them by the name of troubairitz. Their songs are frequently a poetic response to the troubadour, often more down to earth than those of their male admirers. They speak their mind, addressing their lovers directly, formulating their love or complaining of the unfaithfulness of their admirer. They may even reveal their desire to be united with their lover.

One of the most famous of songs is by the Contessa de Dias, 'A Chanter M'er', written in the Old Provencal language.

> I must sing of what I do not want, I am so angry with the one whom I love, because i love him more than anything: mercy nor courtesy moves him, neither does my beauty, nor my worthiness, nor my good sense, for I am deceived and betrayed as much as I should be, if I were ugly.
>
> I take comfort because I never did anything wrong, friend, towards you in anything, rather I love you more than Seguin did Valensa, and I am greatly pleased that I conquered you in love, my friend, because you are the most worthy; you are arrogant to me in words and appearance, and yet you are so friendly towards everyone else.
>
> I wonder at how you have become so proud, friend, towards me, and I have reason to lament; it is not right that another love take you away from me no matter what is said or granted to you. and remember how it was at the beginning of our love! May Lord God never wish that it was my fault for our separation.

There is a refreshing directness in this song, the countess immediately comes to the point and is not afraid to expose her feelings. Exchanges between troubadours and troubairitz encompassed all levels of love; an adored lady may respond with earthy verses or a passionate admirer may be encouraged toward greater purity of love.

Exercise 4: Troubadour

Write a love song. Prove worthy by your 'extreme readiness of speech', your ability to express soul though poetry. Do not falter even though the object of your love is unattainable! Show your dedication.

Contrary to popular opinion love poetry is difficult to write. It is always in danger of becoming clichéd. Here is an example I have written myself:

Seasons of Love

1
Time bit its lip
When we met
And immediately saw
The threshold of us.

And there we stood,
Empty-handed,
Giving and taking
Nothing but ourselves
As the first smile
Trespassed
Between you and me.

2
What is it that makes the washing of dishes
And the stacking away of plates
So ecstatically normal?

It is you
Arranging the flowers
In an improvised vase,
Teaching the roses to bloom
Among the common greens.

Exercise 5: Troubairitz

You have just received a love poem from an admiring troubadour. Does it meet your expectations or is it too highly pitched, with unrealistic ideals? Too bold? Write a response worthy of a modern troubairitz:

Love Poem by Jennifer Kornberger

1.
I have located you on
the palm of my hand —
the relationship line

you are not one familial groove
but a dance of lines

when I was a child
those lines hovered
about my hands
like faint gypsy music
but by the time I met you
their untamed geometry
was scored below any
common clasp

2.
our hands are the same size
we check regularly
hold them just a little
distance apart to feel
the live strands that course
and splay between us

take them further apart
find the point where the
magnetism ebbs, where the
planet we hold between us
moves into thin sunless space

that's where we start
drawing a new ecliptic
inventing fresh zodiacal signs

surely these chalk stars
are ours
to assemble

Troubairitz by Mags Webster

Can I start by giving you a bit of advice? It's probably a good idea to sign your name at the bottom of your letter, rather than just saying 'an ardent admirer'. Then I will know whether it is Jake, or Harry, or Roger, or John, or one of a half-dozen other boys with whom I am presently corresponding. I don't wish to be rude, especially as your spelling is immaculate compared to other examples I have received; and you have nearly won me over entirely by knowing where to place your apostrophe. But, dear 'ardent admirer' how am I to engage with a phantom? If you want this love to be real, to — how did you put it — 'press your aching heart against mine,' then we have to start with a few basics like, what's your name? Are you over sixteen, and, most importantly, are you one of my students?

The Courtship of God

While troubadour and troubairitz acted within the worldly sphere of courts, they had their counterpart in monastic and conventional culture, where saints rose to the mystical experience of love. Worship of the Virgin Mary and adoration of Jesus were resonant with the highest ideals of troubadour culture. Many mystics became, like Francis of Assisi, troubadours of God. Leading clergyman and founder of the Cistercian order, St. Bernard of Clairvaux, speaks movingly about the experience of mystical love:

> This bridegroom is not only loving, he is love … Love is sufficient of itself; it is pleasant of itself and for its own sake. Love itself is a merit, and itself its own reward. Beyond itself love seeks neither cause nor outcome: the outcome of it is one with the practice of it. I love, because I love; I love, that I may love. A great reality is love, if only it return to its source, if it be restored again to its first beginning, if it be poured back into its fount and ever draw therefrom whence it perpetually flows. Of all the movements of the soul, of all its feelings and affections, it is love alone by which the creature responds to its creator …

> When God loves, he wants nothing else than to be loved; for he loves for no other purpose than that he may be loved, knowing that those who love him are blessed by that very love.

Exercise 6: Sermon on Love

Write a sermon about love. What is its mission in the world? What does it mean to you and what can it mean to others?

Love At Its Most Sublime by Karen Mc Crea
The love of a single person is big enough to change the life of everyone it touches. It is both individually grown and expressed, and carries the universal truth of all time within it and is the truth of all time. It is recognizable in its generosity. Where there is love there can be no enemy for love understands we are not separate from one another, nor indeed are we separate from anything at all. We are a tiny life, made from the stuff of God, carrying the stars in our souls. Love gives everything, and by so doing, finds everything in an inexhaustible circle of of life. It's like breathing - the air we breathe is both inside and outside of us and there is no

> barrier anyway. We are made of spaces held together by love. In the end we understand love makes everything that exists.
> Love is the essence of being and beings are of its essence; such a simple thing it's almost impossible to understand except with love itself.

St. Bernard's contemporary the Abbess Hildegard of Bingen responded to her experience of divine love through writing and composition. Her spiritual vision flowered in a burst of creativity that manifested in many contributions to the culture of her time — as poet and composer, healer, scientist, philosopher and active church politician. Her poetic creations, directed toward the divine, were often illustrated with the most extraordinary visual illuminations.

The Beguines

The courtship of god was not reserved to those living within recognised monastic orders. Widespread religious lay communities such as the Beguines aspired to the same ideal. The Beguines were single, independent women who devoted their lives to prayer and good works. They lived in their own huts on the fringes of cities, took no vows, and had no superiors. They supported themselves with their own work and cared for the poor and diseased. Their lives devoted to prayer frequently led to mystical experience. Hadewijch, a major Beguine, writes in her letters of the inexhaustible nature of divine love:

> Now understand the deepest essence of your soul, what 'soul' is. Soul is a being that can be beheld by God and by which, again, God can be beheld. Soul is also a being that wishes to contend God…the soul is a bottomless abyss in which God suffices to himself; and his won self-sufficiency ever finds fruition to the full in this soul, as the soul, for its part, ever does in him.

Another Beguine, Mechthild of Magdeburg, captured her fusion with the divine in many poems. In the example below the divine bridegroom speaks to the soul:

> I who am Divine
> am truly in you.
>
> I can never be sundered from you;
> However far we be parted
> never can we be separated.
>
> I am in you
> and you are in Me.
> We could not be closer.

We two are fused in one,

Poured into a single mould,
thus, unwearied,
we shall remain forever.

Exercise 7: Love at its most Sublime

The mystics experience love at its most sublime; the soul is utterly consumed in the fiery all-encompassing love of god. Dare to stretch your imagination to the point of utmost transcendence and report on the experience of love in a letter like Hadjewich or in a poem like Mechthild.

The Ladder Of Love by Barbara Stapleton

First God shows the soul the tenderness, the largeness of his heart. The soul rejoices in his closeness enveloping her.

And then God takes away what was given, hides it, pretends it is no longer there.

Then the soul, the whole person must contend, struggle like Jacob with his midnight visitor, until what was promised is retrieved, grasped back with great resolve from the Contender.

But in this contention, this long struggle, the gift is damaged, undone, set awry, but in its hurt something truer, deeper, brighter, shifts into its rightful place.

The Soul becomes Bride. The body rejoices.

And the two become One.

Love at its most Sublime by Allison Ashton

I close my eyes.
The storytelling of meditation begins.
My breath drops to a lower gear.
Down I plummet as coloured mandalas, soft like jellyfish, drift past me.
I come out into a vast, limitless space.
It is velvety darkness with stars flashing gently as far as far as I can see.
My body is no longer here.
All that remains is my rib cage, made of light.
Suspended before me it moves out and in, out and in to the rhythm
and sound of a deep, stertorous breathing.
It continues and continues.
After some time, I come back to the surface of my awareness.
I open my eyes.
I am the universe breathing.

26

The Purgatory of Words

Dante Alighieri was the fulfillment of the troubadouric ideal. Born into the lower aristocracy in 1265 in Florence, he studied rhetoric, philosophy, literature and theology to prepare for a political career. At the age of nine, Dante was taken by his father to the house of a wealthy merchant where he met his host's daughter, Beatrice, who was eight. One glimpse and love for Beatrice ignited his heart. The path of the poet opened out before him and all his poetic work would orbit around the sun of his love.

Dante's love was chaste. Even at the age of nine he knew Beatrice was far above his social rank. He met her only on rare occasions, and when, almost ten years later, she spoke to him for the first time, 'I seemed to behold the utmost bounds of bliss.' When Beatrice married a wealthy banker, Dante's love remained steadfast. But when she died, aged only twenty-four, he was left devastated.

La Vita Nuova

Beatrice was his muse. The young poet had written sonnets in her praise, in a new style that refreshed conventional troubadour poetry with the candour of real feelings. Published under the title *La Vita Nuova* (New Life), alluding to his birth as a poet through his encounter with Beatrice, the collection made his reputation as a poet. It culminates with Dante's vision of the dead and glorified Beatrice:

> In which I beheld things that determined me to speak no more of that blessed one until such time as I could treat of her more worthily. And to this end I study as much as I can, as she well knows. So that, if it please Him by whom all things live to prolong my life for a few years, I hope to write of her what never yet was written of any woman.

The poet fulfills this promise years later when, in *The Divine Comedy*, Beatrice becomes his guardian through the seven spheres of heaven.

Though the feelings that inspired him may be uncommon today, Dante reminds us of the scope and depth of the human soul, its capacity for transformation through the power of love. Love can make not only a poet out of a plain man, but a seer out of a poet. It can purify the soul and lead it beyond the confines of this world, as in this passage from *Vita Nuova* where Dante recalls how Beatrice first greeted him:

> I say that when she appeared from any direction, then, in the hope of her wondrous salutation, there was no enemy left to me; rather there smote into me a flame of charity, which made me forgive every person who had ever injured me; and if at that moment anybody had put a question to me about anything whatsoever, my answer would have been simply 'Love'...

The impact of this experience never faded from Dante's life. His eternal self had awoken.

After the death of Beatrice, his family arranged his marriage to Gemma Donati. Dante engaged himself in politics and soon rose to an eminent position in the Florentine republic. But in an ongoing feud between the Guelfs and Ghibellinis his party, the Guelfs, was defeated, and he found himself banished from his native city.

As a political refugee, Dante experiences all the vicissitudes of the homeless: 'Wandering as a stranger through almost every region to which our language reaches, I have gone about as a beggar.' Nevertheless he manages to write a discourse in which he urges the use of colloquial Italian rather than the Latin of the learned. It was Dante more than any other poet who shaped the Italian language and made it a literary tool. He also wrote on the theory of government and the philosophy of life. He hoped for a new Roman Empire under a just monarch who could guarantee the independence of free city states and championed a church dedicated solely to its spiritual tasks.

The Divine Comedy

Dante is a poet of universal interests, concerned with the foundations of human existence. *The Divine Comedy*, begun in the early years of his exile and completed at the very end of his life when he had found refuge in Ravenna, is one of the great adventures of world literature. The poem explores life after death in vivid and exquisite detail as the poet charts a path through the universe of hell, purgatory and heaven. We can traverse some of this same journey in our own writing.

In the medieval world view hell is a pit beneath the surface of the earth, purgatory a mountain rising in seven tiers, while heaven surrounds the earth in seven spheres. In this hierarchical world everything is ordered according to its moral value.

Hell

Dante's journey starts when he is lost in a dark wood. Trying to escape by climbing a mountain, the poet is confronted by three beasts.

> And lo! almost where the ascent began,
> A panther light and swift exceedingly,
> Which with a spotted skin was covered o'er!
> And never moved she from before my face …
> But not so much, that did not give me fear
> A lion's aspect which appeared to me.
> He seemed as if against me he were coming
> With head uplifted, and with ravenous hunger,
> So that it seemed the air was afraid of him;
> And a she-wolf, that with all hungerings
> Seemed to be laden in her meagreness,
> And many folk has caused to live forlorn!

This is a typical threshold experience that spiritual seekers undergo on their journey to the inner world. Menacing beasts are images of the distorted forces within the human soul that bar the entrance to the spirit world; the dark side of the human being reveals itself in threefold form.

Exercise 1: The Three Beasts

Like Dante you find yourself lost in a dark wood, confronted by frightening beasts. Describe the beasts and your meeting with them in detail. Look for correspondences between the imaginary animals and your own unredeemed forces of soul.

> **The Beast by Jennifer Kornberger**
> What moves toward me in the gloom makes a sound that is the daylight torn in two and being not whole it wails its grief in frayed skeins through mute trees. What moves toward me drags itself, having no legs, but arms overgrown and a stump of a body wrapped in the rotting fur of forest animals. This is half bear, half child, the arms are furred and at the end clinging claws, an open toothless mouth endlessly wailing, reaching for me.

Meeting such manifestations unprepared can be devastating, crippling the will to persevere. Dante himself is brought close to despair by the she-wolf, but finds help in that same moment.

> She brought upon me so much heaviness,
> With the affright that from her aspect came,
> That I the hope relinquished of the height.
> While I was rushing downward to the lowland,
> Before mine eyes did one present himself,

Who seemed from long-continued silence hoarse.
When I beheld him in the desert vast,
Have pity on me, unto him I cried,
Whiche'er thou art, or shade or real man!

Beatrice in heaven has seen Dante's distress and sends Virgil to his aid. Dante now has a mentor who will guide him through hell and purgatory until, at Heaven's gate, Beatrice herself will take the poet further.

Virgil the Mentor

Beatrice's choice is no accident. Virgil was Dante's ideal poetic mentor. His *Aeneid* provided ancient Rome with its national epic and Dante aspired to do the same for medieval Italy with his *Commedia*. Virgil was also held in high esteem as a prophet of Christianity (in his writing he foresaw coming of Christ) and a man of great moral integrity. Popular tradition revered him as a white magician who aided the deceased in their sojourn after death.

Guides and mentors are indispensable on an inward journey. If we look back in our own life we will find a long line of mentors who have led us along our path. Sometimes they are people we meet in life; more often they have, like Virgil, long left the world behind. We meet them in books and artworks. Some loom high above the rest and their influence is permanent. Others lead us for a short while and then fade into the background.

Each good book we read, each poem that inspires us, is a mentor; it teaches us paths that lead beyond ourselves into unknown territory.

Exercise 2: The Mentor

List at least seven people who have led you on your journey through life — a therapist, friend, teacher. Then choose one of these and note down what they meant to you and what you learned from their guidance.

> **Kurt by Sophia**
> I met him on a boat and heard him speak.
> He took responsibility for how he was feeling and the impact of his decisions on his life and the lives of others.
> He led me to the 12 steps.
> He showed me where to go when my Gravity Fails.
> How to surrender.
> To let go.
> To trust that a power

greater than myself
can truly bring me back
to sanity.
He showed me how to confront my demons
by taking stock of my life.

The Passage through Hell

Dante and Virgil arrive at the gates of hell where, with Virgil's power, they cross the Acheron, the river of hell, and enter the first circle of the underworld, limbo. Here the unbaptised and virtuous pagans dwell, including fellow poets Horace and Ovid; Socrates, Plato and Aristotle, and many Greek and Roman heroes.

They descend into the second circle where the lustful are forever blown about by howling winds; Helen and Paris, Tristan, Semiramis and 'voluptuous Cleopatra' are among them. In the third circle the gluttonous wallow in stinking mud and perpetual rain, mauled by Cerberus, the three-headed dog of hell.

In the third circle am I of the rain
Eternal, maledict, and cold, and heavy;
Its law and quality are never new …
Cerberus, monster cruel and uncouth,
With his three gullets like a dog is barking
Over the people that are there submerged.
Red eyes he has, and unctuous beard and black.
And belly large, and armed with claws his hands;
He rends the spirits, flays, and quarters them.

Cerberus represents the insatiable appetite of the glutton, the ravenous desire that now, in hell, attacks them from the outside. The lustful are tossed on a howling wind just as in life they were led and tossed about by their desires.

The tombs of heretics burn in perpetual fire. Passing through the wood of suicides, the poets enter the circle of fraud and malice, filled with seducers, flatterers, sorcerers and thieves. Here usurers sit on burning sand and the blasphemous endure the rain of perpetual fire. Traitors suffer in the deepest pit of hell.

Through this kind of metaphor, or allegory, Dante clothes intense inner experience in the language of his time. Personalities of the past and of his own era symbolise the ways in which the soul deviates from its original state of bliss. Through his portrayal of hell, Dante is able to powerfully explore the abysmal side of human nature.

Exercise 3: Hell

We too are wandering through the provinces of hell. Choose one province of sin and describe the suffering of those caught within it. Try to find, like Dante, a correspondence between a vice and its punishment.

One way to approach this exercise is to follow your guide to a scene of suffering and describe it, and then let your mentor explain the punishment. (Remember that the punishment is no outer torment inflicted on the soul, but the description of the inner state.)

Hell by Jo Lunay

The air stank, the street was strewn with rubbish and bodies and spew. We picked our way in the half-light, tripping in the gloom. My guide explains that there is never sunlight here, only stench-filled twilight.

The moaning got louder as we approached the last hovel, and the smell was so bad I had to hold my sleeve across my face. He was in there, squatting naked on the floor, ankle-deep in his own waste — and the people he had wasted …

He scrabbled around grabbing at objects, holding them up to each other, then throwing them aside, repeating this activity over and over. After some time I began to realise that the objects he groped at and tried to match were pieces of human flesh — limbs and body parts — pieces of a grotesque jigsaw he was trying in vain to reconstruct.

Hell by Julie Dickinson

I tear the salty crisp crackling from the carcass —
crunch and snap and savour
the warm juicy fat that runs down my arms.
The spit rotates, turning, turning, endlessly turning
The faceless face now confronts me

Oh God! I know this face!
I have been betrayed, tricked
into devouring the one I loved —

On Mount Purgatory

From there, passing through the very pits of hell where traitors such as Judas and Brutus are devoured, Dante and Virgil follow the stream of Lethe to the Island of Mount Purgatory. After washing themselves, they enter Mount Purgatory, where sins are purged from the repentant soul as it ascends slowly through the seven tiers.

On the first tier are the proud, bent beneath the weight of stone; on the second the envious with their eyelids stitched closed with wire. On the third, the wrathful are blinded by suffocating smoke and on the fourth the slothful run frantically, reciting examples of zeal to prick their conscience and rid it of its stain. On the sixth are the covetous, bound face down towards the world, and on the last tier, fire purges the lustful of their sins.

Dante has translated each shortcoming into a picture: the slothful engaged in frantic activity. The eyelids of the envious stitched shut, a picture of their blindness, their inability to see beyond their own affairs:

> And as no profit of the sun can reach
> Blind men, so with the aforesaid shades: the fire
> Of heaven is niggard of his light to each;
> For all their eyelids with an iron wire
> Are stitched and sealed, as to a wild young hawk
> That won't be still, men do to quiet her.

Exercise 4: On Mount Purgatory

Explore the realm of purgatory through a person of your choice. Follow them to the appropriate level of their transformation. Find a picture that shows the experience that will eventually liberate them from their fault. You could use again the personality you encountered in hell, thus transforming medieval concept of eternal damnation into the redeeming dynamics of grace.

Purgatory by Jo Lunay

Months later we visited him again. He still squatted as before but now he had cleaned his body and the floor and he had settled on one clear task. But this time there was another in the room. He had pieced this one together, washed each part and joined the parts as neatly as he could. We watched as he bent over the body, gently bathing it, carefully smoothing the seams until it looked quite whole.

The entire time he uttered soothing sounds, the words were indistinguishable but the atmosphere was unmistakable — compassion and the beginnings of self-forgiveness.

Purgatory Nan Connell

and i awake - brittle dry..... spat out
by the raging river - stretched
on the rack of a burning desert - molten
leached - broken - jagged - sculptured - pared

strewn about

my story continues now - la loba/wolf woman
this place in the desert where the spirit of women
and the spirit of wolves meet across time
shapeshifting - sure-footed she leads the pack:
she is in full cry - suffused with song
they arrive; panting in a circle of my abandoned carcus

my story becomes a litany - a poem - and finally a song
they crowd my bones - retrieving - licking
and as the fullest moon bursts its skin, i find my voice

i chant - i shout - i scream
i am singing the song of my soul. i am fleshed out - rising up
as one voice we howl to the moon.

Virgil leaves him here and Dante enters the sacred wood where in a lucid dream he experiences the blissful memory of earthly paradise, the long-lost state of primal innocence. Welcomed by Beatrice, the poet is overwhelmed with love. She leads him to Lethe and he drinks the water of oblivion and so loses all memory of his former sins. Then, drinking from the well of Good Remembrance, his spirit is renewed and he is ready to enter the realms of heaven.

Paradise

The medieval geography of soul coincided with the seven planetary spheres. The moon sphere is the first of the heavens and the furthest from the presence of god. Inconstant souls reside here. The second sphere is governed by Mercury and here souls who had the gift of leadership find their reward. The realm of Venus is occupied by those who were too much governed by their passions, yet were of affectionate disposition. Entering the sun sphere, Dante and his love see the blissful light of wisdom surrounding those who pursued it during their earthly life — the philosopher Thomas Aquinas enjoys intimate communion with other masters of wisdom in the sun sphere. The heaven of Mars strengthens those who gave their life for their faith, and the realm of Jupiter the just. Saturn is the abode of ascetics and contemplatives.

Exercise 5: Paradise

Picture someone in one of the spheres of heaven and describe their life of bliss, in which they reap their reward for earthly labour. Find images that illustrate the levels of spiritual reward. You could use the same personality from the last two exercises, as in the sequence of all three stages culminating in paradise by Mags Webster and by Janet Blagg. Where Mags Webster has cleverly extended the allegory to the computer age, Janet Blagg has used the opportunity to work through issues of personal importance.

Hell by Mags Webster

There is a man there sitting alone at a computer. He is surrounded by gadgets. It seems very sterile. He is concentrating so hard on the screen he does not see me watching him. I feel a heaviness in my hand, as if I am holding a plate of food. The man agitates the mouse, changes the CD in the CD drive; then changes to another CD. Whatever he is trying to do, it seems not to be working. He is getting frustrated. There are all sorts of people gathering round the desk, I recognise many of them, see them moving their lips as if talking to him, but he seems not to notice. Now he is lifting the phone to make a call, he is waving a hand, running it through his hair, pointing to the screen which looks blankly back at him. If I am holding food, it will have gone cold by now. His face is a mask of pain, he moves to embrace the monitor but it repels him. He notices the people standing round the desk but they fade, become ill-defined, vanish into mist. Finally he turns to look at me, but by that time I too am starting to walk away.

Purgatory by Mags Webster

There is a man there sitting alone at a computer. He is surrounded by gadgets. It seems very sterile … The man agitates the mouse, changes the CD in the CD drive; then changes to another CD. Whatever he is trying to do, it seems not to be working … There are people gathered around his desk, the same ones as in Hell, and they still appear to be trying to talk to him. This time, he seems to notice them, and I see his shoulders move, heave, as he begins to cry. The mouse is quiescent in his hand. The screen flickers. If I am holding food, it will have gone cold by now. I put down the plate and move towards him, but before I can get there the people round the desk have become solid, real, and they are switching off the computer, rubbing his back, massaging his shoulders, smoothing his hair. Someone puts a plate in front of him, and immediately he begins to eat. He doesn't look round as I start to walk away.

Paradise by Mags Webster

to: webstermv@purgatory.com
from: doejd@paradise.co.utopia
Paradise is nourishment, soul-food which never gets cold, where love is expressed through the endurance of motherhood, and to be old is to be sacred. We leave behind angles and sharp edges; we speak in colours; we are brimming with light. The more we have suffered, the more joy we experience — and peace, and hope, and laughter. Missing you and wishing you were here xxx

Hell by Janet Blagg

We left the third level, where gluttons stuffed their faces until their bodies exploded, and I held back a sigh of relief. It was where I feared ending up myself. Shelly gave my hand a squeeze. Of course he knew. He squeezed it again, harder, and said, 'Ready?'

As he opened the door my hands flew to my ears. Angry, vociferous, loathing voices, all shouting, shrieking, spitting over each other in a cacophony of hate: You stupid idiot! — Worthless whore! — You make me sick!

Shelly pointed down an endless corridor with cages all along it. We set off, under massive loudspeakers that blared their corroding messages between the bars behind which crouched naked men and women. 'These are the souls who beset their loved ones with anger and scorn,' said Shelly. 'Further on you will see the war mongers.'

In the first cage was a man with long limbs wrapped around him and fingers pressed into his ears. I bent down and looked into the pinched and grey face of my father. I got up and had to turn away from Shelly, I couldn't bear him to witness me witnessing my father. For I am my father's daughter.

Purgatory by Janet Blagg

In purgatory my father stands on a green hillside surrounded by a picture perfect family — Mum, and all us kids, clean and shiny, airbrushed over the seams. We are perfect, a credit to him, to be proud of. But he is invisible to us. He waves his arms, tries to lift us up and hug us. He smiles, but the smile slides by us, we are oblivious. He cannot touch us, move us.

I turn to Shelly, my throat dry. 'What punishment is this?' I say.

'Not punishment,' he replies. 'He is learning that the power of control is far inferior to being a mutual member of a connected whole. As you, my dear, are learning too.'

Heaven by Janet Blagg

'Here we go,' said Shelly. 'Welcome to heaven.'

It was like putting on an old coat, a long lost favourite coat I'd not expected to see again, with treasure still in its pockets. It was mine, heaven, and I was filled with an alien feeling, as if something warmer and more solid than blood ran in my veins.

'Is he here?' I asked.

'What do you think?' Shelly replied. 'You know the rules.'

We walked towards a table where a group of men sat talking animatedly. A child slid past me and ran up to my father. She climbed onto his knee and his fingers ruffled absentmindedly through her hair.

'You might call it tough love,' I said. 'And there was a lot of anger. But despite that, he could love. Thin on the ground it may have been, but he knew how to love.'

The Empyrean

Guided by Beatrice, Dante enters the Empyrean, where god and angels abide in brilliant light among the mystical rose, the wellspring of love. In this exalted sphere, Bernard of Clairevaux, great worshipper of the eternal feminine, becomes the poet's guide. Directing Dante's gaze toward the Holy Virgin, the saint asks the heavenly mother to grant the poet a full vision of god. The wish is granted, and *The Divine Comedy* culminates with the poet standing face to face with god, struggling to express in words what he beholds.

> High phantasy lost power and hence broke off;
> Yet, as a wheel moves smoothly, free of jars,
> My will and my desire were turned by love,
> The love that moves the sun and the other stars.

Beholding the divine, Dante is as perplexed by love as he was when Beatrice greeted him in the streets of Florence. His last lines are the divine octave of his earlier experience. He has found in heaven what he already knew on earth .

Here we leave Dante, the great cartographer of the medieval soul, and turn towards one of the few poets who matched the depth and breadth of his genius: William Shakespeare.

27

The Alchemical Stage

Three hundred years pass between the lifetimes of Dante and Shakespeare, two poets I consider linked through the work of Geoffrey Chaucer. It is well known that Chaucer's *Canterbury Tales* were inspired by Boccaccio's *Decameron*. It is less well known that they provide a down-to-earth version of Dante's vision, especially of Purgatory.

In *Canterbury Tales* characters from all walks of life — a knight, a nun, a franklin and a miller to name a few — entertain each other with tales on their pilgrimage to Canterbury. A pilgrimage was a self-inflicted purgatory, made in this world to reduce the time spent there in the next. Chaucer's characters are not yet true individuals — they are still largely defined by their social status — but they are on their way to it. He avoids creating stereotypes by describing his pilgrims in their particulars as well as by characterising their inner life through the stories they tell.

By contrast, Shakespeare's characters have arrived at individuality. Hamlet, Othello and Portia are all convincingly themselves. Their social status is incidental to their personality and their destiny is the result of inner factors, not outward circumstance. In this they differ markedly from the tragic heroes of antiquity who were victims of their destiny. Oedipus tried with all means to avoid his fate but failed against the greater powers that governed his life. Hamlet, in contradistinction, is able to exercise choice and agency. His task of avenging his father is well within his reach. Nothing hinders him but his inner disposition of soul. Only his constant thinking and doubt holds him back: the cause of his downfall follows from his inability to take action.

> Thus conscience does make cowards of us all; And thus the native hue of resolution is sicklied o'er with the pale cast of thought, and enterprises of great pith and moment with this regard their currents turn awry, and lose the name of action.

Chaucer's characters are on pilgrimage to purge themselves. Shakespeare allows us to experience the dramatic culmination of this process. We see Hamlet finally fulfill his intent, King Lear lay aside his conceit and Othello realise his unfounded jealousy. For all three, death is the final liberation from personal limitations.

Shakespeare's plays can also be seen in terms of the medieval alchemical tradition. The alchemists sought metamorphosis by linking their soul to the processes of the refining of metals. Their true laboratory was their inner life. The alchemist had a deep knowledge of the parallels between the forces of the soul and the forces of nature and used them for personal transformation. Working to purify a metal from all base admixtures, they simultaneously transformed their own soul.

Shakespeare's laboratory is the stage. Like an alchemist he knows which ingredients of soul to mix in order to effect transformation. Like chemical elements, the characters become each other's agents of change.

William Shakespeare

Shakespeare was born in 1564 in Stratford upon Avon and educated in the local grammar school. At eighteen he married Anne Hathaway, with whom he had three children. He later moved to London and established himself as an actor, playwright and co-owner of the esteemed Globe Theatre, favoured by Elizabeth I and James I. Most of Shakespeare's plays were written during his time at the Globe. When the theatre burned down the company moved to the Blackfriar playhouse. In 1612, Shakespeare returned to Stratford a wealthy man, to spend the rest of his life with his family.

That is as much as we know of his life. It seems somehow apt that we know so little of a man who made us know so much about others.

Sonnets of Love

Like Dante and Petrarch before him, Shakespeare has left us a volume of sonnets. These are some of the most beautiful love poems ever written. Like Shakespeare himself, his sonnets are a mystery in many respects. We do not know to whom they are addressed: some to a man, others to a woman. Nor do we know when they were written, though I suspect they originate, like those of Dante, in the early phase of the poet's career.

By Shakespeare's time, the tradition of the troubadours had become clichéd. He sought a new and emotionally real approach, and found it in a typical earthy English manner.

> My mistress' eyes are nothing like the sun;
> Coral is far more red than her lips' red;
> If snow be white, why then her breasts are dun;
> If hairs be wires, black wires grow on her head.
>
> I have seen roses damask'd, red and white,
> But no such roses see I in her cheeks;
> And in some perfumes is there more delight
> Than in the breath that from my mistress reeks.
>
> I love to hear her speak, yet well I know

> That music hath a far more pleasing sound;
> I grant I never saw a goddess go;
> My mistress, when she walks, treads on the ground:
>
> And yet, by heaven, I think my love as rare
> As any she belied with false compare.

In the sonnets, Shakespeare explores the width and depth of love, experimenting with the theme of love from every possible angle. He exercises his devotion like a pianist exercises his craft in etudes (finger exercises). The virtuosity he gains he uses later in his plays. Like no one before him, he is able to access the most varied characters and give them their due without personal agenda. The selfless love that allowed Dante to travel through hell, purgatory and heaven becomes in Shakespeare the means to access the depth of souls.

> Let me not to the marriage of true minds
> Admit impediments. Love is not love
> Which alters when it alteration finds,
> Or bends with the remover to remove:
>
> O no! it is an ever-fixed mark
> That looks on tempests and is never shaken;
> It is the star to every wandering bark,
> Whose worth's unknown, although his height be taken.
>
> Love's not Time's fool, though rosy lips and cheeks
> Within his bending sickle's compass come:
> Love alters not with his brief hours and weeks,
> But bears it out even to the edge of doom.
>
> If this be error and upon me proved,
> I never writ, nor no man ever loved.

Hamlet

Claudius has poisoned his brother, the king of Denmark, to obtain the throne and marry the queen. Soon after the funeral, prince Hamlet encounters his father's ghost who tells him about his uncle's foul deed and asks him to avenge his death. The rest of the play shows Hamlet trying to gain proof of the murder and take revenge as he wavers between indecision and resolve and entangles himself in endless doubts and complications that lead to tragic ends. He stabs the father of the girl he loves, and she in turn drowns herself in a stream. Claudius plots for Hamlet to be killed in a duel, but his plans backfire and he and the queen die together with Hamlet in the tragic culmination of the play.

These are the bare bones of the play. The plot itself does not account for the unceasing popularity of Hamlet — one of the most performed plays in the world. The real drama is inside Hamlet. The fascination of the play rests on his unique individuality and his effect on his environment.

Hamlet, in spite of all his indecision and mental agony, is an extremely likeable character, a 'noble soul' who wrestles with the corruption of his uncle, the weakness of his mother and the shallow morality of the court. But most of all he wrestles with his own doubts and over-thinking that prevent him from taking decisive action.

Imagine you are Hamlet, heir to the throne; a scholar and soldier and much loved by your people. Your father has been a great king, and you deeply admire him. You are studying at Wittenberg, a university in Germany, when news is brought that your father has died. You return for the funeral, only to discover your mother has married your uncle, a man you have always mistrusted. Now you see him sitting next to her in your father's place, wearing the crown that should be yours.

Your world shatters. You expected to find your mother and the court in funereal mourning, but you arrive to a marriage feast with your swaggering uncle giving speeches. Your father's courtiers smile at their new lord, everyone feasts and is merry. You give voice to your despair:

> O, that this too too solid flesh would melt, thaw and resolve itself into a dew! Or that the Everlasting had not fix'd His canon 'gainst self-slaughter! O God! God! How weary, stale, flat and unprofitable, seem to me all the uses of this world! Fie on't! Ah fie! 'Tis an unweeded garden, that grows to seed; things rank and gross in nature possess it merely. That it should come to this! But two months dead: nay, not so much, not two: so excellent a king; that was, to this, Hyperion to a satyr; so loving to my mother That he might not beteem the winds of heaven Visit her face too roughly … Frailty, thy name is woman! — O, God! A beast, that wants discourse of reason, would have mourn'd longer — married with my uncle, my father's brother, but no more like my father than I to Hercules: within a month she married! O, most wicked speed, to post with such dexterity to incestuous sheets! It is not nor it cannot come to good: but break, my heart; for I must hold my tongue.

You encounter your father's ghost, which begs you to avenge its death. You are overcome by intense hatred for your uncle and disgust for your mother. But doubt creeps in: What if the spectre was sent from hell to deceive you? What if it is an illusion, a figment of your disappointment, a projection of your hate? You need proof, and pretend to be mad to gain time. You discover that old friends spy on you for the new king. Even Ophelia, your former love, is used by her father to spy on you. Your mother is part of the plot, and except for your friend Horatio, you can trust nobody. Caught between doubt and indecision, between disappointment with the world and with yourself, you ponder the meaning of life in a corrupt world.

> To be, or not to be: that is the question: whether 'tis nobler in the mind to suffer the slings and arrows of outrageous fortune, or to take arms against a sea of troubles, and by opposing end them? To die: to sleep; no more; and by a sleep to say we end the heart-ache and the thousand natural shocks that flesh is heir to, 'tis a consummation devoutly to be wish'd. To die, to sleep; to sleep: perchance to dream: ay, there's the rub; for in that sleep of death what dreams may come when we have shuffled off this mortal coil, must give us pause: there's the respect that makes calamity of so long life; for who would bear the whips and scorns of time, the oppressor's wrong, the proud man's contumely, the pangs of despised love, the law's delay, the insolence of office and the spurns that patient merit of the unworthy takes, when he himself might his quietus make with a bare bodkin? Who would fardels bear, to grunt and sweat under a weary life, but that the dread of something after death, the undiscover'd country from whose bourn no traveller returns, puzzles the will and makes us rather bear those ills we have than fly to others that we know not of? Thus conscience does make cowards of us all …

Exercise 1: Hamlet's Monologue

Creep like Shakespeare into the very soul of a troubled young man. Use the historical Hamlet or a more contemporary soul. Write a monologue that distils his disgust with the world and his unending doubts.

Hamlet's Monologue by Sean Burke

My forehead burns, but my hands are cold. The wind is cold. Like a ghost. And the queen's bed is too, too warm. How can this be, when my father's corpse is not yet cold? His flesh hosts no worm, yet his own bed feeds a parasite.

Denmark remembers how the death of a King was once remembered. How spring would come; a consolation. How summer would bring the harvest. The leaves would fall with the last tears. The winter would be endured. The memory of a King is worth a year. But here spring is late. Shall she come at all without me? Will it be forever winter, while my hands are cold?

Hamlet's Monologue by Jennifer Kornberger

There is a table in my room where once I used to sit and write. There are pens on the desk, liquids in amber bottles line the edge. The table is made from a tree that once stood in an inaccessible forest. A forest so thick and sour that men with bulging angry trunks and scarred arms swore they would not hew wood in that region until midsummer, or a season marked by some distant and favorable moon.

That malevolent forest has grown here overnight — it surrounds this castle, branches weep through the windows, boughs break on the battlements. In the lower buildings it is dark already. But nobody can hear the false cackle of twigs as they walk on the floors, nobody sees the decayed leaves dropping into the festive dishes, the scorpions creeping between the sheets. My mother thinks she wears a gown of clean silk but a dark bird nests at her breasts and a streak of brown blood drips down her calves.

Even if I sat at this table there is no one to whom I can write of this.

When a troupe of actors arrives at the court, you stage a play that involves a murder like the one you suspect your uncle to have committed. During the performance, you observe his reaction, see how he pales and leaves in distress at the murder on stage. You have your proof. The spectre has told the truth. Now is your time to take revenge without tainting your conscience. You hurry after Claudius and find him alone in the chapel, praying. You stand behind him, the dagger in your hand. But wait! Though this brute has murdered your father, if you kill him now, in the middle of prayer, he might go to heaven instead of hell. You leave, your deed undone, and go to your mother with your proof.

> HAMLET: Look you now, what follows: here is your husband; like a mildew'd ear, blasting his wholesome brother. Have you eyes? Could you on this fair mountain leave to feed, and batten on this moor? Ha! Have you eyes? You cannot call it love; for at your age the hey-day in the blood is tame, it's humble, and waits upon the judgment: and what judgment would step from this to this? ... O shame! where is thy blush?
>
> QUEEN GERTRUDE: O Hamlet, speak no more: thou turn'st mine eyes into my very soul; and there I see such black and grained spots as will not leave their tinct.
>
> HAMLET: Nay, but to live In the rank sweat of an enseamed bed, stew'd in corruption, honeying and making love over the nasty sty, —
>
> QUEEN GERTRUDE: O, speak to me no more; these words, like daggers, enter in mine ears; no more, sweet Hamlet!
>
> HAMLET: A murderer and a villain; a slave that is not twentieth part the tithe of your precedent lord; a vice of kings; a cutpurse of the empire and the rule, that from a shelf the precious diadem stole, and put it in his pocket! ...

Exercise 2: Hamlet and his Mother

Write your own dialogue exploring the dramatic tension between mother and son (or a father and a daughter), in a similar situation (life is full of them). Do not take sides. Give each character their due.

Hamlet and his Mother by Mags Webster

H: So how many times a night does he screw you, Mother? It's disgusting, you don't even think whether anyone can hear …

G: How dare you speak to me like that? Since your father died I haven't even looked at another man until now. And now you come into my house to wreck my one chance of happiness.

H: Happiness? Don't confuse happiness with your grunting, heaving lust, Mother, oh yes, I've heard you both, it makes me sick. And as for not looking at another man since Father died … how did he die, Mother?

G: What do you mean?

H: I mean, wasn't it a little strange he was driving your car when it happened? He never drove your car, but you asked him to take it to the garage for a service didn't you?

G: Hamlet, you don't know what you're saying. Your father died in a senseless accident, and your uncle has been kindness itself, and if our feelings have developed, I hardly see it is your business. You're never at home, and when you are you use the house like a hotel. I hope when you get to my age you will understand that desire is not the province only of the young.

H: Oh don't try to bounce this back on me and my failings — after all I am your son, you made me what I am …

G: Oh poor Hamlet. Still denying responsibility for yourself and trying to throw the blame on everyone else? Grow up, little boy. People die, people move on. So what if you hear us making love? It's time you found your own place anyway.

Romeo and Juliet

Romeo and Juliet is concerned with the tragedy of romantic love. There is a long-running feud between two families, the Montagues and the Capulets. When Romeo, a Montague, and Juliet, a Capulet, meet at a party and fall in love at first sight, the scene for tragedy is set.

Imagine yourself Juliet. You glimpse the love of your life only to discover that he is the son of your family's mortal enemy.

> JULIET: Go ask his name: if he be married. My grave is like to be my wedding bed.
> NURSE: His name is Romeo, and a Montague; the only son of your great enemy.
> JULIET: My only love sprung from my only hate! Too early seen unknown, and known too late! Prodigious birth of love it is to me, that I must love a loathed enemy.

But seeing Romeo, you have met with something greater and more powerful than all your bonds with your family. That same night, thinking yourself alone on your balcony (not knowing Romeo is nearby), you give voice to your feelings.

> JULIET: O Romeo, Romeo! wherefore art thou Romeo? Deny thy father and refuse thy name; or, if thou wilt not, be but sworn my love, and I'll no longer be a Capulet.
> ROMEO [Aside]: Shall I hear more, or shall I speak at this?
> JULIET: 'Tis but thy name that is my enemy; thou art thyself, though not a Montague. What's Montague? it is nor hand, nor foot, nor arm, nor face, nor any other part belonging to a man. O, be some other name! What's in a name? That which we call a rose by any other name would smell as sweet; so Romeo would, were he not Romeo call'd, retain that dear perfection which he owes without that title. Romeo, doff thy name, and for that name which is no part of thee take all myself.
> ROMEO: I take thee at thy word: call me but love, and I'll be new baptised; henceforth I never will be Romeo.

There and then you decide to marry in secret. A friar is found and the next day the marriage is celebrated. That night, you are impatiently waiting for your new husband to come and consummate your marriage.

> JULIET: Gallop apace, you fiery-footed steeds, towards Phoebus' lodging: such a wagoner as Phaethon would whip you to the west, and bring in cloudy night immediately. Spread thy close curtain, love-performing night, That runaway's eyes may wink and Romeo leap to these arms, untalk'd of and unseen. Lovers can see to do their amorous rites by their own beauties; or, if love be blind, it best agrees with night. Come, civil night, thou sober-suited matron, all in black … come, gentle night, come, loving, black-brow'd night, give me my Romeo; and, when he shall die, take him and cut him out in little stars, and he will make the face of heaven so fine that all the world will be in love with night and pay no worship to the garish sun …

Exercise 3: Waiting for Romeo

Try to inhabit the soul of a strong young girl impatiently waiting for her love. Try to imagine her whole range of feelings and give them voice.

Juliet by Morgan Yasbincek

I can't stay, I can't stay. I can't be here when he comes. I'll leave a note, tell him I'm not sure now. It was the heat of the night, the moon, the blooms on the balcony. I thought I was ready for love, the simple delight of kisses and coy play. But this is no coy play. It is a cataclysm that has made a swoon of me. I cannot bear even the minutes of time. This day has been fraught with time, the tedious motion of hours and minutes and yet the ticking seconds terrify me. It is immanent. This love has made me into more than myself and that strange vine reaches for him with easing tendrils even as I plan to flee. It is a delicious agony, terrifying, mysterious — and into which all is already lost.

Juliet by Kristina Hamilton

Will this day never end? Mother prattles on about what is on the menu for the evening meal. The servants break into the privacy of my room. My childish cousins play childish games. This used to be my life, but now all is changed. Romeo comes tonight.

Through mishaps and messages gone astray, the plans of the lovers fail. Juliet feigns death, and Romeo, believing her dead, kills himself at her grave. When Juliet awakens from her induced sleep and finds Romeo dead at her side, she too takes her life.

Richard III

Richard is one of the most fascinating characters of the Shakespearean pantheon. In him we meet evil genius. A hunchback, physically distorted from birth, Richard feels excluded from a life of love and so is determined to hate and prove a villain. Ambitious for the crown he plots the deaths of his brothers, Edward the king, and Clarence, next in succession. He woos a woman in front of her husband's coffin, a man he has just slain. Richard is a master of intrigue, skilled at exploiting fears and weaknesses. At the start of the play his monologue reveals his character and intent.

> Now is the winter of our discontent made glorious summer by this sun of York; and all the clouds that lour'd upon our house in the deep bosom of the ocean buried ... and now, instead of mounting barded steeds to fright the souls of fearful adversaries, he capers nimbly in a lady's chamber to the lascivious pleasing of a lute. But I, that am not shaped for sportive tricks, nor made to court an amorous looking-glass; I, that am rudely stamp'd, and want love's majesty to

strut before a wanton ambling nymph; I, that am curtail'd of this fair proportion, cheated of feature by dissembling nature, deformed, unfinish'd, sent before my time into this breathing world, scarce half made up, and that so lamely and unfashionable that dogs bark at me as I halt by them; why, I, in this weak piping time of peace, have no delight to pass away the time, unless to spy my shadow in the sun and descant on mine own deformity: and therefore, since I cannot prove a lover, to entertain these fair well-spoken days, I am determined to prove a villain and hate the idle pleasures of these days. Plots have I laid ... to set my brother Clarence and the king in deadly hate the one against the other ...

Exercise 4: Richard III

Feel into the soul of this man, distorted from birth and mocked behind his back. Try to understand his discontent and hatred, his passion for revenge. Dive into the abysmal realm of a thwarted but brilliant soul.

Richard III by Sean Burke

I shall not be the victim of nature twice. This twisted body shall never be straight. Twice scoured Christendom, and none have been found to make my limbs new. Every promise came with a charlatan attached.

   But fouler chance it was that placed me two steps from the throne. If it were more, say, six, or even four, I would not stir. But two steps! The gods were not content with twisting my fingers, but had to place a golden cup just out of reach.

   I will not endure this double disfigurement. I'll hoist this unwilling frame onto the throne. I will drink from that cup, and I care not whether it runs with blood.

Richard III by Peter Stafford

Do you out there in nature's fine paradise understand me? Me, and my wretched being ... understand how it is to be shut out by the light of beauty, of freedom of limb, speech and inherited finery? No, and you never will ... for your imagination ends with your guilded mirror's love for. But, very quietly, hark ... listen well for I will tell you... How I will devise a means of bringing you to understanding. I will plan something especially for your darkness's delight ... Evil you would call it ... But what do you know ...? You of beauty stature and grace — What friend is evil to you? — none! ... but I have endured its lethal kinship saturating my every pore and waking thought across the fetid waste of all my ill-favoured years. Now I can not but train its fallow desire upon you.

28

Landscape and Soulscape

Dante's poetic horizon extended beyond the material world, and Shakespeare dealt with the essential within a human being. With the Romantics — Wordsworth, Coleridge, Shelley, Keats — we arrive at the biography of the poetic, where poetry becomes self conscious.

The Romantics awake to themselves and begin to reflect on their own soul life, their creative process and their mission as poets. Becoming self conscious is always accompanied by a process of emancipation: the Romantics distanced themselves from outdated modes of poetry as well as from the dominating scientific views of their time.

Science and Classicism

The world had changed since the times of Dante and Shakespeare. The earth was no longer at the centre of the cosmos, surrounded by spheres of angelic beings. It was just another planet in a mechanical universe. Copernicus, Galileo and Kepler had pushed the earth from its ancient throne and Newton had installed the new government of reason, safeguarded by physical laws and mathematical formulation.

The once spiritual universe had become a great clockwork, governed not by god but by the law of gravity. Reason, it was hoped, would soon explain everything and solve all problems. By the time of the Romantics, science had produced the industrial revolution and its by-products: the unchecked growth of cities and a class of impoverished workers chained to the rhythms of the machine, Blake's 'dark satanic mills'.

In this universe devoid of soul and imagination, poetry had fled to its own province, a forest of Arden far from the vicissitudes of scientific conception. Classicistic poetry established its own rules of conduct, much like the elaborate rituals at the European courts: a language which kept itself apart from ordinary use and everyday speech.

Pope and Johnson produced poetry that sounded elevated and refined, but was often artificial. Their aim was not to share personal insight or feelings but to treat poetic topics of interest in the best possible style: 'What oft was Thought, but ne'er so well Exprest' (Pope). They saw themselves as virtuosos of literary form, masters of verse and meter. The Romantics rebelled against this attitude just as they rebelled against the domination of the rational intellect. They aimed for a 'real' language, understood by all and without artificial decorum.

The Romantic Poet

In the Romantic conception, the poet was not just a virtuoso, but a human being endowed with a responsive soul, a deep feeling life and the power of the imagination, and called upon to share this surfeit of feelings, insights and concern with others. In the preface to *Lyrical Ballads* William Wordsworth asks himself: 'What is a poet?' In his answer he does not mention poetic skill or any other literary aptitude. He focuses on inner aliveness, sensitivity, and the power of the imagination to add to reality what is lacking:

> He is a man speaking to men: a man, it is true, endowed with more lively sensibility, more enthusiasm and tenderness, who has a greater knowledge of human nature, and a more comprehensive soul, than are supposed to be common among mankind; a man pleased with his own passions and volitions, and who rejoices more than other men in the spirit of life that is in him; delighting to contemplate similar volitions and passions as manifested in the goings-on of the Universe, and habitually impelled to create them where he does not find them. To these qualities he has added a disposition to be affected more than other men by absent things as if they were present.

Exercise 1: What is a Poet?

What makes someone a poet or writer? By what attitudes of soul do you recognise a poetic personality?

What is a poet? by Mags Webster

The poet lies back in the sunshine, bleeding to death. She feels the warmth just as she feels the wounds, and she wraps a cloth of words around each feeling. Life is not incremental, she experiences the whole thrust of its energy. Her head can trick her into using language to distance the emotions while her heart crouches like a burning coal in the grate of her chest, searing the real feeling into her soul. She bears the marks of one who sees and is impelled to tell of what she sees; she wears the scars under the velvet of her skin and each touch of the nib to paper is like the knife teasing the lips of the wound. She is a creature of joy and sorrow converging like mighty oceans, and through the faultline of her mind she pulls a single thread to say: it is like this, and like this, and like this.

What is a Poet? by Nandi Chinna

a poet is not made

of rote revisions
alphabetic chantings
and marching in unison to salute a flag
a poet is a leaf
of a particular mottled complexion
falling through the afternoon sky
a poet is the flotsam
washed up on grey sand
after a night of storms

a poet waits at the bus stop
in summer when the grass
is dry and sharp and feels heavy
so heavy that the need to lie down
on the verge is almost irresistible

a poet opens their eyes
and there is the whole world
inside the cavity of the skull
in frames and pictures and breeze
water lapping and sunlight
many different shades and reflections
a place where things are broken …

Poetic Childhood

For Wordsworth, childhood was a sacred source of inspiration and imagination, a kind of paradise lost and never quite regained, an echo of the sublime experience of the spirit before birth. He described this in **'Intimations of Immortality from Recollections of Early Childhood'**:

> There was a time when meadow, grove, and stream,
> The earth, and every common sight,
> To me did seem
> Apparell'd in celestial light,
> The glory and the freshness of a dream.
> It is not now as it hath been of yore;—
> Turn wheresoe'er I may,
> By night or day,
> The things which I have seen I now can see no more.
>
> The rainbow comes and goes,

And lovely is the rose …
Waters on a starry night
Are beautiful and fair;
The sunshine is a glorious birth;
But yet I know, where'er I go,
That there hath pass'd away a glory from the earth …

Exercise 2: Recollections of Childhood

Can you recall intimations of immortality — childhood memories infused with celestial light, innocence, a closeness to the elements?

Recollections of Childhood by Jennifer Kornberger

I see it in the boy what I had once
the slippery cloak of dawn, the shiver
of a branch, the way a rock
admonishes the sky, tolling the
stations of the day through bees
and cicadas and blowflies
as if all the world were thin amber
wings and an iridescent hum.

Summer of Bliss by Janet Blagg

Even then, aged nine or ten, I was self conscious. But it was a delicious self consciousness, that summer I left my large and unhappy family and entered the secret world of Great Aunt Mary and Great Uncle Stan, deep up a disused local railway line in Somerset, where Uncle Stan had been the last Station Master.

Beyond the station buildings which were mine to make-believe in, a stream overgrown with watercress, all mine. I was living in the Railway Children. I was the heroine. I was the only child and treated very seriously.

From the station master's cottage to the neighbour, a walk on open lane skirting a rounded hill, all soft and green. I am carrying a basket of eggs, carefully. I am reflecting on how good it is to be the substitute child for these nice old people whose only child is long grown up and gone. I sleep in her room.

I remember the strange smell of the cutlery drawer; and a visit to a yet more distant family with a great doll's house, and still me the only child. I remember more ordinary incidents of this short holiday than I do of the rest of my childhood put together.

Landscape

Finely tuned to their environment, the Romantic poets experience the tension of their age, the growing alienation of humanity from nature. William Blake captured the sinister side of city life in his poem, **'London'**:

> I wander thro' each charter'd street.
> Near where the charter'd Thames does flow
> And mark in every face I meet
> Marks of weakness, marks of woe.
>
> In every cry of every Man,
> In every Infant's cry of fear,
> In every voice: in every ban,
> The mind-forg'd manacles I hear
>
> How the Chimney-sweeper's cry
> Every black'ning Church appalls,
> And the hapless Soldiers sigh
> Runs in blood down Palace walls
>
> But most thro' midnight streets I hear
> How the youthful Harlots curse
> Blasts the new-born Infants tear
> And blights with plagues the Marriage hearse

Appalled by the decadence of city life they often sought refuge in the simplicity of rural life. Nowadays such longings are popular, but at the time they were a new element in the feeling range of the soul who for the first time felt estranged enough from nature to enjoy it again.

But the Romantics do not just long for what is lost. The past cannot be restored. An earlier humanity and the intensity of childhood experiences cannot be simply restored. Their appreciation of nature adds a new, active element through the use of the poetic imagination; by dint of effort a new link is forged that would otherwise not exist.

Wordsworth consciously elaborated on his experiences through his imagination. He regularly recalled his encounters with nature, refreshing his memory and adding to it through creative activity.

> I have said that poetry is the spontaneous overflow of powerful feelings: it takes
> its origin from emotion recollected in tranquility: the emotion is contemplated
> till, by a species of re-action, the tranquility gradually disappears, and an
> emotion, kindred to that which was before the subject of contemplation, is
> gradually produced …

Many of Wordsworth's poems were written by such recollections in tranquility, long after the initial experience. His poetic approach is perhaps the first conscious attempt at meditation developed directly out of the artistic praxis. His poem *'Daffoldils'* originated in this technique, as the poem itself testifies.

> I wandered lonely as a cloud
> That floats on high o'er vales and hills,
> When all at once I saw a crowd,
> A host, of golden daffodils;
> Beside the lake, beneath the trees,
> Fluttering and dancing in the breeze.
>
> Continuous as the stars that shine
> And twinkle on the milky way,
> They stretched in never-ending line
> Along the margin of a bay:
> Ten thousand saw I at a glance,
> Tossing their heads in sprightly dance.
>
> The waves beside them danced, but they
> Outdid the sparkling waves in glee:
> A poet could not but be gay,
> In such a jocund company.
> I gazed — and gazed — but little thought
> What wealth the show to me had brought;
>
> For oft, when on my couch I lie
> In vacant or in pensive mood,
> They flash upon that inward eye
> Which is the bliss of solitude;
> And then my heart with pleasure fills,
> And dances with the daffodils.

Seeing into the Life of things

This 'flash upon the inward eye' is more than a mere memory; it is an active process taking hold of the poet's soul and arousing the feeling of bliss. For Romantic poets, nature represents the landscape of the soul: the inner and outer worlds correspond. For Wordsworth, daffodils relate to bliss, lightness, cheer; the gentle hills and valleys of the Lakes relate to a sense of harmony and wholeness. When, after five years, he revisits the River Wye above *'Tintern Abbey'*, he reflects on the deep sustaining influence his former encounter had had for him during his absence.

> … Though absent long,
> These forms of beauty have not been to me
> As is a landscape to a blind man's eye;
> But oft, in lonely rooms, and 'mid the din
> Of towns and cities, I have owed to them
> In hours of weariness, sensations sweet,
> Felt in the blood, and felt along the heart;
> And passing even into my purer mind,
> With tranquil restoration; feelings too
> Of unremembered pleasure — such, perhaps,
> As may have had no trivial influence
> On that best portion of a good man's life:
> His little, nameless, unremembered, acts
> Of kindness and of love. Nor less, I trust,
> To them I may have owed another gift,
> Of aspect more sublime — that blessed mood,
> In which the burthen of the mystery,
> In which the heavy and the weary weight
> Of all this unintelligible world
> Is lightened; that serene and blessed mood
> In which the affections gently lead us on,
> Until, the breath of this corporeal frame
> And even the motion of our human blood
> Almost suspended, we are laid asleep
> In body, and become a living soul,
> While with an eye made quiet by the power
> Of harmony, and the deep power of joy,
> We see into the life of things …

The experience became a doorway to his own deeper nature, to the best in himself, and led him towards the threshold where his greater self, the living soul, saw 'into the life of things'.

Exercise 3: Recollection in Tranquility

Recollect your favourite place in nature. See it with your inward eye, in all its details. The picture may simultaneously recreate the feelings you once had and perhaps others you were not aware of. Describe the landscape and all the feelings and thoughts associated with it.

Recollections in Tranquility by Anthony Hart

Up high on the hill, a sou-wester blowing in great bursts down snowcapped mountains, punching into the sea scattering waves and spray. On my left, a peninsula jutting into the ocean, and behind me, the range stretched south into the distance. Whilst standing atop this hill, with the elements roaring on all sides, a sudden loneliness like nothing I'd ever felt, came, and wrenched my fragile emotions into great heart bursting sobs of grief. Grief for the loneliness he had to endure forever, for all eternity. This God, my God, how vast his loneliness was, for that is how the world is made. Created from the longings of a heart so immense, so immortal, so in love, so alone, that the mere quiver of a spoken being is enough to yield gusts of creation so strong they shatter all resistances, all knowing. My heart was not mine any more, it was his, or hers, everyone's, and in one bright moment it held that God-grief, that aloneness so always alone …

Landscape by Mags Webster

Peel back my skin: what is there? A long red dusty road that stabs into acid blue; miles of white sand fringed by the lace of the ocean; cool dark interiors of pine trees; the mottled flanks of mountains; the sea mist rolling in over farmland; the vast plate of land stained with gravy, the road scratching through it; secret places, mystery of a dark continent; shapes moving beneath the waves where the coral flares and blooms. There are no neat landscapes or pretty scenes: just dust, heat, raw elemental energy, rock face, timber, tang of wet leaves, smack of water and a vast, untroubled moon. This is my country, this is myself, unexplored, unknown and I a traveler with no compass and no map, just the desire to move forward and discover, to ask the land to take care of me as I journey. I will hold your hand as I take my first steps and you will let me lead the way, walk just behind my shoulder, give me water when I need it, discover for yourself the geography of this land, and then show me what wonders you have uncovered.

Soulscape

Our choice of landscape is inevitably a soulscape, a revelation of a deep longing for being one with the world, a paradise long lost and temporarily regained in active recollection. To find a landscape corresponding to the interior of the soul is one path the romantics explored. The other is the opposite gesture; to express the interior life by means of similes and metaphors gleaned from nature. Both ways were much used in Romantic novels such as those of the Bronte sisters and in gothic novels. In his *Biographia Literaria* Coleridge describes how he and Wordsworth followed the two paths for the Lyrical Ballads:

… my endeavours should be directed to persons and characters supernatural, or at least Romantic; yet so as to transfer from our inward nature a human interest and a semblance of truth sufficient to procure for these shadows of imagination that willing suspension of disbelief for the moment … Mr. Wordsworth, on the other hand, was to propose to himself as his object, to give the charm of novelty to things of everyday, and to excite a feeling analogous to the supernatural by awakening the mind's attention to the lethargy of custom, and directing it to the loveliness and the wonders of the world before us.

Coleridge's *Ancient Mariner* and *Kubla Khan*, are both intense inner experiences expressed by means of metaphors gleaned from human life and nature: they are soulscapes. *Kubla Khan* projects the dynamics between the abysmal depths of the human soul and its pure heavenly counterpart in to an imaginary landscape.

In Xanadu did Kubla Khan
A stately pleasure-dome decree:
Where Alph, the sacred river, ran
Through caverns measureless to man
Down to a sunless sea.
So twice five miles of fertile ground
With walls and towers were girdled round:
And there were gardens bright with sinuous rills,
Where blossomed many an incense-bearing tree;
And here were forests ancient as the hills,
Enfolding sunny spots of greenery.
But oh! that deep romantic chasm which slanted
Down the green hill athwart a cedarn cover!
A savage place! as holy and enchanted
As e'er beneath a waning moon was haunted
By woman wailing for her demon-lover! …

A damsel with a dulcimer
In a vision once I saw:
It was an Abyssinian maid,
And on her dulcimer she played,
Singing of Mount Abora.
Could I revive within me
Her symphony and song,
To such a deep delight 'twould win me,

That with music loud and long,
I would build that dome in air,

That sunny dome! those caves of ice!
And all who heard should see them there,
And all should cry, Beware! Beware!
His flashing eyes, his floating hair!
Weave a circle round him thrice,
And close your eyes with holy dread,
For he on honey-dew hath fed,
And drunk the milk of Paradise.

In this strange and oriental landscape we plunge into the sunless sea of soul, tumult and prophesies of war, to emerge to a vision of the holy and pure, the Abyssinian maid and the poet feeding on the milk of paradise.

Exercise 4: Soulscape

Recall a state of soul that had a powerful impact on you in your past and describe it as if it were a place in nature. You need not label your rich and unique interior world with a known landscape. Use your imagination to create a new one.

Soulscape by Nandi Chinna

Was it a desert there? Dry and hot and dusty with a road so littered with small round stones that your feet slide and scrabble, tripping and slipping. And the tyres on wheels rattle over the surface skidding in crazy zig zags and curves. A brittle road that leads to a city.

Before you can get to those towers of steel that glint red in the dusty sunlight, you encounter a sea of flapping detritus. Cans, bottles, plastic bags, torn garments, rotting carcasses, car bodies torn up and smashed, batteries leaking acid into the soil. This bright flatness mapped out by the orange and green of tidy bags, tumbles out in a 20 kilometre radius from the city's gates.

Amongst this debris people wander, tearing open the plastic bags to pick through their contents. Smoke from fires mingles with a smell that is almost unbearable. The smell of the empire. The shitty arse of the empire. The wasteland of success.

You may have to stop here for a while but be careful. People here have nothing, and nothing to lose. Their dogs are thin and pale and expect that you will throw rocks at them ...

You might get to the gates of the city. You might even be persuaded to trade favours with the guards, to give the last things up, your body even. Your language. You might get inside that citadel. But you might not.

What is poetry?

Many of the romantic poets had vivid interest in the act of poetic creation itself. Much of Coleridge's later work is highly philosophical, attempting a theory of poetic creation. Both Keats and Shelley wrote about poetry and aimed to understand the process of artistic creation and what part imagination played in the sum totality of the world. In these attempts poetry became self conscious (a theme that Owen Barfield has brilliantly explored in many of his works.)

Exercise 5: What is Poetry?

What do you do when you create poetry? Where do words come from, and what is the function of your imagination? Is it purely subjective capacity or can it touch a greater, universal truth?

> **What is poetry? by Martina Chippindal**
> When I write poetry a door is opened.
> I instantly recognise something.
> Invited into its surroundings
> I dust its surface,
> look at what sits beneath,
> turn it over and place it
> against the skin of my cheek.
> It is refreshing in the heat of summer.
> It stills me.
> I sit …
> and the shape of my back fits its contours.
> It holds me.

29

The Pact with the Devil

Goethe is not usually counted among the Romantics, but there is much in his work that allies him to the deeper intentions of this movement. Born in 1749 in Frankfurt, his mother was artistic and his father was a wealthy merchant committed to his son's education. Goethe learned to speak English, French and Italian and read Latin, Greek and Hebrew. Despite suffering a breakdown and long illness, he graduated as a lawyer. But the spirited young man had poetic ambition.

Prone to falling in love, he found himself in a painful triangle. When he extricated himself he poured his anguish into a novel that loosely resembled his personal situation. *The Sufferings of the Young Werther* immediately struck the nerve of the time and became not only a bestseller, but an icon. The character Werther, who kills himself for love, became a cult figure and his style of dress became the fashion of the day. Young men suicided in Werther costume, a copy of the book in their pocket. Napoleon, who Goethe met later in his life, read it eight times.

The Germany of Goethe's time was no unified political state, but a great number of independent kingdoms and city-states. The young archduke Karl-August of Sachsen-Weimar invited Goethe to be his mentor, and at the age of twenty-six Goethe moved to Weimar, where he was to stay for the rest of his life, taking on the mentorship of the archduke as well as responsibility for many offices of state.

Goethe lived a long, full and intense life and produced masterpieces in all literary genres: poems and ballads, novels and verse epics, plays and tragedies, fairy tales, essays and autobiographical writings. It was the height of German classical culture and he knew almost every poet, artist, and statesman personally — including Byron and Napoleon, Beethoven, Haydn, Humboldt, Schopenhauer and Hegel — and maintained a long and poetically productive friendship with Friedrich Schiller, Germany's second literary giant. Goethe was active in almost every branch of human endeavour and one of the last great geniuses to encompass art, science and politics.

Goethean Science

Goethe had a passion for science and contributed much to such diverse fields as botany, animal morphology, meteorology, geology and the theory of colour. It was Goethe who discovered the magenta spectrum. He himself thought his Theory of Colours the most important of his works. And against the prevalent opinion of authorities in anatomy, he proved the existence of the intermaxillary bone in the lower jaw.

But his importance as a scientist does not lie in his accidental discoveries but in pioneering an approach to science that was so far ahead of its time that it failed to make the impact it deserved: the artistic imagination as a scientific tool. He systematically pursued what Wordsworth had tentatively begun through his method of Recollections in Tranquility. This technique allowed Goethe to 'think with nature' rather than about her, and so to 'see into the life of things'. He understood that nature is a great artist and that it can only adequately be understood by the artist within the human being.

Faust

Goethe's greatest literary contribution is his drama Faust. He took the story of the medieval magician and scholar Doctor Faustus and his pact with the devil, and gave it new dimensions of meaning. He was not the first to adopt Faust for the stage: the first German drama ever was a version of Faust by Roswita von Gandersheim, a nun in the early middle ages. Christopher Marlowe's Dr Faustus was contemporaneous with Shakespeare, and Goethe himself encountered the story as an adaption of Marlowe's version. But Goethe's treatment differs markedly from the medieval flavour of Marlowe's play. His Faust is a modern character, an archetype that we will easily recognise as ourselves.

Faust: Part One

The play opens with a conversation between God and the devil Mephistopheles, who complains about the misery of the world.

> MEPHISTOPHELES: … On suns and worlds I can shed little light,
> I see but humans, and their piteous plight.
> Earth's little god runs true to his old way
> And is as weird as on the primal day.
> He might be living somewhat better
> Had you not given him of Heaven's light a glitter;
> He calls it reason and, ordained its priest,
> Becomes more bestial than any beast.
> THE LORD: And do you have no other news?
> Do you come always only to accuse?
> Does nothing please you ever on the earth?
> MEPHISTOPHELES: No, Lord! I find it of precious little worth.
> I feel for mankind in their wretchedness,
> It almost makes me want to plague them less.

When Mephistopheles shows nothing but contempt for the pitiful state of humankind, God mentions Faust, whom he holds in high regard. Mephistopheles does not think much of Faust and is convinced that he could easily turn him away from God.

> THE LORD: Do you know Faust?
> MEPHISTOPHELES. The doctor? …
>   Forsooth! He serves you in a curious fashion.
>   Not of this earth the madman's drink or ration,
>   He's driven far afield by some strange leaven,
>   He's half aware of his demented quest…
> THE LORD: Though now he serve me but in clouded ways,
>   Soon I shall guide him so his spirit clears…
> MEPHISTOPHELES: You'll lose him yet! I offer bet and tally,
>   Provided that your Honour gives
>   Me leave to lead him gently up my alley!

God trusts the good in Faust more than the evil that Mephistopheles is able to tempt him with.

> THE LORD: So be it; I shall not forbid it
>   Estrange this spirit from its primal source,
>   Have licence, if you can but win it,
>   To lead it down your path by shrewd resource;
>   And stand ashamed when you must own perforce:
>   A worthy soul through the dark urge within it
>   Is well aware of the appointed course.

Exercise 1: Prologue in Heaven

At this moment God and the Devil are meeting again, discussing a quite interesting topic: yourself. Write what you hear them say about you.

God and the Devil by Jill Whitfield

God and the Devil sit sipping coffee, engrossed in lively conversation. God points out a tall, capable-looking woman at a nearby table. She is on her own, stirring the froth of her cappuccino into the coffee. She seems distracted.

'Do you know that woman over there?' he asks.

'Which one?' The Devil follows God's gaze. 'Oh her! Yes, I've noticed her from time to time. Or, should I say,' he says with a smirk, 'she's noticed me!'

God raises one eyebrow. 'I doubt she's noticed you much. Her hands are too full to wander far from my path.'

'Ah,' says the devil, leaning back in his seat. 'That's when my best work is done! Load them up, have them believing they can do anything, and everything, then start to remove the tent pegs one by one.' He grins. 'They don't know they're missing at first. Till all that's left are the four corners. Then I just whip up a bit of weather and, hey presto, over she goes like a giant tumbleweed.'

God is unconvinced. He glances at the woman who seems to be wondering where her coffee has gone. She's scraping the bottom with a teaspoon, distracted.

'I don't think she even tasted that coffee,' mutters God to himself. 'I think it's time for a quiet word with her guardian angel. And some better tent pegs!'

Faust in his Study

It is Easter Saturday and the aged scholar is in his study all by himself, surrounded by Gothic vaults and books. He is pondering his life, painfully aware that all his knowledge and erudition have brought him no closer to nature and real life.

> FAUST: I have pursued, alas, philosophy,
> Jurisprudence, and medicine,
> And, help me God, theology,
> With fervent zeal through thick and thin.
> And here, poor fool, I stand once more,
> No wiser than I was before.They call me Magister, Doctor, no less,
> And for some ten years, I would guess,
> Through ups and downs and tos and fros
> I have led my pupils by the nose—
> And see there is nothing we can know!
> It fair sears my heart to find it so.
> True, I know more than those imposters,
> Those parsons and scribes, doctors and masters …

Faust suffers under the dead weight of intellectual knowledge. In the past, knowledge was transformative. It led to experience, to the source of life and the spiritual origins that govern the world. But now, like every modern human being, Faust is barred from experiences that alchemists and visionaries like Dante accessed. He feels caught in the maze of the intellect, buried beneath books, stuffed with facts and useless detail.

Exercise 2: Faust in his Study

Faust expresses for the first time a state of mind that is now familiar. There is no need to slip into his skin because we all wear it already. The intellect has taken hold of us all and we live in a world permeated by its forces. As a contemporary Faust reflect on your state of mind and the painful separation from the forces of nature and the divine.

Faust in his Study by Sean Burke

There are, as you may or may not be aware, 3672 different areas of unique knowledge, which may be classified into 39 separate areas of study, or 42 if one prefers the Eastern approach. Using the latter, I have created a schema whereby the bases of ethical action in relation to the 46 major sub-headings in each area of study can be cross-referenced with aspects of astrology, the human senses, colour, taste, mineral type, temperament, day of the week, economic cycle, and the incidence of revolutionary outbreaks in Central and South America. By the time you read this note, I will be dead. Please do not overfeed the goldfish.

Faust realises that his unfruitful search for knowledge has cost him the best of his years. Painfully aware of the superficiality of intellectual knowledge he seeks deeper experience by means of magic:

> So I resorted to Magic's art,
> To see if by spirit mouth and might
> Many a secret may come to light;
> So I need toil no longer so,
> Propounding what I do not know …

Faust succeeds in conjuring forth the Spirit of the Elements. But the presence of this spirit proves too much for the unprepared Faust:

> SPIRIT: Who calls for me?
> FAUST: [face averted] Appalling vision! …
>   I cannot bear you! Woe!
> SPIRIT: With bated breath you yearn to meet me,
>   To hear my voice, to gaze upon my face;
>   Swayed as your mighty soul-pleadings entreat me,
>   I yield, am here! What horrors base
>   Now seize you superman! Where's the soul's call you hurled?

Rejected by the Spirit of the Elements and crushed by his visions, Faust considers suicide to open the doors to the spirit. Raising the poisoned draught to his lips, he hears the Easter bells of a nearby church, and, touched by childhood memories, refrains from the deed.

The next day a black poodle follows Faust back to his study. Here it reveals itself as Mephistopheles and offers his services to Faust. Faust is cautious, knowing the devil offers nothing for free, whereupon Mephistopheles declares his bargain: he will serve Faust in this world if Faust will serve him in the next.

> FAUST: No, no! Old Nick's an egoist — it's hard
> To picture him in any special hurry
> To be of service for the love of God.
> Spell out just what the bargain turns upon;
> Not safely is such servant taken on.
> MEPHISTOPHELES: I shall be at your service by this bond
> Without relief or respite here on earth;
> And if or when we meet again beyond,
> You are to give me equal worth.

Faust however doubts if the devil will be able to satisfy his needs.

> What is, poor devil, in your giving?
> Has ever human mind in its high striving
> Been comprehended by the likes of you?

Faust wants more than the pleasures of this world. He seeks more than the world is able to offer. When Mephistopheles remains confident that he can satisfy Faust's desires, Faust offers a bet: if he is ever satisfied with what this world can offer him, if ever he can be lulled into complacency, then he will surrender his soul to the devil.

> FAUST: Should ever I take ease upon a bed of leisure
> May that same moment mark my end!
> When first by flattery you lull me
> Into a smug complacency
> When with indulgence you can gull me
> Let that day be the last for me!
> This is my wager!

Exercise 3: The Pact with the Devil

The meeting with the devil who tempts us with his services in this world, but requires repayment in the next, is worth exploring. There is a payoff for any form of temptation. Every passion we have also has us: we use our computer and soon it uses us. The advantages of technology come with a long tail of destruction. For every comfort we gain, a loss is incurred; we drive our car and forget to walk.

Write a dialogue between you and your particular devil. The devil is an expert on your weaknesses and knows how to exploit them.

Faust's Pact with the Devil by John Stubley

I want to talk to the devil. Tell him it's OK.
Tell him it was all a long time ago, a place far away. Nowhere. Now. Here.
I want to sit down beside him with all the oceans and all the mountains and all our lives in front of us.
I want to tell him everything is going to be fine.
I want to point out the waves, finger the highest peaks
and tell him that everything will be forgiven, blessed, accepted.
I want to take his hand and lead him into it,
melting closer as the waters and the snow overflow us.
I want to tell him there's nothing more to be scared of, nothing left
to fear. I want him to believe me.
I want to believe it myself.
For this I would give anything.

Dealing with the Devil

Faust senses that the devil and all he can provide by means of this world will never completely satisfy him. In this, Goethe's Faust differs from all previous versions: he gets entangled in Mephistopheles' snares, but never entirely succumbs to temptation.

From the moment of their pact, Mephistopheles accompanies Faust constantly. He leads his master through all the stages of human experience available in this world, like Virgil led Dante through those of the afterlife, starting at the witches' kitchen where the aged scholar is made young again. Returning to the world, the rejuvenated Faust falls in love with an innocent girl, Margaret. He enlists Mephistopheles' help to gain her affection and soon the pair are lovers.

But the devil's help proves fatal: to aid the nightly meetings of the lovers, he procures a sleeping draught for Margaret's mother that ends her life. He engages Faust in a duel with Margaret's brother in which the latter is killed. Faust has to flee the town, not knowing that Margaret is pregnant. While Mephistopheles keeps him away, Margaret is publicly shamed for her pregnancy and accused of her mother's death. She is imprisoned and, driven to despair, kills her own child. Faust tries to save her, but Margaret, seeing Mephistopheles at his side and sensing his true nature, refuses to follow Faust into freedom, preferring death.

Faust's love affair ends in tragedy. Because of his alliance with Mephistopheles his passion for a young and innocent girl brings death to her and her family. Part One ends leaving Faust in despair and guilt.

Faust: Part Two

In Part Two Faust, with Mephistopheles' help, enters the sphere of power and politics. At court they endear themselves to the emperor by assisting him in his need for funds. Mephistopheles invents paper money that can be printed without recourse to actual value. Faust stars as a magician and organises magnificent spectacles to entertain the court. The emperor asks him to conjure from the underworld the spectres of Helena and Paris, the male and female ideals of antiquity. Mephistopheles agrees only reluctantly to help Faust on this adventure, for it entails a great descent in time, back to the Mothers, a realm that Mephistopheles resists entering.

> MEPHISTOPHELES: Goddesses sit enthroned in reverend loneliness,
>   Space is as naught about them, time is less;
>   The very mention of them is distress.
>   They are — the Mothers.
> FAUST [starting]: Mothers!
> MEPHISTOPHELES: Are you awed?
> FAUST: The Mothers! Why, it strikes a singular chord.
> MEPHISTOPHELES: And so it ought. Goddesses undivined
>   By mortals, named with shrinking by our kind.
>   Go delve the downmost for their habitat, Blame but yourself that it has come to that.

Descent to the Mothers

Faust descends and returns with the apparitions of Helena and Paris. The court watches the pair appear. Seeing Helena, Faust is seized by passionate love. When Paris threatens to lead her back to the underworld, Faust seizes her. There is an explosion, Helena and Paris dissolve into a mist and Faust is left unconscious on the ground.

Mephistopheles takes Faust back to his old study. Here his former apprentice Wagner is creating a human being in a retort. The newborn being, Homunculus, takes Mephistopheles and the still unconscious Faust back to Greek antiquity. Faust awakens, encountering sphinxes, centaurs, and nymphs. He meets the seer Manto and witnesses discussions between the philosophers Anaxagoras and Thales.

I have always been intrigued by Faust's journey to the Mothers. Maybe because as writers we undertake such journeys to bring heroes or heroines of the past into our own time. The artists of the Renaissance voyaged to ancient Greece for inspiration. The Romantics rediscovered the spirit of the Middle Ages. Modern writers often travel to India, China or Japan to infuse their poetry with new life.

Exercise 4: The Return to the Mothers

Journey back to the sources of your inspiration, the Mothers, creators of time. Describe your meeting, or what you experienced through them.

The Mothers by Edward Laurs

100 canoes carving the ocean.
I sit at the helm of the lead ship.
Kupe The Navigator by my side whispers in Aroha's ear
She is the muse of the wearied warrior's arms. She wails out a karakia to Tangaroa, father of the Oceans, beseeching him to soften his skin, calm his mind to enable the oars to cut deeper into his waves.

The stars are pulling us South. Away from Hawaiki, to Aotearoa - the land of the long white cloud. As passenger I watch the fire in the eyes of the waka's engine. 60 Men. Real Men. Full moko chart the stories of their triumphs, their heritage. Their names destine their future. They are creating a future – these nation builders. These glorious innovators. The bravery overwhelms me as we are plunged further and further South. The abyss of blue widens. Fuelled by the dream of the hope of a new land - rich in soil, veined with rushing rivers and a sun shining with the warrior's own spirit.

The Homunculus by Jennifer Kornberger

Inside me a tiny homunculus lives in the chambers of my heart. He is humming and he's writing a book about what he knows. It is called 'The Great Mothers'. Every so often he dips his quill into my blood. The words surf around like antigens. Some days I feel my immunity to all the dung of this world humming like that homunculus and I pat my heart so he feels my encouragement to keep on writing.

Faust meets Helena in Sparta and carries her back to medieval times. He courts her and wins her love and she bears a son, Euphorion, the graceful embodiment of poetry. But when Euphorion, like Icarus, attempts to fly and fails, he and his mother vanish from Faust's life.

Philemon and Baucis

Faust returns to the emperor who is at war with a rival. With Mephistopheles' help he procures three allies, representing the primeval forces of violence. When the war is won with their help, Faust asks to be rewarded with the gift of coastal lands, on which he aims to found a new society, a community of free human beings.

Soon the work proceeds. But an old couple, Philemon and Baucis, stand in the way of these grand plans. The pair represent the innocent part of humanity, the naive, powerless and poor who stand in the way of great enterprises; indigenous societies and the last parts of pristine nature to fall. When Faust asks Mephistopheles to relocate them, the devil employs violence and Philemon and Baucis are killed.

Though inspired by the ideal of human freedom and an equal society, to achieve it, Faust must destroy the lives and happiness of others in a tragic clash between progress and conservation, culture and nature.

Exercise 5: The Price of Progress

The conflict between Faust and Philemon and Baucis is omnipresent nowadays. We all take part in it just by living in western society. Enjoying the means of modern technology and the comforts of civilisation we side with Faust. Suffering the devaluation of our environment and our innocence, and plagued by worldwide inequality and exploitation of the poor, we join with Philemon and Baucis.

Let the conflict inspire a piece of writing that reflects the enormity of the problem, the violent means and tragic ends that it entails.

The Price of Progress by Mags Webster

Listen up: I have good news. Everyone is going to be happy. We're all going to live to be a hundred, and nobody is going to get Alzheimer's. Everyone is going to have great sex, beautiful, loving children, good-looking parents. If you work, it really will be 9 to 5. We're all going to be super healthy, so we don't need doctors, nurses, dentists, psychologists, hospital porters or specialists. We're going to be born with all the knowledge we need, so we won't need teachers, academics, school-dinner ladies or philosophers. Once we've built all the accommodation, we won't need architects, surveyors, builders, bricklayers, electricians or plumbers. We'll all be really happy staying in our homes entertaining ourselves, so we won't need musicians, poets, playwrights, actors, composers, dancers or novelists. Food will be free and available from a central source, so we won't need farmers, truck drivers, fruit-pickers, checkout staff or shopkeepers. We'll abolish money so we won't need accountants, bankers or tax officials (although they will have to wear badges to state what they did in a previous life). So everything will be perfect, in a dull, overcrowded, selfish sort of a way.

The Price of Paradise by Nandi Chinna

It's amazing what you can do these days
my father rode a too big bicycle five miles
across dirt tracks to school
sometimes he rode a pony
he had ice delivered by the iceman
on a cart pulled by a horse

and milk was ladled out from a can
into a jug held out at the back gate
his best friend lived in a house
made of hessian with a dirt floor
his mother made bread and preserved fruit
he bought lollies from big jars
served out into rolls of paper
and no one stole his bicycle
when he leaned it against the wall

but it's amazing what your can get these days
it's all wrapped up in plastic
it's all made in big steel warehouses
where machines mix and fold stamp roll wrap and pack

it's all grown and made in other countries
brought here on ships and trucks and trains
packed on shelves in brightly lit display cabinets
each item individually wrapped for health and safety

I eat it
it tastes like dust

Faust grows old in pursuit of his dream and is struck by blindness. Mephistopheles fools him into believing that his great project has been completed. Faust rejoices in the achievement and admits that now he is content — so losing the bargain. Faust dies and Mephistopheles rejoices, convinced that Faust is now his. But the heavens open and descending angels rescue the immortal soul of Faust. Angels announce that sa oul who ceaselessly strive, can be redeemed.

Faust has lived a full life, though caused much devastation in his wake. We see Faust'ascend through the spheres of heaven, guided by the saints. He encounters Margaret who has all the while protected him with her love and now directs him toward the eternal feminine as the highest aim of adoration. The play ends with the lines of the Chorus Mysticus:

> All that is temporal
> Is but a parable;
> The unattainable
> Here becomes action.
> Human discernment
> Here is passed by;
> The eternal feminine
> Draws us on high.

30

Western Edge

In England, Victorian poetry succeeded the Romantic impulse. The freshness of Shelley and Keats, Wordsworth and Coleridge, gives way to the mature and masterful poetry of Alfred Lord Tennyson. Tennyson is a master of rhyming as well as epic poetry. The poet laureate of the Victorian age wields his poetic sceptre will unequalled skill. Poems like 'The Lady of Shalott' and 'Crossing the Bar' will remain all-time favourites of poetry lovers. In his work, 'In Memoriam,' (a work written after the passing of his friend Arthur Hallam) Tennyson sustains powerful rhyme as he plots the journey of the soul. He frequently turns to ancient myth and medieval legend. His verse epic 'Idylls of the Kings' is a masterpiece.

Ralph Waldo Emerson

While the poetry of Tennyson flourished in England, new impulses stirred abroad. America, having won political independence in the late 18th century, was now preparing to find its cultural identity. The Transcendentalists, a group of New England poets, writers, thinkers and social activists, were the first to sound the clarion call of cultural independence.

Central to this movement was the poet-philosopher Ralph Waldo Emerson. Born in Boston, Massachusetts, Emerson studied at Harvard and after taking up a teaching position became a Unitarian minister, but he soon resigned, unable to reconcile his broad thinking with the mindset of his church.

On return from a trip to Europe, where he met Wordsworth and Coleridge, he began a successful career as a public lecturer and essayist. The new state was in need of inspirational presenters and Emerson fitted the mould. He carefully prepared his lectures and revised them for publication as essays. Addressed to the general public, they retained their broad appeal in print.

Though Emerson was an acclaimed poet, his lasting contribution to the biography of the poetic is his body of essays: they are philosophical masterpieces that originate from a sphere of poetic inspiration. His philosophy is not a finely wrought system, but an intuitive discipline. He invites his readers to be active, present and independent in thought. His writings are doorways to spiritual self-reliance, to the evidence that active thinking can provide for itself. For Emerson, thinking IS a poetic participation in the 'over-soul' that encompasses nature and mind.

The American Scholar

Emerson's first essay *'Nature'* soon became the bible of the transcendentalist movement. It was soon followed by *'The American Scholar,'* an essay now widely recognized as America's Declaration of Cultural Independence. Emerson begins his address with an image from Indian mythology:

> It is one of those fables which out of an unknown antiquity convey an unlooked-for wisdom, that the gods, in the beginning, divided Man into men, that he might be more helpful to himself;
>
> The old fable covers a doctrine ever new and sublime; that there is One Man,—present to all particular men only partially, or through one faculty; and that you must take the whole society to find the whole man. Man is not a farmer, or a professor, or an engineer, but he is all. Man is priest, and scholar, and statesman, and producer, and soldier. In the divided or social state these functions are parceled out to individuals, each of whom aims to do his stint of the joint work, whilst each other performs his. The fable implies that the individual, to possess himself, must sometimes return from his own labor to embrace all the other laborers…

For Emerson this all-embracing activity is the intuitive thinking:

> In the right state he is Man Thinking. In the degenerate state, when the victim of society, he tends to become a mere thinker, or, still worse, the parrot of other men's thinking…

Emerson proceeds to explore the function of science for the scholar:

> To the young mind (he means earlier cultures) everything is individual, stands by itself. By and by it finds how to join two things and see in them one nature; then three, then three thousand…But what is classification but the perceiving that these objects are not chaotic, and are not foreign, but have a law which is also a law of the human mind? …
>
> He (the scholar) shall see that nature is the opposite (meaning the complement) of the soul, answering to it part for part. One is seal and one is print. Its beauty is the beauty of his own mind. Its laws are the laws of his own mind. Nature then becomes to him the measure of his attainments. So much of nature as he is ignorant of, so much of his own mind does he not yet possess. And, in fine, the ancient precept, "Know thyself" and the modern precept, "Study nature," become at last one maxim…

For Emerson true science unifies the world, makes whole what is separated. True thinking thus is to the world what the thinking Human being, that is, the scholar is to the separate professions.

Emerson's whole message is one of spiritual activity, independence, self-reliance and authenticity. His essay articulates the ideals that underpinned the founding of the United States by asserting the sovereign rights of the Scholar, as the representative human being, to think for himself, to innovate in thought, to go beyond established opinions. He establishes the thinking human being as a nation unto itself, endowed with its own laws and particular mission.

Exercise 1 Global Scholar

Emerson believes that our thinking can know the world and improve it. What do you think about thinking? In your response attempt to think as actively and poetically as Emerson: in the absolute present, unrestricted by what you already know or have been taught, listening to nothing but the self-evident, self-sustaining activity of your thinking. Try to surprise yourself with new insights. If essays are not your style, write a poetic response.

Global Thinking by John Ryan

I
a global scholar is Gaia
        is consciousness
                as environment
                        is planetary ethics
                    with technology
              as sense
    is poiesis-making
an animalistic infusion

II
a global scholar acknowledges Earth as animal consciousness is one who thinks syncretically who sees knowledge as enlivening current of world whose body is transcendental who queries intuition as serious fact in determining the real.

III
(Pulse)
seed heart
    always evaporative
  and undiminishing
occupying my corridors of thinking

>   a bivalve sea fresh
>   physis grown with earth
> prana finger throb and settle
>   this is fragrant
>   sonic fission
> the gut pulse sig-
>   nals this
>   bleeding a
> live.

The Global Scholar by Jennifer Kornberger

The Global Scholar has developed the common sense - being the sense for what is common. The commonality of the head with the globe for instance, or the head with the cupola of the sky. She sees the stars as tracks of animals and hunts down their meaning in a pond, a puddle, in all reflective surfaces. She locates the common sense not as Averroes did, behind the retina, or as Leonardo did - in the ventricle of the brain - but in the wind, with the knowledge that each breath draws the Milky Way closer.

Henry David Thoreau

In Emerson the new nation had found a national sage. In Henry David Thoreau, it would find its first prophet. Thoreau was a poet, writer, activist, anarchist, philosopher, social critic, naturalist and historian. He was fourteen years younger than Emerson and one of the philosopher's closest friends. It was Emerson who encouraged his young, restless and eccentric protégé to keep a regular journal and thus sparked his literary musings. Emerson was a poet in his thinking, Thoreau in his way of leading his life. His deeds are poetic stimulants, his attitudes an on-going inspiration.

Living in the Woods

Thoreau's major work, *'Walden, or, Life in the Wood's*, is an account of an experiment. Thoreau withdrew for two years, two months and two days into solitude to find himself as a writer. He built himself a small cabin with minimal means on a patch of land near Walden Pond that belonged to Emerson. His aim was to live simply and as close to nature as possible. During this time he sustained himself through his own farming efforts and kept only sparse company. His 'time out' was part social experiment, spiritual quest, writing retreat, nature experience and exercise in self-reliance. He was no doubt one of the first 'conscientious drop-outs'.

I went to the woods because I wished to live deliberately, to front only the essential facts of life, and see if I could not learn what it had to teach, and not, when I came to die, discover that I had not lived. I did not wish to live what was not life, living is so dear; nor did I wish to practice resignation, unless it was quite necessary. I wanted to live deep and suck out all the marrow of life, to live so sturdily and Spartan-like as to put to rout all that was not life, to cut a broad swath and shave close, to drive life into a corner, and reduce it to its lowest terms, and, if it proved to be mean, why then to get the whole and genuine meanness of it, and publish its meanness to the world; or if it were sublime, to know it by experience, and be able to give a true account of it in my next excursion.

Walden condenses his two-year quest into a one-year narrative that follows the changing seasons. It is an inspirational book, a manual for simple living with instructions about how to cheaply build a dwelling as well as detailed accounts listing all costs involved. Walden is perhaps one of the first self-help books. Thoreau is also a gifted naturalist whose love for his environment is infectious. His writing is wide ranging and mixes accurate observation, social criticism and philosophic thought.

Exercise 2: Walden

All writers have their Walden, an ideal place to contemplate themselves and the world; a place to withdraw and get work done. This place may be real or imaginary, close or far away, already visited or only dreamt of. What and where is your personal Walden? And why do you go there? What do you do in your time out?

Walden by Edward Laurs

At first a single studio – isolated, unconnected. A place where time blurred into those hours between 1 and 4 am… where nothing ever happens, although when it does it is unforgettable.
Then as I grew, this place alive with literature, film and music… the gourmandizing of culture – all I could devour.
It became a cave I slunk into – separate – alone. Became filled with frustration…a consciousness of the shortness of life.

Out of the cave I came and breathed. I discovered oceans which embraced, washed and woke me. Forests that humbled with their size, near infinite diversity, ability to adapt and the lusciousness of their scent. And rivers. Great highways, both traditional and informational. Transmitters of things: trade, of thoughts, and secrets.

Outside is where it is. By stepping away from what had been laid down I could finally dig deep and enter me.

Un-Walden by John Stubley

I realise I have no Walden, as Thoreau or others may have it. The walls of this membrane are permeable; my hut, open to the wind. Light need not wait to some hour of the day to steal its way across my floor; dust does not gather itself; no fly rests on the window, still.

I have only a few moments come morning, come evening, come the balance of the day, should the day balance that way. Here my hut has a chance to find me in the otherwise dark woods. Here a hut has a chance, warm, a lamplight alight on a table-top, a chair for working fair hours away. Here is a hut that finds me, some moments; a hut where the world can gather, until it passes, and the world rolls, rounding itself into the un-walls of my hut once more.

Civil Disobedience

During this time at Walden Pond Thoreau was imprisoned for refusing to pay tax. His refusal was a conscientious act, a means to protest against the American state that professed freedom but allowed slavery. To pay, he felt, would be to support the corruption of the state. Against his will, a relative paid the outstanding fees and Thoreau was released after one day. This principled refusal resulted in Thoreau's famous essay on 'Civil Disobedienc', a poetic milestone of social activism. *Civil Disobedience* became a major influence on political thought and a source of inspiration to social activists such as Leo Tolstoy, Mahatma Gandhi and Martin Luther King.

Thoreau believed, 'That government is best which governs not at all'. He asks 'if there can be a government where majorities do not rule, but conscience,' and noted that:

> The mass of men serve the state thus, not as men mainly, but as machines, with their bodies. They are the standing army, and the militia, jailers, constables, … etc. In most cases there is no free exercise whatever of the judgment or of the moral sense; but they put themselves on a level with wood and earth and stones;… Such command no more respect than men of straw or a lump of dirt. They have the same sort of worth only as horses and dogs. Yet such as these even are commonly esteemed good citizens. Others, as most legislators, politicians, lawyers, ministers, and office-holders, serve the state chiefly with their heads; and, as they rarely make any moral distinctions, they are as likely to serve the devil, without intending it, as God. A very few, as heroes, patriots, martyrs, reformers in the great sense, and men, serve the state with their consciences also, and so necessarily resist it for the most part; and they are commonly treated as enemies by it.

Thoreau's distinction between mindless masses and the conscientious reformers is the exact complement to Emerson's differentiation between Man Thinking (the American Scholar) and a mere thinker… the parrot of other men's thinking.

Today when ignorance and complacency are epidemic, Thoreau's stand is as inspiring as it was then. Our society readily accepts the status quo and is little inclined to change it. Writers and poets tend to be socio-sensitive. They have an acute sense for injustice, and quickly register inconsistencies in the fabric of society. They are often the first to speak out.

Exercise 3: Literary Disobedience

This exercise is your chance to explore the meaning of civil disobedience in the life of the writer. What are your thoughts about the state of society? What do you really stand for? What do you think is worth fighting for?

Civil Disobedience (Man's Best Friend) by John Stubley
We have let slip the dogs of the economy; unchained them before training them. And so, now, we are forced to tame them on the run; as they fly by, as they devour us, as we ride them. And when we manage to do so, every once in a while, we find that it is ourselves we tame, also. And we can become men in such moments, serving other men, with best friends between us; with best friends now heeled.

Civil Disobedience by Liana Christensen
The German people have been much on my mind of late as I watch in horror while my nation sinks deeper and deeper into a complacency fat with fascism. I'm a pacifist. Yet here we are just past Remembrance Day and I can't help thinking of those who died for the idea of freedom. What do their ghosts make of their homeland where now we have concentration camps in remote deserts and think nothing of tearing a mother from her newborn infant?

What was it like if you were even half awake in Germany watching the gathering darkness, feeling overwhelmed, appalled, powerless?
I know.

We will be judged by history.

Enter: The American Poet

As soon as the Transcendentalists set the stage of cultural America, Walt Whitman appeared on the scene, producing a new poetic style that is as wide, broad, generous and open as his country. We sense the fresh, confident and entrepreneurial spirit of a new nation surging through his lines; we can feel the prairies in the cadence of his lines and the pulse of New York in his '**Song of Myself'**.

> I celebrate myself, and sing myself,
> And what I assume you shall assume,
> For every atom belonging to me as good belongs to you.
>
> I loafe and invite my soul,
> I lean and loafe at my ease observing a spear of summer grass.
>
> My tongue, every atom of my blood, form'd from this soil, this air,
> Born here of parents born here from parents the same, and their parents the same,
> I, now thirty-seven years old in perfect health begin,
> Hoping to cease not till death.
>
> Creeds and schools in abeyance,
> Retiring back a while sufficed at what they are, but never forgotten,
> I harbor for good or bad, I permit to speak at every hazard,
> Nature without check with original energy.

There is something unashamed and refreshingly over-confident in his lines. Whitman is a self-proclaimed prophet of himself and his nation. His language breaks with continental ties and finds a daringly American tone. He claims new poetic ground, does away with tradition, invades new and hitherto taboo territories by idolising himself, his body, his nation. He makes himself the poet he wants to be.

> …Walt Whitman am I, a Kosmos, of mighty Manhattan the son,
> Turbulent, fleshy and sensual, eating, drinking and breeding;
> No sentimentalist—no stander above men and women, or apart from them;
> No more modest than immodest.

Exercise 4: Song of Yourself

This is your chance to do the same, to expand confidently into verse. Be unashamedly yourself. Confess without remorse, speak without inhibition. Claim your poetic place because it is yours. Speak of yourself and in doing so create yourself. Like Whitman, create the poet you want to be.

> **Song of YourSelf by John Stubley**
> The song of myself is nothing other than the song of *your*self; your best song; your best self. It cannot be otherwise. Without your singing, no notes would I sound abroad; without your being, no I to find. In your melodies, the melodious I. In your

rhythms, my heart-beats too. In your harmonies, the bridge that comes to harmonise us both.

Take your place upon such a stage as this. I hold it open for your song, for your Self

The Closet Genius

Complementing Whitman's energetic, broad sweep of expression, we find the intimate and courageous poetry of Emily Dickinson. Dickinson is as introvert and reserved, as Whitman is boisterous and forward. Emily Dickinson was born in Amherst, Massachusetts. She did not marry, spent her life within the confines of her family home and eventually retreated from society altogether. Withdrawing permanently to her room she created her own domestic Walden. Her shyness extended to her poetry. Only a handful of poems were published during her life. When she died she surprised her relatives with an inheritance of 1800 poems.

Like Whitman, Dickenson is a daring innovator. She explores an utterly personal style of expression. Her language is extremely economic, almost clipped. The hallmark of her work is a disarming honesty. She has the courage to plumb the depths of emotion with scrutiny. As her emotions become objects to herself a subtle humour emerges:

I'm Nobody! Who are you?
Are you — Nobody — Too?
Then there's a pair of us!
Don't tell! they'd advertise — you know!

How dreary — to be — Somebody!
How public — like a Frog —
To tell one's name — the livelong June —
To an admiring Bog!

Here too is a break with European conventions, a turning away from clichés and an attempt to embrace immediate reality. A new, sensitive, female authenticity comes to the fore. Dickinson speaks of everyday events in everyday language. It is in many ways the first really personal poetry.

Exercise 5: Who are you?

I believe that every great poet explores one aspect of the universally human. In the case of Emily Dickinson it is personal honesty. This no-nonsense approach to herself is reflected in her concise, matter-of-fact writing style. Following her example will help us to bring some balance to the previous exercise:

Ponder your personal life, and recall things you rarely talk about: hidden hopes, small and large disappointments closeted away, limitations and difficulties never shared in public. Profess to them in a small poem. Be honest, factual, clear.

Who are you? by John Ryan

I am a shoe
with uncooperative glue
no, a shrew
that tunnels the new
lawn

I dissolve like salt
in the blue
pool and am profusely kind to

willy wagtails
crusader bugs
bush roaches
even the slugs

that gnaw on the mail
may they always prevail
too, to do what they do
like me and you.

Who are you? By Ann Harrison

You look like me,
you walk like me
so little difference.
We have eyes,
nose,mouth,hair.
We are human,yes,
so you are me but are you.....
like me.
Difficult to know.

Back in England

Back in England, Gerard Manly Hopkins' fate paralleled that of Emily Dickinson. His poetry too went unnoticed by the public until after his death. Born into a well-to-do and highly artistic family, Hopkins studied in Cambridge. Ascetic by nature and spiritually inclined, he converted to Catholicism and eventually joined the Jesuit order. (The monastery was his Walden.) Throughout his life he struggled to reconcile his poetic ambitions with what he perceived to be his spiritual duties, and even forbade himself from producing poetry for several years.

Hopkins was a daring innovator, using older rhythmic structures to escape convention. He is one of the first poets to consciously work with the qualities of sound, searching for new dimensions of expression as he explores the parallels between nature and language. Revisit his masterpiece 'God's Grandeur' in chapter one. In 'Inversnaid' too, the poet is at one with the elements, and his words cascade like water over the lines.

> This darksome burn, horseback brown,
> His rollrock highroad roaring down,
> In coop and in comb the fleece of his foam
> Flutes and low to the lake falls home …

Hopkins is a master of the onomatopoeic style. His poems are meditations cast into sound. He lives into experiences where sound and world coincide. In *'Pied Beauty'*, his celebratory tone and attention to details resonate with Whitman's work.

> GLORY be to God for dappled things—
> For skies of couple-colour as a brinded cow;
> For rose-moles all in stipple upon trout that swim;
> Fresh-firecoal chestnut-falls; finches' wings;
> Landscape plotted and pieced—fold, fallow, and plough;
> And áll trádes, their gear and tackle and trim.
>
> All things counter, original, spare, strange;
> Whatever is fickle, freckled (who knows how?)
> With swift, slow; sweet, sour; adazzle, dim;
> He fathers-forth whose beauty is past change:
> Praise him.

Exercise 6: Poetic Soundscape

Allow Hopkins' work to inspire you. Recall an intense experience in nature and relive all the sensation. Ponder the quality of light, the rustle of the wind, the wash of the sea.

Translate colour into vowels, landscapes into a consonants. Make us taste luscious green grass by means of words and hear the sounds of clouds. Explore the resonances between language and world.

Soundscape by Karen McCrea
The roaring ocean
driven by storming black darkness
smashes into the land,
pounds the pier relentlessly,
bites, swallows in one greedy gulp,
its shrieking splinters.

Rain lacerates the blackness
Knifing earthwards,
thrashing trees,
stabbing fields,
ripping earth
into sharp edged ridges

Fury meets ferocity,
hour after hour,
until, spent, the howling gale

drops to a soft sussuration, ushering in
a pink-rinsed dawn, the sea settling as
day creeps quietly over the horizon
and a single woolly cloud
rolls through the sky,
the last remnant of the storm.

Soundscape by Stuart Wallis
Golden dusk light kisses
Your majestic flank

Sensuous curve of corkscrew
Horns held majestically aloft
I lower the cold instrument of
your demise
To gaze enviously at your timeless beauty.

31

Tracing the Beloved

It may seem surprising that the medieval Islamic-Persian mystic Rumi is among the most widely read poets in the western world. But Rumi is like a rare spice missing from the table of western writing. More than any other poet Rumi speaks the language of the soul, reminding us of a vocabulary we have forgotten. Champion of the heart and its power, he is also master of love and his path to the beloved is paved with verse.

Rumi is one of the many mystics whose ecstatic experience of the divine broke through in poetry, like St Francis, Basho, Milarepa, Kabir. For these mystics, the higher self is always poetic: closeness to God was at the same time a participation in creative activity. In Rumi we meet the soul of Persia, a culture blessed with great poets such as Omar Khayam and Hafiz, and the essence of Sufism, the mystical dimension of Islam.

Traditional Islam hopes for a meeting with God in paradise. The Sufi sought union with God in this world because God had created the world to be loved and known by his creation. The seed of his love was felt to be present in all manifestations of the world, drawing the Sufi back towards the creator. However that first spontaneous love between creator and created is disrupted in the course of time. Hafiz expressed it thus: 'O wine giver, pour me a cup and pass it around for love seemed easy at first, but later the difficulties arose.'

The first step on the Sufi path was thus the annihilation of the self that obstructed union with God. The second was to become an instrument of the divine will of God. The third and fourth levels bring the ability to guide others, even the dead.

At the time of Rumi's birth around 1200 his father was a well-known mystic. When Rumi was still a small child, his father fell out of grace with the local king and the family had to leave. For many years they travelled, finally settled in Konya, Anatolia. The long journey seemed to mirror the Sufi tradition that sent the spiritual apprentice travelling from country to country, apprenticing himself for a while to a teacher, to learn his trade, listen to his teaching, and study the way he conducted his life. Sufi masters often taught by means of stories and example.

When the family met the mystical poet Faridoddin Attar, he immediately recognised the spiritual gift of the young Rumi and prophesied: 'This boy will spark a fire of divine exultation.

Exercise 1: Hidden Teachers

Veneration and readiness to learn are prerequisites for the spiritual path. With this in mind everyone and everything can become a teacher: a writer we have never met, an inspiring artist we have seen only once, a family member or close friend. Great teachers can appear in humble garb or even disguise: the lady at the till, the neighbour's cat, a tree in the backyard, a river, a mountain: Remember some of the hidden teachers you have met in your life and what they have taught you:

> **The Hidden Masters by Ann Reeves**
>
> From the woman next door I learned the power of a joyful greeting.
> A friendship 20 years old taught me to plumb for truth,
> and gave me the courage to speak it.
> A seamstress showed me the virtue of silence.
> In a Turkish courtroom I saw the power of money,
> and there I learned that truth has greater value.
> A nasturtium showed me cheerful impertinence.
> A rose nobility
> And a lily deep peace.

Awakening

In 1220 Rumi's father became a teacher of Islam in Konya. When he died, Rumi took his place and became a rather orthodox teacher of theology. Then, in a single moment, his world changed. Rumi had been teaching when suddenly a wild looking dervish climbed over the courtyard wall, seized all his books and threw them in the pond. Rumi jumped up to save his precious scripts, but the dervish called out: 'Live by what you know. Speak your own truth and leave all theory behind.'

Their eyes met and Rumi's heart leapt in passionate love. They embraced and Rumi declared, 'The God I have searched for all my life, I have now found in you.' He had found the Beloved. Shamsoddin Tabriz, the dervish and wanderer, became his entry to the divine.

We are immediately reminded of Dante's meeting with Beatrice. But Rumi's experience bears the passionate intensity of the Middle East. The love between the two men is holy, direct and intimate. Each becomes the other's catalyst for divine union, for the ecstasies of love in which each is lost and found in the heart of the other. Rumi began to neglect his duties in favour of his beloved Shams. It is reported that the lovers remained in a state of total intoxication for one hundred and one days.

> The way of love is not
> a subtle argument.

The door there
is devastation.

Birds make great sky-circles
of their freedom.
How do they learn it?

They fall, and falling,
they're given wings.

This poem recalls the first step on the Sufi path, and the powerful conversion that Rumi suffered through his meeting with Shams Tabriz.

Exercise 2: The First Step

The annihilation of the self through the power of love is an experience both remote and close. We suffer it in small doses when we fall in love, which testifies to its existence in the depths of our soul. We lose our selves in the thought of the beloved. To a mystic like Rumi loss is a liberation from the self, freeing the soul from illusion.

Imagine the power of such love, the transformation of all that you are. Write a poem on death and resurrection through the fire of love.

The World's Wild Heart by Jaya Penelope

& you walk in
carrying the night
on your skin &
empty your pockets
of the moon —
an ecstatic orange. I sink
my teeth in & tongue
the world's wild heart
of honey —
Let us throw open every door
& invite the dark in
Why should we be afraid?
for you have planted
the morning in my belly
now watch
me hatch
the sun.

First Step by John Stubley

I see the way you smile — half smile.
I see the way you walk and hold,
the way you turn and
turn and rise. I see
the way you write and type
and stir your coffee white,
the way you phrase and rhyme
and change your never mind.
I see the way you push inwards
and outwards, forwards and through.
I see your criticism, your poetic vision.
I see your terrible distance
so beautiful, so close by.

The Transformative Power of Love

Such love breaks down old habits, shattering the brittle idol of the temporary self. It is a threshold experience in which the old falls away and the new is given wings. The soul is freed and the newborn spirit embraces the world as itself, as in this poem by Rumi:

> Inside this new love, die.
> Your way begins on the other side.
> Become the sky.
> Take an axe to the prison wall.
> Escape.
> Walk out like someone suddenly born into colour.
> Do it now.
> You're covered with thick cloud.
> Slide out the side. Die,
> and be quiet. Quietness is the surest sign
> that you've died.
> Your old life was a frantic running
> from silence.
>
> The speechless full moon
> comes out now.

In this state all boundaries dissolve. The soul and the world are one. The mystic becomes the world, the sky, the clouds, the vast horizon; inhabits the old world anew, embedded in silence and held by a stillness that always is.

Exercise 3: Widening the Self

In rare moments we have inklings of this. We feel closer to nature. Our layers of protection fall away. We expand beyond our skin. We embrace the world and the world embraces us. The romantics longed for this experience. The haiku poets touched on it. The Sufi masters lived in it.

Imagine yourself rooted in silence and poured out into all that surrounds you. Like a mystic, feel encompassed by the world and at one with the trees, the garden, the desert.

> **Consummation by John Stubley**
> Already blessed. Already loved. Already in love.
> Already enlightened, enlivened, entrusted, enabled.
> Already dead.
> Already all of everything's positives
> and negatives
> and all the extremes of the one line that joins
> and rolls on and on with us, for us, as us,
> through the sparkling waterways of the world.
> Already already ALL READY
> for whatever may be,
> maybe.
> But still we search like fish for water,
> like fish for bones.

Chickpea to Cook

The intense love between the two men aroused jealousy among Rumi's students. Sensing the growing animosity, Shams leaves without warning. Rumi is devastated. His extreme anguish turns him into a passionate poet — he curbs the pain into words. He accepts suffering as a teacher, a stepping stone; the labour that accompanies the birth of the new. He has the gift of describing soul transformation in everyday language. Nothing was too mundane — even the preparation of food — to make the divine palatable.

> A chickpea leaps almost over the rim of the pot
> where it's being boiled.
> 'Why are you doing this to me?'
>
> The cook knocks him down with the ladle.
> 'Don't you try to jump out.
> You think I'm torturing you.

I'm giving you flavour,
so you can mix with spices and rice
and be the lovely vitality of a human being.
Remember when you drank rain in the garden.
That was for this.'

Grace first. Sexual pleasure,
then a boiling new life begins,
and the Friend has something good to eat.

Eventually the chickpea
will say to the cook,
'Boil me some more.
Hit me with the skimming spoon.
I can't do this by myself.
I'm like an elephant that dreams of gardens
back in Hindustan and doesn't pay attention
to his driver. You're my cook, my driver,
my way into existence. I love your cooking.'

The cook says,
'I was once like you,
fresh from the ground. Then I boiled in time,
and boiled in the body, two fierce boilings.
My animal soul grew powerful.
I controlled it with practices,
and boiled some more, and boiled
once beyond that,
and became your teacher.'

Exercise 4: Transformation of the Mundane

In 'Chickpea to Cook' Rumi anchors his spiritual experience in the solid world and at the same time sanctifies everyday affairs. The poem is a Jacob's ladder in which meanings travel between heaven and earth. We all experience transformation, in small or large doses. Life itself is a slow cooking of the soul. Each difficult experience cracks one of our shells.

Describe in poetry or story a process of soul transformation making metaphors from any mundane activity you are familiar with. Think of the fact that any process, no matter how profane, can be a parable of transformation when seen through the poetic lens.

Beloved Baltic Pine by Harriet Sawer

On the bluest of days
you reached to pluck the icy sun
and honeyed sap filled your veins.
How straight you lie in welcome on the far side of the world,
with subtle give and gentle dimples,
soft dents of fifty trodden years.
You reach for gold no more,
back dappled in amber light.
It falls in drops through old long frames
and under flaking salmon eaves
the bees are singing to dead spring moths.
Open all doors! Let the wind possess you!
Open all curtains! So even in your endless sleep,
You can still reach for that far sun.

Semi Detached by Martina Chippindal

Click on file
make a quick exit
and shutdown.

Go outside
draw in the air
and fill your lungs.

Climb the stairs
to the man next door.

He has been waiting.

Laid out on the table
days of preparation
to assault your senses

Cumin, coriander and ginger
permeate the meat
mustard seeds explode
turmeric excites the eye
chilli bites

Sit down and taste
the intensity
of living.

Beyond Limitation

Years later Rumi and Shamsoddin met again, and clung to each other, lost in ecstasy. But jealousy flared up again in his students, and Shams is murdered. Rumi ordered mourning robes and began to whirl in search of ecstatic union with his dead beloved. This may have been the origin of the dervish dance that became one of the hallmarks of Sufi practice. From this time, Rumi saw his beloved in everything, in mountains and sea, in cooking pots and sweetmeats.

> I am not alone in singing Shamsoddin and Shamsoddin.
> But the nightingale in the garden sings the same
> And the partridge in the hills
> The day full of splendour is Shamsoddin and
> The heavens are Shamsoddin too ...

He finds him in all the saints of the past: in Christ, Joseph, Mohammed. Like other great mystics, Rumi's soul expands far beyond the confines of his own faith. Love is universal. It cannot be kept in the cage of creeds.

> Only Breath
> Not Christian or Jew or Muslim, not Hindu,
> Buddhist, Sufi, or Zen. Not any religion
>
> or cultural system. I am not from the East
> or the West, not out of the ocean or up
>
> from the ground, not natural or ethereal, not
> composed of elements at all. I do not exist,
>
> am not an entity in this world or the next,
> did not descend from Adam and Eve or any
>
> origin story. My place is placeless, a trace
> of the traceless. Neither body or soul.
>
> I belong to the beloved, have seen the two
> worlds as one...

Rumi has settled in the homeland of mystics, poets and great lovers: the continent of love, the world within the world, the essential human being. I believe it is this quality that makes Rumi so attractive to modern readers. He is the poetic champion of love, liberated from race, culture and language. He pioneers the universal human we all long to become.

Exercise 5: Beyond Limitation

Inhabit the continent Rumi so successfully explored, beyond culture, gender and creed. Inhale the fresh air of that place and exhale it in verses that celebrate the universal humanity at the core of your poetic self.

> **Only Breath by Sue McBurney**
>
> In the beginning
> only breath
> one breath breathes us
> no you no me
> only us beloved
>
> Like birds diving and weaving
> on the same wing
> falling earthward
> one breath sustains us
>
> Like a candle flame
> changing imperceptibly
> we become one
> re-enacting an
> architecture of love
> the thread through time
>
> no religion
> no culture no form
> breath informs all
> no beginning no end
> only me into you into me
> no end, beloved

Transformative Stories

In the Sufi tradition, stories are a means of teaching; they are messengers of god. Many revolve around the lives of holy men and women who represent the divine on earth; others are humorous and paradoxical, intended to shift the awareness of the listener from one plane to another. They are pointers and signposts towards a higher reality.

Playing with convention and form, Rumi often used bawdy or humorous stories like the tale of a young man pretending to be a eunuch and making a living by shampooing naked women in the bathhouse, or the teachings of the wandering dervish in 'The Dervish at the Door':

A dervish knocked at a house
to ask for a piece of dry bread,
or moist, it didn't matter.
'This is not a bakery,' said the owner.
'Might you have a bit of gristle then?'
'Does this look like a butchershop?'
'A little flour?'
'Do you hear a grinding stone?'
'Some water?'
'This is not a well.'
Whatever the dervish asked for,
the man made some tired joke
and refused to give him anything.
Finally the dervish ran in the house,
lifted his robe, and squatted
as though to take a shit.
'Hey, hey!'
'Quiet, you sad man. A deserted place
is a fine spot to relieve oneself,
and since there's no living thing here,
or means of living, it needs fertilising.'
The dervish began his own list
of questions and answers.
'What kind of bird are you? Not a falcon,
trained for the royal hand. Not a peacock,
painted with everyone's eyes. Not a parrot,
that talks for sugar cubes. Not a nightingale,
that sings like someone in love.
Not a hoopoe bringing messages to Solomon,
or a stork that builds on a cliffside.
What exactly do you do?
You are no known species.
You haggle and make jokes
to keep what you own for yourself.
You have forgotten the One
who doesn't care about ownership,
who doesn't try to turn a profit
from every human exchange.'

In this glimpse into the everyday life of medieval Islamic culture comes insight into the struggle between the mundane and the sacred, the struggle of the higher and lower selves in our own soul.

Exercise 6: A Teaching Story

Follow the Sufi tradition of teaching the way of the divine through stories that may be sublime or ridiculous. Make up a story or recall one of your experiences that holds an important teaching.

The Mould-maker by Jennifer Kornberger

A mould-maker travelled the world

he made moulds of people's ears
the inside of ears
the listening part
the rounded inner space
he made them in clay
his collection was huge
a corral of tiny clay creatures
Jewish listening, Christian listening, Muslim listening, Hindi listening
he sat up a huge display — it was his life work.
He invited people to come
and listen to all the ears listening.

After Shamsoddin's death Rumi shared his divine love with the saintlike and illiterate goldsmith Salahaddin. When he too died, Rumi's friend and student Hosamoddin became his companion. When Rumi died in 1273, Jews, Christians and Moslems followed the procession to honour one of the greatest poets and lovers of humanity.

32

Sermon of the East

Western civilisation has, like Faust, taken a journey back in time and gained new inspiration from the meeting with distant cultures. The contributions of Buddha, Rumi and Lo Po have touched many contemporary readers and writers.

Buddha lived 500 years before Christ and founded one of the major world religions. But his doctrine of compassion and peace reaches far beyond religious devotees; it is of universal appeal and makes him revered in both east and west. The Buddha sitting in the lotus position is a global symbol for meditation. The generally tolerant and non-violent attitude of his followers has commanded respect throughout history.

The Birth of Buddha

Buddha was born as Siddhartha Gautama in the foothills of the Himalayas, the first son of Queen Mahamaya and King Suddhadana. His birth was preceded by visions and prophesies: his mother dreamed that a white elephant walked three times around her before entering her womb.

Mahamaya delivered her son in a sacred grove of trees, giving birth in an upright position. The newborn babe immediately took seven strides and, addressing all four directions, called out: 'I am born to achieve enlightenment. This is my last birth in the world of semblance.'

Exercise 1: Birth Chant

Like Krishna, Zarathustra and Taliesin, Buddha is articulate as a babe. He entered this world conscious and aware of his mission. To a degree, this is the case with every human being. We all possess a destiny, a distinct mission, a memory of our initial intentions from long before we were born — but often we forget about them in the course of our lives.

Assume at your birth you were conscious of why you had come, what you intended to achieve. Proclaim your intent to all four directions.

> **First Words of the Hilton Buddha by Janet Blagg**
> I salute the sun on this my 457th incarnation in the world of sin. My purpose, as for the last 456 incarnations: to learn how to love.

I bow to the south, so I may learn to recognise love even in the cold and dark. To the east, so I may receive love in its morning glory. To the north, so I may be a channel for love's flowering. To the west, so, like a quivering deer, I may come to trust in the breath of love.

Soul Song by Judy Griffiths
I thrust firmly from my mother's holding body,
singing notes pure-smelted by many lifetimes.
This is the song of my soul,
titrated from each drop of being,
filtered through the wind, the rain, the sun and
the starry moonlit nights.

I sing of magnificence, of fecundity and of
sorrowful emptiness- the spindles that weave
the threads into that which I am, that whom I be.

I hum the melody of All Time – the breaths and
breadths, the lengths and longness, the
stultifying pressures of 'never-enough-time' ness.

I sway in the rhythm of movement – quickening
from that first moment of conception, through
the stumblings and staggerings, into purposeful
gait and gracefulness.

I dance with the flecks of consciousness,
with the flicker of firelight,
with the sway of the breeze,
with the musical plucking of the brook.

And I tremble in the exquisite knowing of the All That Is

The Four Signs

Gods and spirits shower the newborn child with blessings, and dangerous creatures refrain from harming him. The king's advisors prophesy that his son will become a world emperor or a great spiritual teacher. His father naturally prefers the first option. To deter Siddhartha from spiritual pursuits, he is separated from the world of poverty, suffering and death and brought up in the confinement of the royal palace, surrounded by intoxicating luxury and beauty. To tie him to his worldly career, he is married to princess Yasodhara.

But the gods send four signs to awaken him to his task. During an excursion into the royal park Siddhartha, for the first time in his life, meets a decrepit old man. He cries out: 'Shame on birth, since everyone who is born must grow old and feeble.' On a second outing he encounters a sick man, and on a third a corpse, rotting on the wayside. When on his last visit the young prince sees a wandering ascetic, surrounded by unshakeable tranquillity, he feels the call of destiny.

Exercise 2: Signs on the Way

Like Buddha we all encounter signs that wake us from the sleep of complacency, from the dull and ignorant ways we lead our life. Such signs may come in the form of a life-changing accident or major setback; a breakdown or the death of a beloved; an encounter with suffering or injustice, or with an inspiring personality or a great ideal. A sign is anything that makes us reconsider reality, assess and determine to change ourselves. Signs are the call of destiny. Describe one or more signs that made you feel the call of destiny.

The Four Signs by Annette Mullumby
Surgeons green garbed and goggled
move under water
I lay awake unhinged
numbed hip reddens as
knife needles flesh aside scalps socket
lined with iron
Shuddering blows jammed the dagger into bone
adrenals pump heat sweat

Staggered home with an armful of ghosts
bent on possession
Played a racket of knucklebones on ribs
Air ballooned and whittled
Lungs gasp in straight jacket
Porous skin a door for vagrant things

Sometimes sea washes ghosts away
Body empty as old bone
crumbles to light.

The Sign by Julie Dickinson
The laryngectomy had robbed him of life's speech — he had drifted into unconsciousness, had rejected help or comfort.

The nurses asked me to stay with him and I was willing, but wary of accompanying him on his wheezing, laboured journey. I pondered on this man's lone passage. No friends or relatives visited. I thought of how it would be, unable to communicate apart from awkward words on scraps of paper. The sadness overwhelmed me, time passed — we breathed in harmony.

Suddenly his eyes flicked open and he searched my face. Determinedly he tapped the bed and beckoned. I let my hand rest tentatively beside him — he firmly placed his hand on mine.

The Ascetic
The day his wife gives birth to his son Rahula, Buddha leaves her, resolving to return only when he has found enlightenment. He leaves the luxury of the palace and adopts the life of a homeless monk, with shaved head, robe and begging bowl. Siddhartha joins famous meditation teachers and masters all their disciplines, but he remains dissatisfied.

He adopts strict austerities, living on one grain of rice and one sesame-seed a day until his body becomes emaciated and black.

Eventually Buddha realises that austerity is not the way to enlightenment. He begs for food in the village and soon his body returns to its health.

Mara's Assault
Renouncing asceticism, Siddhartha vows to sit under the sacred Bodhi tree until he attains enlightenment. After forty-nine days he has a vision of demonic intensity. Mara, the god of sensuality, of all passions and desires that bind human beings to the earth, attacks him, sending his sensual daughter Kama to divert Siddhartha from his meditation. When this fails Mara appeals to Siddhartha's duty as a member of the warrior caste. Finally Mara unleashes an army of destruction against Siddhartha.

From all sides wild demons crowd upon him, spitting and biting. Evil snakes and monsters attack. Mara hurls flaming mountaintops, vicious weapons and blazing logs. Storms howl and the earth shakes in its foundations. But nothing disturbs Siddhartha's self-possession and calm.

Exercise 3: The Terrors of Temptation
The image of a spiritual seeker being assaulted by a host of demons appears in both eastern and western traditions. The remaining passions in the soul gather for a last attack. Liberated from the illusion of the sense-world, instincts and desires appear as demons and spectres, monstrous shapes arising from the abyss. In normal life these

realities hide beneath the mask of desires and passions, behind hatred and weakness, and within every habit or obsession that will not let go of us.

Describe such an attack as far as your experience or imagination allows.

Mara's Assault by Annette Mullumby
His skin draws my fingers, his eyes invite
I know men, how to woo, pursue them
My deep brown sleek body exudes jasmine
my breath cinnamon
Now I'm whirling around him, leaning in close
My rubies flickering his face
My silks wafting his body
but he doesn't stir
I move closer whisper magic potions
How can you resist me
I'll give you bliss,
anytime, an easier way, try me.

Damn that's not working
Now I'll show my hagging bag of bones
My teeth ripping that tender flesh
I'll make him do my bidding
My raking nails red track his pure white body

It's futile
He sits in stillness
a mirror
Dare I look

The White Elephant by Annie Wearne
The white elephant stood firm, the four great feet, toes splayed, almost welded into the earth beneath. His tail flicked away tiny flies that tried to bite into his leather hide. A small bird perched high on his back.

   The jaguar approached, slinking seductively, teeth bared. A low growl emanated from her throat. The white elephant raised his trunk and a magnificent roar shook the trees for miles around.

   The jaguar moved nearer, joined by five more, all with teeth bared, hot for blood. Their long nails, talons that could tear a hide into pieces, showed gleaming white. The white elephant did not flinch or move even an inch.

   Where was the fun? Where the chase for blood? The jaguars lost interest after sniffing round him and pawing him a bit.

Absolutely nothing happened. They slunk off back into the jungle. The white elephant nosed around and ate another grain of rice and a sesame seed. The little bird on his back burst into song.

The First Sermon

Mara is defeated and Siddhartha, sinking into untroubled meditation, experiences spontaneous enlightenment. In this state of bliss he recollects all his previous incarnations as a Bodhisattva (a being on the path to enlightenment). With this revelation the Bodhisattva becomes the Buddha, freed from the wheel of rebirth and the grip of Samsara (the entanglement in the world of the senses). Moved by compassion, he returns to the world to preach his doctrine (dharma) — the middle path between severe asceticism and entanglement in sensual life — and soon finds followers from all strata of society. In his first sermon the Buddha teaches the four noble truths that lead to liberation:

> What, monks, is the truth of suffering? Birth is suffering. Decay, sickness and death are suffering. To be separated from what you like is suffering. To want something and not get it is suffering. In short the human personality, liable as it is to clinging and attachment, brings suffering.
>
> And what is the truth of the origin of suffering? It is craving. Craving leads to rebirth, bound up as this is with the search for pleasure and restless greed. It is in craving for sensuality, craving for new life, craving for non-existence and annihilation.
>
> And what is the truth of the extinction of suffering? It is the indifference to and elimination of craving: freedom and detachment from it.
>
> And what is the truth about the Way leading to the extinction of suffering? Just this excellent Eightfold Path that leads to the extinction of suffering:
>
> Right view. Right thought. Right speech.
> Right action. Right livelihood. Right effort.
> Right awareness. Right meditative concentration.

Buddha's sermon rings a modern note. From the vantage point of his spiritual attainment he becomes the supreme analyst of the human soul. He is the first psychologist. The Eightfold Path of Right View, Thought, Speech, Action, Livelihood, Effort, Awareness and Concentration is central to his doctrine. It leads the seeker on a pilgrimage through inner virtues until their soul is purified from undue attachment to the world.

Each of the eight elements is an expression of the middle way, the balance between the extremes. Practised long enough it liberates the self and the soul pours forth in universal compassion.

Exercise 4: The Eightfold Path

Imagine you are the Buddha. Followers are eager to learn about the 'excellent Eightfold Path'. Many are willing to tread it, but need more guidance: What is 'right action' or the 'right word'? Explain the nature of each of the eight steps. If eight explanations are beyond your present state of poetic enlightenment, try at least two or three.

Right Action by Kristina Hamilton

Right Action (Right Deed): Prepare your action with considered thought so that the deed will be born at the right time and the right place. A misplaced deed is like a child lost in the dark unable to find his way home. A hasty deed is like an actor who takes his bow before the curtain rises. A deed performed too late is like serving over-ripe fruit to a guest already sated.

Right Awareness by Jill Whitfield

When you are a mother and your children play sport, right awareness means being in the right place, looking in the right direction at the right time when your child does something spectacular because there are no action replays.

Right Livelihood by Jennifer Kornberger

The right livelihood is the one that makes the new money. The new money is so light that your pockets fluff out as though the wind was nesting there. The new money is so bright that you can run your solar car from its rays. The new money is so big you can live in it and roll all over the world

Right Effort by Janet Blagg

Right effort is that effort which is no effort at all.

Right View by Ann Reeves

The right view is many views. First look closely. Concentrate on the small things. Be Alice, looking at small things that grow and grow so that you must climb over them.
Then pick yourself up. See, they've shrunk again, right size.
Now walk to the periphery. Stroll round it. Stop often, gaze at the centre.
Gaze at the point opposite on this wheel that welcomes you.
See the point in the middle. Walk towards it, eyes open now. See, it's coming to you.
Centre and periphery change places.
Do that again, more slowly. Now savour all those points. You've tasted them all, seen from each. You have encircled the circle, centred it, moved it around the heavens. Now you see.

The Spread of Buddhism

When Siddhartha becomes the Buddha, he renounces the untroubled and blissful state of Nirvana. Out of compassion for those still entangled in the world of the senses, he returns to the world and preaches to aid others on their path towards liberation. By the time of Christ, the early Hinayana Buddhism, whose central aim is to find personal liberation, is enlarged by the Mahayana school, which emphasises a deeper engagement with the world through the Boddhisattva vow: not to withdraw to the bliss of Nirvana until all creatures are free of suffering.

Mahayana spreads to the north of India into Tibet, and Hinayana (or Theravada) travels via Sri Lanka into Burma, Laos, Thailand and Cambodia. Both forms of Buddhism eventually reach China and Korea and from there Japan. In each of these places the flexibility of the teaching creates unique responses.

The Koan

One of the most poetic responses is the Koan, a poetic means of enlightenment in Ch'an and Zen practice. The Koans are based on student-master interaction and serve as metaphors for the transcendental, non-dual reality. In the form of a paradox the Koan asserts the identity of opposites. Its aim is to destroy the reality we know and to point to another we are not yet aware of. Administered to a Zen student in the right moment the Koan catapults his mind into a new level of awareness.

The making of Koans developed into a widespread literary practice. In Japan many Buddhist schools were based on Koan curricula. Here are a few examples:

> What is the sound of one hand clapping?
>
> Look at the flower that looks at you.
>
> If you meet the Buddha on the road, kill him.
>
> What did your face look like before your mother was born?
>
> Who is it that carries this corpse around?

A Koan often comes in the form of a question. Yet there is no answer to it. The real answer is the student's awakening to the pure, undivided Buddha-mind, his or her essential nature. Other Koans come in question-answer form such as:

> A monk asked Zhaozou: 'What is the meaning of Bodhidharma coming from the West?' ((Bodhidharma was the great teacher who brought Buddhism to China) and Zhaozou answered: 'The cypress tree in front of the hall.

The answer here is like pulling the carpet out beneath the student's feet to see if he can fly. Koans can also be in story format:

> The monk Sato went to a master and knocked on the door. 'Who's there?' asked the Master. 'It's me, Sato!' 'Go away'.
> The next day Sato came again and knocked. Again the master asked: 'Who's there?' 'It's me, Sato!' and again the master answered, 'Go away!'
> Sato went away, but returned the next day. He knocked again. Again the master asked 'Who is there?' 'Nobody!' 'Ah, Sato! Come in!' answered the master.

Exercise 5: Breaking Through

Koans are not easy to make. They originate from a level of awareness other than the one we are accustomed to. And yet writers draw their best ideas from the same source, albeit unconsciously. With this in mind we may attempt a Koan or even a teaching story. If you find this exercise difficult or impossible, remember Sato's example and keep on trying.

> **Koan by Sofia**
> I break through glass.
> Shattered, I arrive whole.
>
> **Koan by Nan Connell**
> Who is at the house
> where nobody lives
>
> **Koan by Liana Christensen**
> Who is the Buddha in Australia?
> What is the sound of one thong slapping?
>
> **Koan by Helen Mc Donell**
> If you see someone by the road deaf, blind, dumb and lame, say hello to yourself.

33

Subtle Empire

China ranks high in Western imagination: in this utterly different culture every letter is a word and every word an artwork. Nuances of tone determine meaning. Artists will be entranced by the sense of refinement surfacing in delicate artwork, porcelain, silk, jade, lacquer-ware and complicated ornaments. Historians will admire the pioneering achievements of Chinese ingenuity such as paper, printing, gunpowder and compass. Philosophers will think of Confucius and Lao Tse, and writers of master poets such as Qu Yuan, Li Po, Tu Fu and Su Shi.

According to tradition, Chinese history commences with Fuxi, the first emperor. Fuxi is the ancestor of all Chinese and the inaugurator of marriage and regulated work. Most importantly he is the creator of the most ingenious of Chinese inventions: the hexagram-system of the *'I Ching'*, the sacred book of changes.

A Changing Book

The I Ching is often regarded as the oldest book in the world. It is a book of divination and ancient wisdom. I see the I Ching as a poetic work, a kind of creative writing manual of the universe, revealing the grammar that governs the world. To the seeker it gives instruction on how to best fit into the great poem of the world, how to align his or her creative response with the greater creativity of the world.

Central to the understanding of this Book is the notion of Yin and Yang. These concepts refer to the polar and yet complementary forces that constitute the world. Dark and light, male and female, hot and cold, water and fire, earth and air are variations of this foundational duality. Though polar they cannot exist without one another. Taken far enough Yin will turn into Yang and Yang into Yin. They are omnipresent and their admixture determines the nature of all things.

In the I Ching, Yin is represented by broken lines, Yang by unbroken lines. Three lines are combined to form trigrams. The first trigram, Ch'ien, is composed of three strong lines, indicating superabundance of Yang. The second trigram, Kun, is entirely composed of receptive or giving lines, expressing predominance of Yin.

Ch'ien and Kun are father and mother to six more trigrams (three sons and three daughters): Gen (Mountain), Kan (Water), Xun (Wind), Zhen (Thunder), Li (Fire) and Dui (Lake).

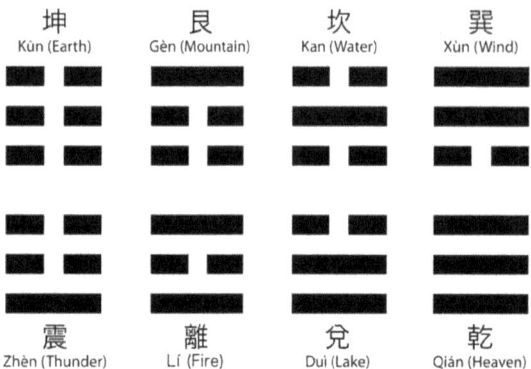

This family of signs is understood as a kind of primal alphabet whose combinations reflect the universal language that governs the world. Each sign is assigned a name, an attribute and a particular place in the family.

The trigram Kan, ☵ ,The Abysmal (or Gorge), for example, corresponds to Water, the direction North, the Second Son in the family and the Ear in the body. Its attribute is The Dangerous and its state is In-motion. The animal associate with Kun is the pig.

The trigram Li, ☲ , The Clinging (or Radiance) corresponds to Fire, the direction Northwest, the Second Daughter, the Eye in the body. Its attribute is Light-giving and its state is Clinging or Clarity. The animal associated with Li is the pheasant.

The combination of two trigrams results in the 64 hexagrams that constitute the I Ching. (Li) ☲ Fire and Kan ☵ (Water), for instance, combine to the Hexagram Wei Chi.

The hexagrams are not static signs, but dynamic signposts of change. When used for divination these signs act like acupuncture points in the body of time, allowing the seeker to flow with the course of events.

In early and more intuitive times the casting of hexagrams was enough to give direction to the one who sought it. At a later stage further explanation was required. The first to provide this was King Wen, the progenitor of the Chou dynasty. Wen added judgements to all signs, translating the language of the cosmos into the idiom of human understanding.

The first hexagram is Ch'ien/The Creative, signifying all that is light-giving, active, assertive, representing the consistency and strength of the spirit. It is related to the divine in the cosmos and in the human being.

King Wen interpreted this sign through the following judgement:

> THE CREATIVE works sublime success,
> Furthering through perseverance. (tr. Richard Wilhelm)

King Wen's son, the Duke of Chou, took his father's impulse further and elaborated on each line of the hexagram. Centuries later Confucius made additional commentaries. Here is a commentary from Richard Wilhelm's sensitive translation:

> …The sage learns how best to develop himself so that his influence may endure. He must make himself strong in every way, by consciously casting out all that is inferior and degrading. Thus he attains that tirelessness which depends upon consciously limiting the fields of his activity.

The second hexagram is K'un/The Receptive, consisting entirely of broken lines.

Kun stands for the soft, dark, yielding, receptive power of Yin. Kun is related to devotion. It represents earth in contrast to heaven, nature in contrast to spirit, space as against time and female as against male. To this hexagram King Wen assigned the following judgement:

> THE RECEPTIVE brings about sublime success,
> Furthering through the perseverance of a mare.
> If the superior man undertakes something and tries to lead,
> He goes astray;
> But if he follows, he finds guidance.
> It is favorable to find friends in the west and south,
> To forego friends in the east and north.
> Quiet perseverance brings good fortune (tr. Richard Wilhelm)

An exerpt from the commentary of the Richard Wilhelm translation reads:

> …The superior man lets himself be guided; he does not go ahead blindly, but learns from the situation what is demanded of him and then follows this intimation from fate. Since there is something to be accomplished, we need friends and helpers in the hour of toil and effort…

I Ching for Writers

The Book of Changes has always invited new interpretations. I believe it is time for a new commentary written for and by poets: an I Ch'ing for writers. Let us begin with Ch'ien, the first sign.

Exercise 1: Commentary on Ch'ien, The Creative

Write a comment, explaining the deeper meaning of this hexagram to generations of future writers. Here is the judgement again:

> THE CREATIVE works sublime success,
> Furthering through perseverance.

Now add your commentary. Rather than addressing it to a sage, create it with the writer in mind. Remember that Ch'ien stands for the active, creative rather than the receptive part of artistic practice. Explore it to the full.

Commentary by Ann Reeves:
To stoop inside is to examine one's instincts and impulses.
One must turn them over, then turn them out, cast them into the sea.
Your own greatness can then carry you to the mountain with need of neither sail nor wind.
The true seeker must strive for the peak alone, with only the moon and her crown to guide her.

Exercise 2: Commentary on Kun, The Receptive

Do the same for Kun. Read again through the judgement: 'THE RECEPTIVE brings about sublime success, Furthering...' (see above) and add your commentary. Explore the soft, receptive and yielding part of creativity.

Commentary by Ann Reeves
Tread backwards to go forward. Do not look down. You must prepare to receive.
The crane stands still.

In the next two exercises we will explore the two complementary hexagrams Kan and Li and produce both the judgement and a commentary. Take your lead from the sparse but profound architecture of oracular judgements. Remember that they are made for a poet by a poet. I recommend that you carefully observe the structure of the signs before you start. Let it seep into you to maximise inspiration.

Exercise 3: Judgement and Commentary on Kan, Water, The Abysmal

In this sign, the trigram water is combined with the trigram water (water above water). Immerse yourself in the meaning of water. Ponder what all things fluid mean for the writer. Cast your insight into a judgement that instructs writers how to conduct themselves in the watery phase of their work. (Remember that judgements are short, enigmatic and powerful.)

Judgement by Ann Reeves
The stillness is of a full moon.
Silver glistens.
Its calm beckons, yet following is imprecise.
Be awake to the gleam.

Judgement by Liana Christensen
The superior writer allows the surface to clear to transparence.

Thus the reader may penetrate to the fire within.
Now write a commentary to elucidate the judgement. Give direct and practical advice.

Commentary by Liana Christensen
Desert sand — no water — no life.
Spring melt — muddy cataracts — no clarity.

Be like a slow-flowing summer river, clear to the depths.
Water is no less powerful for being transparent.

Exercise 4: Judgement and Commentary on Li, Fire

Now do the same with sign 30:

Note how strong-weak-strong pattern of Li contrasts to the weak-strong-weak of Kan.
Formulate a judgement and commentary worthy of Fire above Fire.

Judgement by Ann Reeves
Blow on your own ember.
Your breath is its guardian.
Beware the cold blue tongue.

Commentary by Ann Reeves
Your actions are the fuel that strengthens the flame to brightest gold and strongest red. Warm your feet by the coals

Poetic Culture

Poetry was held in high regard in China. It was treasured for its aesthetic as well as educational value. The Odes, the oldest poetry collection of literature, was one of the five canonical readings for educated Chinese. Confucius recommended the Odes as a means to ennoble the spirit and he was personally responsible for editing its final version. Many works in the Odes are either written by women or use the female voice. Chinese poetry rhymes and was accompanied by music and dance.

In ancient China, emperors and dukes, noble ladies and the learned elite engaged in the practice of poetry. The Zhou Dynasty even established a poetic bureau. Officials went among the peasants to record their songs for the emperor. Listening to folk poetry the ruler informed himself about his subjects and the state of the empire. Poetry helped him to rule according to the mandate of heaven.

The earliest known Chinese poet was Qu Yuan, a high official who lost favour at court. Banished, he lamented the degeneration of his country. When he heard of the ruin of the state he had served, he drowned himself in the Milou river. The unsuccessful attempt of peasants to save the revered poet from drowning was commemorated in a festival that is still celebrated today. Here is the end from his poem **Crossing the River:**

> Now, the phoenix dispossessed,
> In the shrine crows make their nest.
> Withered is the jasmine rare,
>   Fair is foul, and foul is fair,
> Light is darkness, darkness day,
> Sad at heart I haste away.

The Philosophers

In China Yin and Yang are omnipresent. Even in the work of influential philosophers this theme asserts itself: Confucius and Lao Tse are opposites complementing each other on the grand scale of perennial wisdom. Confucius is the supreme teacher of Chinese antiquity, the canonised philosopher and champion of the state; a fervent upholder of what is best in tradition as well as a spirited innovator and humanist. His philosophy emphasises the cultivation of the individual through learning and ethical conduct. He is the advocate of culture, tradition, time-honoured ritual and he regards familial bonds as the foundation of civility. He understands the role of poetry as ennobling the soul and civilising society.

Lao Tse is the opposite. This grand sage, disillusioned by human culture, fled civilisation. He left high office for the simple, natural, unobstructed life in solitude. To him learning and letters spoil the simplicity of the soul and lead it away from true awareness of the Tao, the dynamic flow behind sensory reality. His gesture is markedly on the Yin side of the cosmic scale.

Li Po and Tu Fu

A similar duality can be observed in the two most popular poets of ancient China, Li Po and Tu Fu. Both lived in the eighth century AD, met twice and became friends.

Li Po is a kind of poetic Taoist, a carefree carouser, an eccentric, charismatic genius who spent his fortune on his friends. He cared little about convention and more about wine. His poetry is personal, immediate, fresh. Tu Fu is more serious and intellectual. Slighted in his attempts to embark on a official career and plagued by ill health, his poetry has a melancholy depth. He is often concerned with matters of state, the welfare of people. Living in war-torn times Tu Fu contemplates the fate of peasants and soldiers, puts himself into the shoes of the conscripted and explores their plight, hardship and despair.

Below is one of Tu Fu's longer poems describing the effects of war. He powerfully evokes the reality of war simply by describing its effects. Tu Fu withholds judgement and trusts the situation to give its own verdict. The peasants speak of their plight and thus draw the reader into empathetic resonance. Apart from the references that anchor this work, it could have been written today.

Ballad of the War Chariots by Tu Fu

The carts squeak and trundle, the horses whinny, the conscripts go by,
each with a bow and arrows at his waist. Their fathers, mothers, wives, and children run along beside them to see them off. The Hsien-yang Bridge cannot be seen for dust. They pluck at the men's clothes, stamp their feet, or stand in the way weeping. The sound of their weeping seems to mount up to the blue sky above. A passer-by questions the conscripts, and the conscripts reply:

They're always mobilizing now! There are some of us who went north at
fifteen to garrison the River and who are still, at forty, being sent to the
Military Settlements in the west. When we left as lads, the village headman had to tie our head-cloths for us. We came back white-haired, but still we have to go back for frontier duty! On those frontier posts enough blood has flowed to fill the sea; but the Martial Emperor's dreams of expansion remain unsatisfied.

Haven't you heard, sir, in our land of Han, throughout the two hundred
prefectures east of the mountains briers and brambles are growing in thousands of little hamlets; and though many a sturdy wife turns her own hand at the hoeing and ploughing, the crops grow just anywhere, and you can't see where one field ends and the next begins? And it's even worse for the men from Ch'in. Because they make such good fighters, they are driven about this way and that like so many dogs or chickens.

Though you are good enough to ask us, sir, it's not for the likes of
us to complain. But take this winter, now. The Kuan-hsi troops are not being demobilized. The District Officers press for the land-tax, but where is it to come from? I really believe it's a misfortune to have sons. It's actually better to have a daughter. If you have a daughter, you can at least marry her off to one of the neighbors; but a son is born only to end up lying in the

grass somewhere, dead and unburied. Why look, sir, on the shores of the Kokonor the bleached bones have lain for many a long year, but no one has ever gathered them up. The new ghosts complain and the old ghosts weep, and under the grey and dripping sky the air is full of their baleful twitterings.

I am moved by the power of the last line, a poetic device often applied by Chinese master poets. I have chosen this poem for its compassionate stand and deep humanism. The poet is able to transport himself into the minds of the conscripts and describe the despair of the women and children left behind. The work resonates with the lasting plight of wartime, the endless pain for all involved.

Exercise 5: Words at War

We can sympathize with the sentiment of the eighth century poet. War was always gruesome and is no less today. It is easy to write a polemic against war. It is not so easy to do it poetically. Tu Fu can inspire us to take a compassionate approach. He is able to distil beauty from pain without compromising either.

Use your imagination or report on one of the many conflicts in the world. Follow Tu Fu and powerfully describe war through its effects.

Devastation by Karen McCrea
there are desert places,
harsh, barren, hard places
hollow mothers carry bundles
of bones, that watch them
with the eyes of ghosts-to-be.

empty land holds millions
of these dessicated people, hungry,
while machines as mindless
as the men who sent them
set their teeth into the earth
ripping out what is left, gorging.

in the middle of an abandoned village
a small, lone, lost child,
swell-bellied,
starved to sexless-ness
finds enough water to cry.

silent grief shades the bright sun.

Words at War by Lachlan Mckenzie
Dearest Father,
The Jailer's son joins me for chess Mondays. He plays well but lacking the flair for strategy which you taught me. He plays with cunning but he falls to me often.
March 1870

To Father,
This week I was allowed to till the fields unshackled. There are decent folk amongst the peasants. You should see the fields of wheat!
December 1871

Father.
All is not as you told me. I have lived as a free man this last Spring and, though common, I have found love in the arms of this dark land. Where you spoke often of dogs, Father, I have seen now Winter Wolves. I will not return. This is my last letter.

Poetic Friendships

Poetic friendship is a theme worth exploring. On rare occasions the world conspires to make two geniuses meet. Li Po and Tu Fu, each aware of the other's gift, met several times. Tu Fu wrote seven poems about his poetic equal. Here is one:

> **Thoughts of Li Po from the World's End by Tu Fu** (tr. Hawkes)
> Here at the world's end the cold winds are beginning to blow.
> What messages have you for me, my master?
> When will the poor wandering goose arrive?
> The rivers and lakes are swollen with autumn's waters.
> Art detests a too successful life;
> And the hungry goblins await you with welcoming jaws.
> You had better have a word with the ghost of that other wronged poet.
> Drop some verses into the
> Mi-lo as an offering to him!

The 'other wronged poet' is Qu Yuan, who drowned himself in the Milou river: a remarkable and prophetic line as Li Po too will find his end by drowning. Here is a poem by Li Po addressed to Tu Fu:

> **To Tu Fu From Shantung by Li Po** (tr. Hamill)

You ask how I spend my time ---
I nestle against a tree trunk
and listen to autumn winds
in the pines all night and day.

Shantung wine can't get me drunk.
The local poets bore me.
My thoughts remain with you,
like the Wen River, endlessly flowing.

Exercise 6: From Poet to Poet

Think of a poetic friend, someone who shares your sensitivity and write a poem about him or her. Or explore the option of writing a poetic letter as the one by Li Po.

Poetic Friendship by Karen McCrea
Hello beloved friend,
   greetings from the other side, where I sit indoors wrapped from head to foot against the teeth in the endless winds of this great city. I'm watching the street through the window and the good citizens for all the world look like a shuffling mass of wombles in t heir hats and coats and scarves and gloves, busy with their busy-ness.
   I have found no place here where I can be my first self like I can with you. There is constant buzz here, but i miss the sound of the trees outside your window, the small domestic music of teapots and china cups, of turning pages and scratching pens. I shall light a candle when I get home and by its flickering light remember our two heart beats, in rhythm as sisters.

Letter to a Sister Poet by Liana Christensen
You came bearing unaware
the terrible glory of all
the Celtic stories
fecund with words
from distant shores
and deep springs within

Now you set out again
for the far away
while I remain
sessile
but for all that

content
with the knowing
even dead poets are eloquent
So, what matters a continent?

Li Po's influence is by no means restricted to the Chinese language. Being one of the fathers of modern poetry he is undoubtedly one of the most influential poets in the world. Translating Li Po into English at the beginning of the twentieth century, poetic maverick Ezra Pound changed not only his own style of expression, but that of a whole century. Western poetry has never been the same since. Pound's translations are often criticised by scholars as free style. But the best translation is not measured by linguistic exactitude, but poetic similitude. Below is Pound's celebrated translation of Li Po:

The River Merchant's Wife by Li Po
While my hair was still cut straight across my forehead
I played about the front gate, pulling flowers.
You came by on bamboo stilts, playing horse,
You walked about my seat, playing with blue plums.
And we went on living in the village of Chokan:
Two small people, without dislike or suspicion.
At fourteen I married My Lord you.
I never laughed, being bashful.
Lowering my head, I looked at the wall.
Called to, a thousand times, I never looked back.
At fifteen I stopped scowling,
I desired my dust to be mingled with yours
Forever and forever and forever.
Why should I climb the look out?

At sixteen you departed,
You went into far Ku-to-en, by the river of swirling eddies,
And you have been gone five months.
The monkeys make sorrowful noise overhead.

You dragged your feet when you went out.
By the gate now, the moss is grown, the different mosses,
Too deep to clear them away!
The leaves fall early this autumn, in wind.
The paired butterflies are already yellow with August
Over the grass in the West garden;
They hurt me. I grow older.
If you are coming down through the narrows of the river Kiang,
Please let me know beforehand,

And I will come out to meet you
    As far as Cho-fu-Sa.

The language is refreshingly direct. Much is said, yet there is not one superfluous word or phrase. This poem exemplifies the great sensitivity of Chinese works. Li Po tells a story by means of a letter. He inhabits the soul of a young woman and applies his craft to articulate her feelings. He does this indirectly: the length of absence reflects in mosses grown deep, the pain of separation in the sorrowful noises monkeys make. The soul is reflected in its surrounding. Inner and Outer coincide.

Exercise 7: Poetic Reflections

Be inspired by Chinese sensitivities. Attempt a poem that is as intimate and observant as Li Po's. Detour through detail and environment. Let the outer world speak of the inner. Take the perspective of a young woman or a child to aid your writing.

Poetic Reflection by Stuart Wallis
The sweet coppery scent of
Rain drops mixed with
The dry red dust reminds me of
The perfumed smell of your hair

Cool breeze stirs the leaves.
Termites scurry across the path
With their burdens
Plugging their hole with straw

Black angry clouds build
Menacingly against the deep blue
Sky
The drops roll
Down my face like tears.

Poetic Reflection by Alison Ashton
It was shortly before you turned four that I drove you down the hill to your new home.
The road usually smooth, felt rough beneath the wheels.
On either side, the trees leaned inward, their grey-green boughs coming between the sun and our journey that was to end too soon.
Later, after I returned home, it seemed to me the sun
scorched the hills as it dropped into the advancing night.

Exercise 8: Found in Translation

I am fascinated by how Esra Pound's has changed the course of poetry. Translations are difficult even between related languages. Shakespeare is not the same in German and Goethe's Faust never entirely makes it across the channel of English language. Strangely enough, distance of culture can, as in the case of Pound's translation, help the process (the opposites contain the complement). The original is so far removed that it ends up closer. Knowledge dies and poetry takes precedence.

With this in mind we will try to translate one of the most popular poems of Chinese literature, Li Po's *'Night Thought's*, a work that contains many of the themes dear to Chinese sensitivity: autumn, full moon, night, separation, longing, home and family. So here is your chance to help one of the greatest works of world literature into the English language. Below are two translations of this poem:

Night Thoughts by Li Bai (Li Po) (Tr. H.A. Giles)
I wake and moonbeams play around my bed
Glittering like hoar frost to my wondering eyes
Upwards the glorious moon I raise my head
Then lay me down and thoughts of home arise

Thoughts in a Tranquil Night by Li Po (Tr. L. Cranmer-Byng)
Athwart the bed
I watch the moonbeams cast a trail
So Bright, so cold, so frail,
That for a space it gleams
Like hoar-frost on the margin of my dreams.
I raise my head, --
The splendid moon I see:
Then droop my head,
And sink to dreams of thee --
My fatherland, of thee!

There is room for improvement. Now try your own version. And remember that it is not a matter of accuracy but poetic resonance.

Translation by Karen McCrea
I rise up to behold a wonder,
By my bed - frost-silvered ground!
Deceived by the light of the bright moon
I lay my head back down,
and sink into thoughts of home

34

Threshold Images

In 1912 Ezra Pound published his famous translations of Chinese and Japanese works that changed the course of western poetry. Inspired by Chinese sensitivity and Japanese precision, a group of English and American poets lead by Ezra Pound, Hilda Doolittle and Amy Lowell rebelled against the surviving vestiges of Romantic poetry. Known as the imagist poets, they looked for a poetry of 'precise visual imagery' and succinctness of form without embellishment and false sentiment. In 1912 Ezra Pound declared their intentions in the manifesto we met in chapter ten:

> To use the language of common speech, but to employ the exact word, not the nearly-exact, nor the merely decorative word.
> We believe that the individuality of a poet may often be better expressed in free verse than in conventional forms. In poetry, a new cadence means a new idea. Absolute freedom in the choice of subject.
> To produce a poetry that is hard and clear, never blurred nor indefinite.
> Finally, most of us believe that concentration is of the very essence of poetry

Haiku
The haiku held a strong fascination for the imagists. It exemplified the reduction to essentials. Ezra Pound's *'In a Station of the Metro'* was clearly influenced by haiku. The poet said of it: 'I wrote a thirty-line poem, and destroyed it because it was what we call work of second intensity. Six months later I made a poem half that length; a year later I made the following hokku-like sentence':

> The apparition of these faces in the crowd; Petals on a wet, black bough.

The haiku, a form of Japanese poetry, is strongly influenced by Buddhist tradition with its emphasis on acute awareness, its concentration on essentials and the practice of the right word. The early haiku were often frivolous in content and formed the first part of a collaborative poetry composition called *haikai no renga*, wherein one poet started with a haiku strictly confined to 5 – 7 – 5 syllables per line verse and another followed with the *mora*, consisting of a 7 – 7 syllable per line verse.

Matsua Basho is one of the first masters who lifted the *haiku* from common use into the sphere of art and made it stand on its own. Basho also developed the *haibun*, a travel diary in which the prose narrative is heightened by haiku poetry. Basho's travel journal *'Narrow Road to the Interior'* has become a canonical text in Japanese literature.
Here is an example of from the beginning of his travel log:

> On the twenty-seventh day of the Third Month the moon was thinning. Mount Fuji hid behind the pale light of dawn. Will I ever see the cherry trees of Ueno and Yanaka again? Friends who had gathered the night before boarded the boat to see me off. As we left Senju, my heart grew heavy with thoughts of the long road ahead. I knew the world is transient, and yet, at this crossroad, I wept.
>
> as this spring withers
>   birds sing sadly and fish-eyes
>   are wet with tears
>
> I wrote this haiku to begin my travel diary. We then started off. It was hard to proceed with my friends all standing there in a row, watching us, as we dragged ourselves out of sight.

Exercise 1: Haibun

Take up Basho's example of the haibun (travel journal interspersed with Haiku) and remember an intense experience in nature, on a journey, in a place of significance, in the parting and meeting with friends.

You can start with the prose part (describing the narrative periphery of the event) and then distill it into tight poetic form (the centerpiece). Ideally the first line of the haiku contains 5 syllables, the second 7 and the third 5 again. This form, however, cannot always be maintained, and in the end a good poem is always more satisfying than a second rate, but accurate rendition. What grips us is not the count of syllables but the immediacy of deeper realities caught through poetic awareness.

Alternatively you could start with the haiku and ad the narrative as a supporting framework. Try both approaches and see which works best.

Haibun by Alisson Ashton
It was a warm spring day at Meelup Beach.
A soft breeze caressed the trees behind me.
I sat on a rock with my friend, overlooking the sea.
As I listened to the waves licking the rocks, swirling back and forth, I was drawn by that sound deep into the deepest well of my awareness.
Still and silent.

Listening to waves
lick around rocks;
Inner storm stills.

Haibun by Helen McDonnell
As I walk along the edge of the cliff; waves pounding the jagged rocks below.
Birds nestling in rocky outcrops.
An eagle caught in a thermal hovers above me, wings outstretched
He is so close I feel I could almost reach up and touch him.

A rugged coast line
Majestic eagle rests in space
Our closeness, breathtaking.

Here is some more examples of Basho's works:

Calm and serene
The voice of a cicada
Seeps into the rocks.

The poem transports us into a moment of heightened awareness where we see into the subtle depths of transitory life. For a split second the veil between us and the world is lifted; we are the voice of the cicada seeping into the rock, the serene expanse of evening; the world at standstill.

A haiku is a form of poetic meditation, a splinter of time illuminated by the instant of thought, a moment of oneness caught in seventeen syllables and three lines. Here is another example by Basho:

As the sea grows dark
The voice of the duck
Faintly whitens.

'Faintly whitens' is an acute depiction of synaesthesia, the merging of senses that occurs in heightened states of awareness such as meditation. Traditionally, haikus refer to one of the seasons. In this haiku by Sora, the rows of barley place it securely in time:

A butterfly
Stitching together
The rows of barley.

The haiku reminds me of the precision of Japanese rituals — the clean contours of Zen and bonsais pruned to perfection. Like a Buddhist monk, a haiku thrives on minimal means and offers a perfect literary form to practise Right Word. This example is by Kyoshi:

> The snake flees
> But the eyes that peered at me
> Remain in the weeds.

And two more haikus by Issa, author of the moving *'Spring of my Life,'* haibun (travel journal). Many of his poems are inspired by birds, insects and beast: The second example is typical of Issa's compassionate attitude.

> Cool breeze,
> tangled
>   in a grass-blade.

> Hey! Don't swat:
> the fly wrings his hands
> on bended knees.

Exercise 2: Haiku

Now write a few more haiku. Recall moments of transcendence and put them to pen. Try variation on the same poem. Experiment with leaving out words or using different ones, omit everything that is not essential. Try turning a phrase around. Change the order of lines. Write the same haiku in strict and in loose form.

Here are some examples inspired by the Japanese poets predilection of seasonal themes:

Haiku (Spring) by Jaya Penelope
The eagerness
of the wedding bush
and I, without you?

Haiku (Spring) by Jennifer Kornberger
The sky hails
poppy buds do not open
to such rough hands

Haiku (Summer) by Morgan Yasbincek
Black dog, shot by light
a casualty
on our driveway

Winter by Helen McDonnell
Snowflakes falling
Crystals caught in headlights
Muffled footsteps

Through Pounds translations and the powerful impact of Imagist poetry a new impulse entered the biography of the English language.

From East to West

William Carlos Williams, Western master of the haiku, worked particularly successfully with imagist ideas. Though a twentieth century Basho grown on American soil, Williams is never pedantic with form. The succinctness of his language originates in his attention to poetic detail, his careful observations of life and his insights into the ephemerals of existence. His *'Red Wheelbarrow'* has become an icon of modern poetry:

> so much depends upon
> a red wheel barrow
> glazed with rain water
> beside the white chickens

In a form particular to itself Williams captures in only a few lines the essential quality of the situation. The moment opens into a timeless dimension. Another good example of his style is the following:

> This Is Just to Say
>
> I have eaten
> the plums
> that were in
> the icebox
>
> and which
> you were probably
> saving
> for breakfast

Forgive me
they were delicious
so sweet
and so cold

Exercise 3: Imagist Poetry

William Carlos Williams' use of imagism provides a good training ground to enter modern poetry. It allows us to see the poetry of everyday existence as it asks us to see the familiar with new eyes. Follow his call of poetic awakening and create a short poem that captures the essence of a situation.

(apologies to William Carlos Williams) by Mags Webster
I found your message
under the knife-block:
your words
serrations over my flesh

long after
your scent still penetrates

The Second Coming

One of the first heralds of modern poetry was the Irish poet William Butler Yeats. His work changes considerably during his lifetime. His early work still echoes romantic sentiments, his love for Ireland and the Celtic revival. Meeting Ezra Pound and working closely together with him in Sussex changed his style and outlook. He transcends his nationalism, and rises to universal, even prophetic expression in poems like **'The Second Coming'**:

> Turning and turning in the widening gyre
> The falcon cannot hear the falconer;
> Things fall apart; the centre cannot hold;
> Mere anarchy is loosed upon the world,
> The blood-dimmed tide is loosed, and everywhere
> The ceremony of innocence is drowned;
> The best lack all conviction, while the worst
> Are full of passionate intensity.
>
> Surely some revelation is at hand;

Surely the Second Coming is at hand.
The Second Coming! Hardly are those words out
When a vast image out of Spiritus Mundi
Troubles my sight: somewhere in sands of the desert
A shape with lion body and the head of a man,
A gaze blank and pitiless as the sun,
Is moving its slow thighs, while all about it
Reel shadows of the indignant desert birds.
The darkness drops again; but now I know
That twenty centuries of stony sleep
Were vexed to nightmare by a rocking cradle,
And what rough beast, its hour come round at last,
Slouches towards Bethlehem to be born?

'The Second Coming' is like a tolling of bells, a warning siren. Like a great Leitmotif it precedes many of the themes of modern poetry. The language is hauntingly foreboding, direct. Like a magical invocation, the first line transports us into the dilemma of the modern soul and we begin to spin in the whirlpool of disintegration: 'Turning and turning in the widening gyre ... Things fall apart; the centre cannot hold; Mere anarchy is loosed upon the world ...' These lines summarise a battle that rages in the depths of every human being. At the same time they are acutely prophetic of the political turmoils that wrought unprecedented destruction over Europe and Russia.

The poem has lost nothing of its relevance in our time. The experience of falling apart and the inability to integrate the diverse forces of our soul is epidemic. The spectres of social injustice, economic exploitation and unbridled imperialism have taken tangible form in numerous instances of genocide and a war against nature. Mark the mythical image of a disintegrating sphinx. But Yeats' poem is not just a statement of decay. It is a call to arms. 'The Second Coming' ends with a question. Pointing to the shadow, it involuntarily invokes the light.

Exercise 4: The Second Coming

Let 'The Second Coming' inspire in you a poetic response. Explore the challenges of inner and outer disintegration, the rise of adversarial forces and worldwide challenges. Find pictures and metaphors that illustrate the state of the world and the human soul.

Second Coming by Janet Blagg

The second coming announces itself in a neat package of blood, flown frozen over continents for transfusion into a body rendered numb and glabrous by a lethal cocktail of drugs and radiation. The great god-doctor pulling the puppet strings, holding out a second chance to this ruined body, not yet fifty, never to be fifty.

Sorry dear, I'll get it in a moment, says the nurse, distressed at his tenth failure; but he doesn't get the needle in, the veins have shut down, they've had enough. And no heavenly chorus or snowy dove ascends over this hospital bed, suspended high above the snaking river, the straining city, as I watch the stem cells drip drip dripping down the plastic tubing, through the maddening beeping machines and into the tangle of lines blossoming red at her neck. Is there really any life in those thawed-out cells?

I sit holding a hot hand, wiping my sister's shuddering brow.
No words to chart this drop into pain, vomit, ulceration, disintegration — all in the hope of more, a little more . . . a second chance for more . . . of the same.

Wasn't it enough to break your heart the first time?

The Second Coming by John Stubley
The world roars at me
through the coils and wire
and speakers
of my television.
It streams an endless
vision and re-revision
of an apocolyptic super-vision.

The world rushes at me
through the chips and bits
and windows
of my personal computer.
It downloads and upgrades
from sourceless looters,
romantic suitors, debt-free dupors.

The world rushes through me,
through bones and muscle
and a heart that beats
in a tired chest
that longs for rest
but still hopes —
hopes for the best.

The Human Being Coming Through

D. H. Lawrence was one of the most controversial and influential writers of his time. He was also a poet, and his *'Song of a Man Who Has Come Through'* answers the question posed by Yeats. I count it among those works where the poet, led by the genius of poetry itself, transcends his own limitations and touches on what is universally human.

> Not I, not I, but the wind that blows through me!
> A fine wind is blowing the new direction of Time.
> If only I let it bear me, carry me, if only it carry me!
> If only I am sensitive, subtle, oh, delicate, a winged gift!
> If only, most lovely of all, I yield myself and am borrowed
> By the fine, fine wind that takes its course through the chaos of the world
> Like a fine, an exquisite chisel, a wedge-blade inserted;
> If only I am keen and hard like the sheer tip of a wedge
> Driven by invisible blows
> The rock will split, we shall come at the wonder, we shall find the Hesperides.
>
> Oh, for the wonder that bubbles into my soul,
> I would be a good fountain, a good well-head,
> Would blur no whisper, spoil no expression.
>
> What is the knocking?
> What is the knocking at the door in the night?
> It is somebody wants to do us harm.
>
> No, no, it is the three strange angels.
> Admit them, admit them.

Like 'The Second Coming', this poem describes a threshold experience, but one which awakens to the presence of light, to new possibilities emerging in the human soul: 'Not I, not I, but the wind that blows through me!'

To begin with, these possibilities are 'sensitive, subtle and delicate'. Like the poem itself, they are a 'winged gift', invoking the new paradisal forces found in the Hesperides. Lawrence is aware of the darkness but his poem sees beyond it. At every threshold to the new and unknown, the shadows congeal and our resistances condense into spectres of fear: 'What is the knocking?' But once the unknown power — that 'Not I, but the fine, fine wind that blows through me' — is found, the sphinx of our fears reveals itself as the three strange angels.

Exercise 5: Coming through: Song of the Human Being

Explore this continent of new possibilities. Listen for the 'fine wind that takes its course through the chaos of the world'. Draw the poetic contours of a new world. Meet the threshold and see beyond it.

Song of the Human Being by Diane Marshall
She asked me to save three seats.
One for her and two for her friends.
Agitated, watching, waiting, constantly alert, distracted,
Refusing to let anyone sit in them.

She was there all the time.
Happily sitting down the front
Oblivious to my misery.

It took me days to realise
I needn't have done it.

Song of the Human Being by Mags Webster
This life fits like a comfortable shoe. My tread is sure and I know what to do: put one foot in front of the other. Yes, perhaps I have to stop every once in a while; there is a piece of gravel nagging at my heel: I feel for it with irritable fingers. No point in taking the shoe off; my stride is already interrupted and anyway, there is a knot in my laces: the more I try to unpick it, the tighter the knot becomes. That's life, I think, it's not an easy sort of slip-on experience. But then I wonder what it would be like to cut the laces and kick off the shoes. I consider how good it might be to feel the grass between my bare toes.

Opposite Approaches

Two poets loom large in the first half of the twentieth century: T. S. Eliot and Dylan Thomas, their work occupying opposite poles of the poetic world. Dylan Thomas is Welsh and a bard unburdened by the weight of thought — surely he was dipped in Ceridwen's cauldron. His language has a will beyond himself, wild and elemental, inspired, fresh and braided with surprises. With bold metaphors it weaves Welsh magic into the eloquence of English verse. The poet often turns to the past, soaring high in the lament of loss. *'Fern Hill'* is such a poem, an unmatched invocation of paradise and childhood all in one:

The Writer's Passage

Now as I was young and easy under the apple boughs
About the lilting house and happy as the grass was green,
    The night above the dingle starry,
        Time let me hail and climb
    Golden in the heydays of his eyes,
And honoured among wagons I was prince of the apple towns
And once below a time I lordly had the trees and leaves
        Trail with daisies and barley
    Down the rivers of the windfall light.

And as I was green and carefree, famous among the barns
About the happy yard and singing as the farm was home,
    In the sun that is young once only,
        Time let me play and be
    Golden in the mercy of his means,
And green and golden I was huntsman and herdsman, the calves
Sang to my horn, the foxes on the hills barked clear and cold,
        And the sabbath rang slowly
    In the pebbles of the holy streams.

All the sun long it was running, it was lovely, the hay
Fields high as the house, the tunes from the chimneys, it was air
    And playing, lovely and watery
        And fire green as grass.
    And nightly under the simple stars
As I rode to sleep the owls were bearing the farm away,
All the moon long I heard, blessed among stables, the nightjars
    Flying with the ricks, and the horses
        Flashing into the dark.

And then to awake, and the farm, like a wanderer white
With the dew, come back, the cock on his shoulder: it was all
    Shining, it was Adam and maiden,
        The sky gathered again
    And the sun grew round that very day.
So it must have been after the birth of the simple light
In the first, spinning place, the spellbound horses walking warm
    Out of the whinnying green stable
        On to the fields of praise.

And honoured among foxes and pheasants by the gay house

Under the new made clouds and happy as the heart was long,
    In the sun born over and over,
        I ran my heedless ways,
    My wishes raced through the house high hay
And nothing I cared, at my sky blue trades, that time allows
In all his tuneful turning so few and such morning songs
    Before the children green and golden
        Follow him out of grace,

Nothing I cared, in the lamb white days, that time would take me
Up to the swallow thronged loft by the shadow of my hand,
    In the moon that is always rising,
        Nor that riding to sleep
    I should hear him fly with the high fields
And wake to the farm forever fled from the childless land.
Oh as I was young and easy in the mercy of his means,
        Time held me green and dying
    Though I sang in my chains like the sea.

Exercise 6: Moved by the Muse

Connect, like the Welsh bard, with the elemental power of language. Remember an instance in your life when you were as immersed as Dylan Thomas in his Welsh childhood. Re-experience the intensity of this moment, feel it fully and allow your language to take its pulse. Court a language that has a will of its own. Allow it to be energetic and inspired. Let it move through you; if it takes you on a ride, give it free rein.

The Red Dragon by Meirion Griffith

The lizard, green and black, shone on the crest of the brown rock,
Still as the amazing butterfly for a second only
Brief as a blue woman admired in the brilliantine shining sun.

Entranced like a weak infant, paralysed as a stalking lamppost made no meaning. But moved too quick to see into the dark embracing shade, black as night. As Mrs Black, all in black, moved her arthritic leg a millimetre to the left of the Dragon mounted on the green and white, red as ever on the flag ...
As it lay on the baize, green and white, the red dragon seemed to grow in clarity and, gigantic as a mountain, animate, lifting from the surface on the ground.

Three-dimensional, animal of immense bulk, scarlet, dazzling.

Its plangent breath, white hot as its forked tongue flicked to and fro
between its yellow, drooling, spiked teeth.
Its roar was as the sound of a mighty waterfall, a huge tsunami
engulfing, mesmerising all who stood about.

They shrank into the tiniest size they could imagine,
Lowering their eyes to avoid the scalding stare of the beast.

In contrast to Dylan Thomas, T. S. Eliot's poetry exemplifies the music of ideas. In spite of being a great innovator, his poetry is always measured, educated and contained. In the 'Wasteland' he produced a milestone of English poetry. While Dylan is a drunkard gambling with a dangerous muse, Eliot is a scholar, a meditant on the mantra of words, a monk hidden behind the respectability of an English suit. His *'Four Quartets'* may be the most widely read and commented upon piece of English poetry. As the title suggests, the composition is a variation on musical themes and resonances, point and counterpoint. The last quartet leads the reader to that rare place where the philosophic, poetic and religious meet:

> What we call the beginning is often the end
> And to make an end is to make a beginning.
> The end is where we start from. And every phrase
> And sentence that is right (where every word is at home,
> Taking its place to support the others,
> The word neither diffident nor ostentatious,
> An easy commerce of the old and the new,
> The common word exact without vulgarity, The formal word precise but not pedantic,
> The complete consort dancing together)
> Every phrase and every sentence is an end and a beginning ...

Exercise 7: Poetic Reflection

Follow Eliot through the ladder of words, the mirror of poetic reflection, conclusion, insights and carefully wrought ideas, until a gate opens into the ephemeral of poetic experiences. Here is a contemporary call by Jennifer Kornberger:

Rosacea by Jennifer Kornberger

> The spirit speaks slowly to the soul, one word can take a choir of years.
> When you are spelled by spirit you will know the first sound
> early on the morning of your unremembered choosing
> as though the muslin gauze you hung at your window

was stained by the song of migratory birds....

Eliot meditation on words culminates in his poetic epiphany, the grand and moving lines that end the **Four Quartets**:

With the drawing of this Love and the voice of this Calling:

We shall not cease from exploration
And the end of all our exploring
Will be to arrive where we started
And know the place for the first time.
Through the unknown, remembered gate
When the last of earth left to discover
Is that which was the beginning;
At the source of the longest river
The voice of the hidden waterfall
And the children in the apple-tree
Not known, because not looked for
But heard, half-heard, in the stillness
Between two waves of the sea.
Quick now, here, now, always —
A condition of complete simplicity
(Costing not less than everything)
And all shall be well and
All manner of thing shall be well
When the tongues of flame are in-folded
Into the crowned knot of fire
And the fire and the rose are one.

35

Choir of the New

Modernism

Eliot and his work have become an icon of modern poetry. While he began to cross the threshold into the spiritual, other writers extended literature into hitherto unexplored areas. D. H. Lawrence's *Lady Chatterley* broke sexual taboos and entered the sphere of intimacy.

James Joyce's 'Ulysse's appeared in 1922 and became a milestone of literary innovation. The novel echoes the structure of Homer's *Odyssey*, but confines itself to a single day, 16 June 1904, in working class Dublin, and records the internal monologue of Leopold Bloom — his thoughts, pictures, memories, plans and hopes, mingled with the events of a normal day. Joyce created a new style that mirrored the dynamics of the modern mind: its incessant self talk, clatter of ideas; the multiplicity and fragmentation of the soul. Below is a section that parallels the Lotus Eaters:

> The far east. Lovely spot it must be: the garden of the world, big lazy leaves to float about on, cactuses, flowery meads, snaky lianas they call them. Wonder is it like that. Those Cinghalese lobbing around in the sun, in dolce far niente. Not doing a hand's turn all day. Sleep six months out of twelve. Too hot to quarrel. Influence of the climate. Lethargy. Flowers of idleness. The air feeds most. Azotes. Hothouse in Botanic gardens. Sensitive plants. Waterlilies. Petals too tired to. Sleeping sickness in the air. Walk on roseleaves. Imagine trying to eat tripe and cowheel. Where was the chap I saw in that picture somewhere? Ah, in the dead sea, floating on his back, reading a book with a parasol open. Couldn't sink if you tried: so thick with salt. Because the weight of the water, no, the weight of the body in the water is equal to the weight of the. Or is it the volume is equal of the weight? It's a law something like that. Vance in High school cracking his fingerjoints, teaching. The college curriculum. Cracking curriculum.

Exercise 1: Flow of Consciousness

Experiment with flow of consciousness writing. Record all thoughts, images, feelings, impressions — whatever occupies your mind for a period of time. Do not make it fit any pre-imposed order, style or form. Let the inner flow of images break the linearity of thought and mirror the convoluted, fragmented and continuously changing dynamics of your inner monologue. Reveal the kaleidoscope of your mind.

Flow of Consciousness by Nandi Chinna

How can I concentrate when there are musicians on the tv playing guitars and looking beautiful like their fathers and mothers. How remarkable the resemblance. Then the birds rattle the bars of their cages causing me pain oh yes everything comes back to that eventually. As I sit in a blue chair in a safe place with all the technological advancements, no cause for complaining. A big wave rose up you should have seen the breakages and splintered houses that engulfed the beaches and crawled up hillsides. Crawled. Food left over from indulgent feasts lays on bench tops, scraps. Flies land there, cockroaches can't run fast anymore they are drunken louts on linoleum skidding and sliding. It was Christmas. Dead to the world at 5 am the stray chicken started clucking and choofing outside the bedroom window. Oh god it's dawn. Not much to complain about. Shall I make a cup of tea. Oh the earth is drying out now since I went away all the grass is dead and brittle, it's summer again so. So suddenly. I can't bear birds in cages. Don't complain about it. Somewhere in the world it is a different time of day and the globe keeps spinning changing time everywhere. I'm here at dawn near the sea …

The innovations of James Joyce reflected the increasing fragmentation of the modern mind. Many poets followed his lead and experimented with language. One of the most successful was e. e. cummings, who stretched the elasticity of language as he explored new forms. Through a mix of playfulness and originality he created a highly idiosyncratic expression:

> i thank You God for most this amazing
> day: for the leaping greenly spirits of trees
> and a blue true dream of sky; and for everything which is natural which is infinite which is yes
> (i who have died am alive again today,
> and this is the sun's birthday; this is the birth
> day of life and of love and wings: and of the gay great happening illimitably earth)
>
> how should tasting touching hearing seeing breathing any— lifted from the no of all nothing— human merely being doubt unimaginable You?
>
> (now the ears of my ears awake and now the eyes of my eyes are opened)

Tuned to the parallels between sounds and nature, cummings invokes spring through the vowel e — 'the leaping greenly spirits of trees' — in a daring and yet totally fitting construction. A phrase like 'and for everything which is natural which is infinite which is yes' gains momentum through the total lack of punctuation. His surprising use of syntax resonates with the theme of his poem: an inner rebirth that changes his perspective on the world. The renewal he experiences in his soul is reflected in the refreshed language.

Exercise 2: Poetic Experiments

Experiment with the structure of language. Use the freedom language has gained in the twentieth century and integrate it in a poem or small piece of prose on any theme. You could try cummings' example of a rebirth to match your birthing of new expression.

(happy) new year by Mags Webster

this world is blessed with moist new fruiting
and everyhow it shimmers in the secret
of leaf and real beginnings; I hear
this laughter spinning out a single note
the sky accepts (most graciously) its weight of tears
and in the bloodquake of a whispered word I feel
the sonnetting of trees
(the wolfish lick of wind)

Poetic ex 2 by Nandi Chinna

This morning smells like light
licking at the tips of leaves
shudder green the songs of birds
dreamed in the darkness
pictures of music into eyes and ears
and fingertips that pull aside curtains
an audience to this

tastes like steam inhaled fragrance
of sacred bitter leaves cling
to hands thrown with great reverence
into porcelain waiting with time
on clocks on walls in houses ticking
ringing whistling water
scalds leaves and bubbles brown
held in my hands I sip
these tender gifts

The Beat Generation

A world ends with T. S. Eliot and e. e. cummings. Eliot could rely on the stability of English society and find meaning in conventional religion. But this changes with the poets of the Beat generation. After the second world war old values have become clichéd, confidence has turned to doubt, Yeats' prophesies have come true: 'Things have fallen apart, the centre could not hold and mere anarchy was loosed upon the world …'

Inspired by psychoanalysis, surrealist writers had already experimented, like Joyce, with the flow of consciousness. They used it to access the unconscious. The Beat poets used a similar method to break the barrier of the intellect. Jack Kerouac's 'spontaneous prose' and the poetry of Allen Ginsberg, Gary Snyder and Diane di Prima explore the pain and ecstasies of the post-war generation.

In the 1950s Jack Kerouac's travel novel '*On the Road*' became an icon, capturing, like Goethe's 'Sufferings of the Young Werther', the sentiments of its generation. Kerouac's spontaneous prose echoes the improvisational style of jazz. And while Joyce remained outside Leopold Bloom, Kerouac is his own hero. He is his prose:

> 'Where we going, man?'
>   'I don't know but we gotta go.' Then here came a gang of young bop musicians carrying their instruments out of cars. They piled right into a saloon and we followed them. They set themselves up and started blowin. There we were! The leader was a slender, drooping, curly-haired, pursy-mouthed tenorman, thin of shoulder, draped loose in a sports shirt, cool in the warm night, self-indulgence written in his eyes, who picked up his horn and frowned in it and blew cool and complex and was dainty stamping his foot to catch ideas, and ducked to miss others — and said, 'Blow,' very quietly when the other boys took solos. Then there was Prez, a husky, handsome blond like a freckled boxer, meticulously wrapped inside his sharkskin plaid suit …

Kerouac, Ginsberg and Gary Snyder were rebels exploring the fringes of society through sex, drugs, alcohol and meditation. With the Beat poets poetry enters sub-culture and fraternises with the desperate and homeless. Ginsberg's '*Howl*' is symptomatic of the time; the poem is a barometer of pain, social injustice and the desperation beneath the skin of American life. It scratches the wounds festering beneath the veneer of society; the madness and the suffering among the down and out. It is a poet's outcry and a journal of despair:

> I saw the best minds of my generation destroyed by madness, starving hysterical naked,
> dragging themselves through the negro streets at dawn looking for an angry fix,
> angelheaded hipsters burning for the ancient heavenly connection to the starry dynamo in the machinery of night,

who poverty and tatters and hollow-eyed and high sat up smoking in the supernatural darkness of cold-water flats floating across the tops of cities contemplating jazz,
who bared their brains to Heaven under the El and saw Mohammedan angels staggering on tenement roofs illuminated
… who cowered in unshaven rooms in underwear, burning their money in wastebaskets and listening to the Terror through the wall,
who got busted in their pubic beards returning through Laredo with a belt of marijuana for New York …

'Howl' hurls us into a state of rebellion. Some safety valve has burst. Nightmares ride into the world. Reality is purgatorial, normality a form of hell. The poet is not aloof. He is part of the misery. He suffers and names the suffering. His language is direct and improvisational. We are hit by the drumbeat of fragments, the cascade of pictures; we are electrified, shocked, driven by the lines, drugged by the intensity. Such poetry is courageous. It does not talk about. It partakes. It is rough but compassionate. The poet has come to a place of suffering. He has asked the question: What ails thee? And tells us the answer he got.

Exercise 3: The Beat of Extacy and Agony

Write a piece in the intense style of the beat generation. Take your lead from the ecstasy of Kerouac or be inspired by Ginsberg's agony; or mix them one with the other as Mags Webster in the piece below:

On the road, On the bed by Mags Webster
there's this thing about sleep, the big burning treacle of it, the drowning-bubble of closed-eyes ecstasy, the folding-down of limbs into sheets which knot like vines and caress with lovers' hands, the bed which rocks its cradle-angels around your head, their breath is melting through the pillow into your ears, along the channels of your brain to tell you all the lullaby-things you've forgotten are a part of this subterranean world, and the dream-peoplers stomp behind your eyelids pressing little planets into the spaces in your skull, their timing is so perfect you can't even feel they're there on this mushroom-cloud of sleep which drifts its lazy fingers down your spine until your bones take root and start to make patterns of their own and thread back up through your skin, which reaches out across the bed like some elaborate beast and takes the oxygen out of the world and pours it down your throat, telling you it's OK, it's OK, we're going to shut you down, we're going to push you through the wall of doze and you are going to sleep-land, baby

Loba and the Emergence of the Feminine

Diane di Prima's *'Loba'* assembles surviving fragments of feminine spirituality and identity in poetic form. She visits the Wolf Goddess, Kali, Inanna, Lilith, Iseult and Guinevere, Persephone and Ariadne. She claims the female archetypes for herself, her life and her work as a poet. She actualises aspects of the eternal feminine, resurrecting them from the grave of myth. Here is one of her poems to the Indian goddess Kali:

> Because you love the burning grounds
> I have made a burning ground of my heart, O Kali,
> That you, Beloved, may dance there unceasingly.
> Nothing burns in my heart but funeral fire
> Nothing dwells there now but the ashes of the dead.
> O Mother, who dances on Lord Shiva's corpse,
> Come, swaying to the sound of drums,
> Enter my heart's ash:
> I await you with closed eyes

Di Prima pioneers a journey that every human being needs to undertake, a pilgrimage as important for men as it is for women — the liberation of the feminine within the soul.

Exercise 4: The Liberation of the Feminine

Choose any female archetype or heroine and give her voice. Identify with her power or reveal her presence working within your soul.

Woman in the Wilderness by Jennifer Kornberger

> The man child has in turn given birth to you, woman.
> Do not let anyone say you are beautiful
> lest you remember how to grieve.
> There is a chasm in the earth in the wilderness
> where they said I would find you.
> Are you seeking me or I you?
>
> When you come to claim me be so unknown
> that I will have to leap to your conclusion.

Grace Darling (1815–1842) by Julie Dickinson

> A modest tablet commemorates her deeds.
> When on the night of a howling furious gale,
> she took her father's row boat and saved nine shipwrecked sailors

clinging to the rocks with bloodied hands and broken finger nails.
Five times she battled the tempest and brought them to safety.
Be-medalled brave daughter of a lighthouse keeper.

Men now counted, sketched, elevated to
'Valiant Survivors' storied objects placed in 'heroic epic',
focus of endless conversation at the tavern,
etched into topic for folklore.

Grace stowed her boat, dried her clothes
served her father's dinner, darned his socks
and as habit demanded, retired to bed.
The waves stilled, the storm abated
And Grace subsided beneath her daughterly duties.

New Voices

In the twentieth century the poetic voice of women powerfully emerges. Anna Akhmatova opened western readers to the depth and suffering of the Russian soul under Stalin.

> It was a time when only the dead smiled, happy in their peace … Stars of Death stood over us, and innocent Russia squirmed under the bloody boots, under the wheels of black Marias.

The voice of Ingeborg Bachman shook post-war Germany from sleep:

> Do not decree faith on this race, stars, ships and smoke are enough; it is concerned with things, determines stars and mathematical infinity, and a trait, call it trait of love, emerges more purely from it all. The heavens hang limp, and stars come loose from the juncture with moon and night.

Confessional Poetry

Following the Beat poets, Ann Sexton and Sylvia Plath explore themes that were hitherto taboo — shame, despair, depression and anger. Their poetry acts as a private confessor, a therapy by means of words. Readers become intimate with the poet's soul. Confessional poetry is autobiographical. It is courageous writing that shuns neither trauma nor death. Both Sexton and Plath suffered frequent breakdowns and each ended their own lives. The confessional poets walk an inward path. Their poems are carefully crafted rather than spontaneous outpourings. Consider Ann Sexton's poetic response to the suicide of Sylvia Plath:

O Sylvia, Sylvia,
with a dead box of stones and spoons,
with two children, two meteors
wandering loose in a tiny playroom,
with your mouth into the sheet,
into the roofbeam, into the dumb prayer,
(Sylvia, Sylvia
where did you go
after you wrote me
from Devonshire
about raising potatoes
and keeping bees?)
what did you stand by,
just how did you lie down into?
Thief —
how did you crawl into,
crawl down alone
into the death I wanted so badly and for so long,
the death we said we both outgrew,
the one we wore on our skinny breasts,
the one we talked of so often each time
we downed three extra dry martinis in Boston,
the death that talked of analysts and cures,
the death that talked like brides with plots,
the death we drank to,
the motives and the quiet deed? ….

To give words to anguish is one way of dealing with it. We do not need to follow these poets to the endpoint of despair, but we can learn from them the archeology of soul, the courage to speak when we are numbed, to face our demons and shape the chaos of sufferings into meaning.

Exercise 5: The Confessional

Find a painful event in your own biography and give it poetic shape. Call up a spectre of your past, liberate it from its mute prison, give it voice on paper. Infuse it with the life of language.

Dream by Desma Kearney

an angel nests in bones
she is song without sound
a skeleton washes her feet

the waking
finds me without the structure of a bed
below, nor ceiling where it should have been
above me. the street is gone and I am searching
for a mirror — to see if I exist
but there are no objects here, there is nothing
the world that has not given way to white
motionless coldless winter
silent territory that is a mirror
and I notice
I leave no footprints
and I notice
I have lost everything

a skeleton nests in feathers
in silent service, an angel
sings his feet

Confession by Nandi Chinna

In the chair
I give up the footsteps heavy clatter
take off my shoes
and lay back, ok, ready
for the final injection
the shock treatment

but all that happens is words
gurgling up from a deep stream
they come up fast like a well
sunk a spurting geyser
spits them onto the floor
where they squirm like guilty secrets

the weight of words rising
leaves me light I am not bound
to the chair I am free to leave at any time
yet time and again I choose
to return.

Narrative Poetry

Narrative poetry is as old as language. However, the concise narrative poem is young. Cotinuing in the tradition of the confessional poets, Sharon Olds has developed the narrative furhter. Her work captures events, perceived through the lens of poetry.

Like a good short story, a narrative poem often culminates in a surprising end or a poetic insight that opens up new possibilities of meaning. This kind of poetry needs careful composition, a subtle orchestration of events leading to the final revelation. Then the poem takes hold of us and suddenly we are in the heart of the matter, stunned, shocked, surprised, moved, as by **Sharon Olds in 'A Week Later'**.

> A week later, I said to a friend: I don't
> think I could ever write about it.
> Maybe in a year I could write something.
> There is something in me maybe someday
> to be written; now it is folded, and folded,
> and folded, like a note in school. And in my dream
> someone was playing jacks, and in the air there was a
> huge, thrown, tilted jack
> on fire. And when I woke up, I found myself
> counting the days since I had last seen
> my husband-only two years, and some weeks,
> and hours. We had signed the papers and come down to the
> ground floor of the Chrysler Building,
> the intact beauty of its lobby around us
> like a king's tomb, on the ceiling the little
> painted plane, in the mural, flying. And it
> entered my strictured heart, this morning,
> slightly, shyly as if warily,
> untamed, a greater sense of the sweetness
> and plenty of his ongoing life,
> unknown to me, unseen by me,
> unheard, untouched-but known, seen,
> heard, touched. And it came to me,
> for moments at a time, moment after moment,
> to be glad for him that he is with the one
> he feels was meant for him. And I thought of my
> mother, minutes from her death, eighty-five
> years from her birth, the almost warbler
> bones of her shoulder under my hand, the
> eggshell skull, as she lay in some peace
> in the clean sheets, and I could tell her the best
> of my poor, partial love, I could sing her

out with it, I saw the luck
and luxury of that hour.

At first we are not sure what the poem is about. We are kept in suspense, only slowly let in to the poem's core — the complications of love and disappointment, the achingly sublime end with the poet's realisation at the deathbed of her mother.

Olds tells so much in so little space. We are confronted with the distillate of her life and the power of feelings. We feel the wing-beat of her muse move the stagnant air of her past and turn it into that 'fine, fine wind that takes its course through the chaos of the world …' (D. H. Lawrence). Poems like this are purgatorial: they leave us changed.

Exercise 6: Narrative Poem

Try to tell a story within the limitations of a poem. Or start off with a longer version and then shorten it. Experiment with how much you can leave out without obscuring the plot. The story need not be extraordinary. As in Olds' poem, it is the poetic insight that counts.

Adelaide September 2004 by Jennifer Kornberger
The taxi driver was upbeat about Adelaide water
some of us still live to be 100 he crowed, but
when your number's up, it's up, hey?
Yeah, I said and we drove up Montfiore Road
and there was a traffic jam and a bicycle on
its side, a bin wheeled out to shield the body of a
boy from any more traffic
no ambulance yet but a policeman doing his duty
next to the covered one, wondering if
it was his duty to answer the mobile phone
ringing in the dead boy's pocket.

Sharon Olds is one of many women writers who are shaping the new landscape of poetry. With Elisabeth Bishop, Adrienne Rich and Denise Levertov she is part of an emergent female voice in American poetry, contemporary with the Australian Judith Wright. More recent Australian poets like Judith Beverage and Morgan Yasbincek are navigating the depths of female experience with the haunting precision of their poetic means. Here is a recent work by **Morgan Yasbincek:**

she takes you down from this cross in silence lest the weight
of a word shatter your bones
each of your wrists she cradles in the palms of her hands as she releases
them from the ropes, eases the fibres out of the burnt skin

she kisses your hands and, your mouth, the womb which
gave her her children and the feet which carried her life
she lets your weight fall onto her, heavy as a body

as she washes you a moon opens the night with her inquiry and even
so it is found that mercy has closed the doors of its kingdom, the elohim
weep behind them and the earth has let go of time

she pries the nails from the wood, takes an axe and cleaves the cross
at its centre, she chops the cross into pieces and sets a fire

in this fire she burns the prayers of gratitude for your tenacity, your
daily effort, your translations of heat to life, she lays your purple
robes across the sun and

all this she does in silence for now that you are gone
nothing will ask and nothing
will answer

Women are increasingly claiming the poetic ground that is rightfully theirs.. But the emergence of the feminine voice is by no means restricted to women. We may also find it in male poets. Rainer Maria Rilke is a striking example. His life and work testify to the poet's spiritual quest for the feminine side of his own soul. In the original German his poems possess an almost unearthly quality, a perfect balance between language and image and an unprecedented ease in the flow of words.

It is easy to imagine Rilke's poems pre-existing in the poetic heaven long before he wrote them — his ability to 'hear' them a function of a fine-tuned receptivity and depth of soul that is one of the marks of the universal feminine. Interestingly, the integration of the feminine in Rilke's soul was foreshadowed in his middle name, Maria.

In the last of his *'Sonnets to Orpheus'* Rilke admonishes us to:

   Walk in and out of transformation.
   What terrifies you most?
   If drinking is bitter, become wine …

36

The Imaginal Age

The biography of the poetic is inevitably linked with the life of the imagination. The further we go back in time the more the imagination rules supreme. Gradually it starts to dwindle as a cultural currency and become the province of artists, writers, poets. The fairies that populated Shakespeare's plays, the order of angels and saints that inhabit Dante's universe, fade. The world of the senses becomes the only world.

The death of imagination has not gone unsung. The most influential work of Spanish literature, *'Don Quixote'*, has this death as its theme. Written by Miguel de Cervantes (a contemporary of Shakespeare) during Spain's Golden Age this novel tells the story of Don Quixote de la Mancha, a county gentleman obsessed with the reading of chivalric novels:

> In short, his wits being quite gone, he hit upon the strangest notion that ever madman in this world hit upon, and that was that he fancied it was right and requisite, as well for the support of his own honour as for the service of his country, that he should make a knight-errant of himself, roaming the world over in full armour and on horseback in quest of adventures, and putting in practice himself all that he had read of as being the usual practices of knights-errant; righting every kind of wrong, and exposing himself to peril and danger from which, in the issue, he was to reap eternal renown and fame. Already the poor man saw himself crowned by the might of his arm Emperor of Trebizond at least; and so, led away by the intense enjoyment he found in these pleasant fancies, he set himself forthwith to put his scheme into execution.

Don Quixote has read too many novels. He imagines himself a knight when knighthood has long since vanished. He chooses a local peasant girl (who knows nothing about it) as his lady and renames her Dulcinea. He imagines a local inn to be a castle and mistakes ladies of light virtue for noble women. He persuades Sancho Panza, a simple farmer to become his squire and together they ride into one humiliating adventure after another. They are laughed at, led by the nose and often sorely beaten.

But Don Quixote remains steadfast. He upholds his noble ideas in spite of ridicule and abuse. His vivid imagination mistakes windmills for giants and so he attacks them. He gets so involved in a puppet play that he intervenes with his sword. The humorous situations increase in part two of the book, when the knight and his servant meet many who have already read part one; they know of his delusion and play practical jokes on the knight and his loyal quire.

Exercise 1: Colliding with Reality

The experience of clashing with reality is common for children. At one point or another their imaginal world comes into conflict with the intellectual world they inhabit. The tooth fairy dies and Santa Claus is dismantled.

Artists, writers and idealists often have such experiences later in their lives when their work is ignored or ridiculed. And so do inventors, innovators and great scientists. (The imagination that is out of touch with the world of today is often in touch with the world of tomorrow.)

Recall such an experience in your childhood or adult life. Remember when you were at odds with the status quo, a world without imagination, ideals, and hope.

> **Colliding with Reality by Ann Harrison**
> They are foot prints! They are, look two of them and see the glass is empty and the cake is gone? He is real!!
> No He's Not!! That was dad.
> So dad's Father Christmas?
> Know stupid! Dad just pretended.
> But why? He didn't have to because if he had just waited a bit longer he would have seen him and then everything
> would be alright. Poor dad!

Imaginal History

The Spain of the 17th and 16 centuries had has left its imaginary childhood long behind (and with it the great ideals of the chivalric age). The Spain of Cervantes' time subscribed to realities. The swift conquests of the Mayan and Inca cultures by a few hundred Spaniards testify to this fact. The Indians' real disadvantage was not their less advanced weaponry, but their mindset: like Don Quixote, they still lived in imaginal conceptions of the world and thus became easy prey for the realistic, profit hunting conquistadors. (Peter Schaeffer's 'The Royal Hunt of the Sun' brilliantly explores this theme.)

But the story does not end here. History shows that conquerors are often conquered in turn by the culture they vanquished. The realistic Spanish that settled in the Americas became affected by vigorous imaginative elements of their new home. The poetry of Pablo Neruda bears witness to the vibrant life and poetic possibilities emerging in Latin America.

Poetry by Pablo Neruda
And it was at that age ... Poetry arrived
in search of me. I don't know, I don't know where
it came from, from winter or a river.
I don't know how or when,
no they were not voices, they were not
words, nor silence,
but from a street I was summoned,
from the branches of night,
abruptly from the others,
among violent fires
or returning alone,
there I was without a face
and it touched me.

I did not know what to say, my mouth
had no way
with names,
my eyes were blind,
and something started in my soul,
fever or forgotten wings,
and I made my own way,
deciphering
that fire,
and I wrote the first faint line,
faint, without substance, pure
nonsense,
pure wisdom
of someone who knows nothing,
and suddenly I saw
the heavens
unfastened
and open,
planets,
palpitating plantations,
shadow perforated,

riddled
with arrows, fire and flowers,
the winding night, the universe.

And I, infinitesimal being,
drunk with the great starry
void,
likeness, image of
mystery,
felt myself a pure part
of the abyss,
I wheeled with the stars,
my heart broke loose on the wind.

Exercise 2: Poetic Calling

Every writer will have had a calling to take up the pen. This moment is precious and initiatory and often changes the course of their lives, the way they see the world. Celebrate this moment in a piece of writing like Pablo Neruda. Do it justice.]

Calling by Helen McDonell
The glass vase cracked and shattered into a thousand pieces.
Water flowed and found its own peaceful space.
The flowers fell and their petals, now loose, floated on the breeze
finally coming to rest.
A breeze lifted the lace curtain catching one of the petals,
lifting it higher and higher.
The sun shone piercing the glass, the water and petals
and all became a glorious kaleidescope of mesmerizing colours.
Words began to flow like water, landing like the petals, gently on the page.

Poetic Calling by Ann Harrison
I saw the rain falling and splashing in shallow puddles, all in slow motion.
I saw the swans reach across the lake and I felt the same wind on my face
that filled the sails on their backs.
I saw the trees bend in grace and I worried for the flight of the birds in this bold storm.
I became one with all of this, and realized I was living with a rhythm and timing too eloquent to dismiss, and the only way I could speak of these events was to take them into my soul, and then lay them on paper to bring them alive again.

Magical Realism

Neruda is not the only one whose heart broke loose with the wind. He is a contemporary of a number of Latin American authors who broke with the conventions of realism and thus changed the course of world literature: Gabriel García Márquez (One Hundred Years of Solitude), Isabel Allende (The House of the Spirits) and Laura Esquivel (Like Water for Chocolate). The result was magical realism, a style that has in the meantime gained worldwide popularity.

Magical realists anchor their writing in detailed everyday reality and add fantastical elements such as time shifts, impossible happenings and improbable situations. Linear narratives give way to a tapestry of interlaced events, parallel worlds, and multiple meanings. Spirits intervene. The dead come to life. Magic happens. The extraordinary and the ordinary mix.

Jorge Luis Borges

The father of this style was the Argentinian writer and essayist Jorge Luis Borges, whose literary fame rest on short story collections that explore themes such as time, labyrinths, libraries, mirrors, magical creatures, fictional writers, literary forgeries. Borges is a writer's writer, a literary innovator, a poetic thinker.

Interestingly enough, one of his first breakthrough stories into the new style was *Pierre Menard, Author of Don Quixote*. It is a make-believe literary review on the work a fictional French author Pierre Menard who recreates parts of Cervantes' Don Quixote by copying it word for word. The author of the review compares a passage written by Cervantes

> '…truth, whose mother is history, rival of time, depository of deeds, exemplar and advisor of the present, and the futures counselor.'

with the same passage written by Menard centuries later:

> '…truth, whose mother is history, rival of time, depository of deeds, exemplar and advisor of the present, and the futures counselor.'

and finds the contrast striking. For the same is not the same in a different time and context. Or is it?

In this piece Borges reviews fictional author who is challenging literary convention by copying a third author (Cervantes) verbatim. We have entered the labyrinth. Reality is severely challenged. So are notions of authorship, originality, and identity

Exercise 3: Reviewing Reality

What do you think about Menard copying a passage of Cervantes and claiming it as art? And what do you think about Borges writing a fictional review of Menard's work?

Assume familiarity with Menard's (or Borges') work, critique it with gusto, agree or disagree with other authors (fictional or real) who have commented on their writings. Quote from reliable sources (that may not exist). Show the expertise you don't have. In other words, treat the fiction as reality, reality as fiction. Make the concoction sound believable, convincing.

> **Review by Liana Christensen**
> Lately we have been much vexed with the question of originality – and never more so than with the *oeuvre* of Mon. Pierre Menard. Really, these empty gestures of replicant postmodernity would amuse, were it not all so tediously predictable. Much as they like to claim such practices as *avant-garde*, it is nothing more than literary theft, a tart tricked out in fake finery plying the oldest trade in the world. Such empty gestures have always been the mark of the second rate.
>
> Of course, I am familiar with the Chinese defence – and clearly I have the utmost respect for the necessity of long, literary apprenticeships, in which the novice writer walks in the shoes of the great. After all, ontogeny recapitulates phylogeny in more than just the biological field. But this is mistakenly applied as a defence for plagiarism. The best writers will use their heritage, granted, but must always move beyond into new territory. That is the mark and measure of a true artist.

The Labyrinth of Libraries

Borges had a predilection for labyrinths and libraries (perhaps because the modern library is a labyrinth of the present age). Our next exercise takes its inspiration from libraries, and the maze of books they contain.

Exercise 4: The Maze of Books

Imagine yourself in a vast library. See yourself walking through endless aisles of books. Walk deeper and deeper into the heart of a bookish labyrinth. Dust has settled on the shelves. Look behind the spider webs. One book attracts your attention. The light is dim but you can read the title on the spine. What do you read? Write it down.

Below the title is the author's name. It is identical to yours. Write it down also (it is important that you physically print your full name at this point).

Ocean's Grip by Jill Whitfield

Exercise 5: Three Headings

Intrigued by the coincidence (if coincidence it is) you open the book and read the first three chapter headings. What do they say?

Chapter 1: The Edge of Today

Chapter 2: A Glimmer of Turquoise

Chapter 3: White Horses

Exercise 6: The Summary

You search for an introduction and find a summary at the back of the book. What does it say?

Jennifer grew up by the estuary. Every day she watched the fishing boats leave and return. She watched jetskes flying by, and yachts gliding gently. Every day, Jennifer fought the urge to follow them. She knew that once she gave into it, she would never return.

Exercise 7: The Author

Below the introduction is a short biography of the author who shares your name. His/her biography looks familiar to your biography (or is it the same?). Read what you see there and write it down.

About the author:

Jill Whitfield lives in Tasmania with her husband, three children and two dogs. Ocean's Grip is her fourth novel, exploring the allure of the ocean's deep. She doesn't remember a time when she couldn't swim but she does remember sailing with her father and being enchanted by the dolphins that raced with the yacht. She is still afraid of the dark

Exercise 8: Chapter Three

You open the book at random and find yourself somewhere in the middle of chapter three. Write what you read.

Chapter 3: White Horses

The door to the cottage was already open when Jennifer awoke. She could hear horses neighing. Her heart thumped and she sat up abruptly. No other sounds out of the ordinary called, and she started towards the door. The neighing sounded again, closer now.

Outside on the front lawn, the lawn that reached down to the water's edge, four horses stood. Three grazed greedily but the other looked directly at Jennifer. They were white, all of them, with long graceful tails and manes. Something about their hooves wasn't right, but Jennifer felt her eyes drawn straight into the liquid pools of black that looked at her, and she couldn't tell what.

A soft nicker called to her. It sounded like the lapping of water against the shore.

Exercise 9: The Review (optional)

In the back of the book there are two newspaper clippings. They contain reviews of the book you have just read (and have partly written). What do the journalists say about the book? What do they say about you?

>Review:
>Astonishing! The ocean will never again be the same to you.

Here is a complete exercise all in one:

Filamental

by

Liana Joy Christensen

This volume treats of the seventy-seven paths of dissolution and the fifty-five paths of integration. It is a work of re-membrance, fully referenced and thoroughly researched.

Liana Joy Christensen was born in a library. She is a dedicated reader of trees and stars. Although not, herself, filamental, she has verified knowledge of that realm, and has received authorization to speak from the Three Voiceless Beings.

Chapter One: Incarnate

Chapter Two: The Ruby of Dressa-Laura

Chapter Three: Time Sweeps Leaves from the Stairs

. . . We all know the celestial stairs. Those who are new to Realm Nine may take them for a story, a half-fragment of a dream that vanishes at dawn. Those who watch for the first separation know that in this instant a goldfish gleams that opens its mouth and spits forth the ruby of Dressa-Laura.

It is on the journey down the stairs when this first, uncertain stirring of knowledge that the celestial stairs are real begins. It is that slender thread which will wind across millennia, eventually drawing us home to the filamental state. .

Review
No doubt we are in the hands of a master storyteller here. Christensen's book captures the soul and imagination. It beguiles the mind, too, but not entirely. It seems somewhat churlish, given how much pleasure the reading affords, to question the accuracy of some of her alleged scholarly references. But that is the book's main weakness. It cobbles a vision from moth wings and ant trails, but with such an unreliable guide as a narrator, it is not to be fully trusted. My recommendation? Read it for joy, but don't be fooled by its pseudo-scholarly patina. You need to do the hard work of systematically tackling *The Annotated Annals of All the Realms* if you wish to be properly informed about the filamental.

Inklings of Imaginations

Borges is a master of plots that undo reality to open doorways for the imagination to re-enter. Latin American writers were the first to follow. English-writing authors took longer to catch onto the trend. In the western world the imagination had first to enter under cover of children's books. Not surprisingly, the beginnings of modern children's fantasy in England coincided with the beginning of magical realism in Latin America. Pivotal to this were The Inklings, a literary group at Oxford University, who met between 1930 and 1949. They shared a strong interest in fantasy writing and the revival of myth. The group included the two life-long friends, Owen Barfield and C. S. Lewis, as well as J. R. R. Tolkien and Charles Williams. C. S. Lewis's series *The Chronicles of Narnia* and Tolkiens' *Lord of the Ring* have become modern classics of imaginal writing. After the second world war children's fantasies started to proliferate: Michael Endes *Neverending Story* and *Momo*, Pullman's *Northern Lights,* and Rowling's *Harry Potter* series have captured vast audiences starved for imaginative content.

   Children's fantasy and magical realism have much in common, but are not the same. Children's fantasy is less beholden to reality. And perhaps because of this, it captures deeper realities: the 'mental fight' behind the scenes. Many such stories have the loss and resurrection of the imagination as their theme. (My chapter on Imaginal Literacy in *Global Hive – Bee crisis and compassionate ecology* explores the profound dimensions of this genre.)

In the work of Nigerian writer Ben Okri incorporates many of the features of magical realism, but goes even further. His first book, 'The Famished Road' is a breathtakingly vibrant account of the writer's childhood in Africa. Inner and outer worlds, real vision and childhood fantasy mingle in a astonishing, overwhelming staccato of events.

In newer works such as 'Astonishing the Gods' and 'Starbook,' Okri approaches pure imaginations. These works are imaginary tales in the tradition of Goethe's 'Beautiful Lily and the Green Snake'. Okri does not see himself as a magical realist, and rightly so. He does not add imagination to reality, but reality to the imagination. His stories are accurate metaphors and initiatory tales.

I believe that we are witnessing a worldwide resurrection of Imagination from the grave of rationalism. And this will have consequences not just for literature and arts. Goethe has already pioneered the imagination as a cognitive tool and applied it to the life sciences.

I have worked with a group of experienced writers along Goethean lines and have witnessed them arrive independently at the same in-depth insight about copper, silica, sunflowers or *Eucalyptus caesia* — subjects about which none had detailed foreknowledge. It was revelatory to me, familiar though I am with the powerful potential of Goethe's approach. The writers were equally astonished to find they were able to use the imagination as an objective tool. This experience has left me with no doubt that we stand at the dawn of a new era, an Imaginal Age that will find a new balance between intellect and imagination, science and art.

Bibliography

All of the texts you need to work the exercises are contained in the chapters. The following reading list is for those who wish to study further. The books are listed in the sequence followed in the course.

Literary Works

This Little Puffin, Finger Plays and Nursery Games, E. Matterson. Puffin, 1987.
The Orchard Book of Nursery Rhymes, Faith Jaques, Orchard Books, London, 1990.
The Brothers Grimm, The Complete Grimm's Fairy Tales, Routledge and Kegan Paul, London, 1975. In particular:

>Briar Rose
>Hansel and Gretel
>Mother Holle (Mother Frost)
>The Goose Girl
>Ferdinand the Faithful and Ferdinand the Unfaithful
>The Fisherman and his Wife
>The Water of Life
>The Crystal Ball

Hindu Scriptures, trans. R. C. Zaehner, Dent, London,1968.
The Epic of Gilgamesh, trans. N. P. Sandars, Penguin Classics, Harmondsworth, 1960.
Robert Graves, *The Greek Myths*, Penguin Book, 1992.
Bullfinch Mythology, The Modern Library Paperback Edition, New York, 1998.
Larousse World Mythology, Hamlyn Publishing Group, London, 1973.
Sophocles, *King Oedipus*, Penguin Books, Harmondsworth, 1947.
Sophocles, *Antigone*, Penguin Books, Harmondsworth, 1947.
Homer, *The Odyssey*, trans. E. V. Riev, Penguin, London, 1991.
The Love Songs of Sappho, ed. Paul Roch , Penguin Books, Harmondsworth, 1991.
Plato, *The Last Days of Socrates* (*Apology*), trans. Hugh Tredennick and Harold Tarrant, Penguin Books, London, 1993.
The Holy Bible: King James Version.
Pistis Sophia, G. R. S. Mead, Kessinger, 1997.
The Gospel of Mary of Magdala: Jesus and the First Woman Apostle, Karen L. King, Polebridge Press, 2003.
Ovid, *Metamorphoses*, Translated by Horace Gregory, The Viking Press, New York, 1958.
Roger Lancelyn Green, *Myths of the Norsemen*, Puffin Books, London, 1970.

The Celtic Vision: Selections from the Carmina Gadelica, ed. Esther de Waal, Darton, Longman and Todd, London, 1987.
Wolfram von Eschenbach, *Parzival*, Penguin Classics, London, 1990.
Dante Alighieri, *The Divine Comedy*, trans. D. L. Sayers, Penguin, London, 1955.
The Essential Rumi, trans. Coleman Barks, Penguin Books, London, 1995.
Geoffrey Chaucer, *The Canterbury Tales*, Penguin Books, Harmondsworth, 1962.
The plays of William Shakespeare.
Johann Wolfgang Goethe, *Faust*, Norton Critical Edition, New York, 1976.
Henry David Thoreau, Walden and Civil Disobedience, Penguin Books, New York, 1983.
The Portable Emerson, Penguin Books, new York, 1981.
Walt Whitman, Leaves of Grass, The New American Library, New York, 1958.
Emily Dickinson, Selected Poems and Letters of Emily Dickinson, Doubleday, 1959.
Tu Fu, Selected Poems, Foreign Language Press, Peking, 1990.
Lao Tse, Tao Te King, Reclam, Stuttgart, 1976.
Issa: Sakuo Nakumura's Daily Issa Blog http://sakuo3903.blogspot.com/ http://thegreenleaf.co.uk/hp/issa/00haiku.htm
Issa, The Spring of my Life, Shambhala, Boston 1997
Miguel de Cervantes, Don Quixote, Harper Perennials, New York, 2005.
Jorge Louis Borges, Fictions, the Penguin Press, London England, 1999.

Books on Creative Writing

Horst Kornberger, *The Power of Stories*, Floris Books, Edinburgh, 2007.
Paul Matthews, *Sing Me the Creation*, Hawthorn Press, Stroud, 1994.
Julia Cameron, *The Artist's Way*, Pan Books, London, 1994.
Natalie Goldberg, *Writing down the Bones*, Shambhala, Boston, 1986.
Jean Houston, *The Search for the Beloved*, J. P. Putnam's Sons, New York, 1987.
Kenneth Koch, *Wishes, Lies and Dreams*, Harper & Row, New York, 1970.

Works by Rudolf Steiner

How to Know Higher Worlds: *A Modern Path of Initiation*, Christopher Bamford, Anthroposophic Press, Hudson, 1995
Theosophy: *An Introduction to the Spiritual Processes in Human Life and in the Cosmos*, Anthroposophic Press, Hudson, 1994.
An Outline of Esoteric Science, Anthroposophic Press, Hudson, 1997.
Intuitive Thinking as a Spiritual Path, *A Philosophy of Freedom*, Anthroposophic Press Hudson, 1997.

Works by Owen Barfield

Romanticism Comes of Age, Wesleyan University Press, Middletown, 1986.
A Barfield Reader, ed. G.B. Tennyson, Floris Books, Edinburgh, 1998.
History in English Words, Lindisfarne Press, Hudson, 1967
Saving the Appearances: *A Study in Idolatry*, Harbinger Books, New York.
Speakers Meaning, Wesleyan University Press, Middletown, 1984.

About the Author

Horst Kornberger is an interdisciplinary artist, poet, writer, lecturer and researcher in the field of imagination and creativity. Born in Austria in 1959, Horst began his career as a visual artist before studying Speech and Drama in England, Goethean Studies in the United States and Waldorf Education in Australia.

Horst is a director of The Writing Connection where he pioneers creative, biographical and environmental writing. He is also co-director of Creativity Consultants Worldwide and Theatre of the Sea. He lectures internationally on themes of education, ecology, creativity and the use of the imagination as a healing and community-building tool. He lives with his family in Western Australia.

Horst's interdisciplinary artwork can be viewed at www.horstkornberger.com.

Books by the same author
The Power of Stories – Nurturing Children's Imagination and Consciousness
The Call the Poetry – a manual for everyone
Global Hive – What the bee crisis teaches us about building a sustainable world
The Delphi Project – Collective Imagination and its uses

www.ingramcontent.com/pod-product-compliance
Lightning Source LLC
Chambersburg PA
CBHW062125160426
43191CB00013B/2201